WHO FIGHTS FOR REPUTATION

Princeton Studies in International History and Politics

Series Editors

G. John Ikenberry, Marc Trachtenberg,
and William C. Wohlforth

For a full list of books in this series see
http://press.princeton.edu/catalogs/series/psihp.html

Recent titles

Who Fights for Reputation

The Psychology of Leaders in International Conflict

Keren Yarhi-Milo

PRINCETON UNIVERSITY PRESS
PRINCETON AND OXFORD

Published by Princeton University Press,
41 William Street, Princeton, New Jersey 08540

In the United Kingdom: Princeton University Press,
6 Oxford Street, Woodstock, Oxfordshire OX20 1TR

press.princeton.edu

ISBN 978-0-691-18034-2
ISBN (pbk.) 978-0-691-18128-8

Library of Congress Control Number 2018942729

British Library Cataloging-in-Publication Data is available

This book has been composed in Adobe Text Pro and Gotham

Printed on acid-free paper ∞

Printed in the United States of America

10 9 8 7 6 5 4 3 2 1

To Ariel, Jonathan, and Daniel

CONTENTS

FIGURES AND TABLES

Figures

Tables

ACKNOWLEDGMENTS

The first two chapters of this book were drafted in Kenneth Waltz's old office on the thirteenth floor of the International Affairs Building at Columbia University, where I spent my academic sabbatical. The idea of writing a "reductionist" theory about the importance of leaders, while in the former office of the master of "structural" theories in international relations, was both ironic and at times intimidating.

The idea for this book came from rereading Robert Jervis's *The Logic of Images in International Relations*. Most insights I have had in my career can be traced back (at least in my mind) to something I had read in this great book. The fact that Bob was three doors down the hall when I developed the ideas in this book made the process even more joyful and productive. Bob, as always, has been extremely supportive, helpful, and insightful.

I am especially grateful to all the presidential historians who were kind enough to fill out my survey and code, among other things, the self-monitoring tendencies of the presidents they had studied. I would not have been able to write this book without their willingness to share their expertise. The survey experiments presented in chapter 3 were made possible thanks to my friend Josh Kertzer, who taught me a lot about experiments, and made the process of working together so much fun. Mark Snyder, the father of "self-monitoring" in social psychology, was a valuable source of information and insight during the early stages of this book. I benefited enormously from his advice and support.

Throughout the process I was lucky to receive comments and engage in conversations with some of the brightest minds in the field of international relations. At the Hoover Institution, I received crucial feedback on early chapters from Jim Fearon, Sarah Kreps, Condoleezza Rice, Ken Schultz, Mike Tomz, Jessica Weeks, and Amy Zegart. Throughout the process of writing this book, I kept referring back to their guiding questions and comments. My colleagues at Princeton University were extremely supportive and offered valuable feedback on the manuscript at various stages. I thank especially Joanne Gowa, Christina Davis, Robert Keohane, Melissa Lee, Tali Mendelberg, Rafaela Dancygier, and Gary Bass. Tom Christensen deserves my most profound gratitude for his constant encouragement, support, and insights.

I thank the Arnold A. Saltzman Institute for War and Peace Studies at Columbia University for providing the perfect intellectual environment to kick off this project; the Hoover Institution at Stanford University for making the summer of 2016 both productive and fun; and the Center for International Security Studies, Mamdouha S. Bobst Center for Peace and Justice, and the Woodrow Wilson School of Public and International Affairs at Princeton University for their generous financial support.

I presented versions parts of this book at political science departments at several universities including University of Chicago, Dartmouth College, Duke University, Harvard University, the Ohio State University, University of Pennsylvania, University of Southern California, University of Virginia, University of Wisconsin–Madison, and Yale University. The input I received from students and faculty at each of those departmental seminars significantly sharpened the manuscript and my thinking. I want to thank Dick Betts, Steve Brooks, Austin Carson, Peter Clement, Dale Copeland, Allan Dafoe, Peter Feaver, Page Fortna, Chris Gelpi, Avery Goldstein, Rick Hermann, Marcus Holmes, Michael Horowitz, Andy Kydd, Marika Landau-Wells, Debbie Larson, Ed Mansfield, Roseanne McManus, Dipali Mukhopadhyay, Jon Pevehouse, Daryl Press, Tonya Putnam, Jonathan Renshon, Steve Rosen, Elizabeth Saunders, Randy Schweller, Alex Weisiger, and Bill Wohlforth for their extremely insightful conversations about the book, as well as their suggestions on how to revise the manuscript.

I am especially grateful to Allison Carnegie, Bob Jervis, Josh Kertzer, Jack Levy, Brian Rathbun, Jack Snyder, and Rachel Stein for carefully reading an earlier version of this manuscript, dedicating an entire day to discussing it, and offering immensely helpful constructive criticism about how to improve it. I left this workshop very encouraged that I could bring this book to the finish line.

Throughout different stages I was very fortunate to work with superb research assistants. Their contributions can be found on each and every page of this manuscript. I owe a special thanks to Rohan Mukherjee, Sondre Solstad, Hans Christian Boy, Mindy Haas, Ted Rappleye, Audrye Wong, Martha Jachimski, Richard Gagliardi, Lawrence Liu, Doyle Hodges, Zenobia Chan, and Joshua Zuckerman.

I thank Eric Crahan from Princeton University Press for believing in what this book was trying to do, and for helping me figure it out. His guidance and insights were so valuable, and the efficiency of the entire team at PUP made the publication process very pleasant. I was also lucky to receive detailed and thoughtful comments from two anonymous reviewers to whom I will remain indebted. Teresa Lawson and the editing team at Princeton University Press were incredibly helpful in polishing this manuscript.

Last but certainly not least I would like to thank my family and my dear friends in Israel and the United States for helping me keep my sanity during this process. My political science friends were also a constant source of support and encouragement, not only while writing this book, but also during the tenure process.

I dedicate this book to three very special men in my life. Ariel, my husband, has always been my rock and my compass. I could not have wished for a more loving, supportive, kind, and funny partner. There is no doubt in my mind that I could not have done any of this, let alone complete this book, without his constant encouragement, faith, and assistance. My little munchkins, Jonathan and Daniel, whom I love more than words can express, deserve a medal for their patience and eagerness to help. They popped into my office to check how many pages I wrote each day and even volunteered to type some; they made me laugh during the stressful days; they crossed their fingers that my colleagues would like this book; and they were always thirsty for my "stories" about US presidents. I hope that one day they will read this book and maybe will understand why their very different self-monitoring tendencies made so much sense to me, and how much I thought about them even while I was locked in my office writing this book.

WHO FIGHTS FOR REPUTATION

1

Introduction

"Some countries' leaders play chicken because they have to,
some because of its efficacy."
—THOMAS SCHELLING, *ARMS AND INFLUENCE*

In August 2012, an armed rebellion against the Syrian government escalated into civil war. Reporters quizzed President Barack Obama about whether he would deploy military force to prevent chemical weapons in the hands of the Syrian military from being used against the rebels or stolen by extremist groups. The president famously replied that use or transport of chemical weapons by the Assad government would constitute "a red line" for the US government.[1] A year later, a neighborhood in Damascus was attacked with sarin gas, killing more than fourteen hundred civilians. The US government had evidence of the Syrian government's responsibility.[2] President Obama reportedly ordered the Pentagon to prepare an attack on the Syrian military's chemical weapons facilities but then had second thoughts. In an unexpected move, Obama sought congressional authorization for the strike, knowing full well that in the gridlock of Washington, such authorization would not be forthcoming. According to one analyst, "the president having drawn that red line realized that he had no appetite for direct military engagement in Syria."[3] Having engaged the United States' reputation for resolve, the president was unwilling to use military force and stand firm.

In the end, Russia brokered a deal with the regime of Bashar al Assad whereby the latter would hand over its chemical weapon stockpiles to an international agency. Although Washington proclaimed this outcome a victory, the episode invited strong criticism of the US president from various domestic and international quarters. In March 2015, when the Syrian government used chlorine gas against civilians, many were quick to point out that Assad had been emboldened by Obama's failure to follow through on the "red line" declaration two years prior.[4] In recent decades, even when the United States has not made commitments or drawn any explicit red lines, it has faced criticism for weak responses to crises, such as Putin's intervention in Crimea or China's provocative actions in the South China Sea.[5]

Without access to primary documents that detail Obama's decision making, we should be prudent in our assessments about the role reputation for resolve played in his decision making during the crisis with Syria.[6] In an interview with Jeffrey Goldberg in the *Atlantic*, published in April 2016, President Obama offered readers a glimpse into his thinking when he dismissed the importance of fighting for face. As Goldberg notes, Obama would argue within the White House that "dropping bombs on someone to prove that you're willing to drop bombs on someone is just about the worst reason to use force."[7] And yet, the contrast between Obama's reasoning and that voiced by other Democratic presidents is stark: in 1993, when President Clinton attempted to bolster public support for the military operation in Somalia, he did so on reputational grounds, arguing that if the United States were to "cut and run,"[8] its "credibility with friends and allies would be severely damaged," and "our leadership in the world would be undermined."[9] The United States must leave only "on our own terms," he argued, and show the world that "when Americans take on a challenge, they do the job right."[10] Similarly, in the midst of the Vietnam War, President Lyndon Johnson responded to the private pleas of George Ball and other advisors to withdraw the troops by stating, "But, George, wouldn't all these countries say that Uncle Sam was a paper tiger?"[11]

Leaders in other countries and other eras have differed in their concerns about saving face. British leaders in the interwar period, for example, were deeply divided over whether their country should oppose the growing encroachments of Germany and Japan. While some, such as Neville Chamberlain, rarely raised concerns about Britain's reputation for resolve in the mid-1930s, other members of his cabinet, as well as Winston Churchill, often raised such concerns when debating policy choices. The historical record suggests, too, that leaders and their closest foreign policy advisors often hold divergent views about whether reputation for resolve is worth fighting for.

What explains such variations in concern about reputation for resolve? Most existing explanations have focused on features of the strategic environment or the specific crisis situation.[12] This book provides an alternative analytical framework that focuses on psychological dispositions and beliefs of national leaders.[13] Importantly, by attributing variation in willingness to fight for reputation to variation in individuals' self-monitoring—a stable trait with both genetic and early childhood environmental influences—I show that fighting for reputation has prepolitical origins. Leaders and publics, I argue, take foreign policy personally. International relations constructs, such as the inclination to fight for face, are built on this foundation.[14]

Explaining variations in willingness to fight for reputation for resolve is not a mere academic exercise, but one that has important implications for understanding US conflict history as well as contemporary policy debates about military interventions and the application of military coercion. A leader-level theory on the psychology of leaders also has some predictive value: it allows us to form expectations about the crisis behavior not only of acting leaders but also of presidential candidates and lower-level policy makers who might assume that position in the future. Such expectations about which leaders will fight for reputation could significantly affect their opponents' decisions about whether and when to challenge them. Moreover, as a function of the psychological nature of the theory, it can be easily applied to understanding what segment of the electorate cares about reputation for resolve and would therefore impose costs on leaders who fail to fight for reputation. The theory and its findings thus allow us to identify more precisely which types of citizens are likely to be successfully mobilized to support "contests of face"; it thereby yields a richer understanding of how reputational considerations shape public opinion toward the use of force.

Scholarly work in international relations has long debated the question of whether a nation's reputation for resolve *should* matter. But in so doing, scholars have failed to reconcile the answers they offer with the equally important observation that leaders vary in their concern for reputation for resolve. Thus, a better understanding of the sources of such variation sheds important light on when reputation would matter, and in whose eyes. The novel theory I offer, grounded in individual dispositions, is thus an attempt to revisit the psychological roots of reputation, while focusing on the actors that matter most in international crises.

How Leaders Matter

At the core of this book is the claim that the dispositions or psychological traits of individuals significantly shape their understanding of "the logic of images" in international relations, as Robert Jervis laid out in his seminal work.[15] Consequently, their dispositions also affect the willingness of those individuals to fight for "face." This book is a part of the renaissance of the study of the psychology of leaders in international politics, but it also diverges in important ways.[16]

Tracing policy preferences back to leaders and their decision making is not a new exercise in the field of international relations.[17] Individual leaders have always played a central role in the work of historians of diplomacy, foreign policy, war, and international crises. Scholarly work has long established that leaders are especially influential during international crises where there is a strong role for authority at the highest levels of government.[18] In such times, choices are likely to be made by the key decision makers and are likely to be less affected by bureaucratic compromise or by the preferences of mass publics and special interests.[19] During crises, the latitude with which a leader can make decisions grows as the institutional and normative restraints that usually operate in a democracy wane. A leader's behavior during a crisis, then, aligns more closely with his or her own dispositions, beliefs, and perceptions of the nature of the crisis.[20] This is not to argue that other actors or organizations are irrelevant to the crisis decision-making process, but that they are best seen as moderating the effect of a leader's own preferences. Hermann and Kegley write that, "[as] even a cursory reading of diplomatic history will attest, leaders' personal characteristics can reinforce or downplay the effect of formal governmental institutions or cultural norms in crises."[21] In the case of the United States, which is the focus of this book, strong informational advantages coupled with the unique ability to act unilaterally in the international arena make the president "the most potent political force in the making of foreign policy."[22]

Still, for many years scholars have treated individual-level explanations of international politics as "reductionist," while leaving open the question of the extent to which leaders can explain the foreign policy of states.[23] Political scientists, though writing about the importance of leaders during the 1970s and 1980s, only recently began to find a new appreciation for the role of leaders, delving deeper into the psychology of leadership to understand the microfoundations of first-image explanations of international politics. While there is a growing consensus that leaders can play a decisive role in foreign policy outcomes, the manner in which they affect these outcomes remains contested.[24] Byman and Pollack set the stage for the most recent wave of scholarship on leaders by arguing that "the goals, abilities, and foibles of individuals are crucial to the intentions, capabilities, and strategies of a state."[25] Scholars have sought to unpack *how* leaders' beliefs have shaped the strategic choices of states. For example, Kennedy examines the individual-level sources of "bold leadership" among states, using the examples of Nehru and Mao;[26] Saunders demonstrates how presidential causal beliefs about the nature of threats have shaped the contours of US military interventions.[27] My own work demonstrates how leaders' beliefs shape their selection and interpretation of interstate signals of intentions.[28] More recently, Horowitz and colleagues look at a much larger set of cases to find how leaders' backgrounds affect their behavior in international conflict.[29]

Rather than focus on a leader's background, causal beliefs, psychological biases, or bargaining skills, as many do in the recent scholarship, I set forth an argument here that draws a causal link between a particular psychological trait called self-monitoring and foreign policy behavior. Numerous other psychological traits might also be associated with certain types of decision making. Similarly, there is likely more than one characteristic that can affect the foreign policy behavior of a president. Indeed, much of the earlier work on leadership styles has focused on how the interactions of several characteristics of leaders[30]—such as openness to information, sensitivity to political contexts, and underlying motivation—or their background[31] or formative experiences[32] shape a range of foreign policy behaviors[33] and processes.[34] Yet, as significant as those studies have been in establishing leaders as authoritative decision units that should be taken seriously, they were limited by the methodology and research designs they employed to test the theory.[35] In trying to build on these studies' core insights, the researcher's task, as Jervis aptly puts it, is to develop careful theoretical expectations about which particular trait or characteristic should influence a particular outcome; derive hypotheses about how it should affect a leader's decision making; and measure it carefully and independently of the outcome we wish to explain.[36]

With those guidelines in mind, this book sets out to explain why some leaders fight for face while others do not. Importantly, this book is utterly agnostic about whether leaders were correct to worry about reputation for resolve or whether their policies were effective in shaping others' beliefs about their resolve.

What Is Reputation for Resolve?

In international relations, reputation refers to the belief that others hold about a particular actor. A state's reputation for *resolve* is the belief that during crises, the state's leaders will take actions that demonstrate willingness to pay high costs and run high risks, and will thus stand firm in crises.[37] Leaders who project or protect a reputation for resolve signal that they are willing to use military instruments in order to affect others' beliefs about their willingness to stand firm. Reputation for resolve is important in crisis bargaining because it portrays an image of toughness and strength that, in and of itself, can help the leader to be more effective at coercing or compelling the other side into submission.

As conceived in this book, the primary audience to which a leader signals resolve is his or her country's adversaries, potential challengers, and allies. Other audiences are important as well. Maintaining a good reputation for resolve should also bolster the credibility of the leader in the eyes of allies who are looking for evidence that he or she will stand firmly in their favor in a crisis that affects their interests.[38] Finally, prior research has shown that domestic audiences are likely to punish leaders who seem to undermine their country's reputation for resolve under particular circumstances. At the heart of the theory of audience costs—defined as "the domestic price that a leader would pay for making foreign threats and then backing down"—is the notion that by backing down, they put at stake the nation's reputation for resolve.[39] While recent literature has called into question the premise that domestic audiences punish leaders for being inconsistent, there is also plenty of evidence that domestic audiences care about national honor and reputation for resolve, and that domestic audiences are willing to impose costs more generally on incompetent or inconsistent leaders.[40]

For all those reasons, maintaining "face" or a "reputation for action," according to Thomas Schelling, is "one of the few things worth fighting over."[41] Thus, the United States committed to the defense of Berlin, for example, to avoid losing face with the Soviets—in other words, to avoid the "loss of Soviet belief that we will do, elsewhere and subsequently, what we insist we will do here and now" because "our deterrence rests on Soviet expectations."[42] Defending this reputation, according to Schelling, is more valuable than the strategic value of any particular territory. "We lost thirty thousand dead in Korea," as Schelling put it, "to save face for the United States and the United Nations, not to save South Korea for the South Koreans, and it was undoubtedly worth it."[43]

Signaling one's willingness to fight for purely reputational reasons can, however, be costly and risky, and it requires some degree of deception. This is because contests over "face" in their purest form are conceptually different from struggles over things that have intrinsic material value, such as territory, natural resources, or economic interests. The two can coexist: fighting for a particular piece of territory could be important both for its intrinsic material value and for the signaling value inherent in the act of displaying resolve. But conceptually, at least, contests that are purely about reputation for resolve would arise even when strategic or material interests have little importance.

The existing literature offers three main insights about the conditions that raise concern about reputations for resolve and that can generate reputation-building behavior.[44] I treat those as scope conditions for my theory. The first refers to the idea of observability. For reputation to be a plausible concern, there needs to be at least one target audience (preferably more than just one such audience) that can observe the present actions (or nonactions) of the country in order to determine how it might behave in the future.[45] Second, reputation becomes a concern only if leaders believe that they will engage in a future interaction that would be informed by past behavior. A third necessary condition for reputation-building behavior is that some degree of uncertainty must exist about the preferences of the country. Without this uncertainty about how the government is likely to react, governments would not have incentives to invest in reputation for resolve. I argue that even in the presence of all these necessary conditions, we still observe significant variations in leaders' willingness and likelihood to fight for reputation.

This book diverges from traditional studies about reputation building by starting from the premise that fighting for "face" is most likely under a leader who believes strongly in the importance of his or her own and his or her country's image, leading the leader to be a more resolute actor who will risk escalation or war even over nonvital issues. The history of US foreign policy suggests that most leaders see value in actually fighting for reputation for resolve. However, we still lack an explanation for what it is about these leaders that makes them willing to take these costly or risky actions, often against the judgment of their advisors. Conversely, why we do occasionally encounter leaders who are reluctant to fight for reputation even when their advisors think they should?[46] The political science literature currently lacks the microfoundations for understanding what it is about leaders, and individuals more generally, that makes them willing to take risks or support policies not to achieve intrinsic material value, but rather purely for the sake of demonstrating resolve.

Fighting for reputation for resolve is akin, but not identical, to fighting for "credibility," although I use the terms interchangeably, as decision makers often do. Analytically, however, one way to think about the relationship between the two is to follow Shiping Tang's formulation in which credibility is defined as a combined assessment based on perception of capabilities, perception of interests, and a reputation for resolve.[47] Viewed in this manner, a loss of reputation for resolve affects overall credibility. Importantly, however, fighting for reputation is *not* just about fighting in situations where the credibility of one's explicit commitments or verbal threats are at stake.[48] Rather, to fight for a reputation for resolve, as I operationalize it in this book, is *to threaten, display, or use military force* in situations where a leader believes his or her actions will affect the beliefs formed by international audiences about his or her firmness.

The Reputation Debate in International Relations and Its Limits

For many decades, owing to the prominence of systemic approaches to the study of international politics, the field of international relations has resisted treating leaders as the central unit of analysis. There are important exceptions, and in many ways this study is built on the shoulders of these inspirational works.[49] In recent years there has been a resurgence in the study of psychology in international relations. Scholars have demonstrated how leaders' emotions, causal beliefs, cognition, experience, and background, to name but a few attributes, shape the conduct of their foreign policy decision making. This study highlights another way in which a leader's attributes play a critical role in his or her conduct of intentional crises. By showing why some leaders may fear being seen as irresolute, while others put much less value on reputation for resolve, this study provides evidence of reputation and its effect on states' actions in foreign policy crises.

Why is a reputation for *resolve* important? This concept can be traced back to the writings of Thucydides and beyond, but it gained momentum during the Cold War in the context of deterrence theory, which argued that it was necessary for the United States to respond to Soviet probes around the world in order to prevent further aggression.[50] A similar logic applies in crisis bargaining situations. That is, according to this view, a state must consistently demonstrate that it is willing to stand firm and fight in order to credibly signal its commitments and deter future challengers. If a state backs down, adversaries will infer that it would be likely to do so again in the future, and, hence, they will be more likely to challenge it. In addition, allies will infer that the state would be less likely to uphold its commitments to stand by them in a crisis. As a result, theoretical arguments have emphasized the central role of creating a reputation for resolve, based on the assumption that actors perceive commitments as interdependent.

At the same time, a debate has emerged about the empirical importance of reputation, and whether observers draw inferences about reputation for resolve based on past actions.[51] Most of these criticisms, however, are based on the examination of historical records and focus on specific crises. During a crisis, leaders will focus mainly on new information revealed by actions at the time, such as military mobilization or crisis negotiations.[52] The information on reputation gained from observing past behavior prior to the crisis would already have been available and incorporated into existing assessments of the adversary. These shared beliefs and common knowledge will not usually be stated explicitly, leading to an underrepresentation bias in historical records.[53] An absence of references to past actions in documents or statements does not necessarily mean that reputation is irrelevant.[54] Indeed, a more recent empirical study finds that reputation for resolve still matters. Weisiger and Yarhi-Milo show that countries that backed down in the past are significantly more likely to be challenged in the future, whereas countries that stood firm in previous crises were significantly less likely to be challenged subsequently.[55]

Studies on human behavior and psychology also point to the importance of reputation—not just that for resolve, but also for violence, honesty, keeping commitments, and so on—in many aspects of social life.[56] Economic models of reputation as well as experiments also support the relationship between reputation building and behavior under particular conditions. In particular, scholars have noted that reputation-building actions tend to emerge when there is uncertainty about intentions and when individuals deal with each other repeatedly in similar circumstances.[57] Applying this logic to civil wars, Walter argues that reputation becomes more important when facing a greater number of adversaries.[58] In the context of interstate coercive bargaining, Sechser shows that when facing an adversary that will likely pose future coercive threats again, namely, those that are geographically close, militarily powerful, or have a history of aggression, states will not capitulate in the face of compellent threats because they wish to protect their reputation for resolve when facing such an adversary.[59] Using laboratory experiments, Tingley and Walter find that in later iterations of the game, participants invested more in reputation building and that reputations also had stronger effects.[60] Some recent large-N studies suggest that state behavior is influenced by the interaction between reputation and interests. States with both "strong" and "weak" reputation for resolve face higher rates of resistance to their threats when they have low strategic interests at stake. Thus, the enhanced credibility from having a strong reputation for resolve exists only when there are greater strategic interests at stake. Furthermore, states with a weak reputation for resolve are more likely to issue threats when their strategic interests increase, because they are likely to incur fewer costs for bluffing behavior than would states with a strong reputation for resolve. This is because states with higher reputation for resolve would incur costs to both reputation and strategic interests if caught bluffing, which is a higher cost than that borne by states with weaker reputation.[61]

Recent work has also started to look at how concerns for reputation can vary as a function of culture or strategic environments. For example, Lebow suggests that different countries have had different propensities for conflict, owing to the varying cultural importance of values such as honor and "spirit."[62] Morgan describes the United States as having a culture of reputation, stemming from a "pervasive insecurity over what to do if one's important commitments are challenged."[63]

Despite the proliferation of studies on reputation building, three important challenges remain to our understanding of how reputation for resolve affects crisis decision making. First, there has been little development of theory on the variation in concern for reputation at the individual level, and on the *sources* of such variation. Dafoe theorizes that leaders earlier in their tenure will be more concerned about their reputations as they face longer time horizons and their reputations are less well formed.[64] In addition, US presidents from the South, who are born into a "culture of honor," may be more concerned about reputation for resolve.[65] Zhang argues that US presidents have varying concerns for reputation due to differing individual beliefs about types of reputation and also due to the effects of different war aims.[66] In an experimental work on whether reputations are attached to states or to individual leaders, Renshon, Dafoe, and Huth find that reputations are associated most closely with the actors who are most influential in the relevant decision-making process, that is, the leaders.[67] Recent experimental work also provides new empirical evidence that a threatened loss of status spurs low-powered subjects to escalate commitments over a given task.[68] Finally, using a creative bargaining game based on the market-entry deterrence game, Tingley and Walter find that there is considerable variation in how participants play: many participants invest in reputation even when existing argument tells us that they should not, and others are underinvested in reputation even when the model tells us that they should invest.[69] All this suggests that individuals and states are actively drawing differing linkages between reputation, status, and fighting. Moreover, the revealed variation in agents' responses suggests that conventional theories at the level of the international system or strategic environment are indeterminate and inadequate in explaining when reputation will constitute a driving concern. The theory I advance here turns to the individual level to help explain this variation.

A second limitation of much of the recent wave of scholarship on reputation for resolve is that it has narrowly focused on the context of audience cost models. However, such models specifically explore the reputation costs imposed on leaders by domestic audiences only when they back down from public threats.[70] Yet presidents from Kennedy to Nixon to Reagan to Clinton, and others, frequently and publicly invoked reputational costs in instances where no public threats had been previously made, a phenomenon outside the purview of audience cost theory. By looking at the degree to which reputational considerations affect leaders' decision making, this study moves beyond the audience cost framework and provides a broader understanding of how reputation matters in international politics. Moreover, unlike audience cost models that identify the public as the key audience deterring leaders from backing down, the framework developed here focuses on how the perception of *external* audiences motivates some leaders, but not others, to fight for face. While domestic audiences are, of course, important, I show that they play a secondary role in leaders' calculus of whether to fight for reputation during international crises.

Finally, it has long been acknowledged that reputational concerns are ultimately *beliefs about others' beliefs*, and thus that leaders' assessments about when reputations form are inevitably rooted in psychology.[71] Indeed, the role of psychology has been prominent in earlier studies on reputation: in Mercer's study, the fundamental attribution bias explains leaders' beliefs about when states form reputations;[72] for Tang, the "cult of reputation" is a "belief system" that shapes the behavior of many leaders;[73] and for Snyder and Diesing, it is the "hard-liner" bias that leads hawks to care about reputation and credibility.[74] Much of the recent scholarship, however, has bracketed the role of psychology in explaining reputation building, focusing instead on more tractable variables or proxies such as geographic distance, length of tenure, or the number of adversaries. This study is thus an attempt to revisit the psychological roots of reputation building; at the same time, it departs from earlier work through novel instrumentation that studies more precisely the effect of these predispositions on a willingness to "fight for face."

The Argument in Brief

Under what conditions will leaders be willing to use military instruments to project a reputation for resolve? The greatest willingness to fight for face should be seen among leaders who hold the following four beliefs: First, fighting for reputation is most likely when leaders care about how other leaders perceive them. Without the belief that the perceptions of international actors affect their behavior, fighting for reputation is meaningless. Second, willingness to fight for reputation requires leaders to believe that they can manipulate their own state's reputation. Leaders who think that they do not have the ability to change others' beliefs about them will be reluctant to risk war over nonvital interests for reputational reasons. Third, leaders must be prepared to "misrepresent their interests" in ways that make nonvital issues seem vital to observers. Crisis bargaining often involves actors who are capable of manipulating or misrepresenting their interests and resolve to the adversary in order to coerce or deter. Finally, leaders must want to appear "resolute," steadfast, or strong in the eyes of others during international crises. In order to be driven to fight to project a reputation for resolve, leaders must seek to maximize their image of being firm more than other possible images (such as appearing reasonable, moral, or honest). Leaders who fail to hold these beliefs should be markedly less likely to fight for face than a leader who ascribes to them.

In psychology, individuals who fit the above description are called "high self-monitors," and those individuals are inclined to modify their behavior strategically in order to cultivate status-enhancing images. Low self-monitors, on the other hand, are individuals who, in their everyday lives, are less likely to change their behavior in response to status-based social cues. Other-directedness inclination, a prominent feature of high (but not low) self-monitors, makes high self-monitors significantly more likely to care about their reputation in general compared to low self-monitors. Low self-monitors rather than being concerned about their image, are motivated by a need to establish congruence between their inner beliefs and outer behavior.

While high self-monitors are more prone to care about reputation in general, I argue that in the context of *international crises*, the focus of this book, high self-monitors will be particularly concerned about *reputation for resolve*.[75] This is because the primary motivation of high self-monitors, according to the literature, is to enhance their social status. Different domains feature different social currencies (and hierarchies) of status. For example, high self-monitors will gain status at a cocktail party by being the funniest, most gregarious guest.

In diplomatic meetings, high self-monitors will give a different performance, also strategically designed to establish an image that they believe will enhance their status. High self-monitors are capable of this shift because of their innate ability to control their outward expressions. When high self-monitors are faced with crisis on the world stage—whether in real life or in an experimental setting—the dominant social currency is their image as resolved actors who will not back down, and are even willing to escalate, in order to protect their standing in the eyes of allies and adversaries. In subsequent chapters, I also demonstrate the validity of this claim both experimentally and empirically using historical case analysis. Furthermore, as I show in chapter 3, high self-monitors' desire to appear resolute stems less from tangible or instrumental benefits that reputation for resolve offers, and more from an intrinsic psychological benefit such an image confers in their mind.

Finally, the ability and inclination of high self-monitors to mask their inner beliefs and strategically manipulate their behavior in their everyday life makes them more inclined to use coercive military signals and misrepresent their interests (as well as their willingness to fight). Resolve, more so than honesty or moderation or any other attribute, is the dominant social currency in crises, and reputation for resolve can be cultivated most dramatically in crises without important material interests, so we should expect high self-monitors to intuitively understand the logic of coercive signals designed to manipulate an opponent's inferences about one's willingness to stand firm in these crises. Low self-monitors, in contrast, do not seek to enhance status and are less able and willing to control their outward expressions. Seeking consistency between their beliefs and behavior, they thus will be significantly less motivated to fight primarily for the sake of image when material or vital interests are not at stake.

Self-monitoring is a stable trait among adults, with some genetic origins. The implication of self-monitoring and its effect on a variety of image-related social behaviors has been established in other work.[76] This is the first study, however, that uses self-monitoring dispositions to study the willingness of political leaders to fight for reputation in international relations.[77] Since self-monitoring is intimately linked to the strategic use of impression management, this study thus builds on the insights of the sociologist Erving Goffman that were introduced into international politics through the work of Robert Jervis in his seminal work on the logic of images.

The theory seeks not only to explain concerns about reputation for resolve during crises, but also to explain willingness to apply military instruments to that end. I argue that the effect of self-monitoring is conditioned by an individual's overall attitudes toward the use of force, which, following Herrmann, Tetlock, and Visser, I refer to as hawkishness or military assertiveness.[78] Hawkishness affects the baseline expectations about the overall likelihood a leader will use military force in international crises for any reason. While hawks are expected to use force more frequently than doves overall, I argue that when it comes to fighting for reputation, there are important differences between high and low self-monitor doves, as well as between high and low self-monitor hawks. Unlike the conventional literature, I argue that hawks do not necessarily care more about reputation than doves; although hawks may want to fight more than doves, reputational considerations do not affect all hawks, and certainly not hawks alone. Thus, relying on the hawk-dove dichotomy can mask important variation between leaders.

There are several observable implications that follow from the theory, which I test in subsequent chapters. Most generally, they can be summarized as follows: High self-monitor doves will act more assertively than low self-monitor doves during international crises when they believe their reputation for resolve is at stake. In fact, high self-monitor dove leaders will at times actively seek opportunities to show resolve in order to improve their reputation for resolve. High self-monitor dove presidents are thus more likely to use military instruments overall compared to low self-monitor doves. Yet, given their overall reluctance to see military force as an effective instrument of foreign policy, they are more likely to first seek nonmilitary means to demonstrate resolve such as economic sanctions. Moreover, in explaining their decision to use force in private or in public, high self-monitor dove presidents will likely invoke reputational considerations, such as the importance of demonstrating credibility, strength, and resolve to allies and adversaries. Such considerations are less likely to be salient in the discourse of low self-monitor doves, as they will perceive fighting for face as doubly dishonest and unnecessary. These presidents are likely to resist pressures from their advisors to fight for issues without material implications simply to save face, and they will resist sending signals in crises that are intended to deceive the adversary into believing they will stand firm.

When we turn to the hawks, the difference between low and high self-monitors is perhaps less pronounced in terms of their overall willingness to fight, which could be already very high. Still, we should expect to see systematic differences between the two groups in terms of *what they will fight for*. Both low and high self-monitor hawks view military instruments as important and effective tools in the conduct of foreign policy. Thus they are likely to view high levels of defense spending, modernization and augmentation of one's deterrent forces, and even the use of force when vital interests are at stake, as important and justified policies. But because high self-monitor hawks also believe that standing firm in crises enhances their social standing on the world stage—and because such considerations are known to motivate high self-monitors, but not low self-monitors—high self-monitor hawks are more likely to use military force to demonstrate resolve and enhance that type of reputation, *even when vital or material issues are not at stake*. Moreover, unlike low self-monitor hawks, in explaining their decisions to use military force, high self-monitor hawks will emphasize considerations of reputation, credibility standing, and image in the eyes of adversaries and allies; while low self-monitor hawks will have a different rationale for the use of force, one that emphasizes material stakes and strategic-instrumental logics. High self-monitor hawks can therefore be thought of crusaders, leaders who are far more likely and eager to fight for face compared to all other groups, including high self-monitor doves, who might be more reluctant to use force and escalate in comparison.

Taken together, when we control for hawkishness, we should expect high self-monitor leaders to be more likely to use military instruments during international crises to demonstrate their resolve (as I show in chapter 4). Moreover, we should see that high self-monitor leaders seek to fight for very different reasons compared to their low self-monitor counterparts (as I empirically demonstrate in chapters 3, 6, 7, and 8).

I test my theory on the American presidents during and after the Cold War. Finding variation in concern about reputation for resolve among American presidents poses a hard test for my dispositional theory. Although individuals may differ in their inclination to use force, conventional wisdom would suggest that the foreign policy institutional framework, as well as Cold War concerns, may minimize the effect of individual differences on the use of force. Not only might we expect leaders to exert less control over policy making in democracies than in nondemocracies, but also the particular style of American political campaigning might lead us to assume that all individuals who have come to hold the position of a president are high self-monitors, and thus this trait cannot be used to explain variation in the behavior of American presidents. Moreover, alternative explanations, such as those pointing to the structure of the international system, would expect to see continuity rather than variation in concerns about reputation within the strategic environment of the Cold War period, and then within the post–Cold War period. And yet, in the following chapters, I show that those assumptions are wrong: while more American presidents since 1945 were high self-monitors—an observation that can explain why many of our leaders did fight for reputation for resolve—there still exists important variation in the self-monitoring dispositions of this population of presidents. Moreover, I find that US presidents have exerted strong influence over policy making during international crises, and they have varied in their willingness to fight for reputation.

Testing the Theory: A Layered Methodological Approach

Assessing the causal effects of leaders' traits on their crisis reasoning and foreign policy behavior poses some challenges, but it also provides an opportunity to improve on past attempts to trace the effects of leaders' characteristics on their foreign policy behavior rigorously and systematically. To that end, I use several methods to measure the theory's key variables, trace their causal effects, and evaluate the theory's generalizability. Any single methodological approach I use—experimental and nonexperimental surveys, computerized text analysis, large-N statistical analysis, and qualitative analysis of historical case studies of presidential crisis decision making—comes with its own set of tradeoffs. One method might shed important light on one aspect of the theory, but it might contribute very little to testing other aspects; one method might be rigorous in some dimensions, but more vulnerable in others. The empirical testing of the theory is thus layered, stacked in a logical way to test the theory from the ground up, while recognizing the strengths and drawbacks of each approach. Importantly, *because of data constraints, each method tests different observable implications (although overlapping to some degree) that follow from the theory*. Taken together, these layered methods increase confidence in both the internal and external validity of my theory.

Empirically, I begin with cross-national survey experiments to test the microfoundations of the theory in a controlled setting (see chapter 3, coauthored with Josh Kertzer). Because of the psychological nature of the theory, we should observe support for the theory within the general population. I fielded the experiments in two countries: the United States and Israel. By testing my theory on citizens in two different cultures, geopolitical environments, and domestic political systems, I explore both the replicability of my findings and the generalizability of the theory. Israel also serves as a hard test case, because the presence of a hostile security environment with multiple adversaries should make it more difficult to detect variation in willingness to fight for reputation.

Experimental approaches offer a much clearer window into the microfoundations and causal mechanisms underlying the theory by allowing us to construct controlled crisis scenarios that engage reputational concerns, thereby avoiding the selection problems that can often arise in the study of international crises in the historical record. Survey methods offer important measurement advantages, enabling us to borrow instruments developed by social psychologists and public opinion scholars to capture individual variation in self-monitoring and hawkishness, our dispositional variables of interest. The power of random assignment intrinsic to experimentation allows us to study the causal effects of reputation in a manner that would be difficult with observational data.[79] More broadly, these cross-national survey experiments can help make substantive contributions to the study of public opinion about foreign policy. Political elites routinely "prime" members of the public with reputation arguments, and yet we have little sense of which segments of the public are the most receptive to such priming. The results of these surveys show that hawks are more willing to fight for reputation compared to doves and, consistent with our theoretical expectations, that high self-monitoring doves become significantly more willing to fight when reputation for resolve is at stake. These results strongly suggest that varying levels of self-monitoring among citizens are important predictors of their support for "face-saving" wars.

Chapters 4 through 8 turn to test the theory against the primary population whose behavior the theory seeks to explain—national leaders. To increase our confidence in the validity of the theory, the two key explanatory variables— leaders' self-monitoring dispositions and their beliefs in the efficacy of force— are coded and measured independently of the outcome variable, which is the application of military instruments to project an international reputation for resolve. While I could test experiment participants' level of self-monitoring and attitudes toward the use of force directly, by asking them to take well-established tests that directly measure those factors, it is impossible to do the same with deceased (or even living) American presidents.

Thus, I employ two alternative analytic strategies to measure the key explanatory variables of my theory. First, I use an original survey of sixty-eight presidential historians to obtain a measure of the self-monitoring levels of all American presidents from 1945 to 2008. This research design leverages a propitious property of the self-monitoring scale: that self-ratings and peer-ratings on the self-monitoring scale are intercorrelated.[80] For example, parents can score the self-monitoring tendencies of their children, and colleagues can assess the self-monitoring levels of their coworkers. The judgment of the experts who spent years studying these presidents—their personalities before entering office, leadership styles, historical backgrounds, and so on—thus allows me to measure self-monitoring in a manner that diminishes coding bias and tautological inference. Second, the book uses a variety of proxies to measure a leader's belief in the effectiveness of use of force in international affairs, including party affiliation of the president and computerized and dictionary-based text analysis program (WordScore) of all their foreign policy speeches while in office, excluding those made during all international crises.[81]

In chapter 4, I use the variations in presidents' self-monitoring by turning to a statistical analysis to establish the external validity of the theory. Here, I test the theory on a data set of all militarized interstate disputes in which American presidents have engaged between 1945 and 2008.[82] Using different model specifications and measurements, and by controlling for a host of potential confounding variables including hawkishness, I probe whether the self-monitoring disposition of a US president is a significant predictor of his likelihood to employ and initiate military instruments to demonstrate resolve during international conflicts. Low self-monitor presidents, I argue, should rely less on such instruments compared to their high self-monitor counterparts. Moreover, I probe whether high self-monitor presidents are also more likely to prevail in militarized interstate disputes, owing to their determination to demonstrate resolve.

The statistical analysis provides extremely robust and consistent support for the theory in showing the strong predictive value of leaders' self-monitoring on their international crisis behavior. I find that high self-monitoring presidents engage in and initiate about twice as many militarized interstate disputes that involve coercive military instruments per year, compared to their low self-monitoring counterparts. I also uncover evidence indicating that high self-monitor presidents are more likely to prevail in such disputes compared to low self-monitor ones. Finally, I show that the effect of self-monitoring is larger among the doves than the hawks, as the theory expects. This chapter concludes with a battery of robustness checks, as well as some observations about the relationship between self-monitoring and the selection of US presidents.

Unfortunately, however, this previous analysis cannot shed light on an important link in the causal "chain" of my theory—leaders' *beliefs* in the importance of reputation for resolve, and the role of reputational considerations in motivating decision making and crisis behavior, compared to other contextual variables such as the preferences of domestic audiences or the leaders' belief in the severity of the threat. In chapter 5, therefore, I develop the observable implications of the theory for contemporary documents and secondary literature on past presidents' crisis decision making. I develop alternative explanations against which I test my theory, as well as additional contextual explanations for the crisis behavior that should be evaluated. They include systemic explanations that explain variation in concern for reputation by reference to the polarity of the international system or the advent of nuclear weapons; differences in material cost-benefit calculations shaping the behavior of the president; various domestic political arguments that trace the president's policies to public opinion or his core constituency, or congressional support; and other leader-level alternative explanations. The case analysis allows me to augment the classification of leaders along the dimensions of self-monitoring and hawkishness with several qualitative indicators. Finally, I specify my selection criteria for the international crises studied.

To test the predictions of my theory, I study the crisis decision making of three presidents: Jimmy Carter, a low self-monitor dove (chapter 6); Ronald Reagan, a high self-monitor hawk (chapter 7); and Bill Clinton, a high self-monitor dove (chapter 8). Those presidents were selected for their significant variation in their self-monitoring dispositions and their levels of hawkishness.[83] For each president, I select three or four international crises where material stakes were moderate or low; reputation for resolve could have been at stake; and the use of military instruments and the outcomes varied. The qualitative analysis relies on thousands of primary documents (for Carter and Reagan) as well as memoirs, biographies, oral histories, and other secondary literature.[84] Using such evidence, I process trace the observable implications of monitoring dispositions on the presidents' crisis discourse and behavior, paying particular attention to the extent to which reputational considerations played a role in decision making. In addition to the testing the theory against the crisis behavior of the presidents, I also code the self-monitoring and hawkishness of Carter's and Reagan's main foreign policy advisors, to establish how well the theory can explain their positions about whether to fight for reputation during those crises. Taken together, I am able to show how dispositional differences among the presidents and advisors shape inner-circle debates about the importance of face in international politics.

2

What Types of Leaders Fight for "Face"?

Prior studies of reputation have examined the role of structural and situational factors to explain why reputation for resolve motivates leaders during some crises, but not others. In contrast, the theory advanced here posits that the variation in leaders' self-monitoring dispositions generates significant variation in the degree to which they will use diplomacy and force in international crises, and the extent to which reputational concerns will guide them.

The remainder of this chapter is organized as follows: First, I discuss what self-monitoring is, how and why individuals differ in their self-monitoring dispositions, and the tools that exist to measure this trait in individuals. Second, I offer three causal mechanisms linking self-monitoring with concern for reputation for resolve. Third, I explain how individuals' beliefs about the efficacy of military force have an important intervening effect on whether a given leader will fight for reputation. Fourth, combining these two factors, I classify leaders with regard to their willingness to use military instruments for international reputation into four ideal-types: crusaders, believers, skeptics, and critics. Fifth, I raise testable research hypotheses that follow from this typology, which I then test empirically in the rest of the book by leveraging different methods. Lastly, I explain my choice of US leaders as the main focus of my empirical analyses.

Before proceeding, I should note what is outside the scope of this theory. First, the theory does not address the likelihood of success of leaders' policies during a crisis, regardless of whether they were motivated by reputational concerns. Second, it does not indicate whether leaders were correct in the extent to which they considered reputation for resolve during a particular crisis. Put differently, this is not a theory of when reputation *should* matter. Third, the theory does not predict what specific military instruments leaders would use to project a reputation for resolve. Rather, it seeks to uncover a causal link between concern for reputation and subsequent policies involving military instruments that are consistent with such concerns.

Variation in Impression Management: High and Low Self-Monitors

Leaders engage in impression management in both their personal and professional lives.[1] Impression management is a process by which a person attempts to control how he or she is viewed from another person's perspective.[2] In our private lives, people communicate their nature through their manner of dress, posture, way of walking and speaking, hairstyle, and so on. Self-presentation is fundamental to human nature. The sociologist Erving Goffman's pioneering work on the strategic presentation of self in everyday life has shown how social interactions are akin to theatrical performances in which each person acts out a "line"—a set of carefully chosen verbal or nonverbal signals—in order to project a desired, appropriate image in the current situation and to control the outcome of the interaction.[3]

International relations scholarship has a rich history of applying Goffman's sociological analysis of everyday life to diplomacy and statecraft. Robert Jervis's seminal work on the logic of images established that self-presentation is fundamental to how states (and statesmen) communicate in international politics.[4] Leaders use impression management in the form of signals as an attempt to control their images in the eyes of different audiences. More recently, scholars have adapted these ideas to understand, for example, the public posturing of Arab leaders in the Middle East,[5] the adoption of strategic norms in Europe,[6] and the role of secrecy in international politics.[7]

However, strategic self-presentation is essentially a trait that some have, while others do not. Leaders differ significantly in their inclination and ability to exercise control over their verbal and nonverbal self-presentations, notwithstanding the external incentives to employ impression management. This hinges on their inherent individual level of self-monitoring.[8]

SELF-MONITORING: HIGH AND LOW

Self-monitoring concerns the extent to which individuals strategically cultivate their public appearances.[9] A very large body of scholarship reviews how individuals differ in the extent to which they monitor and control their self-presentation in social situations. Since the original article by Mark Snyder in 1974, self-monitoring has received high prominence in the field of social psychology.[10] A Google Scholar search for articles published after 2010 that cite Snyder's original article yielded 884 results, many of them focused on assessing the impact of self-monitoring on various behavioral outcomes.

The literature distinguishes between two ideal-types of individuals: high self-monitors and low self-monitors. The two differ in both the skill and frequency of their use of impression management.[11] To begin with, high self-monitors are particularly sensitive to cues about the appropriateness of various types of behavior and use them as guidelines to construct their social behavior. They are more socially sensitive and are better able to strategically modify their behavior to a given situation.[12] This can come at a cost: as high self-monitors "act self-consciously to manage the impressions they create . . . they devote substantial cognitive and emotional resources to their social performances."[13] Acting skills, a prominent feature of high self-monitors, are important to a decision maker producing a desired effect on audiences.

Thus, high self-monitors engage in greater expressive control and impression management, displaying greater responsiveness to social and interpersonal cues that indicate the status-enhancing behavior they believe they should pursue. They are frequently concerned with projecting images that can impress their observers, and they adapt their outward emotions and behavior to fit the subtleties of the situation. The self-presentations of high self-monitors "do *not* reflect a passive conformity to others, but an active and strategic means of image projection and status cultivation."[14]

Low self-monitors have been seen as lacking both the motivation and the ability to monitor their behavior.[15] They differ in acting ability: high self-monitors are more likely to be better at expressing emotions on cue than low self-monitors.[16] They also differ in "technique" when engaging in social interactions: high self-monitors are more likely to be better at focusing a conversation on their partner instead of themselves.[17] More importantly, low self-monitors are controlled by their own attitudes: they are less attentive to cues from their social environment and will be less likely to monitor the environment and change their own behavior in order to produce a desired image of themselves.

What motivates the behavior of high and low self-monitors? Existing research on high self-monitoring individuals indicates that they are more often motivated by the need to develop or maintain high social status. In a study measuring differences between implicit and explicit attitudes about social status and consumer products, Czellar found that high self-monitors relied more on brand names associated with higher social status than on immediate reactions about quality when evaluating consumer goods, while low self-monitors based judgments on their implicit initial reactions and evaluations of quality.[18] Similarly, Cheng and Chartrand found that in the context of leader-worker interactions, high self-monitors engaged in more behavioral mimicry and other impression-management techniques to establish affiliation when they engaged with a more powerful other (in comparison to engagement with a less power-ful other); low self-monitors did not vary.[19] Relatedly, physical appearance of partners is an important and salient feature of high self-monitors' social worlds, viewing physical appearance as an important instrument in the facilitation of social status. Attractiveness, on the other hand, is a less salient feature for low self-monitors.[20] Existing research on the motivation of self-monitors suggests that high self-monitors possess both the desire to have high social status and the ability to regulate their expressive behavior in order to realize this desire.[21]

Low self-monitoring may have its own motivational underpinnings. Studies suggest that low self-monitors are more concerned about self-congruence than social status. They presumably derive pleasure and satisfaction from being sin-cere and honest individuals and lack the desire to strategically construct what they perceive as false images of themselves. Low self-monitors choose to inhabit social worlds by fostering honesty or sincerity, so that the faces they publicly display are authentic representations of their inner realities.[22] Importantly, this motivation to behave truthfully and honestly should be distinguished from a strategic image manipulation designed to project a reputation for those traits. Rather, low self-monitors value congruence between their beliefs and behavior not because of the instrumental benefits, but out of a psychological need to maintain a consistent self-image across different situations.

Indeed, these differences in motivation and behavior ultimately imply that high and low self-monitors hold very different views about what constitutes a "self." According to Snyder and Fuglestad, high self-monitors tend to attribute their behavior to situational influences and to define their identities in terms of situational features.[23] Low self-monitors, by contrast, have better articulated self-images that hold consistent in various social situations.[24] They tend to at-tribute their behavior to dispositional influences and to define their identities in terms of enduring dispositions.[25]

WHAT DOES SELF-MONITORING MEASURE?

In the social psychology literature, self-monitoring abilities are typically mea-sured using the Self-Monitoring Scale (SMS), which was created by Mark Sny-der in 1974 and revised in 1986 by Snyder and Gangestad. It contains eighteen true-false questions that ask subjects about various behaviors in which they en-gage in their social interactions.[26] The SMS is a measurement of the observable results of self-monitoring, rather than a simple measurement of either ability or motivation. Since high self-monitors exhibit both ability and motivation, while low self-monitors lack one or the other, the test assesses the extent to which subjects display behavior characteristic of high or low self-monitors.

Analyses of the self-monitoring test show that high self-monitors are more likely to exhibit three behavioral tendencies.[27] The first, *expressive self-control,* is the tendency to act or otherwise voluntarily modify one's outward emotional expressions. In the SMS, questions such as "I would make a good actor," and "I can look anyone in the eye and tell a lie with a straight face" measure this trait. The second, *social stage presence*, is the tendency to draw attention to oneself or to avoid it, and it is measured using such questions as, "In a group of people I am rarely the center of attention," and "At a party I let others keep the jokes and stories going." The third behavioral tendency, *other-directed self-presentation*, is the tendency to act according to what others expect or desire; it is measured with questions such as, "I may deceive people by being friendly when I really dislike them," and "I guess I put on a show to impress or entertain people." (A list of the eighteen questions and the traits to which they correspond can be found in the online appendix.) These characteristics differ from one another, but factor analysis suggests that a single underlying trait affects the presence of all three aspects of self-monitoring.[28]

Several studies suggest that self-monitoring has a substantial genetic component,[29] and that the development of early self-monitoring orientation might be sensitive to specific environmental parameters during childhood.[30] Researchers also agree that self-monitoring dispositions become stable after childhood and do not change substantially during adult life. Self-monitoring is thus better thought of as a trait, rather than a state.[31]

Self-monitoring has been shown to be independent of other characteristics that are typically studied in public opinion. Thus, Snyder notes that factors such as "social class, economic status, geographical location, religious affiliation, and so on" have not been found to be significantly associated with self-monitoring.[32] This reduces the likelihood of bias when applying the concept to political leaders of various socioeconomic backgrounds and ideologies. The only demographic variable that may have an effect on self-monitoring is gender, and the literature remains divided on whether gender has a consistent observable effect.[33] High and low self-monitors can also have virtually any political ideology. A 2004 survey on self-monitoring and political attitudes found that neither Democrats nor Republicans were significantly more likely to be either high or low self-monitors.[34] Work on differences in the distribution of self-monitoring across cultures is still in its infancy.[35]

Finally, for the sake of analytical clarity, it is important to separate self-monitoring and its associated traits from other established traits in psychology. Although self-monitoring may be moderately correlated with other psychological personality constructs such as the Narcissistic Personality Inventory[36] or the "Big Five" personality scale—which tests for extraversion, agreeableness, conscientiousness, neuroticism, and openness to experience—it is widely accepted as an independent trait or disposition whose behavioral implications are distinct.[37] Evidence for this in the case of US presidents is presented in chapter 4.[38]

LEADERS AND VARIATION IN SELF-MONITORING

One might ask whether politicians who have risen to key policy positions already possess high self-monitoring. If so, high self-monitoring might be over-represented in any sample of leaders. The existing literature on self-monitoring has not examined the correlation between self-monitoring and careers in politics. Studies do suggest that individuals who are high self-monitors are more likely to emerge as leaders in group settings,[39] occupy central positions in professional social networks,[40] and have more upwardly mobile careers.[41] Self-monitors do not all tend to become leaders, although they are more likely than low self-monitors to occupy leadership positions in professions involving high levels of verbal interaction[42] and in normative climates that encourage striving for leadership.[43] Thus, we should not be surprised if the population of states' top policy makers would consist of more high self-monitors than low self-monitors. Indeed, as I detail later in this chapter, high self-monitoring is likely to be a particularly advantageous feature in a democratic leader, where winning a popular mandate in free and fair elections is necessary to become the chief executive. Indeed, as chapters 3 and 4 reveal, more US presidents since 1945 were high, rather than low, self-monitors. At the same time, important variation still exists in self-monitoring, not only within the population of ordinary citizens in the United States and Israel, but also within American presidents since 1945.

Moreover, as I note in chapter 9, studying the effect of variation in self-monitoring across leaders is also important in the context of nondemocracies. Among nondemocracies, we may be more likely to observe high self-monitor leaders in personalistic regimes where dictators rely on a cult of personality to generate support for their regime. In such cases, followers identify with a leader based on his or her personality attributes rather than his or her policy agenda. Still, in other types of nondemocratic regimes, such as dynastic monarchies or military regimes, the likelihood of low self-monitors making it to top leadership positions should be higher. The insights gained from studying variation within a democracy, as I do in this book, can be generalized to other contexts.

I am not the first to identify self-monitoring as a feature of leaders. Other work by scholars like Hermann, Keller and Yang, and Preston for instance, has shown that self-monitoring, as a larger basket of traits, can shed light on the decision-making process of leaders as well as a host of foreign policy behaviors.[44] While helpful in highlighting the importance of leaders' traits, such studies are not designed to explain crisis behavior or concerns for reputation in particular, nor do they isolate the effect of self-monitoring in designating leader types. Other than those studies, political science studies that employ self-monitoring are still very rare.[45]

Self-Monitoring and Concerns for Reputation for Resolve

The central argument of this book is that decision makers who are high self-monitors are more likely to be disposed to fight for reputation for resolve compared to low self-monitors. Why? Figure 2.1 outlines the sequential components and effects of the self-monitoring mechanisms.

OTHER-DIRECTEDNESS AND CONCERNS FOR REPUTATION

Other-directedness makes high self-monitors more concerned about the reactions of external audiences in a crisis. Because high self-monitors are more concerned about the perceptions of others, they are likely to be more sensitive than low self-monitors to the reactions of external audiences in crises. Concerned about how others might judge them, they are attentive to signals from allies and adversaries that might give them clues as to how they are perceived. They are consequently sensitive to contexts in which others are drawing inferences about their dispositions and future behavior; reputational costs are greater inducements to high self-monitors than low self-monitors. High self-monitors

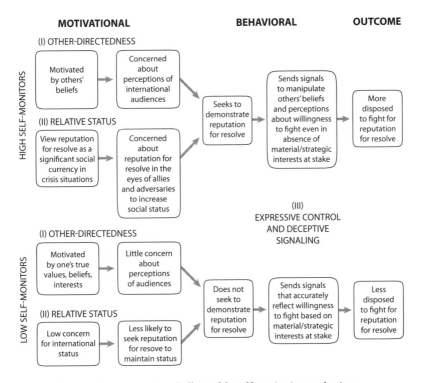

FIGURE 2.1. Sequential components and effects of the self-monitoring mechanisms.

are thus especially willing to fight for reputation when reminded that others are watching them, or when there are reputational costs for backing down.

Theoretically, a high self-monitor leader could be highly attuned to multiple audiences, including domestic constituencies, citizens, advisors, the leaders of other countries, and even citizens of other countries. But in an international crisis situation, which is the focus of this book, the leader will be primarily concerned with how adversaries and allies view his or her actions and the inferences they will draw with regard to his or her country's resolve. This is not to argue that domestic audiences are unimportant; indeed, all else equal, high self-monitors might be more sensitive to perceptions of domestic audiences and public opinion polls compared to low self-monitors. Indeed, domestic audiences might sometimes moderate or constrain the behavior of a high self-monitor. However, the international audience is a more important and constant presence in foreign policy decision making, whereas the effect of the domestic audience on foreign policy, as a constraint or moderating factor, can vary. Therefore, the impact of *international* situational appropriateness dominates the concerns of high self-monitoring leaders during international crises. I return to this point in chapter 5 as well as demonstrate the predominance of international audiences empirically in chapters 6 through 9.

Low self-monitors, in contrast, are significantly less willing to change their behavior based on how others perceive them. They are not disposed to think about their reputation as such, because the beliefs of others rarely guide their behavior. Instead, their actions are motivated by concerns about pursuing policies that reflect their true beliefs and interests. Consequently, their desire to pursue policies simply for the sake of saving "face" over nonvital issues is likely to be significantly lower than that of high self-monitors.

> OBSERVABLE IMPLICATION NO. 1: During international crises, high self-monitors will strategically modify their behavior in order to establish a positive reputation (i.e., image) in the eyes of international audiences compared to low self-monitors.

STATUS SEEKING AND REPUTATION FOR RESOLVE

Having explained the relationship between high self-monitoring and concerns about reputation more generally, I now assess what kind of reputation high self-monitors will seek during international crises. Although actors in international politics can have reputations for any number of traits, including empathy,[46] honesty,[47] consistency, and others,[48] I argue that high self-monitors *in crisis situations* are especially concerned about cultivating their reputations for *resolve*.

To understand why this might be the case, we should recall that, according to the literature, high self-monitors seek to cultivate reputation for things that enhance their social status. High self-monitors' desire for status has been known to shape their choices about everything from the products they buy[49] to the people they date.[50] For example, high self-monitors react more positively to advertisements for products that are associated with prestige (e.g., a luxury car or a fashionable piece of clothing), whereas low self-monitors focus more on intrinsic quality and reliability.[51] This need for a positive public appearance also affects high self-monitors' decision making in romantic contexts: they tend to pursue physically attractive romantic partners to enhance their social standing among peers.[52]

Status, defined as "*attributes* of an individual or social roles, especially those attributes related to position in a deference hierarchy,"[53] varies across domains. Within the realm of international relations, there are multiple status hierarchies, each with a dominant social currency that is relevant for the positionality of the actors within that hierarchy. For example, one such status hierarchy involves the domain of "great powers" or "superpowers," which is based on military and economic might. Great power status is a socially legitimated hierarchy created and maintained by the international system. The states of the international system recognize the prestige inherent in holding great power status, and they behave in ways to achieve that status or shape which states may gain that status.[54]

This book focuses, however, on a different domain within international relations: militarized interstate crises. Within *this* domain, I argue, high self-monitor individuals will tend to regard reputation for *resolve* as the primary means of enhancing social status within the community of leaders on the international stage. Put differently, high self-monitor individuals regard reputation for resolve as carrying significant social currency during international crises. I test this proposition experimentally in chapter 3 and empirically in chapters 7 and 8.

OBSERVABLE IMPLICATION NO. 2: High self-monitors will view reputation for resolve as enhancing social standing in the eyes of allies and adversaries during interstate crises and thus will voice concerns about reputation for resolve during crises.

High self-monitors' beliefs that reputation for resolve increases perceived status should not be necessarily viewed as "pathological," or a sign of high self-monitors' "irrationality." While some studies have questioned the effectiveness of reputation for resolve, as I highlight in chapter 1, there is considerable evidence of the benefits of such reputation. In the context of foreign policy crises, one of the central ways status is accorded is through perceptions of resolve.[55] Reputations for resolve, Dafoe and colleagues argue, establish patterns of deference.[56] Indeed, reputation for resolve and status are intimately linked in the consequences of international crises: a reputation for greater or lesser resolve will influence a state's position in a deference hierarchy.[57] Similarly, status influences reputation by setting expectations of behavior: one's gain in status "will color how others talk about and perceive one's past actions."[58] Other scholarship has also identified the positive effects that a display of resolve has on status. Actors understood to be resolute are more successful at the bargaining table,[59] while leaders who reveal a lack of resolve are deemed to be less competent or less worthy of respect.[60] Using statistical analysis, Weisiger and Yarhi-Milo have shown that countries that back down are more likely to be challenged subsequently, whereas countries that gained a good reputation in past crises are significantly less likely to be challenged subsequently. Carter and Yarhi-Milo also find that dictators who back down from territorial disputes are more likely to be targets of internal coups.[61]

The question whether high self-monitors are "rational" or correct in believing that reputation for resolve will lead to higher status, however, is largely irrelevant for this study. This is because this book seeks to establish the relationship between self-monitoring and willingness to fight for face, rather than whether such tendencies produce the desired outcomes. As a result, this question is outside the scope of this book. At the same time, it is important to consider, conceptually if not empirically, a related question: Do high self-monitors pursue reputation for resolve because they seek status as an end of itself or because they seek to claim the instrumental benefits it could offer? Put differently, do high self-monitors desire to cultivate a reputation for resolve during crises because prestige, standing, or an image of a "winner" offer intrinsic psychological benefits to them; or do high self-monitors seek reputation for resolve also for the sake of more instrumental ends, such as protecting their state from attack in the future through the deterrence benefits of a strong reputation for resolve, or by convincing other weaker states to bandwagon with them through a show of strength and resolve?

Disentangling these two types of motivations, empirically at least, is a difficult task.[62] The literature on self-monitoring, while highlighting status seeking and other-directedness, is informative on whether these are behavioral tendencies designed to achieve other instrumental benefits or whether they are separate goals in and of themselves. Nevertheless, to shed light on this question, I probe the relative salience of the two motivations in the experiments presented in the next chapter. I show that for high self-monitors, image considerations about their country's global standing and global opinion appear to figure more predominantly in their justifications for fighting for face, compared to the more strategic consequences of maintaining a good reputation for resolve. This offers evidence that a reputation for resolve is valued for pure image-based psychological considerations, rather than instrumental ones. The case studies detailing the rhetoric of high self-monitor presidents, however, show that for the most part, these presidents are driven by both motivations. Overall, then, it seems that high self-monitors want reputation for resolve during international crises both because they believe it enhances their social status, and because that increased status has both intrinsic psychological as well as instrumental benefits. This conclusion is consistent with many studies on status seeking, which have found evidence both for status as an end in itself, and status being instrumentally beneficial.[63]

Before we proceed, it is important to acknowledge several scope conditions of the theory. First, while my theory posits that reputation for resolve is what high self-monitors value in crisis situations, the theory does not argue that reputation for resolve is what high self-monitors will necessarily seek to cultivate in other domains. Indeed, *outside of military crisis situations*, reputation for *resolve* may *not* be viewed by high self-monitors as increasing status in the international arena.[64] For example, high self-monitor leaders who are negotiating climate change agreements will not necessarily seek to enhance status by appearing resolved in such settings; rather, they might be more likely to change their outward behavior in order to cultivate a different status-enhancing reputation, such as an image of commitment to environmental issues. Demonstrating commitment to climate change in its domestic policies and regulations can signal that a country will reliably comply with multilateral requirements of climate change agreements.[65] Future work, as I note in the conclusion, could and should test those propositions empirically. Moreover, as I discuss in chapter 9, the intimate normative link between reputation for resolve and social status in crisis situations might be more salient in the mind of high self-monitors during some time periods than others; or some types of international cultures, such as a culture of anarchy, than others.

A second scope condition of the link between self-monitoring, reputation for resolve, and status consideration is that I assume that, to the extent leaders value reputation in private life, they also come to identify with their office—in this case, the presidency—and to value the reputation of the United States accordingly. Presidents then take threats to US reputation for resolve personally, and this concern for the country's reputation is an extension of the concern they hold for their own personal reputation. Put differently, individual-level reputational concerns scale up to the state level through collective identification with the nation. As a result, the theory I advance allows us to move across different levels of analysis: while locating reputational concerns at the individual level, it explains behavior at the national level. Chapters 4 and 6 through 8 show this empirically with leaders and their advisors, and chapter 3 demonstrates this experimentally with citizens. Nevertheless, we should also be open to the possibility that there may not be perfect correspondence between reputational concerns at the leader level and at the national level. For example, a leader from a foreign occupying power may not connect personal reputational concerns to a greater concern with the reputation of the state. On the other hand, personalist regimes, such as that of North Korea under Kim Jong-Un, might display a high degree of congruence between the reputational concerns of the leader and that of the nation, because the fate of the state is directly linked to the dictator's personal fate.

EXPRESSIVE SELF-CONTROL AND SIGNALING RESOLVE IN CRISES

Finally, high and low self-monitors differ in their ability to control their outward behavior, which creates variation in their crisis behavior. High self-monitors are more inclined and able to influence the images others hold of them, partly because they are highly capable of controlling their self-expression and thus can signal such that their desired image is the one perceived.

Just as high self-monitors' other-directedness makes them more sensitive to the perceptions of others, their emphasis on expressive self-control increases their belief in their own ability to shape these perceptions. Mercer notes that actors "may be given reputations, but they do not own them,"[66] yet high self-monitors do believe they can exert control over their own reputations. Self-monitoring thus partially explains the pathology that Mercer, Press, and Tang decry.[67] The key mechanism is a belief in signaling: just as high self-monitors in everyday social situations use signals to change their social appearance and manipulate others' perceptions of them, high self-monitors in foreign policy contexts believe in the power of sending signals to manipulate others' perceptions of their resolve.

High self-monitors are thus natural crisis bargainers. This is because crisis bargaining, especially over nonvital stakes, requires the use of costly signals to manipulate others' perceptions of one's intentions and resolve, and thus dissuade opponents from escalating tensions, or coerce rivals into backing down, through threats or assurances. Thus, if high self-monitors are more likely to value a reputation for resolve, they will also employ policy instruments and signaling that will demonstrate (and even at times inflate) their willingness to fight. Because reputation for resolve is cultivated most dramatically when one is willing to fight for things that do not have vital strategic or material interests, a state's ability and inclination to manipulate others' beliefs that it is willing to fight becomes a central feature of this strategic game.

Furthermore, this strategic scenario implicates the ability of high self-monitors to successfully manipulate and deceive to create certain perceptions in the eyes of the international community in order to inflate the appearance of resolve. To be clear, fighting for reputation involves fighting to project a certain image to other states, *irrespective of the material stakes involved*. In other words, those who fight for reputation will do so irrespective of whether vital or nonvital interests are involved. In contrast, fighting for vital interests involves fighting to secure certain material stakes, *irrespective of the reputational considerations involved*. Of course, it may be that not fighting for vital interests harms a leader's reputation for resolve, or that not fighting for reputation jeopardizes a state's vital interests in the future. In some crises, both reputational and material stakes may be involved. Here I refer to "fighting for reputation" in the sense that a leader is willing to fight for face even if material goals are minimal or absent.

Finally, high self-monitors' need to cultivate an image of resolve in the eyes of their adversaries and allies implies that they will prefer public means to signal resolve to those target audiences. Public demonstration of resolve would allow high self-monitors to project that image quite effectively to multiple audiences. Nevertheless, as I discuss in my work with Austin Carson, under certain circumstances covert means, such as covert military interventions, could offer leaders another effective way to signal resolve to those audiences who can observe their actions, namely the adversary and local allies; while avoiding backlash from domestic audiences who might object to such interventions.[68] In the literature on impression management, this technique of going "backstage" in situations that demand images that are in tension with one another is called "audience segregation," and it allows high self-monitor individuals to project their desired image vis-à-vis a particular target audience.[69]

Thus, all else equal, high self-monitors are more likely, compared to low self-monitors, to be willing to influence others' assessment by inflating their willingness to escalate. Low self-monitors, in contrast, do not possess this same predisposition toward strategic signaling and are more likely to send signals that accurately reflect their actual intrinsic interests. This suggests that high self-monitors should more likely respond to reputational cues by "fighting for face."

OBSERVABLE IMPLICATION NO. 3: To cultivate a reputation for resolve during international crises, high self-monitors will seek to communicate their willingness to stand firm by sending military signals that demonstrate their willingness to fight, compared to low self-monitors.

The Moderating Effect of Military Assertiveness

Self-monitoring implicates the overall propensity or disposition of decision makers to invest in reputation for resolve. Thus, while the theory predicts that high self-monitors should be more willing to fight for reputation, it is important to consider the moderating effect of broader beliefs about the effectiveness of military force. These beliefs, I argue, play an important role in shaping decision makers' willingness to use force in general and thus should be accounted for in a theory that tries to explain the decisions of leader to fight for reputation for resolve in particular.

It has long been recognized that leaders vary in their perceptions about whether military force is an effective instrument in international affairs. The literature generally holds that the efficacy of force is an attribute of the strategic environment in which states operate, which may include the international system as a whole. Keohane and Nye, for example, argue that the efficacy of military force has declined over time as states face more economic threats than security threats.[70] Powell characterizes the efficacy of force as a function of the technology of warfare, which determines the cost of fighting.[71] Changes in technology that raise the objective cost of fighting will reduce the efficacy of military force between states, while changes that reduce this cost will increase the efficacy of force. Conceptualized in this manner, Grieco and colleagues consider the efficacy of force as a source of uncertainty in interstate interactions.[72] This view precedes post–Cold War assessments of the revolution in military affairs and its alteration of the costs of fighting and hence the efficacy of using military force to address, for example, nuclear proliferation challenges.[73]

Although efficacy of force is at times conceptualized as a systemic variable—the product of the state of technology and the strategic environment—the theory discussed in this book is more concerned with the *beliefs* of individual decision makers about the efficacy of force. These beliefs may or may not be accurate assessments of the *actual* efficacy of force, but they nonetheless shape the strategic thought and decisions of leaders. These beliefs can vary across countries, institutions, or time periods. Johnston's definition of strategic culture includes "concepts of the role and efficacy of military force in interstate political affairs."[74] Strategic culture itself is widely shared and slow to change among its adherents; however, strategic cultures vary across time and space, and thus we can see variation in beliefs about the efficacy of force. Martha Finnemore finds that changing conceptions of the efficacy of force over time leads to different views of the utility of military intervention.[75]

Beliefs about the efficacy of force are also found to vary in a more immediate sense across individuals. In the psychology literature, for example, Sell and colleagues find that male strength—both actual and as perceived by others and by oneself—is positively correlated with positive judgments about the efficacy of military force in international affairs.[76] Peter Liberman finds that abstract beliefs about the efficacy of force vary across individuals; he uses these beliefs as a control variable in studies of punitiveness in public attitudes toward external actors,[77] and support for international punishment and torture.[78] Saunders argues that in the case of a US president—Dwight Eisenhower—a "particular set of political beliefs, an understanding of the broader implications of the use of force," caused him to exercise greater strategic restraint than assessments based solely on the strategic environment and domestic politics would have predicted during his presidency.[79]

Beliefs about the use of force, unlike self-monitoring, may change significantly over time through learning. In his study of the development of domestic garrison states, Gurr argues that leaders who find that the use of force has worked abroad will tend to use it more often to resolve domestic conflicts.[80] In the international context, Bennett argues that Soviet leaders did not use force to prevent the Warsaw Pact from falling apart in 1989 because they had formed beliefs about the high cost and low success of the use of force based on prior attempts in Czechoslovakia, Afghanistan, and other places. He argues that even the hard-liners in Moscow held such beliefs about the nonefficacy of force that they were prevented from exercising force to save the Warsaw Pact.[81] Leng develops a theory of crisis bargaining behavior based on the lessons of experiential learning—policy makers overemphasize the outcome of previous interactions with an adversary of relatively equal capacity. If the outcome of that prior interaction is unsuccessful, the state is likely to view the outcome as their own failure to show sufficient strength and resolve, leading the state to employ a more coercive bargaining strategy, emphasizing power and firmness, in the next interaction with that adversary.[82]

A belief in the efficacy of force is perhaps best conceptualized as a subset of hawkishness, as that attribute is usually measured in the political science literature. The overall notion of hawkishness carries with it certain aggressive connotations that may or may not be present in someone who believes in the efficacy of force. For example, in devising a scale of "militant assertiveness," Herrmann and colleagues ask questions that go beyond a pure consideration of force as an instrument of policy into more ideological territory. Questions related to "crime, sexual immorality, and . . . public disorders," "obedience and respect for authority," or the feelings one has upon seeing "the American flag flying" are designed to paint a portrait of hawkishness, of which belief in the efficacy of force is but one component.[83]

Put differently, a belief in the efficacy of force somewhat aligns with some of the instrumental questions considered by Alex George's discussion of leaders' operational codes, or the questions that consider beliefs about the utility of military force.[84] My conceptualization of hawkishness is aligned more closely with Bruce Russett's definition of the hawk-dove spectrum: "hawks emphasize competitive elements, the need to keep up one's military strength to deter war; also they are ready to use that strength periodically. Doves reply with words about the need for cooperation to avoid war and the risks of provoking the adversary. They prefer negotiations for arms control and disarmament to reliance on unilateral action."[85]

Importantly, a belief in the *efficacy* of force in general is neither equivalent to nor a necessary precursor of the willingness to *use* force and is an even weaker predictor of who will fight for reputation, according to the theory I posit.[86] In this regard, my theory differs from how hawks and doves have traditionally been understood in the international relations literature. According to Snyder and Diesing's seminal work on crisis decision making, for example, hawks or "hard-liners" tend to care more about projecting reputation for resolve compared to doves or "soft-liners." They argue that "concern [for reputation] is always voiced by 'hard-liners,'" while "the soft-liner is much less sensitive to resolve considerations."[87] Hawks are presumed inherently to care about reputation for resolve, while doves do not.

In contrast, I suggest that neither doves nor hawks are monolithic in this respect. First, variation in self-monitoring means that some doves are indeed sensitive to reputational considerations. Second, even though low self-monitor hawks and high self-monitor hawks might both be eager to fight, they do so for different reasons, with the latter placing a greater emphasis on reputational considerations. Low self-monitor hawks may be just as bellicose as high self-monitor hawks, but not for reasons of face. Thus, unlike Snyder and Diesing, I would expect to see significant differences both among the doves and hawks about their inclination to fight for reputation, and expect to see some doves (high self-monitor) even more inclined to use force to save face compared to some (low self-monitor) hawks.[88]

LEADERS AND VARIATION IN EFFICACY OF MILITARY FORCE

Beliefs about the effectiveness of military force can result from leaders' individual experiences, or in combination with systemic factors. Such beliefs are therefore likely to vary across leaders owing to ideological differences and differences in professional and personal experiences,[89] pivotal episodes in which one's country has used force and either succeeded or failed; and technological change.[90] For the purposes of this book, I do not engage with the origins of these beliefs.

To measure those beliefs as a moderating factor, I operationalize them in several different ways. In the experimental setting, I draw directly from Hermann and colleagues using only the questions that pertain to assertiveness. In the statistical analysis, I rely on a proxy for beliefs about military effectiveness in the form of political ideology. Lastly, I infer a leader's beliefs on the efficacy of the use of force indirectly, through text-analysis examination of public rhetoric on foreign policy—a measure I also employ as a robustness check in the statistical analysis (chapter 5). In the case analysis, I combine those measures with qualitative factors suggested by Hermann and colleagues that I discuss in further detail in chapter 6. The observable implications resulting from these various operationalizations are similar.

Four Ideal-Type Leaders

Taking into consideration the decision maker's self-monitoring as well as the moderating effect of beliefs about the efficacy of military force produces four different ideal-typical leaders. These are illustrated in table 2.1. The theory I

TABLE 2.1. Ideal-Type Leaders

	Leaders' Self-Monitoring Disposition	
Leaders' Beliefs in the Efficacy of Force	High Self-Monitor	Low Self-Monitor
Force is an effective instrument (hawkish)	Reputation crusader	Reputation skeptic
Force is not an effective instrument (dovish)	Reputation believer	Reputation critic

present is probabilistic rather than deterministic: I argue that on average, high self-monitors are more likely to be concerned about reputation for resolve compared to low self-monitor individuals, and that all else equal, those tendencies could be moderated by overall dispositions about use of force. Taken together, we can expect variation in the likelihood these four ideal-types of leaders will use military instruments to maintain reputation for resolve.

Further predictions are derived using a two-step process: First, which of these four types of leaders are likely to be concerned about reputation for resolve during international crises, and which are likely to see reputational considerations as unimportant or even counterproductive? To answer this question, we consider whether the leader is a high or low self-monitor. Second, what types of leaders will act on concerns for reputation and decide to threaten or use military instruments for reputational reasons? To answer this question, it is important to pay attention to the *interaction* between self-monitoring and beliefs about the efficacy of force.

THE EFFECT OF SELF-MONITORING ON DOVES' WILLINGNESS TO FIGHT

High and low self-monitor doves should exhibit significant differences in their willingness to fight for face, as well as the reasoning they will use in supporting the use of force:

A low self-monitor dove, which I term a reputation *critic*, will doubt both the necessity of fighting for nonvital interests, as well as the importance of reputation in international affairs. The reputation critic will protect only what reflects his or her true interests and will refrain from using force over nonvital issues. Reputation critics would also question whether one's own actions could generate a reputation for resolve in international politics. They are skeptical of the reputation-building process for several reasons: actors may not believe that a leader's actions to protect nonvital interests will be indicative of that leader's behavior over other, more vital, issues. Reputation critics also doubt that international audiences keep track of one's past behavior, but instead they believe that the international community assesses the credibility of one's threats or promises on a case-by-case basis, based on capabilities and interests in any particular crisis. More fundamentally, however, their low self-monitoring inclinations mean they are not wired to think about their image or reputation in general, as those things offer little psychological benefits to them. Thus, fighting for reputation makes little sense in their minds.

The reputation critics' view that military force is not a useful instrument in international affairs further implies that taking costly actions to invest in reputation is both futile and unnecessary. Consequently, reputation critics largely ignore reputational considerations for resolve and focus on calculations of their true interests and capabilities in any given crisis. During international crises in which they do use military force, a reputation critic will not highlight considerations of credibility, standing, or prestige in the eyes of allies and adversaries, but rather those pertaining to the material and strategic interests that are at stake. Finally, compared to believers, reputation critics will be less likely to be influenced by their advisors or other domestic actors who are trying to make the case for fighting for pure reputational reasons.

A high self-monitor dove, which I term a reputation *believer*, will exhibit significantly more willingness to fight for face compared to a reputation critic. A reputation believer will view reputation for resolve as a tool to significantly increase social status on the international stage during crises. Notwithstanding his or her general reluctance to use military force, a reputation believer sees reputation for resolve as constituting a significant social currency during international crises, either because the psychological benefits such a reputation confers in terms of standing and prestige, or also because of the instrumental benefits such a reputation offers. His or her high self-monitoring will thus have a significant effect on his or her willingness to fight even on nonvital issues so as to build and restore reputation for resolve. Reputation believers will cultivate reputation for resolve by utilizing a variety of policy instruments. Nevertheless, because of their belief that military force is not an effective instrument to solve problems, they are likely to first seek nonmilitary means to show resolve during international crises, such as economic sanctions, nonmilitary public threats, or easy-to-attribute cyberattacks, for example. Yet, given that these might be insufficient to cultivate what they perceive as a meaningful reputation for resolve, they are also likely to escalate to the use of military instruments as well.

Importantly, reputation believers will voice reputational considerations for resolve during international crises in their private and public justifications to using force. Concerns about credibility, standing, and prestige will likely be repeated themes in their explanation of why they fight. During international crises, although reputation believers are likely to be most concerned about cultivating a reputation for resolve in the eyes of international audiences, they will actively monitor public opinion and will try to find ways to satisfy and appease domestic opposition without compromising reputation for resolve.

Finally, reputation-based justifications for fighting, when voiced by advisors, or domestic or international actors, will be more likely to resonate with reputation believers, compared to reputation critics.

In sum, there are two key observable implications that follow from the discussion above. First, high self-monitor doves (reputation believers) will be significantly more likely to fight, even for nonvital issues, compared to low self-monitor doves. Second, they are more likely to highlight reputational considerations when they use military force compared to low self-monitor doves.

THE EFFECT OF SELF-MONITORING ON HAWKS' WILLINGNESS TO FIGHT

Compared to the doves, the effect of self-monitoring on hawks' general inclination to fight should be smaller. This is because hawks are already predisposed to using military instruments in crises by the mere fact that they see military force as an effective instrument to deal with foreign policy problems. Thus, both high and low self-monitor hawks should start with a higher predisposition to use force compared to doves. Still, I argue, high self-monitor hawks—that is, reputation *crusaders*—will be more inclined to fight in a set of crises that do not involve important material or strategic stakes but do involve reputational considerations; low self-monitor hawks—that is, reputation *skeptics*—would be less motivated to fight in these crises. Indeed, in purely reputational crises, high self-monitor hawks should be more likely to use military instruments compared to low self-monitor hawks. Moreover, in explaining their decision to use military instruments, high self-monitor hawks will be significantly more likely to refer to reputational considerations compared to their low self-monitor counterparts.

More broadly, the reputation crusader is likely to advocate the use of force in most international crises, irrespective of whether the issues at stake are reputational or material. Concerns for reputation are also likely to play a significant role in the reasoning a crusader uses to justify his or her decisions on whether to use military coercive instruments. A reputation crusader is therefore less likely than a reputation skeptic to retreat or yield in crises, believing that such actions will lead allies and adversaries to see his or her country as weak and to expect him or her to back down in the future. A reputation crusader is also more likely to seek to protect his or her credibility and prestige even in small crises over nonvital issues. This could be for two reasons: the first being for instrumental reasons—for example, believing that small defeats will have amplified consequences for future interactions on the international stage. Second, an image of resolve enhances social status in the eyes of a high self-monitor, which in turn confers some psychological benefits that are independent from instrumental ones.

Compared to the reputation skeptic, a reputation crusader thus sees the demonstration of force during crises as having an important additional benefit: it allows high self-monitors to increase standing and prestige, something that low self-monitor hawks do not see as an important end. Reputation skeptics, on the other hand, are more likely to weight the instrumental benefits of force, including deterring future conflicts and protecting material and strategic stakes, greater than the reputational ones. Thus, while advocating policies that give more prominence to military force as an instrument of policy, low self-monitor hawks will be less likely to consider or highlight the status-enhancing aspects of reputation for resolve as an important motivation for fighting. As a result, compared to reputation crusaders, the reputation skeptics are likely to resist pressures from advisors or public opinion to fight for face when material or strategic interests are not at stake, and they will be more willing to back down when they no longer believe military force can achieve those strategic/ materialist means.

Importantly, because they are both high self-monitors, the behavior of reputation crusaders and reputation believers will look similar in crises that are purely reputational in nature, notwithstanding their different predispositions regarding the effectiveness of force. The main observational difference between a crusader and a believer when reputation is at stake involves their determination to use military force: all else equal, crusaders will advocate the use of coercive military tools in order to further reputational ends, and they will be optimistic about the ability of such instruments to achieve those desired ends. A believer can be expected to exhibit more reservations about the use of military coercion during crises, especially by seeking more information about the utility of force and the potential for alternative, nonmilitary means of demonstrating resolve. A believer would be expected to choose those nonmilitary means before resorting to the use of force, so long as those alternatives allow him or her to save face.

Whereas reputational concerns drive the reasoning of believers and play a significant role in the reasoning of the crusaders, they play only a minor role in the decision making of reputation critics and skeptics. Owing to their low self-monitoring, the reputation critics and reputation skeptics will be unlikely to fight for purely reputational reasons. Yet, we should expect reputation skeptics to be more likely to initiate the use of force and escalate when material interests are at stake compared to reputation critics.

Main Testable Hypotheses

As I note in chapter 1, in this book I leverage several methodologies to test different observable implications that follow from the theory. I begin with cross-national survey experiments that allow me to test the microfoundations of my theory. Here I am able to manipulate reputational stakes in several different ways and thus am able to test the interaction between self-monitoring and beliefs about the efficacy of military force, both of which I test directly using available instruments. Using the subjects' responses to open-ended questions asking them to explain their decision whether to support the use of force as well as a battery of other follow-up questions, I am able to test differences between how high and low self-monitors reason.

> H1: Reputation crusaders/believers are more likely to fight for reputation compared to reputation skeptics/critics respectively, but the effect of self-monitoring on the doves' willingness to fight for reputation will be stronger than the effect of self-monitoring on the hawks' willingness to fight for reputation.
>
> H2: High and low self-monitors should reason differently in explaining their decision to use force: the former are more likely to raise image-related concerns pertaining to global standing and global public opinion while the latter are more likely to raise non-image-related concerns.

Turning to the statistical analysis of the conflict behavior of US presidents from Truman through Bush 43 (George W. Bush, the forty-third president), I am able to test a different, albeit overlapping, set of research questions. Here I am zooming in on the behavior of leaders rather than the public. Unlike in the controlled experiments where I could manipulate reputational concerns, it is impossible to do so with observational data of US conflict history. Thus, I perform a slightly different test of my theory that looks at the effect of self-monitoring on leaders' willingness to demonstrate resolve in interstate crises. Importantly, because here I seek to demonstrate the effect of self-monitoring on conflict behavior (without distinguishing whether the conflict involves a lot or little reputational concerns), I use different measures to control for the effect of hawkishness of the president in all models. Controlling for hawkishness thus becomes critical because of the potential concern that hawkishness by itself might be endogenous to overall conflict behavior.

The premise in the statistical analysis of US conflict history is that while in any given crisis high self-monitors and low self-monitors should view material interests similarly, they are likely to vary significantly in their concerns for reputation for resolve. Thus, if my theory is correct, then controlling for the hawkishness of the president, this additional concern about reputation for resolve should lead high self-monitor leaders on average to be more motivated to fight than low self-monitor leaders. Consistent with the theory and H1 above, we should also see evidence of differences in the marginal effect of self-monitoring among doves compared to hawks. Specifically, the case analyses will help shed light on the following hypotheses:

H3: Controlling for hawkishness, high self-monitor presidents are more likely to get involved in and initiate the use of military instruments to demonstrate resolve in crises compared to low self-monitor leaders.

H4: The marginal effect of self-monitoring should be more pronounced among the presidents who are doves than hawks.

Finally, the case analysis allows me to process trace more meaningfully the causal mechanisms and shed light on the crisis behavior and rhetoric of the presidents and their closest foreign policy advisors, as well as the explanatory power of alternative explanations and contextual variables. Here, I address the following hypotheses:

H5: High self-monitor/low self-monitor leaders will be more/less likely to seek to use military instruments to project a reputation for resolve, even when they believe vital material or strategic interests are small, and even if domestic audiences or their advisors object/support.

H6: Reputation believers will be more likely to exhibit more initial reservations about the using military force to demonstrate resolve in crises over reputation compared to reputation crusaders.

H7: High self-monitor/low self-monitor leaders will be more/less likely to raise reputational concerns for resolve during international crises in explaining their decision to stand firm (or, occasionally, back down).

H8: The president's advisors on foreign policy who are high self-monitors are more likely to raise reputational concerns in their policy deliberations during crises compared to low self-monitor advisors.

Taken together, the different empirical chapters allow me to establish the importance of self-monitoring in understanding when and why leaders will fight for face.

Why US Leaders?

The empirical analysis in this book focuses on evaluating the theory against the crisis behavior of American presidents from 1945 to 2008, although the theory is generalizable to explain variation in leaders' willingness to fight for face across different regime types and time periods. By focusing on the United States during the Cold War and just after its end, I hold domestic institutions in the United States, and its great power status, relatively constant.[91]

During the Cold War, the United States faced off against the only other superpower, the Soviet Union, in a bipolar international system. While there were significant debates about the scope of the long-term political intentions of the Soviet Union, US decision makers throughout the Cold War focused on the Soviet Union as a global threat with revisionist ambitions. Owing to these consistencies throughout the Cold War, variation in the degree to which crisis discourse and behavior implicates reputational logic cannot be attributed to these types of international systemic factors, as shown in the case analysis.

Several scholars have contended that American crisis decision making during the Cold War was guided by a constant concern about reputation for resolve that did not significantly vary across American leaders. This is partly because Thomas Schelling's writings on the interdependence of commitments, which originated during the Cold War, were quite influential among scholars and decision makers at the time. Empirical works on reputation are rife with anecdotal examples of how US presidents practically obsessed with reputation and credibility.[92] Moreover, nuclear technology brought credibility concerns to the forefront; to the extent that each superpower assessed the other's willingness to run the risks of nuclear war based on its behavior in confrontations around the world, a defeat anywhere was believed to undercut the state's reputation for protecting its allies and vital interests everywhere. International relations scholars have come to accept that there was a Cold War consensus over the importance of investing in international reputation.[93] Thus, the existence of variation in leaders' concerns for reputation and willingness to use force to maintain it during the Cold War provides significant evidence for my individual-level theory.

Focusing on the Cold War period also provides an excellent opportunity to test alternative arguments about structural features of the international system and the pressures of domestic politics. These are explained in detail in chapter 5 and are applied to the case studies in chapters 6, 7, and 8. For example, shifts in the nuclear balance during the Cold War led to predictions that vary from mine as to when reputation for resolve should be salient. Domestic politics also offers distinct predictions, such as regarding the pressure of the "military-industrial complex" to invest in US reputation abroad. Other domestic political explanations would predict that White House incumbents would be more likely to pursue reputation-building policies during election years, as a way of distributing public goods to their potential support base. But during the same period, US public opinion for interventionist policies fluctuated significantly; one can derive predictions for reputational concerns based on these fluctuations.

The end of the Cold War and the emergence of a unipolar system, in which the United States became the de facto sole superpower, brought much consideration about the necessity of reputation for resolve. As I explain in chapter 5, some scholars argue that credibility became less important in a unipolar world; others believe that credibility and reputation for resolve may be equally or even more salient in this environment. This study intervenes in this debate by showing variation in the willingness to fight for reputation under bipolarity and unipolarity.

This book also focuses on the United States because testing the effects of leaders' psychological dispositions on foreign policy in a strong liberal democracy provides a tough test for the theory, for two reasons. First, as some scholars have reasoned, compared to other political systems, leaders in democracies rarely have an independent role in shaping policy. Although the president of the United States has extensive access to information and strong agenda-setting powers on issues of foreign policy, the public and domestic elites have more opportunities to intervene and shape foreign policy than in other political systems. Therefore, dispositions and beliefs of presidents would likely not be decisive in shaping American foreign policy.[94] There are genuine analytical challenges that must be overcome to convincingly demonstrate that leaders play a decisive role in foreign policy, as Jervis correctly points out.[95] To the extent that I show leaders matter in shaping crisis policies in a presidential democracy, the theory has more explanatory power where leaders exert more influence over foreign policy, such as in dictatorships.

Second, given that high self-monitoring might be associated with success in public life, it is likely that high self-monitors are overrepresented in any sample of top leaders in a twentieth-century democracy, in which leaders shape their presentation of themselves on a daily basis. Demonstrating variation in impression management among American presidents is therefore important to showing the applicability of the theory to foreign policy decision making in democracies, and it strengthens the argument that greater variation might exist among nondemocratic leaders.

The case analysis also tests the ability of the theory to explain presidential advisors' judgments about the importance of fighting for face. By showing that variation in foreign policy advisors' self-monitoring dispositions can explain their positions on fighting for credibility, I can show that advisors' personalities matter in understanding how crises are framed to the president.

Finally, while the statistical and case analyses focus on explaining the crisis behavior of US presidents, and to a lesser extent, their foreign policy advisors, cross-national survey experiments allow me to broaden the empirical scope of this book in several ways. First, the experiments broaden the scope empirically beyond the United States to Israel, a small country that is facing a significantly more threatening strategic environment compared to the United States. Also, both experiments allow me to establish that resolve remains the dominant social currency during crises in the eyes of high self-monitors even today, not just during and immediately after the Cold War. Finally, because the experiments are conducted on the public, they show the microfoundations of the prepolitical origins of concerns about that state's reputation for resolve that exist within the general public, not simply within leaders. In this way, the theory is generalizable beyond presidential democracies and even the study of politicians.

This book is about the effect of self-monitoring on leaders' crisis decision making. But ultimately, this is a theory about individuals, whether they are citizens or national decision makers. Because of the psychological roots of the self-monitoring concept, the theory should also be empirically valid in a sample of ordinary citizens. In the next chapter, I confirm the presence of the theory's microfoundations through the use of cross-national survey experiments.

3

Microfoundations

EVIDENCE FROM CROSS-NATIONAL SURVEY EXPERIMENTS

By Keren Yarhi-Milo and Joshua D. Kertzer

This book focuses on the willingness of leaders to fight to maintain a reputation for resolve. The dispositional theory, described in chapter 2, argues that a leader's ability and willingness to self-monitor shapes the policies he or she advocates in crisis situations; I show this holds true empirically in later chapters. But, as with many theories in international security, the microfoundations of these explanatory variables are lacking. We use the term "microfoundations" consistently with its use in economics, whereby aggregated outcomes can be explained by changes on the individual level.[1] The survey experiments discussed in this chapter allow us to test how micro-level causes, namely, individuals' self-monitoring and military assertiveness, affect micro-level outcomes, namely, willingness to fight for reputation for resolve.[2]

In this chapter, we present two cross-national survey experiments that explore the relationship between self-monitoring characteristics, beliefs about the efficacy of force, and concerns for reputation for resolve. The first survey consists of two thousand American adults recruited through Amazon Mechanical Turk (MTurk), whereas the second survey is conducted on a nationally representative sample of Israeli Jewish adults. Both surveys use vignette-based experiments that manipulate reputational concerns. We use instrumentation from social psychology to measure individuals' self-monitoring (a shortened version of the Self-Monitoring Scale), and we ask respondents about their political attitudes and beliefs about using military force.

These surveys are a valuable source of support for the arguments advanced in this book. First, they allow us to establish the parameters of individual-level dispositions and beliefs in foreign policy decision making across two countries, which is likely to provide a firm empirical foundation for the theory. Indeed, the surveys measure the impact of self-monitoring and strategic beliefs among leaders and citizens in different cultures, geopolitical environments, and domestic political systems. Second, the surveys offer important measurement advantages, which enable more direct and accurate measurement of the two independent variables than may be possible with the observational data and expert assessments alone. They thus help us better triangulate how these core theoretical concepts would present themselves outside of the historical record. Third, the surveys offer a window into the causal mechanisms underlying the theory by allowing us to construct crisis scenarios that manipulate reputational concerns in an experimental setting, thereby avoiding the types of selection problems that affect the study of international crises in the historical record. Fourth, and most importantly, based on the different treatments employed in the experiments, we are able to more thoroughly develop the microfoundations of the theory in terms of how self-monitoring interacts with other individual and environmental factors to affect reputational concerns.

To be clear, our survey experiments with members of the public in the United States and Israel act as a baseline verification of the theoretical mechanisms posited in this book. At the same time, beyond testing for microfoundations, the results of the survey also have broader implications related to public opinion on foreign policy, and especially the relationship between self-monitoring and foreign policy opinions regarding wars of choice.

Theoretical Expectations

As explained in chapter 2, the interaction between self-monitoring and hawkishness should lead us to observe unique patterns regarding fighting for reputation.

First, we should expect high self-monitor hawks and high self-monitor doves to be more willing to fight for reputation compared to low self-monitor doves and low self-monitor hawks, respectively. At the same time, we would expect *reputation treatment effects* to be significantly more pronounced among the doves than among the hawks. That is, high self-monitor doves should be significantly more willing to fight when treated with reputational considerations compared to low self-monitor doves, whereas the effect of self-monitoring on the hawks' willingness to fight when treated with reputational considerations should be much less pronounced. This is because, as explained in chapter 2, both low and high self-monitor hawks are already predisposed to fight to achieve other, nonreputational, benefits. Thus, in an experimental scenario material stakes might still be sufficient to induce hawks (but not doves) to fight in the control condition. Put differently, hawks might show no reputation treatment effect because of "ceiling effects," and therefore reputational treatments should have a lesser effect on high self-monitor hawks because such considerations are already incorporated into their initial decision to fight in the control condition. We should not expect ceiling effects among high self-monitor doves given their predisposition *against* the use of force.

As a result, we focus on the doves subgroup, for whom the differences between control and treatment conditions should be more visible in an experimental setting. In chapters 4 and 6 I am better able to demonstrate the effect of self-monitoring on the hawks' willingness to fight using other methodological tools.

> H1: High self-monitor doves primed with reputational considerations are more likely to increase their support for military force compared to low self-monitor doves. High self-monitor hawks are less likely to respond to reputational treatment because of a "ceiling effect" (that is, their already high predisposition to fight for reputation in the absence of reputational primes).

Second, regardless of their overall willingness to fight, a key observational difference between high and low self-monitor doves (i.e., reputation believers and critics), as well as between high and low self-monitor hawks (i.e., reputation crusaders and skeptics), is that high and low self-monitors should explain their decision to use force differently. Indeed, we expect high self-monitor doves and high self-monitor hawks to explain their willingness to fight by referring to reputational considerations, but low self-monitor doves and low self-monitors hawks should highlight nonreputational considerations, such as material stakes or domestic political considerations.

> H2: Image-related considerations should play a significantly larger role in explaining the decisions of high self-monitor doves and high self-monitor hawks to fight. In comparison, non-image-related considerations should guide the decisions of low self-monitor doves and low self-monitor hawks.

Third, in addition to testing the key observable implications above, the survey experiments shed light on additional empirical questions. The theory posits that high self-monitors view reputation for resolve as significant social currency during international crises. In the experimental design, we test this proposition by examining how high self-monitors respond to a treatment that merely indicates that international observers are watching, without detailing the consequences of fighting or backing down. If reputation for resolve is indeed the relevant social currency to establish status within this domain, we should see high self-monitors respond by increasing their willingness to fight, but we do not expect to see the same effect among low self-monitors.

Moreover, the theory sheds light on whether reputation in the eyes of allies or adversaries matters more to high self-monitors. By identifying the observer as an ally or adversary, we can identify whether high self-monitors care more about cultivating status in the eyes of their friends or foes. Finally, the theory left open whether self-monitors are motivated by intrinsic image- or status-related considerations, or whether they primarily focus on the instrumental benefits that reputation for resolve could accord, such as enhancing deterrence and preventing future attacks. To shed light on this question we probe whether high self-monitors' willingness to fight is driven by image-based variables such as global standing, or instrumental benefits such as reducing future attacks or increasing domestic support.

The American Experiment

THE SAMPLE

For the US survey experiment, we used a convenience sample of 2007 American adults recruited via Amazon Mechanical Turk (MTurk) in June 2015. Following best practices, we limited participation to MTurk participants in the United States, who had completed above 50 Human Intelligence Tasks (HITs), and whose HIT approval rate was greater than 95 percent. Although MTurk workers tend to be relatively younger, more educated, and more liberal than the US population at large, they are nonetheless more representative of the general population than many of the other convenience samples used in political science.[3] Experiments using MTurk have been published in all major journals in political science, including the *American Political Science Review*,[4] the *American Journal of Political Science*,[5] and *Journal of Conflict Resolution*,[6] and many well-known studies have been replicated using MTurk.[7]

THE EXPERIMENT

Each experiment consisted of two parts: first, a hypothetical scenario where we primed reputational considerations and gauged respondents' support for the use of military force. After the consent process, subjects saw the following introductory screen:

> The following questions are about U.S. relations with other countries around the world. You will read about a situation our country has faced many times in the past and will probably face again. We will describe the situation and ask you for your opinion on what decisions you would make.

Participants were then presented with a scenario based on the "repel an invader" experiment from Herrmann, Tetlock, and Visser, and Kertzer, asking participants whether they want to defend a smaller neighboring country being invaded by its larger neighbor:

> A foreign government has begun a military invasion, sending its troops across the border of a smaller neighboring country. The United States has an interest in preserving the regional balance of power, and is a trading partner of the smaller neighboring country. Best estimates suggest that if the United States intervened, it would require a moderate use of force to protect the smaller country.[8]

Subjects were randomly assigned to one of four conditions: a control group (in which no additional information was given), and three different reputation treatments, each of which primed participants to think about reputation in slightly a different way. We primed individuals for two important reasons: first, the literature tells us that for high self-monitors to act on their predisposition, they need to know there is an audience before whom they are "performing"; our reputation treatments activate this concern. Second, the literature on public opinion has shown that people even need to be primed to consider core values in unfamiliar contexts.[9] Indeed, values do not translate directly and automatically; they must be made salient in order to exert their influence on opinions, especially given the multitude of potential considerations on any given issue.[10] For most people, the values that ultimately become salient and affect behavior will depend on how that issue is framed, or described in communication, especially in elite discourse.[11] Nevertheless, the same prime should be expected to have a significantly lesser (or no effect) on those individuals who do not have the predisposition to care about that value. Thus, because our experiment was conducted on ordinary citizens who are less familiar with the different potential international ramifications of crisis behavior, we needed to include primes that implicated potential reputational effects in the abstract experimental scenarios presented.[12]

Two of the treatments (*Adversaries* and *Allies*) emphasize reputation costs, but with respect to different international audiences. In the *Adversaries* condition, participants are warned that failing to stand up to aggression will cause America's adversaries to doubt our resolve in the future. In the *Adversary* treatment, subjects are told, "Foreign policy advisors in the White House warn that if we don't stand up to aggression now, our adversaries may doubt our likelihood to stand firm in the future." In the *Allies* condition, participants are given the same warning, but this time in reference to America's allies. In the *Allies* treatment, participants are told: "Foreign policy advisors in the White House warn that if we don't stand up to aggression now, our allies may doubt our likelihood to stand firm in the future." Both of these treatments emphasize negative reputation costs, but with respect to different international audiences. The literature on self-monitoring does not make a clear prediction about whether high self-monitors will care more about impressing their friends or foes, but for empirical reasons we wished to evaluate whether in the context of questions about international politics and reputation for resolve in particular, individuals will care more about impressing either observer.

A third treatment, *Eyes*, simply tells participants that the eyes of the international community are on them. In the *Eyes* treatment, participants are told: "Foreign policy advisors in the White House warn that the eyes of the international community are on us." This treatment is markedly more subtle and is inspired by work on the "watching eyes" phenomenon in social psychology, in which cues of being watched induce behavior in line with social expectations.[13] Unlike the other treatments, the *Eyes* treatment does not specify the identity of the observer or the consequences of not getting involved. By simply asking participants what they would do if they knew someone was watching them, it provides an important test of whether they intuitively value reputation for *resolve* in and of itself, without providing them information about the positive effects of being seen as resolved. Put differently, if high self-monitors do not value reputation for resolve (but rather value reputation for other things), this treatment should not affect their willingness to fight. This treatment is neutral with regard to reputational concerns, and so it allows us to discover the perceived social currency of international crises—those attributes that form the language of international crisis behavior and are valued by the participants in those crises—in the eyes of high self-monitors. Through the *Eyes* treatment, we receive confirmatory evidence, separate from our theoretical expectations, that high self-monitors see reputation for *resolve* as enhancing social status.

Immediately following the scenario, subjects were asked, "If the attacker cannot be talked into withdrawing, should our government use our military to push back the invaders, or should we stay out of it?" They were given two options: "Push back the invaders" or "Stay out of it." They were then asked, "On a scale from 0–100, how strongly do you feel about this?" We combine these branched questions to produce our dependent variable, a continuous scale of willingness to fight that ranges 0–100. The results we report below also hold using dichotomous and decile-based operationalizations of the dependent variable. In the American experiment, respondents were also asked to explain their decisions, in order to gain leverage on how participants defined the situation and their reasons.

The second component of the experiment was a battery of demographic and dispositional questions (administered either before or after the experimental scenario) that included gender, age, education, party identification, ideology, international trust, and interest in politics and international affairs. Following Berinsky and Lavine, we used a three-item version of Snyder and

Gangestad's Self-Monitoring Scale, originally developed for use in the ANES (American National Election Studies).[14] To measure military assertiveness, we used a four-item version of Herrmann, Tetlock, and Visser's military assertiveness scale.[15] See the online appendix for details. Following Berinsky, Berinsky and Lavine, and Klar and Krupnikov, and in order to map onto our hypotheses and observable implications and make our analyses more tractable, we mean-split both the military assertiveness and self-monitoring scales, separating low from high self-monitors, and doves from hawks.[16]

The Israeli Experiment

WHY ISRAEL?

We chose to conduct our follow-up experiment in Israel, which is a hard test case for detecting individual variation in concerns for reputation for resolve. The presence of a hostile security environment with multiple adversaries should make it more difficult to detect variation in willingness to fight for reputation.

Some may also be concerned that a focus on US decision making might stack the deck in favor of an individual-level theory. Arguably, because of its great power status and geographic location, US decision makers were less concerned about homeland security and could afford to debate whether reputation was important. That is, in the absence of a true existential security threat, American decision makers vacillated between fighting for reputation during periods when they were more capable of manipulating the public to think that reputation was important, and ignoring reputational considerations in favor of relying on the United States' significant material capabilities in order to deter threats. However, our experiment in Israel demonstrates that public attitudes are consistent with the theory in a non-US context as well.

Israel provides an important contrast to the United States because Israel is not a country where one might argue, as pundits and scholars sometimes do in the United States, that the public is unaware of or unaffected by foreign policy dynamics. The public in Israel is largely informed on foreign policy issues partly because Israel's population centers have been frequent targets of terrorist attacks, rockets, and missiles. Moreover, all Israeli citizens are required by law to enlist in the military at the age of eighteen and serve a period of three years for men and two years for women. (In practice, however, Israeli Arabs, ultra-Orthodox Jews, and religious women are exempt from serving in the Israel Defense Forces [IDF].) Thus, questions about foreign policy and the use of force are extremely salient for members of the Israeli public, either because of personal experience serving in the IDF, or as a collective who has faced these dilemmas repeatedly over the years. The implications are that the questions we pose to the Israeli public in our experiment should appear plausible, if not likely, making our subjects more likely to develop an intrinsic interest in the survey's questions and scenarios.

Finally, Israel provides a good venue to conduct experiments on foreign policy issues because there is sufficient infrastructure to allow for credibly representative samples of the general population; not all countries have such polling/surveying infrastructure in place. This also helps to correct a noted asymmetry in our understanding of international politics: despite the moniker, the dominance of American scholarship and wide availability of data on US decisions (e.g., the Foreign Relations of the United States series) means that our knowledge of international relations is heavily weighted toward "America-specific" knowledge. A focus on Israel helps to correct for US-centric bias and in doing so gives us insight into the leadership and decision-making process of a popular form of government, parliamentary democracy.

THE SAMPLE

In Israel, we drew a sample from the general public by contracting with an Israeli polling firm, iPanel, which has been used successfully by other recent surveys and experiments.[17] Subjects were recruited through iPanel and participated in the study through a Qualtrics interface programmed by the authors.[18] The sample we obtained is representative of the Israeli Jewish population, and stratified based on gender, age, living area, and education. This study was piloted on September 30, 2015, and fielded October 6–9, 2015. Descriptive statistics for this sample can be found in the online appendix. In addition to standard demographic data, we also asked subjects to complete questionnaires designed to assess their political ideology and beliefs. Many of them mirror instrumentation used in the American survey (e.g., self-monitoring, military assertiveness), while others, like stances on the Arab-Israeli conflict, are particular to Israel.

Figure 3A.1 in the online appendix compares the distribution of the self-monitoring and military assertiveness traits across the Israeli and American samples. We see that the Israeli sample, unsurprisingly perhaps, is generally more hawkish than the American sample. Only 12.8 percent of the participants in the Israeli sample would be considered doves by the standards of the US sample, while only 16.9 percent of the participants in the US sample would be considered hawks by the standards of the Israeli sample. In contrast, both samples display similar distributions of self-monitoring.

THE EXPERIMENT

The Israeli experiment, like the US one, included a hypothetical scenario, followed by several questions gauging respondents' support for the use of military force, as well as battery of demographic questions. Importantly, the sort of "repel the invader" scenario we used in the US experiment is inappropriate for Israel, because this type of foreign military intervention is unlikely given Israel's alliance portfolio and strategic environment. We thus employed a scenario more likely to resonate with the public and decision makers in Israel, in which we asked participants whether they wanted to use force to stop a vessel in international waters suspected of carrying weapons to a terrorist organization. The scenario read:

> Israel's security establishment has intelligence information that an enemy vessel is carrying weapons and money to a terrorist organization that conducted attacks against Israel in the past. The vessel is currently in international territorial waters, and any attempt to take over the vessel will require moderate use of force by IDF soldiers. In such an operation there is a high likelihood that IDF soldiers will be killed, and that rockets will be launched on population centers in Israel as retaliation.

Respondents were then randomly divided into three groups. The pure control group in the Israeli experiment resembles the control employed in the American survey, but the other two treatments differ from their American counterparts. The *Reputation* treatment group primed participants that the eyes of other actors in the region are on them, and that not confronting the threat will cause adversaries to doubt Israel's resolve. This treatment group received the following additional information immediately below the scenario: "Members of the security establishment warn that the eyes of other actors in the regions are watching us, and that if we don't confront this threat now, our enemies will doubt the likelihood we will demonstrate resolve in the future." The *Reputation* treatment thus resembles a composite of the *Adversaries* and *Eyes* reputation treatments from the American experiment.

Finally, the Israeli experiment also included an alternate control, which tells participants that the eyes of other actors in the region are *not* on them, and that not confronting the threat will not cause adversaries to doubt Israel's resolve. It read, "Members of the security establishment say that the eyes of other actors in the regions are not watching us, and that if we don't confront this threat now, our enemies will not doubt the likelihood we will demonstrate resolve in the future." The presence of this alternative control allows us to test an additional treatment effect: instead of solely looking at the effects of priming participants to think about reputation costs (as is the case in the American experiment), we can also look at the effects of *raising* reputation costs by comparing the treatment with the alternative control.[19]

After being presented with the scenario, subjects were then asked whether Israel should use military force to take over the vessel, or whether Israel should let it pass. To probe how strongly the subjects feel about their decisions, they were given a seven-point scale, ranging from "not strongly at all" to "very strongly." In addition, we also presented participants with an open-ended question, letting them use their own words to explain their decision.

The Israeli survey included several additional questions designed specifically to shed light on the causal mechanisms underlying the treatment effects. After participants completed the experimental scenario, we presented them with a battery of questions asking about the effects the decision whether to use force would have on four different causal mechanisms: Israel's standing in the region, the likelihood of being attacked in the future, public support for the prime minister, and global public opinion. Response options for these questions are measured on a five-point scale ranging from "definitely will hurt," to "definitely will help." We administered this instrumentation twice to each respondent for each mechanism: if Israel decides to use force and if Israel decides not to use force. In this manner, we can calculate the *within-subject* effect of fighting for each respondent on each of the four mechanisms.

Importantly, our theory expects high self-monitor doves to care significantly more than others about causal mechanisms that involve one's image in the eyes of others, but not about mechanisms that do not directly implicate their image. Thus, we should expect the largest differences between high self-monitor doves and the rest of the population to occur with respect to Israel's standing in the region—which inherently implicates concerns about image and reputation—and world public opinion toward Israel, which in turn speaks to Israel's global image. The standing consideration should also encourage high self-monitor hawks to fight, but we expect to see less movement in any hawks' willingness to fight simply because of their high baseline willingness to fight; when primed to consider Israeli's standing in the region, hawks may become more willing to fight but also have little room in which to increase their willingness to fight.

In contrast, high self-monitor doves should be less likely to distinguish themselves with respect to mechanisms concerning the likelihood of future attacks and domestic support for the prime minister. Concerns about future attacks involve second-order beliefs about image, in that participants are expected in this mechanism to view past actions as directly affecting others' calculations and behavior in the future. Thus, this mechanism speaks more narrowly about the sources of deterrence beliefs and as such is not where we should expect to find significant differences between high self-monitor doves and other subgroups. Similarly, we also expect that the Israeli public's support for the prime minister, which focuses on domestic politics and not the role of Israel's foreign image, should fail to distinguish our high self-monitor doves and other subgroups.

Main Results

The cross-national public surveys provide remarkably consistent support for our theory that the interaction between self-monitoring and beliefs about the efficacy on force affects the willingness to fight for reputation. This is an important finding: at the level of state leaders, it might be easy to understand why the reputation of the president and the state are closely related. But these survey results show that the same intertwining occurs with *citizens*. The general public attributes their own personal tendencies to care about their image in their private life to their *state*.[20]

Turning to the testing the hypotheses, we should start by noting that our results are consistent between the two samples, even though Israel and the United States differ in geographical location, great power status, level of threat, political and strategic culture, electoral system, and level of hawkishness of the population. More specifically, we find support for H1. Unsurprisingly, hawks are more willing to fight for reputation compared to doves, although hawks and doves choose to fight for different reasons. At the same time, consistent with H1, a particular segment of doves—high self-monitors—become significantly more willing to fight when reputation for resolve is at stake. Even when treated with a mild reminder that the international community is watching, high self-monitor doves are significantly more willing to fight compared to their low self-monitor counterparts. Hawks, on the other hand, are already highly predisposed to fighting in the control condition (with high self-monitor hawks already incorporating reputational considerations into their decision to use force), and thus, as we suspected, treating them with reputational considerations does not significantly increase the high self-monitor hawks' willingness to fight.

We also find significant evidence in support of H2, namely, that high self-monitors and low self-monitors fight for different reasons and in a way that is consistent with the theory. To evaluate this hypothesis, we turn to nonparametric causal mediation models to explore the factors driving our participants' behavior, and Structural Topic Models (STMs) to analyze how they justify their decisions.[21] Using those approaches we show that concerns about image in the eyes of external actors, such as concerns for global standing, makes high self-monitors want to fight. This is true for both high self-monitor doves and hawks. The only difference between them is that the high self-monitor doves need a reputation treatment (albeit a very mild one) in order to make the connection between standing firm in crises and their projected image, whereas high self-monitor hawks make this connection even in the control condition (i.e., without being primed with a reputation treatment). In contrast to high self-monitors, and as expected, intrinsic interests or instrumental variables such as concerns about future attacks and domestic support appear to drive the responses of low self-monitor doves and hawks. Taken together, the results show that high and low self-monitors express systematically different justifications about the use of force when presented with identical treatments. At the same time, we see that among the hawks and among the doves, high and low self-monitors are predisposed to fighting but for very different reasons. These findings provide strong

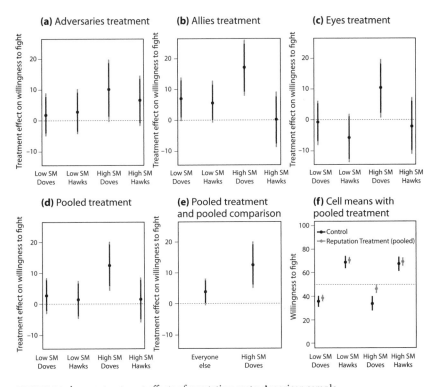

FIGURE 3.1. Average treatment effects of reputation costs: American sample.

support for the causal links stipulated by our theory between self-monitoring and beliefs about efficacy of military force on the one hand, and willingness to fight for reputation on the other.

In the rest of this section, we present our results in three steps. We begin by presenting the average treatment effects, showing how priming participants to think about reputation shapes their willingness to fight. We then look at the roles that military assertiveness and self-monitoring play in explaining variation in willingness to fight. Finally, we bring all three constructs together, showing how high self-monitor doves are more likely to respond to our reputation treatments compared to low self-monitor doves.[22] Moreover, we show in the online appendix that, as expected, the reputation treatment does not have a similar effect on our hawks because of ceiling effects.

Figure 3.1 presents the average treatment effects (with 90 percent and 95 percent bootstrapped confidence intervals) for each of our three reputation treatments in the US survey, conditional on self-monitoring and military assertiveness. The sample is split into low self-monitor doves, high self-monitor doves, low self-monitor hawks, and high self-monitor hawks, and we examine the effect of our reputation treatment across each subgroup. As we note above, our key subgroup of interest is the high self-monitor doves, which represent about 21 percent of the US sample; unlike the low self-monitor doves (who will act consistently with their predisposition against the use of force) and hawks (who should want to fight regardless) we expect high self-monitor doves to respond to the reputation treatment by being significantly more willing to use force.

Our theoretical expectations are empirically supported, as can be seen in panels a–c of figure 3.1: across all three reputation treatments, high self-monitor doves express significantly greater willingness to fight. We see this most strikingly with the *Allies* treatment, but a similar pattern is also evidenced by the *Eyes* treatment, and to a lesser extent, the *Adversaries* treatment. The same pattern is also evidenced in panel d of figure 3.1, when we pool all three reputation treatments. High self-monitor doves respond to the reputation cost treatment by being significantly more willing to fight, while the other subgroups do not.[23]

Two points are worth noting. First, it is key to the theory that we see the same pattern for high self-monitor doves in the *Eyes* treatment (which is neutral with regard to reputational implications) as with treatments that explicitly discuss negative reputational consequences for failing to show resolve. This result shows that high self-monitors in foreign policy crises are explicitly concerned about reputations for *resolve*, rather than other types of reputations; accordingly, resolve is shown empirically to be the social currency of international crisis behavior. If high self-monitors in a foreign policy crisis context were driven by concerns about reputations for honesty, for example, we would not see this effect.

Second, the pattern described above is also evident when analyzing cell means rather than treatment effects. The plot in panel f shows clearly how, consistent with our hypotheses, hawks are willing to fight regardless of the reputation treatment, low self-monitor doves are unwilling to fight regardless of the reputation treatment, and high self-monitor doves display a significant boost in willingness to fight from the reputation treatment (the only subgroup where we see this significant jump).

In the Israeli survey, we observe a strikingly similar pattern of results. Panel a of figure 3.2 shows that, as was the case in the American survey, high self-monitor doves are significantly more likely to fight for reputation when they are reminded of the reputational effects of backing down. On average, the reputation treatment increased Israeli high self-monitor doves' willingness to fight by 9.4 points on a scale of 0–100.

As a robustness check, we calculate reputation treatment effects using the alternate control. Although the results are not as stark, the main pattern holds regardless of the control used: only high self-monitor doves appear to significantly increase their willingness to fight in response to the treatment, and these treatment effects do not significantly differ. To facilitate a more direct

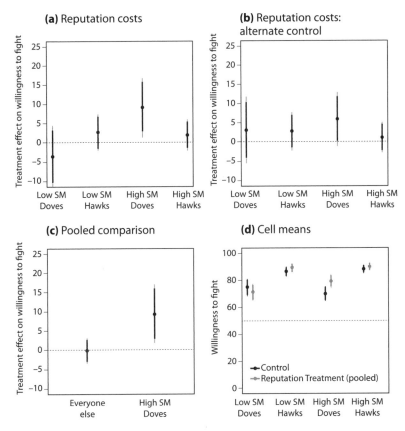

FIGURE 3.2. Average treatment effects of reputation costs: Israeli public sample.

comparison with panel e of figure 3.1, panel c of figure 3.2 pools the non–high self-monitor doves together. As was the case in the American sample, the Israeli high self-monitor doves significantly increase their willingness to fight in response to the reputation treatment, while the other groups do not. The same pattern of results also holds if we pool the reputation controls.

In sum, we find strong support for the claim that high self-monitor doves are more likely to fight when they are reminded of the need for maintaining a reputation for resolve, whereas low self-monitor doves are unmoved. Even a subtle reminder that someone is watching their behavior—without indicating what the desired behavior should be—leads the high self-monitor doves to change their preferences and fight for face. This shows the importance of self-monitoring in affecting an individual's willingness of fight for reputation for *resolve* in particular, as the theory predicts.

Causal Mechanism and Reasoning Evidence

Thus far we have shown that in both the Israeli and American samples, high self-monitor doves respond to the reputation treatment differently from other subgroups of the population. What causal mechanisms might be responsible for these effects? Again, following H2, we expect that high self-monitor doves should be more likely to invoke image-related concerns in explaining their decisions to fight, compared with other participants. We would also expect high self-monitor hawks to be attuned to these image-related consequences to a greater degree than low self-monitor hawks, notwithstanding the ceiling effects. To test these observable implications, we present additional results from both surveys. First, we conduct automated text analysis of open-ended responses on a vignette in the American survey that asks respondents to explain their decision to use military force. Second, we use causal mediation analysis on additional questions in the Israeli survey designed specifically to shed light on the causal mechanisms underlying the treatment.

TEXT ANALYSIS OF OPEN-ENDED RESPONSES

For the American survey, we turn to automated content analysis of the considerations mentioned by our participants when asked to explain their decision to use force in the experimental scenario. Following the measurement of the dependent variable, participants were presented with an open-ended response question, in which they were asked to explain their decision. We use Structural Topic Models (STMs) to explore whether the rationales that our participants offer systematically vary with their levels of self-monitoring, conditional on the experimental treatment and their general predisposition toward the use of force.

Structural topic models are an unsupervised form of automated text analysis, in which each text excerpt is modeled as a mixture of multiple "topics," or distributions of words. Structural topic models differ from supervised text analysis methods in that the model discovers topics in the text without being directed by the researcher. They also differ from traditional mixed-membership models like Latent Dirichlet Allocation (LDA) by leveraging metadata—in our context, information about the author of each open-ended response: their treatment condition, level of hawkishness, and level of self-monitoring.[24]

We therefore estimate a set of structural topic models on our participants' responses.[25] Given our theory, we are interested in the extent to which the rationales offered by high and low self-monitor doves will systematically differ from one another when presented with the reputation treatment. The changes in topic prevalence depicted in figure 3.3 suggest that low and high self-monitor doves who receive the reputation treatments significantly differ from one another on three distinct topics, which, based on representative

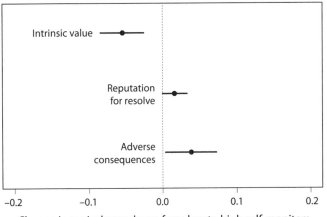

Doves, pooled treatment

Change in topical prevalence from low to high self-monitors

FIGURE 3.3. Structural topic models: American sample.
Structural topic models on the open-ended response participants offer explaining their willingness to use force or not suggest that high self-monitor doves given the reputation treatment differ from their low self-monitor counterparts in three different ways: they're less likely to discuss the intrinsic value of the mission, more likely to discuss the importance of reputation for resolve, and more likely to emphasize the adverse image consequences of interventions.

responses for each topic, we call "intrinsic value," "reputation for resolve," and "adverse consequences."[26]

First, when asked to explain their decisions, high self-monitor doves are significantly less likely than low self-monitor doves to rationalize their decision by invoking the "intrinsic value" of the operation. Low self-monitor doves tend to offer instrumental, rather than reputational, justifications, such as "because the US has an interest in preserving the regional balance of power and also the smaller country is a trading partner," as one respondent wrote. Another participant similarly reasoned, "We want stability in the area and the smaller country is a trading partner. So we do have some interests in the area and should try to protect those interests." Those types of comments reflect a cost-benefit analysis that is based on material calculus of American intrinsic interests in the intervention scenario. This line of reasoning sidesteps the importance of reputation for resolve and the beliefs of others as a motivation for action or inaction. As our theory predicts, these types of comments are significantly more likely to come from low self-monitor doves than their high self-monitor counterparts.

Second, consistent with our theory, high self-monitor doves are significantly more likely than low self-monitor doves to respond to our reputation treatments by raising concerns about reputation for resolve. Echoing Schelling, one respondent warned, "If the US does not push back the invaders, they will continue to the next country and start a domino effect." Another respondent took this logic a step further, arguing, "If we back down it would appear to other countries as a sign of weakness. Other countries might join together and attack us." This line of reasoning is consistent with our earlier findings that high self-monitor doves are more concerned about others' beliefs about their resolve than their low self-monitor counterparts.

Finally, high self-monitor doves were also significantly more likely than low self-monitor doves to refer to the unintended and adverse consequences of attempting to bolster America's image. They often underscored in their responses how interventionist foreign policy could turn external actors against the United States, resulting in a more negative US reputation abroad. For example, as one respondent cautioned, "The United States spends far too much time, energy and money on international conflicts. This isn't America's battle and this is why the world hates America. We go in and tell the rest of the world the way things should be." Indeed, some high self-monitor doves who are clearly adverse to the use of military force conclude that, precisely because of the damage to US reputation and image abroad, an inward-looking policy might be wiser. In the words of one respondent, "In general, I think the U.S. should stop intervening militarily in foreign wars. It seems to backfire much of the time. Also, it often stokes the resentment and anger toward the U.S. around the world, leading to terrorism and other negative consequences."

In sum, just as the experimental results show that high self-monitor doves are more likely to respond to reputational concerns than their low self-monitor counterparts, structural topic models show that high self-monitor doves also express systematically different justifications than their low self-monitor counterparts when presented with identical treatments. High self-monitor doves are more "other-directed" in their explanations, thinking about how their actions could lead external audiences to form a more favorable image of them. The low self-monitor doves, in stark contrast, think about the use of force through a very different lens: they are significantly more concerned about the intrinsic interests to be gained or preserved by using force in this circumstance, rather than any reputational or other-directedness concerns.

CAUSAL MEDIATION ANALYSIS

The Israeli survey included several additional questions designed specifically to shed light on the causal mechanisms underlying the treatment effects. After participants completed the experimental scenario, we presented them with a battery of questions asking about the effects that the decision to use force would have on four different causal mechanisms: Israel's standing in the region, the likelihood of being attacked in the future, public support for the prime minister, and global public opinion. Response options for these questions are measured on a five-point scale ranging from "definitely will hurt," to "definitely will help." We administered this instrumentation twice to each respondent for each mechanism, both if Israel decides to use force, and if Israel decides not to use force. In this manner, we can calculate the *within-subject* effect of fighting for each respondent on each of the four mechanisms, by subtracting the value of the mechanism when Israel does not use force from the value of the mechanism when Israel does use force.

Importantly, our theory expects high self-monitor doves to care significantly more about causal mechanisms that involve one's image in the eyes of others. Thus, we should expect the largest differences between high self-monitor doves and the rest of the population to occur with respect to Israel's standing in the region—which inherently implicates concerns about image and reputation—and world public opinion toward Israel, which in turn speaks to Israel's global image. In contrast, the gap between high self-monitor doves and everyone else should be less likely to manifest itself with respect to mechanisms concerning the likelihood of future attacks and domestic support for the prime minister. This mechanism speaks more narrowly about the sources of deterrence beliefs and thus is not where we should expect to find significant differences between high self-monitor doves and other subgroups. Similarly, the Israeli public's support for the prime minister, which focuses on domestic politics and not Israel's foreign image, should not reveal differences between our high self-monitor doves and all other subgroups.

We also examined the distribution of the Israeli participants' responses to each of the four mechanisms explored: Israel's standing in the world, the likelihood of future attacks, public support for the prime minister, and support from the global public. The split density plots in figure 3A.4 in the online appendix present these distributions. Below, we present the within-subject effect of fighting for our high self-monitor doves, and everyone else, conditional on the reputation treatment assignment, for each of the four mechanisms (figure 3.4). Consistent with H2, panel a shows that high self-monitor doves given the reputation treatment perceive the effect of fighting on Israel's standing in the world to be significantly higher ($p<0.02$) than high self-monitor doves in the control condition. In contrast, the difference between treatment and control in the pooled comparison group does not approach conventional levels of statistical significance ($p<0.11$) despite its much larger number of participants.[27] This pattern for Israeli standing is consistent with high self-monitor doves given a reputation treatment being especially attuned to issues of standing that engage one's image in the eyes of others.

Similarly, panel d explores the effect of the reputation treatment on Israel's global image in the eyes of foreign publics. Here, we see that high self-monitor doves respond to the reputation treatment by being significantly more likely

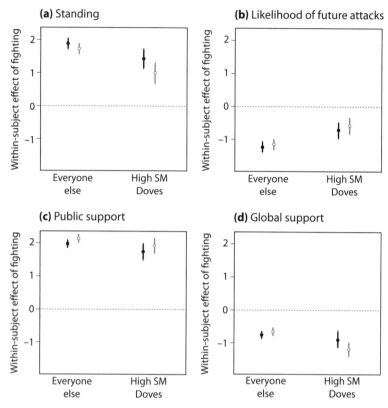

FIGURE 3.4. Within-subject effect of fighting: pooled comparison.
Cell means for reputation treatment in black, for reputation in dark gray. High self-monitor doves presented with the reputation treatment differ from those in the control condition with respect to the effect of fighting on Israel's standing in the region (panel a) and global public opinion (panel d), but not the likelihood of future attacks or public support (panels b and c).

to see the positive effects of fighting for reputation on global public opinion (p<0.04) than high self-monitor doves in the control. In contrast, the effect of the treatment on everyone else is not significant (p<0.16), and the difference in difference between the two groups is significant at the p<0.02 level. Thus, as was the case with panel a, high self-monitor doves respond to the reputation treatment by being particularly sensitive to mechanisms implicating concerns about image.

In contrast, panel b shows that high self-monitor doves given the treatment are no more likely than high self-monitor doves given the control to see fighting as affecting the likelihood of future attacks (p<0.26). We see similarly null results for the public support mechanism in panel c: in general, respondents see fighting as boosting public support, but high self-monitor doves assigned to the treatment do not display a significantly different effect compared to those assigned to the control (p<0.15). Thus, for these two instrumental mechanisms, which focus less explicitly on one's image in the eyes of others, we do not see high self-monitor doves respond in a systematically different way.

We also replicate the above analyses with a more formal nonparametric causal mediation analysis, in which we estimate separate mediation models for high self-monitor doves, and for the pooled comparison group, for each of our four mediators.[28] The average causal mediation effects (ACMEs), presented with quasi-Bayesian confidence intervals drawn from B=1,500 bootstraps in figure 3.5, reconfirm our findings above. For high self-monitor doves, the ACME for standing is significant at p<0.07, and global support at p<0.009; in contrast, the ACMEs for future attacks and public support are not statistically significant at p<0.52 and p<0.31, respectively. In contrast, for the pooled comparison group, none of the ACMEs are significant (standing: p<0.80, global support: p<0.94; future attacks: p<0.68, public support: p<0.23). Once again, then, the results reconfirm: high self-monitor doves respond to the reputation treatment by becoming especially concerned about mechanisms relating to image: high self-monitor doves fight for face, but not for instrumental concerns. As before, the results are the same regardless if we use the just low self-monitor doves as the comparison group rather than the pooled comparison.[29]

Finally, we assess whether high and low self-monitor hawks also differ in why they fight. Even though both low and high self-monitor hawks are willing to fight regardless of the reputation treatment (for evidence of ceiling effects, please see the online appendix), it does not mean that they define the situation in identical ways. Thus, similarly to analysis conducted earlier with the doves, we examine the within-subject effects of fighting on each of the four mechanisms administered in the Israeli data—standing, likelihood of future attacks, domestic public support, and global public opinion—but focusing specifically on hawks in the control condition. Subsetting the data in this manner provides a clear test of how hawks define the situation, even in the absence of a reputation treatment. Consistent with H2, we find a striking pattern, consistent with both the theory and the pattern we observe with the doves: low self-monitor hawks and high self-monitor hawks significantly differ from one another on those mechanisms that implicate image-related concerns (p<0.055 for standing, p<0.043 for global support), but not the mechanisms relating to domestic politics or instrumental considerations (p<0.130 for domestic public support, p<0.318 for likelihood of future attacks).

Substantively, even in the control condition, both high and low self-monitor hawks think fighting will boost Israel's standing, but high self-monitor hawks think the effect will be larger than low-self monitor hawks; similarly, even in the control condition, both high and low self-monitor hawks think that fighting will hurt Israel in terms of global public opinion, but high self-monitor

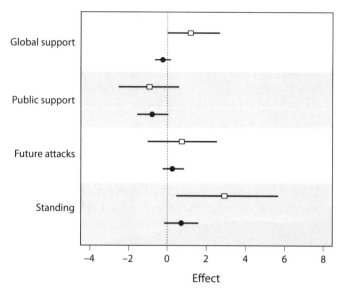

FIGURE 3.5. Average causal mediation effects.
Average causal mediation effects (ACMEs) from a series of nonparametric causal mediation models replicate the findings from figure 3.4: the significant effect of the reputation treatment on the within-subject effect of fighting for high self-monitor doves (depicted here with the open squares) is mediated by concerns about Israel's standing in the world and global support, the two mechanisms that most directly implicate concerns about image. In other words, high self-monitor doves fight for reputational reasons rather than instrumental ones. In contrast, we see no such effect for the pooled comparison group (depicted here with the dark circles).

hawks see the effect as less negative than low self-monitor hawks. In other words, then, another reason why we see this ceiling effect is because hawks (especially high self-monitor ones) already assume the existence of image-related concerns.

Implications

Why are some individuals more willing to fight for face than others? This chapter investigated the theory—linking self-monitoring for concerns about reputation for resolve—by using a set of cross-national survey experiments to explore variation in sensitivity to reputation concerns in a public opinion context. Obtaining almost identical results in each study, we found that the interaction between self-monitoring and general predispositions toward the use of force produces systematic differences in support for the use of force. The findings are not only consistent with the theoretical expectations laid out in chapter 2, but they also allow us to shed light on more specific questions that arise from the theory. For example, we are able to show that even a very mild reputational treatment can make high self-monitor doves want to fight, indicating that reputation for resolve continues to be the primary social currency in their minds. We also show that high self-monitors seem to want to fight because of status considerations in the eyes of international audiences, such as concerns about global standing and global image, more so than strategic or instrumental benefits typically associated with being resolved, such as enhanced deterrence or domestic political support. Finally, we demonstrate that whether the audience is an ally or an adversary does not significantly change high self-monitors' willingness to fight, suggesting that reputation in the eyes of both of these audiences is valued similarly.

These experiments show how the microfoundations of the dispositional theory exist within the general public. These mechanisms, we argue, should operate similarly in leaders' crisis decision making as well. Just as ordinary citizens are often primed with reputational arguments by enterprising political elites, as we shall see in chapters 6 through 8, leaders are often subjected to a similar mechanism where advisors provide reputational cues to a well-informed leader who must make a foreign policy choice either consistent or inconsistent with his or her self-monitoring disposition.

More broadly, however, our findings reaffirm the intimate link between psychological traits and foreign policy decision making even among members of the public. In so doing they also yield a richer understanding of how reputational considerations shape public opinion toward the use of force. We show the existence of an important subgroup of the public—the high self-monitor doves—that goes "against type" when presented with reputational considerations, and actually increases its willingness to fight. We further show that not all hawks are the same, as high and low self-monitor hawks fight for very different reasons, although the former do not need reputational primes to fight as the high self-monitor doves do.

These findings carry significant implications for the ability of leaders to mobilize domestic support for the use of force: when leaders are able to frame an international conflict in reputational terms, a segment of the population that would not otherwise be convinced about the use of force—high self-monitor doves—is likely to become more supportive of military engagement. Although our US study uses a diverse, nonrepresentative sample, our Israeli study does use a nationally representative sample, indicating that high self-monitor doves constitute a nontrivial segment (24 percent) of the population. This suggests that couching military interventions in areas affecting important, but nonvital, interests in language that implicates the country's reputation for resolve—as many leaders have done in a past—is a rational strategy, because it resonates not only with the hawks who already want to fight, but more importantly, with a critical segment of doves: those who are high self-monitors. By identifying a systematic psychological trait that explains variation in willingness to use force to demonstrate a reputation for resolve, we are better positioned to explain what types of citizens and leaders will be more or less likely to seek to fight for face.

4

Self-Monitoring, US Presidents, and International Crises

A STATISTICAL ANALYSIS

In chapter 3, I tested the microfoundations of the dispositional theory using cross-national survey experiments. Public opinion surveys have important benefits, but they also involve some trade-offs for the questions I ask in this book. Specifically, presidents may respond to international crises very differently than ordinary citizens. I therefore also test the theory using observational data of the conflict behavior of US presidents with regard to militarized interstate disputes (MIDs). An important element in testing my leader-level theory is the validity of the measures of the explanatory variables. Scholars in psychology have developed reliable instruments to test the self-monitoring levels of individuals. In the survey experiments, I was able to ask participants to take the Self-Monitoring Scale described in chapter 2. However, it is impossible to do so in the case of American presidents. Instead, I rely on others' coding of the presidents according to the benchmarks listed in the Self-Monitoring Scale, which requires good knowledge of the subjects. Therefore I asked sixty-eight presidential historians to take an original survey on the president each had studied in depth. Among other questions, it contains the eighteen-point Self-Monitoring Test. Classifying the presidents along low and high self-monitors in this way offers several advantages over alternative methods, which I detail below.

The historians' survey suggests that American presidents exhibit variation in their self-monitoring dispositions. I leverage this variation to test statistically whether US presidents' behavior during international crises is consistent with the expectations of my theory. The results provide robust, overwhelming, and consistent support for my argument. The self–monitoring disposition of a US president is a significant predictor of his likelihood of employing and initiating military instruments to demonstrate resolve during international conflict. Low self-monitor presidents not only engage in less militarized interstate disputes, but they are also significantly less likely to initiate such disputes, compared to high self-monitor presidents. Moreover, I present findings indicating that high self-monitor presidents are also more likely to prevail in militarized interstate disputes compared to their low self-monitor counterparts. I present these findings using negative binomial regression, as well as permutation tests. These results remain robust across several model specifications, including when we control for a number of confounders identified with the literature. Finally, this chapter features an online appendix with summary statistics and additional robustness checks.[1]

The rest of the chapter proceeds as follows: I first discuss my hypotheses and the observable implications of my theory when examining the MIDs data set. Next, I detail the procedures and results of the presidential historians' survey I used in order to obtain the self-monitoring measure of the US presidents. I then discuss the control variables used in the regression analyses, including two alternative proxies for the president's level of hawkishness. This is followed by a discussion of the research design, my main results, several robustness checks, and additional observable implications that follow from the theory. This chapter's conclusion summarizes the significance of the results and discusses potential concerns regarding selection effects.

Hypotheses

The theory predicts that we should observe a consistent association between presidents' self-monitoring and their willingness to signal resolve through the employment of coercive military instruments, including the use of force, during international crises. If all else is held equal, high self-monitor presidents should be more willing to influence others' assessments of them through signals of resolve, which will inflate the extent to which others view them as resolved, compared to low self-monitor presidents. Moreover, low self-monitors are less likely than high self-monitor presidents to initiate, or escalate, crises that involve purely reputational issues and will use coercive instruments only when intrinsic interests are at stake. These differences suggest that high self-monitors should be more likely to respond to reputational cues by seeking to fight for face, and therefore we should see greater employment of coercive military instruments during international crises by high self-monitor presidents.

Militarized interstate disputes (MIDs) refer to crisis situations that involve the threat, display, or actual use of military force. The use of these military instruments serves as a proxy for capturing a leader's inclination to demonstrate his or her resolve. Indeed, the threat, display, and use of force are exactly the tools that provide a leader an opportunity to demonstrate "face," because those actions implicate his or her state's reputation for resolve. To be sure, the use of MIDs in order to capture a leader's inclination to demonstrate resolve is not a perfect proxy. This is because there are other, nonmilitary, means by which a leader can demonstrate his or her resolve. Moreover, militarized crises are not necessarily motivated by a leader's concern for reputation for resolve. Thus, while we could expect leaders to believe their reputation for resolve is at stake when employing those instruments, it is hard to establish whether reputational concerns were a *primary* motivation in each instance of the coercive use of military force.[2]

With these caveats in mind, however, I believe it is reasonable to expect that if we control for the presidents' level of hawkishness, high self-monitor presidents should demonstrate, on average, a greater inclination to appear resolved. This is because any given militarized crisis involves a combination of some material interests and some reputational ones. While high and low self-monitors are not expected to differ in their assessments of the material values at stake, they should differ significantly in the importance they attach to reputational costs. Put differently, after we control for hawkishness, in any given crisis, high self-monitor presidents will have one additional motivation to fight (i.e., reputation for resolve) compared to low self-monitor presidents. Thus, all else equal, high self-monitors should be more motivated to demonstrate resolve even in crises where reputation for resolve was not the primary motivation.

Moreover, consistent with previous studies, it is fair to assume that leaders who are concerned about reputation for resolve will engage in and initiate military threats, displays of force, and actual uses of force as a means to signal resolve to adversaries, allies, and domestic audiences.[3] As Fearon has long argued, "leaders and publics have typically understood threats and troop deployments to engage the national honor."[4] Indeed, the foundational notion of the audience cost research agenda is that a leader would incur a penalty from his or her constituency if that leader were to escalate a foreign policy crisis and then be seen to have backed down. Audience costs exist because threats to use military force implicate the state's reputation for resolve.[5] Indeed, Snyder and Borghard have shown that leaders intuitively understand that the threat to use force could tie their hands and implicate their country's reputation for resolve, and therefore those same leaders think long and hard before using such instruments to be certain that they would not retreat from their use of force.[6] For example, displaying military force by stationing troops close to the border, mobilizing forces, or sending an aircraft carrier close to the crisis zone, also provides powerful means of demonstrating resolve or toughness during crises. Those types of instruments are either financially costly to undertake or increase the risk of escalation, so only actors who committed to being resolved will use such a signal.[7]

Turning to the observable implications that follow from the theory, I postulate that leaders who are more concerned about their country's reputation for resolve should, all else equal, be more willing to signal their resolve through the coercive and actual use of military force. At the core of our theory, however, is the notion that not all leaders are created equal, and some leaders come to power with a far greater inclination to fight for face. Specifically, the theory predicts that leaders will systematically vary in their concern for reputation for resolve depending on whether they are high or low self-monitors: high self-monitor leaders are expected to be more concerned about demonstrating resolve through the threat, display, or actual use of force. Thus, if the theory is correct, we should observe the following:

> H1: Because high self-monitor presidents have greater concern for reputation for resolve, they will be more likely to initiate a higher annual rate of MIDs compared to low self-monitor presidents.

The first hypothesis follows directly from the proposition that the use of coercive military instruments is understood as communicating resolve, either by tying the leader's hands, such as by issuing a public threat, or by escalating the conflict by displaying or actually using force.[8] As a result, leaders willing to employ coercive military instruments are also those who are more inclined to care about demonstrating toughness, which my theory identifies as high self-monitors. The low self-monitor leaders are less likely to care about demonstrating their resolve and thus less inclined to employ coercive military instruments.

> H2: Because high self-monitor presidents care more about reputation for resolve, they will be engaged in a higher rate of annual MIDs compared to low self-monitor presidents.

The intuition behind this hypothesis is straightforward. Concern for demonstrating resolve is likely to lead high self-monitor leaders to use military coercive instruments that are particularly strong and costly signals of toughness. In this way, high self-monitors will rely more heavily and more frequently on those instruments, viewing them as good opportunities to influence others' perceptions. Furthermore, in cases where a state poses a challenge to a high self-monitor president, we expect the president to escalate to the actual use of force, rather than backing down, if lesser shows of force fail to settle the challenge. In contrast, we should expect low self-monitors, who care less about affecting others' beliefs about their resolve, to be less inclined to engage in MIDs.

Next, I expect the positive and significant relationship between self-monitoring and engagement/initiation of MIDs to hold when we control for general hawkishness through to use of different proxies. Furthermore, I probe whether this relationship remains when we split the sample into hawks and doves, and evaluate the difference between high and low self-monitoring within each sample respectively. The theory chapter, as well as the results of the survey experiments reported in chapter 3, should lead us to expect to see a greater effect of self-monitoring among dovish presidents, and a positive, albeit more mild, effect of self-monitoring among hawkish presidents, who might be already inclined to show resolve.

> H3: High self-monitoring hawkish or dovish presidents will engage in, and initiate, a higher rate of annual MIDs compared to low self-monitoring hawkish or dovish presidents, respectively. This effect should be more significant among doves than hawks.

Measuring Self-Monitoring Dispositions of US Presidents

WHY SURVEY PRESIDENTIAL EXPERTS?

To obtain a measure of the presidents' level of self-monitoring, I turn to presidential historians. At the outset, it is important to appreciate the value of expert judgments on the dispositions and beliefs of national leaders. While the ideal scenario would be to survey former presidents themselves, only two of America's nine Cold War presidents are alive today: Jimmy Carter and George H. W. Bush. The judgment of experts who have extensively studied the lives of these presidents is therefore a researcher's second-best option. Presidential scholars spend many years studying the personality, leadership style, and background of a president. They interview colleagues, friends, and family members of the president and in most cases spend hours conversing with the president himself. They have significant knowledge that can be utilized to assess a president's disposition and beliefs. With regard to self-monitoring in particular, support for the reliability of presidential experts comes from an early generation of studies finding a significant correlation between self-ratings and peer-ratings on the self-monitoring scale.[9]

Keeping the above in mind, we should expect historians' ideas about the personality traits of the presidents in the study to yield reliable results. The vast majority of the experts surveyed were biographers who had, by virtue of their profession, focused on the entire life of one or more presidents, thus gaining knowledge not only of the presidents' policy choices but also of their personalities before they were elected. This perspective allows the historians to answer questions about each president's self-monitoring abilities with reasonable authority. Moreover, the use of multiple experts for each president is likely to minimize the effects of any biases that individuals might have. Before completing the survey, each respondent was asked to rate his or her level of knowledge of the president; some respondents declined to complete the survey because they felt insufficiently informed to answer the questions it contained. This process of self-selection further strengthens our confidence that our sample contains experts who know their subjects well.

An explicit measurement of self-monitoring is helpful for this study because self-monitoring is not the only factor that affects a leader's decision making: beliefs about the efficacy of force, along with specific factors related to the leader's political situation, will also affect behavior. A study of presidential policy choices would not be able to disentangle self-monitoring from these other factors. In addition, it is easier to compare presidents' levels of self-monitoring based on historians' completion of the same survey using the same scale, rather than to study presidential memoirs and statements alone, especially when seeking to compare across self-monitoring dispositions.

This study is one of the few to use self-monitoring scores to analyze politics, but it is not the only one to use a historians' survey. Studies in political science often utilize expert-generated data in order to measure phenomena for which available behavioral data are inadequate.[10] For example, Braumoeller uses a survey of experts in order to quantify ideal-states of the world for geopolitically powerful nations throughout history, in order to assess the importance of both power and ideology for state decision making.[11] As he argues, surveys allow us to measure the quantity of interest more precisely, whereas behavioral data might be only indirectly or imperfectly related to the phenomena we seek to measure.[12]

SURVEY DESIGN AND IMPLEMENTATION

The sampling frame for the survey included all English-speaking historians or journalists who had published at least one scholarly book on any former US president from Truman to Bush 43 (N=392), as determined by searches through library catalogs and online book retailers.[13] The sample for the survey included all such historians still living for whom e-mail addresses could be found through online searches (N=236).[14] Each of these potential respondents was contacted via e-mail and given a choice of completing the questionnaire electronically or on paper (to be returned by mail). Historians were not notified of the study's topic or hypotheses, and no incentives were offered for the completion of the questionnaire. In some cases, multiple contacts were necessary before a response was elicited. While each potential respondent was contacted with a particular president in mind, a few who had written books on more than one president were asked to complete a questionnaire for each president they had studied.[15] The details of the survey's implementation are summarized in table 4.1.

The survey instrument was divided into two sections. The first contained a commonly used Self-Monitoring Scale (which can be found in the online

TABLE 4.1. Summary of Survey Responses

	Sampling Frame (Number of Living Experts)	Sample (Contactable)	Number of Responses	Response Rate
Truman	43	18	6	33.3%
Eisenhower	50	28	6	21.4%
Kennedy	42	25	12	48.0%
Johnson	27	18	7	38.9%
Nixon	38	22	10	45.5%
Ford	16	11	6	54.5%
Carter	35	22	6	27.3%
Reagan	61	36	7	19.4%
Bush 41	18	15	8	53.3%
Clinton	33	24	9	37.5%
Bush 43	29	17	4	23.5%
Total	392	236	81	34.3%

appendix), modified to apply in the third person to the president before he was first elected president. The second section contained a set of questions about the strategic beliefs and crisis behavior of the president while in office. Thus the first section was designed to measure a president's innate self-monitoring abilities, and the second to measure his beliefs about a host of issues while he was in office. To check for potential bias, respondents were also asked to rate their knowledge of, and respect for, the president they had studied, and the extent to which they shared their subjects' values.[16]

The first section of the survey asked respondents to focus on the president *before* he was elected to public office, and to offer examples from that period to support their answers to the self-monitoring test. In that way I primed respondents to focus on the president's disposition as a person rather than as president and to cue them to think about examples that do not conflate with the president's behavior during his tenure. Measuring leaders' self-monitoring dispositions is not straightforward. In an experimental setting, it is possible to measure the self-monitoring dispositions of an individual by asking him or her to take Snyder's Self-Monitoring Test. The test consists of eighteen true-false self-descriptive statements that describe, among other things, concern with situational appropriateness of self-presentation, attention to social cues, expressive control (which is a key indicator separating high from low self-monitors), the use of this ability in particular situations, and situation-to-situation shifts in expressive self-presentation.[17] Apart from modifying pronouns in the statements to read in third person instead of first person, the eighteen statements used in the survey were taken verbatim from Snyder's test. However, in contrast to the original test, instead of having respondents provide true-false answers to the statements, responses were recorded on a seven-point Likert-scale ranging from *Very Uncharacteristic* to *Very Characteristic*. This is a common modification to the scale in the literature, undertaken originally to facilitate factor analysis.[18] I utilized the modification with the aim of obtaining a more nuanced and fine-grained measure of the assessments of the experts being surveyed. To further minimize bias, respondents were not informed that the statements were part of a test for self-monitoring.

The second section of the survey instrument first asked respondents to rank the relative importance of various factors to the president's decision making in times of general international crisis. The factors included prior commitments, public opinion, domestic interest groups, escalation risks, potential American casualties, personal prestige, and the need to appear resolute. A further set of ten questions, scored on a seven-point Likert-style scale from "Strongly Disagree" to "Strongly Agree," were designed to elicit more detailed information about the crisis behavior of the president with regard to questions of reputation, domestic politics, sincerity, public opinion, vital interests, and the use of force. The complete instrument used for the survey can be found in the online appendix to this chapter.

In Snyder's original study, subjects were categorized as high or low self-monitors using a median split as a cutoff.[19] In order to minimize arbitrary classification through median splits or an excessive numbers of score brackets, I have chosen to categorize presidents as high and low self-monitors based on their scores relative to the midpoint of the scale. On the Likert-style scale I employed for my survey (score 1–7, where 1 is "very uncharacteristic" and 7 is "very characteristic"), the neutral (midpoint) score is 72 (a score of 72 is equivalent to selecting 4, indicating "neither characteristic nor uncharacteristic," for all eighteen questions). Using the sample distributions from the historians' surveys for each of the presidents, I have tested whether each president scored statistically significantly higher or lower than 72 at the 95 percent level.[20] For ease of interpretation, I normalize the scores on a scale of 1 to 100, such that a score of 50 is the neutral score; presidents who are scored significantly higher or lower than 50 are classified as high or low self-monitors, respectively. The results are presented in figure 4.1.

Figure 4.1 indicates that Kennedy, Johnson, Reagan, and Clinton were significantly high self-monitors, while Ford, Carter, and G.H.W. Bush (Bush 41) were significantly low self-monitors. The remaining presidents—Truman, Eisenhower, Nixon, and George W. Bush (Bush 43)—cannot be classified as statistically different from the midpoint score and, hence, could be thought of as in an intermediate category between low and high. Figure 4.1 highlights considerable variation in reported self-monitoring abilities between presidents, and often between successive administrations. For example, Johnson was twenty points higher on the self-monitoring scale than his successor, Nixon,

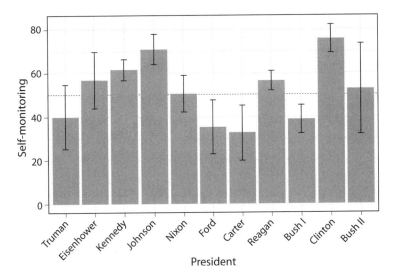

FIGURE 4.1. Self-monitoring scores of US presidents.
The results from a survey of seventy presidential historians shows that some presidents are scored as systematically higher self-monitors than others. John F. Kennedy, Lyndon Johnson, Ronald Reagan, and Bill Clinton are high self-monitors, while Gerald Ford, Jimmy Carter, and George H. W. Bush are low self-monitors. The plot displays 95 percent confidence intervals, classifying presidents based on whether their scores are statistically significantly different from the scale midpoint, denoted here with the horizontal black line.

and the difference between them is statistically significant at the 95 percent level. A similar transition in the opposite direction is visible between Carter and his successor, Reagan, the latter being almost twenty-four points higher on the scale than the former, a difference that is also statistically significant. Johnson, in fact, stands out as the highest self-monitor, while Carter emerges as the lowest self-monitor.

The responses show important variation in the first independent variable. Still, the small sample size of experts limits one's ability to establish a more exact representation of each president's self-monitoring score. For this reason, I take the absolute numbers as only rough estimates. However, the survey responses have greater value in terms of showing relative levels of self-monitoring among the presidents in the study. For example, even though Harry Truman (n=6) is not a significantly low self-monitor, in relative terms he is lower than his successor Dwight Eisenhower (n=6).[21] With more data points, their relative positions would become even clearer; however, given the dearth of available data, it is helpful to classify presidents as high and low self-monitors based on how they compare to other presidents, along with supplemental qualitative data from presidential memoirs and biographies, as I do in chapters 6, 7, and 8. As table 4.1 shows, the overall response rate for Bill Clinton and George W.

Bush (43) was slightly lower than that of the other presidents.[22] Of all American presidents since Truman it appears that Clinton emerges as the highest self-monitor, followed by Johnson.

ROBUSTNESS OF THE MEASURE

One concern about studying presidents' self-monitoring scores may be whether those scores simply correlate with the other so-called Big Five personality traits: neuroticism, extraversion, openness to new experiences, agreeableness, and conscientiousness.[23] However, psychological research has shown that self-monitoring is not merely a composite measure. In the case of US presidents, Rubenzer and Faschingbauer administered to experts a personality test for each president.[24] The study measured the classic Big Five personality traits. Each president received a percentile score. Comparing these scores with the self-monitoring scores generated by this survey using correlation tests and linear regression shows that only one of the five personality traits that Rubenzer and Faschingbauer measured (agreeableness) was significantly correlated with self-monitoring ($r=-0.64$, $p=0.032$). Furthermore, this trait was significant only in a bivariate context; a linear regression model regressing the self-monitoring scores on each of the personality traits, including a composite measure "character," did not yield statistically significant results. The results of this test further buttress the findings suggesting that self-monitoring is a distinct factor, uncorrelated with other individual differences.

A second concern is that scoring the Self-Monitoring Test might vary based on whether a continuous scale or a dichotomous (true/false) scale is used for each question on the test. The literature is divided as to which scale is most appropriate. Multiple studies have used variations of a continuous scale, allowing for respondents to agree or disagree more or less strongly with the statements on the test.[25] However, Snyder and Gangestad, the creators of the Self-Monitoring Test, have consistently offered only "true" and "false" as possible answers.[26] Dichotomizing the data changes my classification of Ford from a significantly low self-monitor to a low, but not significantly so, self-monitor ($p=0.0506$).[27] However, in order to remain true to Snyder's eighteen-item Self-Monitoring Test from which the questions were derived, I use the dichotomized data for calculations described below.

Third, along with measures of self-monitoring, the first section of the historians' survey also asked the historians to rank their knowledge of the relevant president, their respect for that president, and the similarity of their values to those of that president. Using their responses, I checked for biases based on differences in knowledge by comparing the unweighted mean scores to the mean scores weighted by knowledge level. The differences between the weighted and unweighted averages were small and not statistically significant, although only two of the experts ranked their knowledge as less than 5 out of 7 (one for George H. W. Bush and one for Clinton). I then checked if there was a significant difference in mean self-monitoring scores between historians who had more respect for a president (score 5, 6, or 7) and those who had less respect (score 1, 2, or 3) as compared to the median score of 4. The result of the difference-in-means test was not statistically significant, although only ten historians rated their respect for their respective president as less than 4 (of these, four took the survey for Nixon, one for Johnson, three for Clinton, and one for George W. Bush). I carried out the same test for congruence of values between respondent and president and again found no significant difference-in-means between those who shared and those who did not share the president's values, although only nineteen of the eighty-one surveys indicated a dissonance between the values of the historian and those of his or her respective president.

Fourth, one additional concern arises from the potential unreliability of experts with a hindsight view of a presidency: that of post hoc bias. The experts being surveyed are answering the questions in hindsight, that is, they are fully aware of how each president's term and life played out. This knowledge may introduce bias into their assessments. I have tried to minimize this source of bias by, first, explicitly asking respondents in the first section of the survey to focus on the life of the president *before* he was elected to the White House. In addition, I asked respondents to give explicit examples about the behavior of the president before his tenure to support their answers to the questions in the self-monitoring test. These minimal primes may mitigate tendencies toward post hoc bias in the coding of self-monitoring.

Finally, and relatedly, we might be worried that, even though the historians were never told the topic of the project or the nature of the Self-Monitoring Test, they might have been thinking about the president's concerns for reputation for resolve (our outcome variable) while answering the self-monitoring survey, whether consciously or not. If so, our self-monitoring scores might be confounded. I should highlight that such a risk is very small, as the self-monitoring test does not in any way cue respondents to think about foreign policy, and certainly not reputation in crisis behavior. Nevertheless, to evaluate whether this is a valid concern, I asked the historians at the end of the survey to answer several questions about domestic and international politics, including a question that approximates my outcome variable of interest.[28] Reassuringly, there was not a great deal of variation in these assessments, indicating that the historians were not inferring self-monitoring from crisis behavior of the president. That their assessments somewhat differ from the results of this study about which presidents chose to fight for reputation should be expected: these historians are not necessarily experts on the foreign policy of the presidents they studied. Many of them concentrated more on the early personal life of the president, his relationship to members of his family, or his domestic, economic, and social policies.[29]

Research Design

To test the hypotheses about the relationship between self-monitoring and crisis behavior, we need data that captures US involvement in and initiation of militarized international conflicts. I therefore use the widely employed MIDs data set, which identifies all "united historical cases in which the threat, display or use of military force short of war by one member state is explicitly directed towards the government, official representatives, official forces, property, or territory of another state."[30] This data set, despite its limitations, is appropriate for testing the theory given that presidents demonstrate their resolve through military means during crises that don't necessarily escalate into wars. Following Cohen and Weeks, and like Dafoe and Caughey, I dropped fishing disputes from the analysis, which are widely seen as providing negligible information about international disputes as conceptualized here.[31]

Our key explanatory variable is the presidents' self-monitoring scores, which are coded based on the historians' survey. In order to test my theoretical predictions, I categorized presidents as either high or low self-monitors. For the purpose of the statistical analysis, presidents were categorized into high and low self-monitors based on their location above or below the midpoint self-monitoring score of 0.5 on the 0 to 1 scale (which incidentally also divided the two groups at the median score). The categorization is motivated theoretically: rather than expecting the effect of self-monitoring level to be linear, I expect relatively high self-monitors to be systematically different from relatively low self-monitors. In the robustness checks available in the online appendix, I show the results are robust to alternative categorizations of self-monitoring, including treating self-monitoring level as a continuous variable in the regression analysis. Figure 4A.1 in the online appendix summarizes the self-monitoring scores of the US presidents (from 1945 to 2009) from highest to lowest.

I consider two dependent variables: the number of militarized interstate disputes in which a US president either initiated (DV1) or engaged (DV2) in any given year. I thus create a dependent variable that indicates either the number of MIDs in which a president was involved in a given year (DV2), or number of MIDs initiated by a US president in a given year (DV1). In addition to conducting the analysis at the president-year level, in the online appendix I consider the number of MIDs at the presidency level by aggregating all MIDs in which the president was involved or that he initiated during his administration. MIDs are assigned to the president under whom US involvement in the MID began. Importantly, because presidents do not enter and leave office on

January 1, for the data presented at the president-year level, I annualize the MID rate accordingly and weigh observations by the proportion of the year the president served.[32]

I have taken two approaches to analyzing this data: negative binomial regression and permutation tests. To avoid the assumptions of negative binomial regressions, which may be problematic in this case, I employ permutation/randomization tests both with and without matching.[33] Permutation tests assess whether the null hypothesis of no difference between high and low self-monitor presidents is likely given the data we observe. Specifically, if we consider all the possible ways in which the labels "high self-monitor" and "low self-monitor" could have been distributed among presidents, these tests determine how likely it is that we would find a result as supportive of our hypothesis as the one we actually observe.[34]

This randomization inference is naturally conducted at the president level. I also do this same test after making sure the sets of high and low self-monitor presidents included in the test were evenly "matched" on a number of important covariates. In brief, matching offers a statistically rigorous way of balancing high and low self-monitor presidents on potentially confounding dimensions. For instance, we might find that on average, low self-monitor presidents were slightly more likely to take power during economic recessions. Through matching, we can then increase the statistical weight placed on low self-monitor presidents who did not take power during recessions. We then end up with a "matched" sample, in which high and low self-monitor presidents were similarly likely to take power during a recession, for the subsequent analysis.

The statistical analysis uses monadic data with president-year as the unit of analysis. This unit is best suited to my argument, because the theory focuses on how a particular psychological construct that varies among US presidents affects their conflict behavior. Focusing on dyad-year would be more appropriate if I were testing how the interaction with other leaders or countries affects the likelihood of such conflicts. However, as a robustness test, I use dyadic data, which allows me to control directly for the attributes of other actors, as well as changing power relations or alliance relationships between the United States and the other country in the dyad. Given our interest in MIDs between the United States and other states in the international system from 1945 until 2009, I constructed a yearly data set of all dyads involving the United States under a given president and one other country in the period, and I investigated both MID involvement and MID initiation. This dyadic president-dyad-year data was analyzed using logit regression models because the dependent variables—MID initiation and involvement—are dichotomous.[35] My objective in this analysis has thus been first to see whether there is a relationship between self-monitoring level and willingness to fight for reputation, and then to see if this relationship remains when I "stack the deck" against finding a statistical relationship between the two. I do the latter by including a wide set of proxies for alternative explanations as controls in the regression analysis, employing several different statistical techniques relying on different assumptions, and matching high and low self-monitors on important covariates ahead of permutation tests.

Control Variables

In the regression analyses presented below, I include as predictors several potential confounders pertaining to the hawkishness of the president, other presidential characteristics, the international conflict environment, the domestic environment, and time trends. Specifically, I control for the following sets of covariates, both in one model, and in several smaller models using only some of these covariates.[36]

HAWKISHNESS

To measure the hawkishness of presidents, I rely on two alternative proxies: the first captures military assertiveness indirectly by proxying it with political ideology, using a dummy variable indicating whether the president was from the Republican or Democratic Party. A host of survey experiments on the US public suggest a high correlation between high scores on military assertiveness and voting for the Republican Party.[37] Thus, controlling for the political party of the president also allows me to distinguish the impact of hawkishness from the impact of self-monitoring.[38]

A second proxy for hawkishness is obtained by applying a widely used text analysis method called WordScore to the public foreign policy speeches of all US Cold War presidents.[39] WordScore is a scaling technique originally devised for discerning relative policy positions along various policy dimensions from party manifestoes. The method has been shown to approximate expert judgment about party positions closely in different political and linguistic environments, and it has been successfully used both for cross-sectional and time-series analysis.[40] WordScore is a dictionary-based technique: given a set of reference texts with preassigned numerical policy positions (for example, "extreme left" and "extreme right" might be translated into −10 and +10), the technique counts all word occurrences in the reference texts and computes the conditional probability (relative frequencies) of encountering a given word in a particular reference text.[41]

Specifically, I collected all public speeches on foreign policy delivered by each Cold War president during his time in office (see table 4.2). This included all inaugural, farewell, State of the Union, and UN General Assembly addresses held by the American Presidency Project (APP) website.[42] I manually inspected each address and discarded all paragraphs without foreign

TABLE 4.2. Number of Major Foreign Policy Addresses by US Presidents, 1945–92

President	Years in Office	Number of Speeches
Truman	1945–53	15
Eisenhower	1953–61	33
Kennedy	1961–63	19
Johnson	1963–69	34
Nixon	1969–74	20
Ford	1974–77	8
Carter	1977–81	14
Reagan	1981–89	46
Bush (41)	1989–93	10
Total		199

policy or defense-related content[43] so as to ensure that the analysis recovers the correct variable of interest, that is, military assertiveness. This strategy resulted in a total of 199 addresses from 1945 (President Truman) to 1992 (President George H. W. Bush) (see the online appendix for list of speeches). Because this measure could be constructed only for Cold War presidents (who all faced the Soviet Union as the main source of threat) it reduces the presidents I can consider. Moreover, since G.H.W. Bush was president during a transition period, he cannot be considered a truly Cold War president, and his scores should be taken with caution.

These speeches range from a total of 3,286 unique words (Ford) to a total of 7,533 unique words (Reagan). I ran the WordScore algorithm on all the speeches of each president, specifying a −10 value for the two most dovish speeches I identified, and a +10 value for the two most hawkish speeches I identified. In each other evaluated speech, words that did not show up in any of the four reference speeches were not scored. The sum of the WordScores of words present in any of the four reference texts yielded a "raw score" for each unseen speech. The mean of this raw score for the speeches of each president represents a rough measure of whether a president's speeches were collectively closer to the dovish reference speeches selected (lower on the military assertiveness scale) or to the hawkish reference speeches selected (higher on the military assertiveness scale).

A crucial aspect of the WordScore research design is thus the selection of reference texts that constitute clear-cut examples of the two extreme values of the policy position under investigation. This analysis uses four reference texts including, on one end of the scale, two presidential speeches widely seen as conveying a low level of military assertiveness or, put differently, that are not assertive in tone and that place more emphasis on political and diplomatic

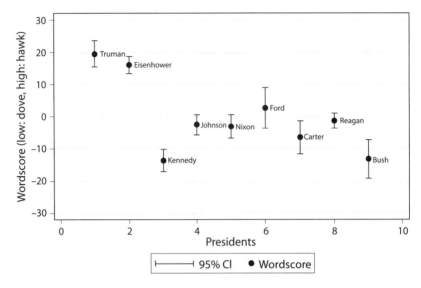

FIGURE 4.2. Cold War presidents' military assertiveness WordScores.

solutions than on military instruments. On the other end of the scale, I select two speeches that place a great deal of emphasis on military instruments and are assertive in nature.[44]

In order to avoid a time trend in this text analysis (for example, by choosing a dovish speech from early in the Cold War and a hawkish speech from late in the Cold War as reference texts), I choose two hawkish and two dovish reference texts—one of each from early in the Cold War and one of each closer to the end. Multiple reference texts from across the time period in question help to eliminate the time trend that otherwise could be seen in the data. For reference texts for hawkish speeches, I use Harry Truman's March 12, 1947, address to Congress regarding the Truman Doctrine, and Ronald Reagan's March 8, 1983, "Evil Empire" speech. For reference texts for dovish (or less militarily assertive) speeches, I use John F. Kennedy's 1963 American University commencement address, and Ronald Reagan's 1988 speech at Moscow State University. A detailed explanation for the selection of those speeches can be found in the online appendix.[45]

Figure 4.2 depicts the results of the WordScore analysis based on each president's foreign policy speeches (with the raw scores rescaled to approximate the variance of the reference texts, as suggested in Laver and colleagues).[46] The horizontal axis shows the presidents in chronological order, and the vertical axis shows each president's WordScore on the military assertiveness scale relative to the four reference texts. Reagan's public speeches (excluding the two reference speeches) place him in the middle on the military assertiveness scale,

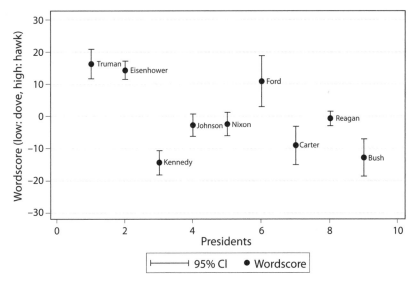

FIGURE 4.3. Cold War presidents' military assertiveness WordScores, excluding crises.

given the 95 percent confidence interval. George H. W. Bush and Kennedy (excluding his American University reference text) have the lowest average military assertiveness score, while Truman and Eisenhower have the highest. The confidence interval bars indicate, however, that many of Reagan's public speeches on foreign policy are more militarily assertive in tone than those of Bush (41), Kennedy, or Carter.[47]

Importantly, however, a president's public speeches may not be truly independent from the outcome I seek to explain, that is, whether he chooses to fight for reputation. Thus, for example, more militarily assertive speeches might be used strategically to signal toughness during an ongoing crisis or immediately following a crisis. To deal with this concern, I identify all moments of Cold War–related crisis using the International Crisis Behavior (ICB) data set.[48] A list of all those crises can be found in the online appendix (table 4A.4). I then exclude all speeches delivered during the period from the day a crisis was triggered until sixty days later (losing about one-fifth of the total number of observations). The results of analysis of the remaining speeches are depicted in figure 4.3. The relative positions of the presidents remain similar along the military assertiveness dimension, showing that the analysis is robust to the exclusion of crises. In the online appendix, I also report several additional robustness tests.

Importantly, the main regression tables (tables 4.3 and 4.4) report results using both party affiliation as well as foreign policy rhetoric as proxies for hawkishness. However, because the foreign policy rhetoric measure could be constructed only for Cold War presidents, it reduces the number of presidents

TABLE 4.3. Self-Monitoring Level and MID Involvement (Wilcoxon-Mann-Whitney Exact Test, No Matching, Weighted by Presidency Length)

Difference in mean annual MID rate	2.03*	p-value:	0.002882

*p<0.1

TABLE 4.4. Hawks, Doves by Self-Monitoring Level and MID Involvement Rate (Wilcoxon-Mann-Whitney Exact Test, No Matching, Weighted by Presidency Length)

Hawks Only			
Difference in mean annual MID rate	2.06*	p-value	0.03047
Doves Only			
Difference in mean annual MID rate	2.30*	p-value	0.0283

*p<0.1

significantly. Thus, I use party affiliation as my main proxy for hawkishness. Nevertheless, all results are also robust to using the text-analysis based proxy for hawkishness, and they are reported in the main regression tables as well as the online appendix.

OTHER PRESIDENTIAL CHARACTERISTICS

To make sure that the patterns detected were not due to some other feature of presidents, I controlled for a range of other plausible presidential characteristics. Scholars have highlighted the importance of leaders' military and political experience, although studies have reached different conclusions about the direction and mechanisms by which experiences affect their crisis behavior.[49] I control for this by including military and executive experience prior to taking office.[50] Age of the president when taking office is also included, given previous work suggesting its importance.[51] I also control for presidents' total tenure.

INTERNATIONAL STRATEGIC ENVIRONMENT

To alleviate the possibility of MIDs covarying with international conflict trends, I included as other predictors the worldwide number of MIDs, the worldwide number of wars, USSR/Russian MIDs, and the USSR-US Composite Index of National Capabilities ratio in the current year (all from the Correlates of War Project). To consider the possibility of selection effects, in which high self-monitor presidents are elected in conflict-prone time periods, I also included as controls the number of MIDs in which the United States was involved in the one, three, and five years prior to the president taking office, as well as the number of MIDs in which the United States used force in the one, three, and five years prior to the president taking office (in both cases reporting the latter).

DOMESTIC POLITICAL ENVIRONMENT

Existing work shows that aspects of the domestic political environment are likely to contribute to US involvement in militarized disputes.[52] Gelpi and Feaver find that, as the percentage of veterans serving in the executive branch and the legislature increases, the probability that the United States will initiate militarized disputes declines. I considered this possibility by controlling for the percentage of the political elite that are veterans of the armed forces (following Gelpi and Feaver). Finally, I control for whether the United States was in a recession in the year in question (utilizing National Bureau of Economic Research definition and data); whether the government was unified (0 or 1);[53] and the logged number of causalities in the preceding US war as a measure of war wariness.[54]

TIME TRENDS

To correct for time dependence, I follow standard practices and include US peace years, peace years squared, and peace years cubed.[55] This is a strong test, because the only variation in my independent variable of interest is temporal (varying by president). Following a wide range of work that focuses on politics during the Cold War, I also included a Cold War indicator. Finally, I included time served in office as another known predictor.[56]

Main Results

SELF-MONITORING AND NUMBER OF MIDS

Figures 4.4 and 4.5 plot the number of MIDs per year for high self-monitor presidents versus low self-monitor presidents. The relationship between a president's self-monitoring disposition and US involvement in MIDs is striking. Consistent with the theory, high self-monitor presidents are involved in significantly more disputes. Figure 4.4 is pooled, and figure 4.5 separates the presidents by their party affiliation.

The figures show a strong relationship between self-monitoring level and number of MIDs on an annual basis, providing support for H2. Importantly, high-self monitors are involved in more MIDs regardless of whether they are

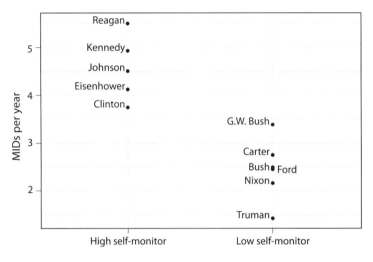

FIGURE 4.4. Self-monitoring scores and average number of MID involvement per year.

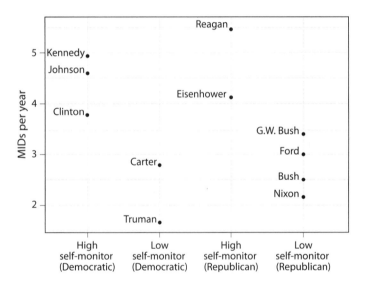

FIGURE 4.5. Self-monitoring scores and average number of MID involvement per year (by party).

Democrats or Republicans, with this score perfectly separating the two groups. How likely is this result simply due to chance? Or more precisely, if we assume self-monitoring scores are unrelated to the number of militarized disputes, how likely is it that we would end up with such a neat division into these two groups? A permutation test shows that it is highly unlikely to see this relationship between self-monitoring and number of MIDs by chance; indeed, as table 4.3 shows, the difference in the mean annual MID rate between high and low self-monitor presidents is highly significant, having only about 1 in 1,000 chance of appearing by chance.

The substantive difference between the two groups is not slight. As shown in figure 4.6, the United States was involved, on average, in 3.5 MIDs per year from the end of World War II to the beginning of the Obama presidency. For low self-monitor presidents, this number was lower, with an annualized MID rate of approximately 2.2, whereas their high self-monitor peers were involved in on average 4.3 MIDs yearly. In other words, high self-monitor presidents are on average involved in *twice* as many militarized disputes per year as their low self-monitor counterparts. The left panel of figure 4.7 shows the average effect of self-monitoring on the mean annual rate of MID involvement, whereas the right panel shows those initiated by the United States. The figure indicates that there is a statistically significant difference between high and low self-monitors in the direction expected.

Importantly, that the magnitude of the effect of self-monitoring on number of MIDs remains even if I use party affiliation may be taken as a proxy for level of hawkishness. Specifically, as reported in table 4.4, a high self-monitor Democratic president is on average likely to be involved in 2.3 more MIDs per year

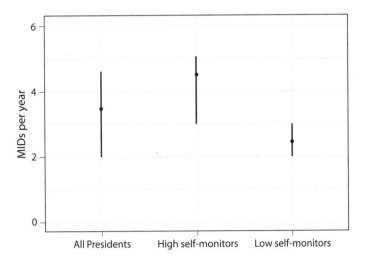

FIGURE 4.6. Self-monitoring scores and yearly number of MID involvement.
Note: MID rate by president-year and type, with error bar indicating twenty-fifth and seventy-fifth percentile, and dot indicating the median. Observations are weighted by the proportion of year served to account for changes in office during the year. This figure shows that low self-monitor presidents are involved in a many fewer MIDs. Note that the top seventy-fifth percentile of low self-monitor president years saw as much MID involvement as the twenty-fifth percentile of high self-monitor president years. N=63 president-years, 31.05 low self-monitor president-years, 31.95 high self-monitor years.

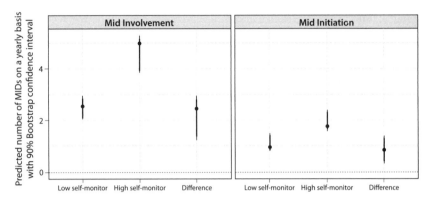

FIGURE 4.7. Average effect of self-monitoring on the mean annual rate of MID involvement (left panel) and those initiated by the United States (right panel).
Note: The red dot denotes the observed difference between the means, while the dark bars represent 90 percent and 95 percent bootstrap confidence interval (B=10,000). As seen, there is statistically significant difference between high and low self-monitors, with high self-monitors both engaging in and initiating more militarized disputes.

compared to a low self-monitor Democratic president. Similarly, a high self-monitor president from the Republican Party is on average likely to be involved in 2.0 more MIDs per year compared to a fellow low self-monitor Republican president. These results are consistent with the theory in that self-monitoring continues to be a strong predictor of the crisis behavior, regardless of level of hawkishness. Thus, the results provide strong support for H3 and continue to hold even when we use an interaction term between self-monitoring and hawkishness.[57]

Next, I conduct negative binomial regression at the president-year level. The regression framework allows me to control for a host of potential confounding factors identified in the literature. Model I in table 4.5 shows the relationship between self-monitoring and number of MIDs using all these predictors by group at the president-year level. Whereas Model I uses party affiliation as a proxy for hawkishness, Model III replicates the analysis using the WordScore results reported above. Recall that because the text analysis was appropriate only for the clearly Cold War presidents, the number of observations is smaller using this model specification.[58] Regardless of the hawkishness proxy I employ, the results indicate strong support for H2: the self-monitoring disposition of a president is a strong predictor of his likelihood to engage in interstate crises that involve military coercion. Put differently, US presidents who are high self-monitors were more likely to either initiate or respond to militarized interstate disputes in order to signal their resolve using military coercive means.[59]

TABLE 4.5. Self-Monitoring and Annual MID Involvement and Initiation, Negative Binomial Regression Models

	Model I	Model II	Model III	Model IV
	Annual MID Involvement Rate	Annual MID Initiation Rate	Annual MID Involvement Rate *(with Text-Based Hawkishness Measure)*	Annual MID Initiation Rate *(with Text-Based Hawkishness Measure)*
High self-monitor president	0.386***	1.004***	0.481**	2.701**
	(0.125)	(0.328)	(0.239)	(1.341)
US in recession in current year	0.03	0.104	0.115	0.608
	(0.209)	(0.621)	(0.242)	(0.702)
Unified government (0 or 1)	−0.12	−0.202	−0.100	−0.337
	(0.092)	(0.453)	(0.141)	(0.553)
Log (US casualities in last war)	−0.033	−0.051*	−0.247	0.280
	(0.034)	(0.027)	(0.214)	(0.428)
Number of US MIDs in five years preceding inauguration	0.002**	0.003	0.011	−0.078
	(0.001)	(0.002)	(0.021)	(0.084)
Number of US MIDs with use of force in five years preceding inauguration	−0.001	0.006	−0.013	0.348***
	(0.013)	(0.013)	(0.026)	(0.128)
Number MIDs worldwide in current year	0.004	−0.008	0.004	0.018*
	(0.012)	(0.013)	(0.012)	(0.010)
US-USSR CINC ratio	−0.008	0.197	0.262	1.636
	(0.131)	(0.236)	(0.400)	(1.605)
President has experience from executive branch (0 or 1)	−0.028	0.281	0.063	0.110
	(0.379)	(0.427)	(0.055)	(0.099)
Number of USSR MIDs in current year	0.099***	0.153***	0.149	−0.329
	(0.033)	(0.05)	(0.265)	(0.970)

(continues)

TABLE 4.5. (*continued*)

	Model I	Model II	Model III	Model IV
	Annual MID Involvement Rate	Annual MID Initiation Rate	Annual MID Involvement Rate *(with Text-Based Hawkishness Measure)*	Annual MID Initiation Rate *(with Text-Based Hawkishness Measure)*
President's age upon taking office	0.015	-0.002	0.030**	0.087
	(0.033)	(0.034)	(0.015)	(0.100)
Length of time in office	-0.028	-0.084*	-0.015	0.012
	(0.031)	(0.05)	(0.030)	(0.107)
Hawkishness of president	0.054	0.849	-0.019*	-0.144
	(0.561)	(0.564)	(0.011)	(0.094)
Cold War	-0.044	0.086	n/a	n/a
	(0.196)	(0.341)		
Peace years	-0.029	-0.144	0.120***	-0.084
	(0.086)	(0.137)	(0.161)	(0.569)
Peace years squared	0.013	0.028	-0.012***	0.004
	(0.012)	(0.026)	(0.023)	(0.104)
Peace years cubed	-0.001	-0.001	0.0002	-0.001
	(0.0005)	(0.001)	(0.001)	(0.005)
Constant	-0.018	-1.064	0.994	-11.659**
	(1.706)	(2.169)	(1.485)	(5.693)
Number of observations	71	71	50	50
Log likelihood	-112.154	-81.374	-77.323	-52.197
Akaike Information Criterion (AIC)	260.308	198.749	188.645	138.394

Note: Unit of analysis is president-year. Observations are weighted by proportion of year served. Robust standard errors in parentheses, clustered at president level.

*p<0.1
**p<0.05
***p<0.01

SELF-MONITORING AND INITIATION OF MIDS

The results thus far suggest strong support for H2. The self-monitoring disposition of a president is a strong predictor of his likelihood to engage in militarized interstate disputes. Recall that Model I of table 4.5 pools initiators and targets together. In most cases, even when the United States was targeted, the president in office still had opportunities to avoid the crisis and its escalation, and in some cases it is unclear who initiated the crisis.

To test the predictions of H1, Models II and IV of table 4.5 evaluate whether the US president was the one who initiated the threat, display, or use of force in the dispute to the best of our understanding.[60] I run a similar analysis, now examining the effect of self-monitoring only on those MIDs that were initiated by the United States. Model II uses party affiliation as a proxy for hawkishness, whereas Model IV uses the president's rhetoric in foreign policy speeches obtained through the text analysis WordScore reported above. I find robust results consistent with the theoretical exceptions: in support of H1, we see that high self-monitor presidents are more likely to initiate the use of military coercion against other countries compared to low self-monitor presidents (with the effect being statistically significant at the $p<0.01$ level).

In figure 4.8, I visualize the magnitude of these effects by a series of simulations based on these estimates. As seen, the model suggests a substantially higher annual MID involvement rate and MID initiation rate for high self-monitors. With all other covariates set to their means (if continuous) or modes, a high-self monitor is expected to be engaged in about 60 percent more MIDs compared to a low self-monitor. Figure 4.8 also indicates that a high self-monitor president is predicted to initiate more than twice as many MIDs as a low self-monitor counterpart, with the number of MID initiations increasing from an estimated 1.3 to 3.5. In both models, the difference between the high and low self-monitors is statistically significant at the $p<0.01$ level.

To test H3, I evaluate the difference self-monitoring makes on initiation of MIDs among the hawkish presidents and dovish presidents. We should be mindful, however, that splitting the sample reduces our degrees of freedom and thus likelihood of finding statistically significant effects. With those caveats in mind, we still find substantial results that are consistent with H3. The results of the permutation test are shown in table 4.6. They reveal that when looking exclusively at MID initiation, the difference between high and low self-monitor presidents is large and significant among the doves. Dovish presidents are significantly more likely to initiate MIDs if they are high self-monitors, initiating about six more MIDs per presidential term, on average. In contrast, as the theory expects, and consistent with the results of the survey experiments, the effect of self-monitoring is positive but lower within the population of hawks.

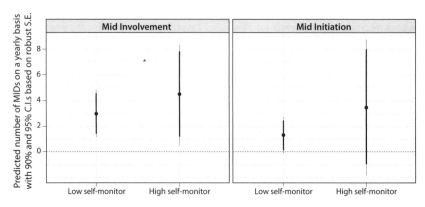

FIGURE 4.8. Predicted annual MID rate for low and high self-monitor presidents.
Note: The red dots present the predicted annual MID involvement rate (left) and initiation rate (right) based on simulated data. The solid line is the model prediction 90 percent confidence interval, and the dotted line the 95 percent confidence interval, both based on robust standard errors. The simulated data sets all covariate to their mean (for continuous variables) or mode levels. The difference between high and low self-monitors is in both cases statistically significant at the p<0.01 level.

TABLE 4.6. Hawks, Doves by Self-Monitoring Level and MID Initiation Rate (Wilcoxon-Mann-Whitney Exact Test, No Matching, Weighted by Presidency Length)

Hawks Only			
Difference in mean annual MID initiation rate	0.512	p-value	0.302
Doves Only			
Difference in mean annual MID initiation rate	1.519*	p-value	0.009

*p<0.1

Using a regression analysis with an interaction term between self-monitoring and hawkishness (instead of controlling for hawkishness) I similarly find that the effect of self-monitoring on MID initiation is larger among the doves compared to the hawks (see online appendix).[61]

DYADIC ANALYSIS OF MID INVOLVEMENT AND INITIATION

Militarized disputes can also be considered dyadically. Instead of thinking about how many MIDs the United States was involved in or initiated over a given year, I considered the likelihood that a dispute was initiated by the United States against any one other country. To probe whether this decision is more likely to be made by high self-monitor presidents, I conducted logistic regression on country-dyad-years involving the United States, incorporating a wide range of potential confounders in addition to cancelling out time-invariant dyad characteristics through dyadic fixed effects. The fixed-effects model takes into account the possibility that time-invariant omitted variables specific to the directed dyads could be affecting the results. Importantly, this model implies that dyads involving the United States where no dispute occurred during the sample period are dropped from the analysis entirely because there is no variation on the dependent variable. Thus, all countries that had peaceful relations with the United States during this period are no longer in the data, leaving only those that were involved in at least one MID with the United States.

In the dyadic models, I am able to include additional standard controls indicating whether the other country in the dispute was a US ally, or a USSR/ Russia ally, its level of democracy (using its Polity2 score, a widely used measure of regime position on the autocratic-democratic dimension), whether the other country in the dyad was in a civil war, the similarity of its alliance portfolio to that of the United States (weighted global s-score), its imports and exports, its gross domestic product on a per capita basis, and its Composite Index of National Capabilities score (CINC).

The results of the dyadic analysis (table 4.7) suggest strong support for the theory and are remarkably consistent with the monadic analysis presented above. The president's self-monitoring level is a highly significant predictor of crisis behavior in all models, with a higher level of self-monitoring being associated with a higher probability of both MIDs involvement and initiation. Robustness tests included in the online appendix give almost identical results using alternate model specifications. Importantly, self-monitoring continues to be a statistically significant predictor of crisis behavior even when using the alternative proxy for hawkishness based on the foreign policy rhetoric of the Cold War presidents.[62]

Looking at the coefficients of the control variables, we observe that in addition to self-monitoring, there are several other predictors of MIDs involvement and initiation. For example, the United States appears to have been more involved in MIDs during the Cold War, but the Cold War is not a predictor of MID initiation by US presidents. We also observe that the United States was significantly more likely to be involved in and initiate military coercion against autocracies as well as less powerful countries (both statistically significant relationships at conventional levels). Importantly, the party affiliation of the US president does not seem to be a significant predictor of either his MID involvement or MID initiation, although the positive sign of the coefficient suggests that Republican presidents, rather than Democrats, are involved in and initiate slightly more MIDs.

TABLE 4.7. Self-Monitoring and MID Involvement and Initiation, Dyadic Logistic
Regression Models

	Model I	Model II
	MID Involvement	MID Initiation
High self-monitor president	0.4302***	1.1989***
	(0.1646)	(0.338)
Republican president	0.1352	0.4939
	(0.1497)	(0.3925)
Year	0.0260**	0.0682**
	(0.011)	(0.0285)
Cold War	7.6545**	2.3837
	(2.974)	(3.2567)
Peace years	−0.0172	0.0858
	(0.1105)	(0.2092)
Peace years squared	0.0081	−0.0068
	(0.0221)	(0.0435)
Peace years cubed	−0.0006	−0.0006
	(0.001)	(0.0019)
Target is US ally	0.6802	1.6577
	(0.955)	(1.1507)
Log (no. of casualties in last US war)	−1.5284***	−0.338
	(0.559)	(0.5433)
Worldwide no. of MIDs in current year	−0.0059	0.0016
	(0.0073)	(0.013)
Polity2 score of other country	−0.1259**	−0.1326***
	(0.0564)	(0.04)
Target in civil war	1.0605**	−0.007
	(0.444)	(0.6558)
Target USSR ally	0.3685	0.1174
	(0.2487)	(0.5283)
Alliance portfolio similarity	−4.0284***	−4.9963
	(1.2588)	(3.2383)
GDPPC of other country	−0.00002	−0.0001
	(0.0001)	(0.0001)
CINC of other country	−66.4835***	−71.4814***
	(22.4781)	(25.2805)
Constant	−40.1950*	−130.8420**
	(20.8307)	(55.1277)
Dyad fixed effects	Yes	Yes
Number of observations	5,022	5,022
Log likelihood	−307.316	−156.869
Akaike Information Criterion (AIC)	918.631	617.7376

Note: Unit of analysis is president-dyad-year. Robust standard errors in parentheses, clustered at president level.
*p<0.1
**p<0.05
***p<0.01

PERMUTATION TESTS

The regression results clearly show that high self-monitor presidents are more likely to be involved in and initiate militarized interstate disputes compared to low self-monitor presidents. But can the striking differences in US conflict behavior under high and low self-monitor presidents support that the differences were caused by the self-monitoring attributes? I believe such an inference is credible, and likely. In the case of the United States, the literature has long suggested that, as a general rule, presidents are not elected based on their conflict or risk propensity. Indeed, in the cases I examine in this book, presidential selection occurred primarily on the basis of economic and other domestic issues, more so than concerns about potential militarized disputes.[63] More importantly, as Dafoe and Caughey observe, "Even when foreign policy does matter, the international situation on Election Day is often a poor guide to what will unfold over a president's term."[64]

TABLE 4.8. Self-Monitoring and Militarized Disputes Involvement and Initiation (Wilcoxon-Mann-Whitney Exact Tests with Genetic Matching)

MID Involvement

Matching	Difference in Annual MID Rate	P-Value
No matching, weighted by president length	2.0293***	0.0028
Matched on number of US MIDs in five years prior to taking office	2.3149***	0.0011
Matched on number of worldwide MIDs in year of taking office	1.8300***	0.0006
Matched on whether nation at war in year of taking office	1.9208***	0.0001
Matched on military experience	2.0424***	0.0005
Matched on party affiliation	2.2172***	0.0007
Matched on all the above	2.0308***	0.0006

MID Initiation

Matching	Difference in Annual MID Rate	P-Value
No matching, weighted by president length	0.8307*	0.07822
Matched on number of US MIDs in five years prior to taking office	1.0801***	0.008479
Matched on number of worldwide MIDs in year of taking office	0.7290*	0.0587
Matched on whether nation at war in year of taking office	1.0271***	0.00318
Matched on military experience	0.8896**	0.0243
Matched on party affiliation	1.1206***	0.0055
Matched on all the above	1.0290***	0.0024

*p<0.1
**p<0.05
***p<0.01

One could still wonder whether high self-monitor presidents are systematically elected in different circumstances than low self-monitor presidents, and whether this correlation underlies the apparent association between self-monitoring and propensity to engage in militarized disputes. Many of the variables in the statistical models account for this possibility by incorporating information about conflict history, the international strategic environment, and domestic political factors.

To further alleviate selection concerns, I employ a set of permutation tests with matching (table 4.8), in order to determine whether there being no difference between high and low self-monitor presidents is likely given the data we observe. Presidents were matched on number of key variables that can affect the selection of high versus low self-monitor presidents: US MIDs in the five years prior to their taking office, number of worldwide MIDs in the five years prior to taking office, whether or not the country was at war when the president took office, party affiliation, and whether or not the president had military experience, as well as including all the above.[65] The results indicate that the association between self-monitoring and number of MIDs remains robust, both in statistical strength (p-values) and magnitude. Furthermore, even when restricting the sample to only US-initiated MIDs (bottom part of table 4.8), the association remained meaningful, both statistically and in magnitude.

Robustness Tests and Extensions

To ensure the findings are not driven by particular coding choices or the inclusion of certain presidents, I conduct several robustness checks (see online appendix). First, I conducted several analyses on subsamples. In one, I replicate the results considering only the top and bottom four self-monitoring scores. In another, I included only presidents with self-monitoring score 95 percent confidence intervals fully below or fully above the midpoint. Finally, I used a continuous measure of self-monitoring instead of a dichotomous one. In all cases, the results remained robust and largely unchanged in magnitude. I also replicated the results with Cold War presidents only. As reported in the online appendix, the results continue to provide support for the theory using these alternative subsamples.

Second, I conduct several additional tests to rule out selection effects, with results in all cases providing robust support for the theory. Thus, in addition to controlling for the number of MIDs in five years before the president took office, I replicate the analysis in table 4.8 while controlling for number of MIDs in the previous three years as well as only the previous year. Moreover, if one suspects that a more contentious international environment is driving the association, one would expect to observe high self-monitor presidents being targeted significantly more than low self-monitor presidents. As reported in the online appendix, in which I replicate table 4.5 using MIDs in which the United States was targeted, this does not seem to be the case. There is no statistically significant association between high self-monitor presidents and the United States being targeted by more MIDs. This provides further corroboration that different conflict behavior is driven by the self-monitoring levels of US presidents, and not the international circumstances into which they are elected.

Finally, the results are also robust to eliminating president-year weights and the use of Poisson regression instead of negative binomial regression. The results also remain when running the analysis at the president level instead of president-year, although given the small number of observations, I can include only a smaller number of control variables in such models.

The preceding analysis provides strong evidence that high self-monitor presidents are more likely to be involved in and initiate international militarized disputes. But are other outcomes associated with such disputes related to the president's self-monitoring disposition, as well?

Finally, readers may wonder whether high self-monitors are more likely to engage in or initiate MIDs that involve the actual use of military force. Recall that the theory advanced in this book does not argue that high self-monitor presidents inherently believe in the effectiveness of military force more than low self-monitor presidents. Rather, I argue that high self-monitor presidents tend to care more about reputation for resolve and are therefore more likely to use a host of military coercive tools including, but not limited to, the actual use of military force to signal their resolve in international crises. The analysis in this chapter provides strong support for this claim. At the same time, if high self-monitor presidents care more about demonstrating resolve, they should show an overall higher inclination to use military force occasionally compared to low self-monitor presidents.

To assess whether this is the case, I replicated table 4.5 but restricted the analysis to only those MIDs in which force was actually deployed (that is, excluding those MIDs that involved threats or demonstration of force). Put differently, I probe whether high self-monitors were engaged in and initiated a larger number of MIDs that involved the use of force. The results of that analysis (table 4.9) suggest that even when we control for hawkishness of the presidents, high self-monitor presidents were involved in more MIDs that included the actual use of military force compared low self-monitor presidents.[66] The analysis further reveals that Republican presidents are more likely to use force compared to presidents from the Democratic Party, as the coefficient is positive and statistically significant for both MID involvement and initiation.[67]

Because the analysis earlier in this chapter revealed that high self-monitors are known to be involved in and initiate a larger number of MIDs compared to

TABLE 4.9. Self-Monitoring and Annual MID Involvement and Initiation in Which the United States Used Force, Negative Binomial Regression Models

	Model I	Model II
	Annual MID Involvement Rate	Annual MID Initiation Rate
	(Use of Force Only)	(Use of Force Only)
High self-monitor president	1.190***	9.743***
	(0.293)	(3.074)
US in recession in current year	−0.754*	−1.290*
	(0.423)	(0.707)
Unified government (0 or 1)	0.280	0.425
	(0.570)	(0.510)
Log (US causalities in last war)	−0.056	−0.088**
	(0.043)	(0.041)
Number of US MIDs in five years preceding inauguration	−0.049***	0.700***
	(0.019)	(0.261)
Number of US MIDs with use of force in five years preceding inauguration	−0.375***	0.911**
	(0.063)	(0.410)
Number MIDs worldwide in current year	−0.024	−0.056**
	(0.019)	(0.026)
US-USSR CINC ratio	−0.648***	−0.259
	(0.218)	(0.543)
President has experience from executive branch (0 or 1)	0.044	0.179***
	(0.047)	(0.064)
Number of USSR MIDs in current year	2.607***	−5.741*
	(0.576)	(3.152)
President's age upon taking office	−0.169***	0.127
	(0.045)	(0.119)
Length of time in office	−0.039	−0.217**
	(0.105)	(0.095)
Republican president	2.555***	7.173***
	(0.683)	(1.641)
Cold War	−0.850**	−6.486***
	(0.423)	(1.903)
Peace years	−0.166	−0.308*
	(0.206)	(0.167)
Peace years squared	−0.004	0.031
	(0.038)	(0.032)
Peace years cubed	0.001	−0.0002
	(0.002)	(0.001)
Constant	11.086***	−24.031**
	(2.501)	(12.168)
Number of observations	71	71
Log likelihood	−72.131	−46.622
Akaike Information Criterion (AIC)	180.263	129.243

Note: Unit of analysis is president-year. Observations are weighted by proportion of year served. Robust standard errors in parentheses, clustered at president level.

*p<0.1

**p<0.05

***p<0.01

TABLE 4.10. Presidents' Self-Monitoring Scores and Outcome of MIDs (Wilcoxon-Mann-Whitney Exact Tests with Genetic Matching)

Matching	Difference in MIDs Outcome	P-Value
No matching, weighted by president length	0.0445	0.2123
Matched on number of US MIDs in five years prior to taking office	0.097 ***	0.0001
Matched on number of worldwide MIDs in year of taking office	0.0679 **	0.0386
Matched on whether nation at war in year of taking office	0.0533	0.1371
Matched on military experience	0.0573 *	0.0719
Matched on party affiliation	0.0972 ***	0.0001

Note: Analysis conducted at the MID level, permutations at president level.
*p<0.1
**p<0.05
***p<0.01

low self-monitor presidents, I probed whether military force is used in a higher proportion of their total MID involvement. That is, do high self-monitors use more force because they are simply involved in more MIDs, or do they use force in a larger proportion of their total MIDs as well? Here, further permutation analysis *at the MID level* (see online appendix), reveals that in any given MID, high self-monitor presidents are not more likely to use force compared to low self-monitor presidents. Taken together, the regression results and permutation tests allow us to infer that high self-monitor presidents have engaged in and initiated MIDs that involved the use of force *more frequently* than low self-monitor presidents, but high self-monitor presidents do not use more force as a proportion of the MIDs in which they engaged compared to low self-monitor presidents (as table 4A.9 in the online appendix shows).

Finally, I evaluate whether high self-monitor presidents are also likely to "win," or obtain a favorable outcomes, in MIDs. I follow Dafoe and Caughey in coding the MID outcome as an "ordinal variable with three levels, 'US loss' (−1), 'draw' (0), and 'US win' (+1), where the first and third categories are disputes that ended in a victory or yield by one party. The average of *outcome* is equivalent to the proportion of victories minus the proportion of defeats."[68] The matched permutation tests below (table 4.10) provide suggestive evidence that high self-monitor presidents are more likely to "win" the disputes in which they engage, especially when matched on circumstances. Specifically, we find a difference of ten percentage points in the average outcome of disputes between high and low self-monitor presidents.[69] One potential explanation is that high self-monitor presidents—who according to the theory are far more concerned about reputation for resolve and are probably more skilled at projecting resolve—are also more likely to take whatever means necessary to signal resolve and avoid defeat, humiliation, and damage to that reputation. Moreover, given their greater ability for deception, their signals of resolve might be seen as more credible, leading the other side to back down. Future work, however, should further investigate the crisis dynamics of self-monitoring and the degree to which reputational concerns affect the outcome of those crises.

Discussion

Is a US president's self-monitoring score a strong predictor of the likelihood that he uses (or responds to a challenge by using) military instruments intended to project resolve in international crises? Consistent with the theoretical expectations of the theory, we see a remarkably robust finding that high self-monitor presidents engage in, initiate, and prevail in more interstate conflicts that involve coercive military instruments compared to their low self-monitor counterparts. These results imply that the high self-monitoring inclination of the US president is a more important predictor of his crisis behavior than whether the president is a Democrat or a Republican.

Beyond their statistical significance, the results indicate that the difference in US conflict behavior under high self-monitor presidents compared to low self-monitor presidents is meaningful. Consistent with H1 and H2, I find that high self-monitor presidents are involved in almost twice as many MIDs and initiate twice as many MIDs. I also find that MIDs under high self-monitor presidents are about 10 percent more likely to end favorably for the United States, suggesting that high self-monitors might be able to convince their opponents to back down by demonstrating resolve. At the same time, we find that high self-monitor presidents are not more likely to resort to actual force in any single dispute compared to low self-monitor presidents, though the vastly higher number of MIDs under such presidents means that high self-monitor presidents deploy force more overall. Finally, we also find support for H3. The effect of self-monitoring is statistically significant in all models, even when we control for the hawkishness of the president. At the same time, the effect of self-monitoring is a more significant predictor of MID involvement and initiation among the population of dovish presidents than hawkish ones. This is consistent with the results of the survey experiments reported in chapter 3.

While the results are robust, readers might be concerned about the existence of potential selection effects, due to path dependence in the empirical record. It could be argued that, given cycles of strong isolationist and proretrenchment tendencies in American strategic thought and public opinion, low self-monitoring presidents were more likely to be elected following particularly salient American misadventures in the international arena, such as the Vietnam War. Low self-monitors, it might be argued, might be elected in more peaceful periods internationally. Conversely, the internationalist strain of American public opinion might favor a high self-monitoring president in elections that follow a period of salient external success for American foreign policy. High self-monitors might also be elected at times where the strategic environment is more contentious. In this manner, the preferences of the American electorate, coupled with the success or failure of past American foreign policy, or even the nature of the strategic environment, might act as an omitted variable in the analysis, leading individual presidents' dispositions and beliefs to be intervening variables. American presidents might therefore be selected into office by an underlying nonrandom process that is linked to their willingness to use force to project a reputation for resolve.

However, this potential selection effect is not especially problematic in this case, for three reasons. First, there are multiple theoretical steps required to link the preferences of voters on fighting for reputation and the election of a president who holds similar preferences, especially in the United States, where election is indirect. In order for the selection argument to hold weight, we would have to assume that voters are (1) aware of the self-monitoring dispositions of their leaders, (2) able to identify the relationship between those self-monitoring dispositions and likely international behavior of a candidate (particularly, his or her willingness to fight for reputation), and (3) likely to use this particular characteristic as the primary reason for their vote. These conditions are unlikely to hold in any democracy, especially since most voters are not single-issue voters, much less ones who prioritize the willingness to use force to project reputation for resolve. Moreover, as I show in the cases, Carter, Reagan, and Clinton were all elected primarily based on their domestic economic agendas, not on their foreign policy goals.

Second, the pattern of selection of high and low self-monitor presidents does not appear consistent with such a selection story. While it is certainly true, for example, that President Carter, who was elected shortly after the Vietnam War ended and served during détente with the Soviet Union, was significantly less likely to fight for reputation than President Nixon, this pattern was not systematically seen with other presidents. President Clinton, a high self-monitor, was elected at a time the strategic environment was far from contentious, for example. Moreover, in the statistical analysis presented in the previous chapter, I took several steps to ensure that selection was not driving the results. First, I controlled for a host of variables in all the regression analyses pertaining to the international strategic environment in the years leading up to the presidential election. Second, even when presidents were matched on these variables, the results indicate that self-monitoring continues to be a strong predictor of conflict behavior. Third, I show that high self-monitors are not significantly more likely to be targeted in MIDs compared to low self-monitor presidents who are in power, providing further evidence that the effect of self-monitoring on crisis behavior is due to "treatment" rather than "selection."

Finally, and importantly, I do not argue that self-monitoring has no effect on the election of leaders in the United States. To the contrary, my argument is that given the way leaders are elected in the United States, high self-monitors are more likely to be elected presidents than low self-monitors. Crucially, however, this is not because of high self-monitors' stances on foreign policy or reputation for resolve, but rather due to their ability to effectively relate to different segments of the population, especially through their performance during presidential debates and other campaign events. Low self-monitors, as a whole, are less likely to have the skills to excel at campaigning and thus are less likely to get elected as presidents. We are likely to see low self-monitors become presidents at times when the public has reduced trust in the government and craves leaders who are honest and sincere, or when those individuals have a unique background or experience that compensates for their low impression-management skills. But this type of selection should not systematically affect the outcome I study here, which is whether those leaders fight for reputation for resolve in international politics. Put differently, the preferences of the electorate may be a deeper cause of my outcomes of interest, which is why I treat them as an alternative variable for explaining when leaders fight for reputation. But the evidence clearly demonstrates that the selection of high or low self-monitor individuals to the presidency is because of their willingness to fight for reputation.

5

Approaches to Testing the Theory with Case Studies

The robust association between self-monitoring and crisis behavior offers strong support for this book's theory. However, the statistical analysis can explain only so much on its own. In this chapter, I explain how I use historical case studies (chapters 6, 7, and 8) as part of a layered methodological approach.

Case analysis allows me to examine more fine-grained qualitative measures of the independent variables (self-monitoring dispositions and attitudes about the use of force) and the dependent variables (use of military instruments) than quantitative coding can provide. I use process tracing—based on primary documents, wherever possible—to examine how leaders made decisions during international crises. I also use process tracing to examine alternative and other contextual explanations for leaders' behavior in those crises. Finally, a key component of this case analysis is the self-monitoring and hawkishness characteristics of the presidents' main foreign policy advisors, which allows us to examine judgments about the appropriateness of fighting for reputation in a given crisis. Looking at the independent variables for the main foreign policy advisors also allows me to examine the extent to which they advocate reputation-based policies to the president and the salience of those arguments in the president's crisis decision making. Taken together, the president-advisor comparisons offer several means of gaining analytical leverage and an opportunity to generalize the theory beyond US presidents.

In this chapter, I first discuss qualitative measures of self-monitoring disposition and hawkishness used in the historical case studies. I then set forth the observable implications of my theory, in terms of the discourse I expect to see and the policies that should be chosen, as well as implications for alternative and contextual arguments. Next, I discuss the criteria for which presidents I studied in depth, and for which international crises I focused on. Finally, I explain how evaluating the self-monitoring, hawkishness, and policy recommendations of the presidents' main advisors offers several significant benefits to the research design.

Measurements in Case Studies

MEASURING SELF-MONITORING AND MILITARY ASSERTIVENESS

I validate the self-monitoring measure obtained from the experts' survey by using the self-monitoring scale to inform the key aspects of the case studies. I rely on primary documents, including from the prepresidential period, in order to assess the relevant dimensions of self-monitoring disposition. This method allows me to avoid conflating a president's innate disposition with his decision-making behavior during the crises studied.[1] I also use secondary literature, including memoirs written by the presidents and their key advisors, as well as biographies and autobiographies. In particular, I look for information about decision makers' behavior in social situations and diplomatic interactions. The literature on self-monitoring shows that people can recognize high or low self-monitors among their peers with some degree of success.[2] Thus, accounts by people close to the decision maker constitute valuable information about the self-monitoring dispositions of the decision maker. I code a president as a high (or low) self-monitor based on three observable measures: expressive self-control, other-directed self-presentation, and social stage presence. Details on these are offered in the online appendix. Based on these three components, I validate qualitatively each president's self-monitoring disposition. Importantly, a president who can be classified as a high self-monitor according to Snyder's scale, for example, might still exhibit variation among these three clusters of behaviors. Such a president might be very high on social presence, for instance, but less so on the other-directedness dimension.

The text analysis of the presidents' public foreign policy speeches reported in chapter 4 provides a useful measure of their beliefs concerning the effectiveness of military force. In the case studies I also undertake a fine-grained qualitative analysis along additional dimensions that can serve as proxies for a president's underlying beliefs.[3] Specifically, I use three observable implications to code a president as believing strongly in the efficacy of force: a preference for higher military spending, a preference for covert military action, and a preference for military solutions over diplomatic ones. I discuss how I operationalize these measures in more depth in the online appendix. They are not exhaustive, but they are prominent indicators in all conventional scales to measure individuals' views about the effectiveness of military force.

In coding the above three measures for each president, I follow a two-step process designed to maximize internal consistency. First, for each president, I code each of the three measures by looking at his prepresidential record of speeches, writings, memorandums, and other private papers. This step is important to establish a baseline level of belief in the efficacy of force, which could change after an individual begins his presidency and assumes responsibility for foreign policy, among other things. Second, I code the same three measures for the period following the presidential election until the crisis that is the focus of study. This second step is crucial for measuring deviations from the baseline level of beliefs after the president is elected and assumes office. Since the focus of my empirical research is the use or nonuse of military force for reputational purposes in international crises, I do not code the above measures for the crisis periods themselves, in order to avoid endogeneity in measuring this independent variable.

Coding these measures of military assertiveness must not be conflated with the outcome I seek to explain. That is, a president's statement calling for protecting reputation using force needs to be distinguished from a president's conveyance of beliefs about the efficacy of force more generally, for nonreputational ends. I address this potential for endogeneity in two ways. First, I measure a president's beliefs about the effectiveness of force *before* he came to office, in order to create some temporal separation between this measure and the outcome to be explained. To guard against the crisis situation itself altering the beliefs of a president, I code each president's beliefs from the time he took office to the time of the first crisis in question. I then trace the evolution of beliefs between the first crisis and subsequent crises chosen for analysis, looking for changes in rhetoric or actions that would point to a shift in the president's beliefs. Second, I look at indicators that are broader in scope than willingness to use force to project resolve, in order to address the president's core beliefs about the effectiveness of force.

In sum, the dependent variable is the use of military instruments for reputational reasons, not the propensity for fighting in general. Beliefs about the effectiveness of military force capture the president's views regarding use of force *in general*. Thus, as the theory suggests, those views might affect the propensity to fight for reputation, but that effect is deterministic, because it interacts with the president's self-monitoring disposition.

Observable Implications

The theory predicts that variations in disposition and belief among decision makers will lead to variation in concern for reputation for resolve, and thus to variation in presidents' willingness to use force to maintain a reputation for resolve in international crises. The basic unit of analysis in my qualitative research is a particular president in a particular international crisis. For each crisis, I assess whether the president views the crisis as having the possibility to affect his country's reputation for resolve, and whether the president is willing to use military instruments to project a reputation for resolve in the crisis. I assume that if a leader is willing to use instruments of military force to project a reputation for resolve, or if he views the present crisis as providing an opportunity to establish or rebuild a reputation for resolve through military force, we should expect to see the president voice this belief in private discussions within his administration, in his writings or memoirs, and through the policies he adopts or rejects during the crisis.[4]

Before we proceed, it is important to clarify three limitations of using qualitative analysis to test this theory: First, this theory is one where the causal relationships are probabilistic rather than deterministic. That is, I do not argue that high self-monitoring presidents will always care about reputation for resolve and will always be willing to fight for reputation. Rather, I argue that they are more likely to do so in comparison to low self-monitoring presidents. Second, the historical record rarely if ever provides "smoking-gun" evidence. In the case of this psychological theory, we would not expect a decision maker to discuss his or her self-monitoring inclinations in the context of his or her crisis policies. Thus, process tracing does not focus on the causal link between self-monitoring and concerns about reputation, but rather on the mechanisms that link presence or absence of reputational concerns with crisis policies. Finally, the case analysis for low self-monitoring presidents is more challenging compared to high self-monitoring presidents. This is because the analysis seeks to uncover the absence of reputational concerns from the low self-monitor president's discourse and to explain "nonevents" such as the decision not to employ military instruments. The case analysis can, nevertheless, shed important light on the validity of the theory by triangulating evidence and carefully assessing when the absence of evidence can serve as evidence. Below I detail the strategies used to test the observable implications in the case analysis.

DISCURSIVE EVIDENCE

Three related types of reasoning are consistent with the logic emphasizing reputation for resolve. The theory predicts that reputation crusaders and believers will be more likely to use these three types of reasoning in private and public statements, and that reputation skeptics and critics will be likely to either ignore or resist such reasoning in private or public discourse.

The first type of reasoning is concern with the idea of appearing "weak," "irresolute," or "lacking in credibility" vis-à-vis external actors in the current crisis. We should expect reputation crusaders and believers to voice, repeatedly and consistently, in public and in private, concerns that not standing firm in a particular crisis will adversely affect others' perceptions of American resolve and credibility in the current crisis, thus affecting the crisis outcome. Reputation skeptics and critics should, on the other hand, voice skepticism about the importance of "face" in a particular crisis or claim that appearing resolute could harm American interests.

A second line of reasoning links a president's current crisis behavior to others' assessments of his country's character. Consequently, a president may argue that backing down in a particular crisis will lead observers to expect similar behavior in future, dissimilar crises. Accordingly, using coercive military instruments is seen as giving a signal of inherent resolve and strength. Observers would draw the inference that a leader used those instruments because he or she is resolute and would be less likely to face additional challenges in the future. Conversely, not using coercive military instruments is seen as a signal of inherent weakness that would motivate future challengers, possibly on issues of intrinsic value. Overall, we expect that reputation crusaders and believers will believe that the actions of the United States in one particular crisis have implications in other times and possibly in other places for future crises.

The third line of reasoning that may be used by reputation crusaders and believers has to do with status considerations. This would be consistent with the results of the experiments reported in chapter 3, in which high self-monitors identified "standing" and "global image" as the key reasons driving them to fight for reputation. In addition to high self-monitors' perception of an intimate link between reputation for resolve and status concerns, reported in chapter 2, if a greater or lesser reputation for resolve will affect a state's position in a deference hierarchy, then a state's position in that hierarchy may be jeopardized if the state refrains from using force in a crisis, even if the state suffers no material losses.[5] In other words, loss of status could be another concern that pushes high self-monitor leaders to use force for reputational considerations. Thus, reputation crusaders or believers should be more likely to refer to status concerns more generally during international crises, compared to reputation skeptics or critics.[6] Importantly, crisis discourse focusing on current defeat allowing for adversaries' strategic benefit against vital interests is less compatible with my view of reputational considerations.

CRISIS POLICIES

In addition to discursive evidence, I also look at the crisis policies the presidents rejected or adopted. The theory does not expect all decision makers to be equally willing to use coercive instruments to project a reputation for resolve. Reputation crusaders and believers are expected to take costly actions to project a reputation for resolve, including mobilization of troops, a ground invasion or bombing campaign, a public threat to use force or actual escalation, or issuing a nuclear alert. We would expect reputation skeptics and critics to refrain from taking such costly actions solely to project a reputation for resolve.

All else equal, we expect crusaders to be most willing of the four types to use military instruments to protect reputation for resolve. The believers will more often advocate using force or the threat of force when reputation for resolve is believed to be at stake. Because believers have weaker beliefs than crusaders regarding the effectiveness of military force, they might be less confident of the ability of military force to produce the desired outcome. They are therefore more likely to be cautious about the use of military instruments and might first try nonmilitary solutions if they think these could effectively signal resolve or maintain reputation for resolve.

In contrast, reputation critics are expected to refrain from using military instruments for the sake of reputation for resolve. They are likely to resist calls for using military instruments just to project resolve, both because they believe that reputation is not worthy of conflict and because of skepticism in the effectiveness of using force more generally. Finally, reputation skeptics are more likely to see the utility of using military instruments, but they will be reluctant to use these instruments for reputational reasons alone. They will be more likely to use military force if material or important strategic interests are also at stake.

While these observable expectations are likely to hold in most cases, we must consider the possibility that even crusaders or believers might refrain from taking costly military actions in some crises where reputation for resolve could be implicated. First, as I discuss in the section below on domestic political explanations, preferences of domestic actors might affect the ability of high self-monitor presidents to pursue reputation-guided policies. Second, high self-monitor presidents might refrain from pursuing reputation-guided policies if they believe that taking such action could result in a net negative effect on the state's reputation for resolve. It is possible, for example, that a leader may perceive the military balance to be extremely skewed in favor of the adversary, in which case fighting could not prevent a defeat and damage to a reputation for resolve.[7] In such circumstances, it might be more beneficial for a reputational reasons to involve third parties—other countries or international institutions—as mediators to help settle the conflict in a manner allowing the state to save face for the sake of future potential crises. Similarly, we might see reputation skeptics, or even critics, occasionally choosing to use coercive military means. This would be consistent with the theory when there is evidence indicating that the use of such instruments was justified on *non*reputational grounds, such as when true vital interests are perceived to be at stake.

Alternative and Other Contextual Explanations

While the theory presented here focuses on leader-level variables, there are additional factors that could influence when leaders will fight for reputation. Some are clear alternative arguments for why and when leaders would fight for reputation; others should be treated more as contextual variables in explaining the policy choices of leaders in any given crisis. My theory does not imply that these alternative arguments do not matter. Rather, these explanations mask important individual-level variation in concern for reputation for resolve, cannot explain the behavior of presidents in reputational crises, and/or lead to predictions inconsistent with actual behavior.

MATERIALIST CALCULATIONS

Decision makers are influenced to use force for reputational concerns by material features of their environment. The first two explanations are more systemic, pertaining to how the distribution of power, and particularly perceived nuclear power, can increase or decrease the baseline concerns leaders have about reputation for resolve. The third explanation pertains to whether the decision to use force is driven by truly reputational concerns, or mainly by the cost-and-benefit calculations of unitary rational actors.

Polarity of the International System

Some explanations predict that the structure of the international system would shape concerns for reputation. These theories expect all US presidents under certain international balances of power (bipolarity or unipolarity) to voice similar concerns regarding the need to defend reputation for resolve. That is, individual variation in decision makers' dispositions and strategic beliefs should not lead to variation in concern for reputation as long as structural conditions are held constant.

As explained in chapter 2, scholars reach different conclusions as to how polarity should affect concerns for reputation for resolve. According to Kenneth Waltz's version of systemic theory, defending reputation for resolve by fighting in areas without US vital interests is not a rational strategy.[8] Still, the stakes during Cold War crises in the periphery, writes Robert Jervis, was "not physical or material power, but each superpower's image of the other, and particularly of its resolve. Under bipolarity any dispute becomes a test of wills as the superpowers fear that a failure to prevail will lead others to draw inferences about their future behavior."[9] Put differently, reputation for resolve during the Cold War should have been a constant concern of the two superpowers' leaders because contests over face provided important signals of willingness to bear costs and run risks. Such actions supposedly served as a focal point in others' assessments of the ability and reliability of each of the superpowers.

Predictions about the role that reputation for resolve should play under unipolarity, however, vary significantly. Tang posits that the strategic environment under unipolarity actually resembles that of a "chain store paradox" game, in which the superpower is the monopolist, while all the rest of the world is the potential challenger.[10] In that case, we would expect the lone superpower to defend its reputation even more adamantly than under bipolarity. Christopher Fettweis argues that "the credibility imperative survived the transition from bipolarity to unipolarity." This is because concern for reputation for resolve remains embedded in policy making.[11]

Other scholars, however, envision a different relationship between unipolarity and reputational concerns. David Lake and Patrick Morgan both contend that reputational concerns should be less salient under unipolarity: "since multipolarity and unipolarity systems are less competitive [than bipolar systems], reputation for resolve will be less central for the great powers."[12] Similarly, Christopher Layne argues, "the passing of the Cold War and the emergence of multipolarity mean that US policy need no longer be driven by a morbid obsession with establishing credibility in secondary regions in order to demonstrate the reliability of US security commitments in more vital areas."[13] Robert Jervis also acknowledges that it is unclear whether the reputational effects of behavior will continue to apply in unipolarity. This is because the main audiences of US credibility are no longer the USSR and a small number of allies, but under unipolarity, the number of actors the United States needs to impress is much larger. Thus, attention to US actions should be diffused, diluting the effect of reputation for resolve.[14]

These divergent perspectives do not provide a clear prediction about whether reputation for resolve should be a less salient consideration in the minds of post–Cold War US presidents. My dispositional theory would expect to see variation among American post–Cold War presidents, but both schools of thought outlined above would expect a similar level of concern for reputation within each group of presidents, stemming from the structure of the international system.

The Nuclear Balance

In addition to the polarity of the international system, scholars have pointed to the advent of nuclear weapons as a particularly relevant systemic variable for leaders' concerns for reputation for resolve. According to Jervis, the ultimate threat in the nuclear age is all-out nuclear war.[15] When two adversaries both possess secure second-strike capabilities, the credibility of a nuclear threat significantly diminishes, because the implementation of such a threat would lead to the destruction of both the state and its adversary. In such conditions, a state's reputation for resolve over nonvital interests might become a crucial indicator that could cause a leader to form expectations about the behavior of its adversary in future crises.

Accordingly, we should expect leaders to be especially concerned about reputation for resolve in situations of Mutual Assured Destruction (MAD), and to be less concerned about reputation for resolve when their state possesses a nuclear monopoly or first-strike capabilities. Some might argue that even within MAD, we could observe fluctuations in concerns for reputation for resolve, driven largely by assessment about the relative balance of nuclear capabilities: leaders of states with nuclear superiority might be more relaxed about the need to project resolve, compared to leaders of states who believe they are losing their nuclear advantage. In contrast, my theory would expect to observe high self-monitor leaders who wish to fight for reputation even when the nuclear balance is clearly in favor of the United States, and to observe low self-monitor leaders resisting wars of face even when their nuclear balance shifts to their opponent's favor.

Material Cost-Benefit Calculus

My dispositional theory posits that some types of decision makers will be more likely to use military instruments when they perceive little material gains because they view reputational considerations as critical. From a purely materialist cost-benefit calculation perspective, leaders will fight when material benefits outweigh the cost/risk of using force. For the materialist hypothesis to receive empirical support, we should observe decision makers focusing on information pertaining to the material costs and risks of pursuing policies, and updating their beliefs in response to new information of that kind.[16] Moreover, if decision makers advocate using military instruments in cases when no clear material interests are at stake, or make contrary arguments in policy debates, this would be evidence against the materialist explanation.

The dispositional theory I advance does not predict that leaders will be solely or automatically guided by their dispositions and beliefs, without regard for material costs and benefits. When the material cost of building or protecting one's reputation for resolve is extremely high and potential for success is extremely low, for example, we should expect even reputation crusaders to hesitate before executing their policy preferences. Conversely, if the cost of building or protecting one's reputation for resolve is very low, and the likelihood of success is estimated to be quite high, reputation skeptics (and even possibly critics) might pursue a policy that would have positive reputational externalities, regardless of their dispositions and beliefs. Within the large class of crises for which the probabilities and costs of protecting reputation are ambiguous, however, individual leaders' dispositions and beliefs should be more influential.[17]

DOMESTIC POLITICAL EXPLANATIONS

Domestic political considerations might shape decision makers' concern for reputation and could constrain a president's decision whether to use military instruments to fight for reputation. A number of explanations link domestic political consideration to foreign policy, each highlighting a different causal mechanism and different observable implications about when leaders will fight for reputation. As I explain below, some versions of domestic political explanations are more in tension with my argument, while others are either orthogonal or complementary to my dispositional argument.

Preferences of Domestic Actors, and Diversionary Motivations

First, leaders might invoke reputational concerns to appease the public, to pacify their core constituency, or to divert public opinion from other issues. Leaders are not truly concerned about reputational considerations but rather employ reputation for resolve to sell their policies domestically.[18] Diversionary motivations for war would be consistent with this explanation; leaders will resort to war even when vital strategic interests are not at stake in order to "distract popular attention away from internal social and economic problems and consolidate their own domestic political support."[19] Thus, leaders might pursue belligerent foreign policy and cite reputational concerns for fighting when their domestic support is weak. Rather than being genuinely concerned about reputation for resolve, according to this argument, leaders fight because they believe that initiating or escalating an international crisis could lead to a "rally around the flag" effect that increases their domestic standing. Even in the absence of diversionary motivations, leaders could use reputational arguments to appease the preferences of core constituents who may believe their country's standing and credibility were eroding.

Regardless of the particular leader's motivation, according to those types of domestic political explanations, leaders fight in response to public opinion or to shape it in ways that give them greater standing domestically. Because public opinion shifts over time, leaders have different core constituencies, and leaders may have different incentives over time to distract the public with war, we might see variation in when leaders will claim to fight for reputation. In particular, two key observable implications emerge from this line of argument.

First, to probe whether leaders invoked concerns for reputation for resolve during crises because of domestic political considerations, we look at whether the following groups have expressed concern for reputation for resolve: the public, through public opinion polls; the president's key constituency, such as his party voters; interest groups that form the core of his electoral base; and congressional leaders from his own party.[20] Leaders who raise reputational justifications for intervention, although public opinion or their support base are *against* using military instruments to project credibility, would be evidence against this particular domestic political explanation. Also, leaders who fight for reputation when their domestic standing or legitimacy is not threatened might be inconsistent with diversionary motivations. Second, decision makers' private writings and arguments should allow us to probe the extent to which domestic political motivations were present. If leaders speak of reputation only in public, this should increase our suspicion that reputational arguments were invoked to garner the public's support.

The Role of Regime Type

A second line of domestic political arguments treats domestic actors' preferences about protection of reputation for resolve as constant rather than variable, at least in democracies. Thus, these arguments explain why democratic leaders will be more likely to care about reputation for resolve more than some autocratic leaders. To be sure, this topic has been a subject of debate in the literature and is far from settled. Selectorate theory suggests that leaders in democracies—who need larger winning coalitions—are more likely to invest in reputation since their political survival depends on producing public goods, such as national security, whereas autocrats are better able to maintain their (smaller) winning coalitions by providing them with private goods.[21] Along similar lines, audience cost theory suggests that leaders in democracies are likely to face domestic audiences who would penalize them for backing down after publicly escalating a conflict.[22] This is because reneging on a threat not only shows that the leader is incompetent in foreign policy issues, but that he or she put the nation's reputation for resolve at risk.[23] Others scholars, however, have contested this argument, showing that domestic actors in some types of autocracies also impose audience costs on their leaders for backing down in crises.[24]

These arguments offer two clear observable implications. First, leaders of democracies should be either as willing, or even more willing, to fight for reputation compared to leaders of some types of nondemocratic regimes. Since the empirical focus of this book is on leaders of democracies, testing this proposition is outside its scope. Second, reputation for resolve is a public good that domestic actors constantly demand of their leaders. Accordingly, and contrary to the predictions of this book's theory, we would expect to see uniformity rather than differences in concern for reputation for resolve among leaders of democracies.

Finally, it is important to emphasize that the theory I advance in this book does not dismiss the importance of domestic actors. Rather, I argue that high self-monitor presidents, while motivated to project resolve to increase their status internationally, are likely to be more mindful of the preferences of the public or their core constituencies than are low self-monitor presidents. This is because they are essentially strategic actors who seek to cultivate desired images—at times multiple images—that they think can increase their status. Thus, if the preferences of domestic audiences strongly oppose policies that increase resolve, this may place the high self-monitoring president in a dilemma. High self-monitoring presidents could use several strategies to deal with this multiple-audiences dilemma. They could decide to ignore the preferences of domestic audiences and pursue their policies despite domestic dissent: for example, they might pursue covert military action that can be observed by the adversary and local allies but not by domestic audiences, allowing the president to signal resolve while avoiding punishment by the public. Finally, where domestic actors, such as Congress, cease necessary support for the pursuit of reputation-building policies, high self-monitoring presidents might be forced to pay a reputational cost. Still, we should observe them taking initial steps to resist pressure from such domestic actors. If they are forced to cease their reputationally guided policies, they do so in a face-saving manner.

This argument is thus different from one that is purely rooted in domestic politics in that, first, I expect low and high self-monitor presidents to differ in the extent they take domestic political considerations into account when formulating crisis behavior. High self-monitor presidents are more likely to care about public opinion, for example, compared to low self-monitor presidents. Second, while high self-monitor presidents could be mindful of domestic preferences, they are unlikely to "cut and run" to appease domestic preferences, or to pretend to care about reputation just to conform to the demands of the public. Rather, reputational motivations will be an important concern for a high self-monitor president even when he is forced to moderate or cease reputation-guided policies because of domestic pressures.

INDIVIDUAL-LEVEL EXPLANATIONS

Southern Presidents

Dafoe and Caughey predict that southern US presidents are more averse to backing down from violent conflict than nonsouthern presidents, as inheritors of a multigenerational "culture of honor."[25] While this explanation draws on societal-cultural variations between, as well as within, countries, the observable implications can be manifested at the individual level. Thus, as Dafoe and Caughey argue, southern presidents are more likely to use force in militarized interstate disputes, have longer disputes, and, when they do win those disputes, are more likely to have done so by forcing their opponent to back down. They expect southern leaders to exhibit greater concerns for reputation for resolve, and to resort more quickly to force when that reputation is at stake.

Importantly, this explanation is not necessarily in direct tension with the argument I advance here. Indeed, high self-monitor presidents from the South could be significantly more likely to fight for face compared to presidents who are low self-monitors or are not from the South. This is because socializing within a culture of honor may lead high self-monitors to be even more strongly motivated to fight for face as they might believe an appearance of "resolve" and "honor" would be especially instrumental in cultivating their social status.

Historical Analogies

Another explanation for variation in leaders' concerns for reputation would point to the role of salient historical events, such as the Munich crisis, that leads some leaders to believe in the importance of reputation for resolve. Put differently, some leaders may have concerns for reputation because they are influenced by available schemas that serve as powerful heuristics.[26] Studies have shown that there is a tendency to learn from events that have a major

TABLE 5.1. Observable Implications

	Materialist	Domestic Politics	Individual Level	Dispositional Theory
Will leaders differ in concern for reputation when faced with an identical crisis situation?	No	Possibly	Yes	Yes
What affects willingness to use coercive military instruments to project reputation for resolve?	Polarity of the system; nuclear balance; rational calculations of materialist costs and benefits	Preferences, interests, and emotional responses of domestic actors	Southern culture; influential historical events	Leaders' self-monitoring and beliefs about the effectiveness of military force
When will leaders use coercive military instruments to project reputation for resolve?	When international system is bipolar or unipolar (although see debate); when nuclear balance is seen as unfavorable or eroding; when materialist benefits outweigh material costs	When domestic actors pressure leaders or when leaders believe it will improve their domestic support and legitimacy	Southern presidents and leaders who are influenced by an historical event pointing to importance of reputation for resolve will be more likely to fight for reputation	Reputation crusaders and believers will be more likely to fight for reputation than reputation skeptics and critics

impact, affect the individual or his or her society directly, occur recently in time, and are observed firsthand and at a formative period in a person's life.[27]

This approach, then, should lead to variation among leaders in their concerns for reputation, not because of their strategic beliefs or dispositions, but rather because of the varying influence of these analogies. Because leaders may also invoke analogies to support policies chosen for other reasons, it is tricky to trace their causal role in decision making. Still, if leaders' policies are driven by lessons from the past as the rationale for pursuing reputation-guided policies, we should expect them to refer to the historical events they believe are influential and salient; to mention them in their private writings and crisis deliberations; and to link their preferred crisis policies to these historical events.[28]

As with the case of southern presidents, because of the subjective nature of analogical reasoning—in both the observation and interpretation of experience—there might be an interaction effect between self-monitoring and the type of salient analogies.[29] For example, high self-monitors might be more likely to gravitate to analogies that emphasize the importance of reputation, and of reputation for resolve particularly during crisis situations. Low self-monitors might select analogies, or interpret historical events, such that the lesson learned is one of how reputational wars can backfire, for example.

Table 5.1 lays out the observable implications of the various theories discussed above, as well as of the dispositional theory I present in this book.

Selection of Presidents and Crises

For the qualitative section of this book, I focus on the crisis behavior of three American presidents: Jimmy Carter (chapter 7), Ronald Reagan (chapter 8), and Bill Clinton (chapter 9). Those presidents were selected, first, because the results of the historians' surveys show that those presidents exhibit variation in their self-monitoring dispositions. While Carter is clearly classified as a low self-monitor president, Reagan and Clinton both score as high self-monitor presidents.[30] Second, they also vary in their beliefs about the effectiveness of military force. The military assertiveness scale, based on text analysis of presidential speeches, suggests that we can reliably classify Reagan as being higher in assertiveness than Carter. Qualitative evidence presented in the following chapters supports this classification. The text analysis of the public speeches was not applicable to those speeches delivered by President Clinton because his presidency began when the Cold War was already over, and thus his foreign policy discourse cannot be compared to that of Cold War American presidents. However, qualitative evidence I present in chapter 9 marks Clinton as low on the military assertiveness scale.

These presidents represent three of the four ideal-types presented in this book (see table 5.2). The one missing type, a low self-monitor hawk, is not

TABLE 5.2. Typology of Presidents by Self-Monitoring and Military Assertiveness

		Self-Monitoring Disposition of Leaders	
		High Self-Monitor	Low Self-Monitor
Leaders' beliefs in the efficacy of force	Force is an effective instrument	**Reputation crusader** Ronald Reagan	**Reputation skeptic** —
	Force is not an effective instrument	**Reputation believer** Bill Clinton	**Reputation critic** Jimmy Carter

analyzed in the case analysis because presidents that can be clearly classified as low self-monitor hawks are extremely rare in our sample. In fact, the historians' survey, combined with the text analysis, identify only President Ford as a low self-monitor hawk among the Cold War presidents. But this is not a good case to study in depth. Ford was not an elected president and served for only two and a half years. As a result of the circumstances that brought Ford into power—and his short term as president—National Security Advisor Henry Kissinger, Nixon's chief foreign policy advisor, dominated Ford's foreign policy.[31] Furthermore, the fact that only one president in our sample can be classified clearly as a low self-monitor hawk might suggest that this combination of dispositions is less prevalent among leaders, and thus might be less significant to study in depth. Nevertheless, in the case study of crisis behavior of Reagan and his advisors (chapter 7), I am able to shed light on the behavior of a low self-monitor hawk by observing the crisis decision making of Secretary of Defense Weinberger, who according to biographical evidence appears to fit the description of a low self-monitor hawk.

Selecting presidents from both the Cold War and post–Cold War periods also allows me to show the applicability of the theory across different systemic conditions. Specifically, showing that presidents continued to care about reputation in the post–Cold War era, as in the case study of President Clinton, cuts against the claim that reputational concerns are no longer important when the international system lacks another superpower to deter, or allies to impress and fight over, or that the US obsession about reputation and credibility was an inherent feature of the superpower struggle for allies and the Third World, bipolarity, or the nuclear conditions during the Cold War.[32] Lastly, I choose two southern presidents (Carter and Clinton) and one nonsouthern president (Reagan) to probe the theory that southern presidents are inherently more likely to use force.

For each of these four American presidents, I select three or four international crises faced during his administration. In selecting the crises, I follow several criteria: First, the concern for US reputation for resolve in each crisis must be plausible. This means that reputational considerations were known to have been raised by the president, his advisors, the opposition, or other parties. Not all international crises or military disputes involve concern for reputation. Second, both the outcome and the military instruments used vary. In this way, we avoid selecting on the dependent variable by examining only uses of force, or uses of certain kinds of force. For example, Reagan used ground forces followed by withdrawal in Lebanon, but he deployed air strikes in Libya. This spectrum of military technologies, as well as the inclusion of cases where the use of force was rejected or limited, shows that the theory explains both the use and the nonuse of military instruments.

Third, concerns for reputation for resolve could also be present in a crisis that involves either vital or nonvital interests. In practice, concerns for reputation would be more visible in shaping actions in parts of the world that are manifestly not worth the risk involved in using force. Indeed, scholars have long noted there is a loose inverse relationship between the rhetorical employment of the imperative of credibility or reputation for resolve and the presence of a vital, tangible national interest.[33] This is because when tangible national interests are clearly at stake, policy makers are likely to focus their private and public discussions on those tangible issues, because more important things are at stake. This implies that the absence of reputation-based discourse as justification would not necessarily imply a leader's absence of concerns about reputation. Disentangling the role of reputation in such crises would therefore be a difficult task even if primary documents were available.

As a result, crises that do not involve clear tangible interests vital to the United States offer a better universe of cases to evaluate the extent to which reputational considerations shape policy choices. In such crises, we essentially control for interests and are thus better able to examine the independent causal role of reputational considerations. All the crises I focus on involve places that, while varying in their strategic or reputational importance, did not pose a significant risk to a vital US interest.[34] This means that reputational considerations could have been what tipped the balance toward the use of force, where we see military instruments employed. However, I am mindful that decision makers may have deemed places that lack obvious vital importance as, in fact, having such importance. Therefore, we focus on the reasoning for the use or nonuse of force, rather than focusing on the geographic location alone, in order to see whether the decision makers' actions were primarily based on reputational considerations.

Lastly, evaluating numerous crises within each presidency allows us to test the validity of competing as well as additional contextual explanations for each president. For example, variation in the time of the crisis relative to the president's tenure in office can shed light on whether reputational concerns

TABLE 5.3. Selected International Crises

Leader	Likely Type	Crises
Jimmy Carter	Reputation critic	Soviet activities in the Horn of Africa (1977–79) Soviet brigade in Cuba (1979) Soviet invasion of Afghanistan (1979–80)
Ronald Reagan	Reputation crusader	Intervention in Lebanon (1982–84) Invasion of Grenada (1983) Soviet war in Afghanistan (1980–86) Bombing of Libya (1986)
Bill Clinton	Reputation believer	Intervention in Somalia (1992–94) Invasion of Haiti (1994) 3rd Taiwan Straits crisis (1995–96)

are indeed more prevalent during crises earlier in the president's tenure. According to Dafoe, leaders are more likely to be concerned about reputation early in their tenure when their reputation is less well formed.[35] According to this theory, we should expect leaders to exhibit more concerns for reputation during their first year in office (and to pursue policies that are consistent with such concerns), and to be less concerned about reputation later in their tenure.

The selected crises within each presidency (see table 5.3) also vary in public opinion and congressional support, which allows me to evaluate some domestic political explanations as well.

President-Advisor Comparisons

For Presidents Carter and Reagan, I code the self-monitoring and hawkishness of their two main advisors on foreign policy and evaluate the extent to which their crisis policy recommendations are consistent with the prediction of the theory.[36] Thus, I essentially test the theory on both the presidents and their main advisors, thereby contributing also to our understanding of dynamics between the president and his inner circle during crises.[37]

The focus on advisors serves several analytical purposes. First, I can generalize the theory beyond presidents and show its applicability to lower-level officials. Second, I am able to demonstrate how differences in the self-monitoring tendencies of the president and his advisors shape their (un)willingness to fight for reputation, and that these differences cannot be attributed to situational variables or access to information during crisis. Third, it allows me to offer a new explanation about why (and when) relationships between some presidents and their inner circles are more prone to debates about the importance of fighting for face than others. A national security inner circle that is populated with high self-monitors is more likely to raise and push reputation for resolve arguments during crises compared to an inner circle of low self-monitors.

Finally, a focus on advisors helps me evaluate whether the president raised the reputational concern, or whether the president was urged by an advisor to consider reputation. The theory would predict that low self-monitor presidents would not raise reputational considerations on their own, and would resist or dismiss such concerns when raised by their advisors. Conversely, I expect high self-monitor presidents to act on reputational considerations independently from, or sometimes as a result of urging by, an advisor. This is because high self-monitor presidents, although intuitively "wired" to be concerned about international image, might nonetheless lack the nuanced understanding of the potential effects of an international crisis on that image. Thus, I expect them to be susceptible to image-type urging by an advisor.

6

Jimmy Carter and the Crises of the 1970s

"I would never again get militarily involved in the internal affairs of another country unless our own security was directly threatened. . . . We don't have to show that we're strong. We are strong."

—JIMMY CARTER, INTERVIEW ON PBS, MAY 6, 1976

Jimmy Carter faced several international crises during his presidency that many observers argue risked the United States' reputation for resolve. Unlike those of most of his predecessors or successors, Carter's discourse and policies seem to show that he was not motivated by projecting resolve for the sake of reassuring allies or intimidating adversaries. In fact, evidence from primary documents reveals that Carter's behavior during international crises corresponds closely to the reputation critic ideal-type. A reputation critic exhibits the outward behavior we would expect from low self-monitors who generally do not believe that military force is a valuable instrument to solve foreign policy crises. President Carter may be the only president since 1945 who well fits this ideal-type. The experts' survey discussed in chapter 4 and other biographical information in this chapter indicate strongly that Carter's personality is that of a classic low self-monitor. Text analysis of Carter's foreign policy speeches reported in chapter 4, combined with other qualitative measures, confirms that he embodied more dovish tendencies about the use of force than did other American presidents.

This chapter reinforces the classification of Carter as a reputation critic using additional qualitative evidence in the form of Carter's personal diary and prepresidential speeches, memoirs written by his advisors, and other secondary literature. It also uses available biographical evidence to illuminate the self-monitoring tendencies of Carter's closest advisors, National Security Advisor Zbigniew Brzezinski and Secretary of State Cyrus Vance. It then utilizes more than ten thousand newly declassified primary documents to provide important insights into Carter's beliefs, preferences, and decision making during three international crises. The documents also illuminate the attitudes and policy preferences of Carter's advisors, as well as the influence of other domestic actors and the American public.

This chapter supports a number of empirical implications that follow from the theory. First, the evidence clearly indicates that Carter's decision making and policies were not motivated by a concern about reputation for resolve and credibility. When challenged by the Soviet Union in the Horn of Africa, Cuba, and Afghanistan, Carter did not use reputation-based discourse, nor were his decisions shaped by considerations of reputation for resolve. For example, Carter declined to escalate the conflict between Ethiopia and Somalia militarily, or to deploy an aircraft carrier as a show of resolve to allies in the region. Carter also declined to link the Soviet brigade in Cuba to larger US-Soviet bilateral relations, and he resisted urging from throughout the government to link the fate of SALT II negotiations to a Soviet withdrawal. Furthermore, although he pursued more hawkish policies in response to the Soviet invasion of Afghanistan, he never used military force. Far more important than appearing "tough" or "resolved" in crises that did not involve important material stakes, Carter sought to pursue foreign policy that truly and honestly reflected his beliefs and US material interests. This is remarkably consistent with how the literature portrays the behavior of low self-monitors, and their emphasis on sincerity and congruence between the inner self and outward expression regardless of the circumstances. Carter emphasized the importance he attached to truthfulness in his public rhetoric but was also visibly disturbed by Brzezinski's *private* suggestions that the administration pursue deception as foreign policy simply to impress the Soviets, quashing any attempts by Brzezinski to develop those points further.

Second, although Carter was a low self-monitor, his national security advisor, Brzezinski, exhibited a fairly high self-monitoring disposition, as shown later in this chapter. Consistent with that disposition, Brzezinski repeatedly and consistently highlighted to the president that Soviet challenges presented a threat to US reputation for resolve, and he urged Carter to think about how his actions might hurt US standing and reputation for resolve in the eyes of adversaries and allies. The theory predicts that Carter, owing to his low self-monitoring, would resist policy options that would demonstrate greater resolve simply to impress international audiences. Carter's private statements and correspondence with Brzezinski reveal that the two did not see eye to eye on this issue, with Brzezinski consistently more concerned with reputational implications than Carter. To be sure, Brzezinski was not the only one pushing the president to think about reputation, as the intelligence community also presented evidence indicating that the Soviets perceived Carter as weak. That Carter was largely unaffected by such considerations or "primes" is consistent with the experimental results discussed in chapter 3. In experiments that manipulate reputation costs, we see that low self-monitor doves are more often guided by their predisposition toward resisting the use of force, and tend to remain unconvinced, despite arguments based on reputational risks, to resort to force.

In contrast to Brzezinski, biographical evidence suggests that Carter's secretary of state, Vance, exhibited a low self-monitoring disposition. Consistent with that disposition, Vance's crisis decision making indicates that he repeatedly resisted both Brzezinski's rhetoric and policies that intended to highlight the importance of reputation for resolve. Rather, Vance suggested a more pragmatic approach that highlighted material cost-benefit calculations, not reputational ones. Importantly, then, my theory offers a novel lens through which we can understand the tensions between Brzezinski and Vance, as well as between Brzezinski and Carter, that go beyond different views about the Soviet Union. These distinctions are further fueled by fundamental differences in their personalities that shaped their outlooks about the importance of "face" in international politics more broadly.

Third, a dispositional theory might suggest that a president's behavior in international crises would demonstrate general continuity over the course of the administration. Yet, as many scholars have observed, Carter underwent a significant transformation in his assessments of Soviet intentions following the invasion of Afghanistan; his policies toward the USSR became more hawkish as a result.[1] I argue, however, that this reading of Carter and the dispositional theory are *not* in tension. As the documents indicate, in the aftermath of the invasion, Carter came to believe that the Soviets possessed expansionist goals and thus feared that the Soviets would challenge other regimes in the Middle East and the Persian Gulf, posing a threat to US vital interests. It was his concern over those vital material interests—rather than concern over "image" or overall "standing"—that prompted Carter to make use of new policy tools to deter further Soviet adventures in that strategically important region. Thus, even during the crisis in Afghanistan we continue to see Brzezinski and Carter reason very differently. Whereas the former viewed the crisis primarily as a threat to US reputation for resolve, the president only highlighted the threat the Soviet Union now posed to US material interests. Those material concerns, I show, forced Carter to consider more hawkish crisis policies that he had previously rejected. However, even when Carter considered more hawkish policies that were intended to deter and punish the Soviets, he still did not resort to military force and did not use military instruments to the same extent that Reagan later did, as I show in the next chapter.

Finally, methodologically, Carter provides a difficult test case for the dispositional theory I propose for several reasons. My argument counters that of Dafoe and Caughey, predicting the opposite outcome for Carter—notwithstanding his southern origins, Carter should be significantly less concerned about projecting a reputation for resolve, even compared to his advisors. It is also a hard test case for the dispositional theory because Carter's rise to power coincided with a peculiar political climate in the history of the Cold War: the American public, disillusioned with the entire political system following the Watergate political scandal, desired a sincere, idealistic candidate. Thus, it could be argued that Carter's choices were driven by the preferences of the electorate, rather than Carter's own psychological disposition. But as we shall see, there is evidence that the opposite is true: US public opinion changed to favor the use of force almost as soon as Carter came into power, and it shifted even more in that direction in reaction to Soviet adventurism in Africa and Central America and the fall of the shah in Iran. Still, Carter did not change his approach toward crises of resolve with the Soviet Union.

This chapter proceeds as follows. I first analyze Carter's self-monitoring tendencies and his attitudes toward the use of force. I then use biographical evidence to establish the self-monitoring tendencies of Carter's two main foreign policy advisors: Brzezinski and Vance, and derive predictions about their likely crisis decision making. Next, in the online appendix I explore factors that led to Carter's election in 1976, highlighting the special circumstances that enabled a low self-monitor politician to emerge as president of the United States. A review of Carter's policy choices gives special attention to his actions during the Soviet and Cuban intervention in the Horn of Africa, the discovery of a Soviet brigade operating in Cuba, and the Soviet invasion of Afghanistan. Finally, the chapter addresses alternative and other contextual explanations for Carter's crisis decision making.

Classifying Carter: Self-Monitoring and Military Assertiveness

Based on the results of the historians' survey and text analysis of Carter's foreign policy rhetoric presented in chapter 4, Carter comes close to the ideal-type of a low self-monitor dove. In the rest of this section, I use several carefully selected qualitative indicators of his self-monitoring and military assertiveness (laid out in chapter 5) to confirm this classification.

CARTER AS A LOW SELF-MONITOR

Jimmy Carter's self-monitoring tendencies were assessed by a group of presidential scholars (n=6) who completed the eighteen-item self-monitoring test.

Carter scored an average of 32.9 on the 100-point scale, with a margin of error of 12.1. This score is statistically significantly different from the midpoint of 50 and places Carter firmly in the low self-monitor category. Generally speaking, low self-monitors are more concerned with upholding their "true dispositions and attitudes in every situation" rather than adapting their behavior to their current environment.[2] Low self-monitors tend to show great consistency in their social interactions across different social settings; they express their emotions honestly even at a cost to their social standing; they care more about being sincere and true to their beliefs than about elevating their social status.[3]

One hallmark aspect of a high self-monitor is expressive self-control, or the ability to use public performances and imitations of different affects to adapt to a given situation. Carter was not known for his ability or desire to put on different performances to appeal to a wide range of audiences. Indeed, Carter did not see his speeches as efforts to convince others that they should vote for him; instead, he believed, as Randall Balmer notes, that "all [he] needed to prevail was to present his case, and his superior qualifications, to the voters."[4] Carter firmly believed that "the purpose of politics is to establish justice in a sinful world," and he was not shy about voicing his displeasure with lobbyists and other politicians who worked primarily for their own benefit.[5] At a May 4, 1974, gathering of alumni for the University of Georgia Law School's "Law Day," in a speech about the criminal justice system, Carter "lit into lobbyists . . . [and] lawyers," especially those who had derailed his attempts to pass an ethics bill that would help reform Georgia's prison systems.[6] Carter's speech was not flattering to his immediate audience, but instead an unvarnished presentation of the truth as he saw it.

Carter's tendency to avoid performances in favor of blunt truth telling continued well into his presidency. His low self-monitoring tendencies and unwillingness to soften his message to fit the demand of the electorate ultimately hurt him in the polls. Perhaps the most infamous example of an unpopular Carter speech is his "Crisis of Confidence" or "Malaise" speech, delivered on July 14, 1979, in which he argued that the United States faced many problems because of a loss of moral strength, "the loss of a unity of purpose for our nation."[7] When his advisors expressed worry that telling the American people that their way of life was flawed or decaying, Carter replied, "I just don't want to bulls——t the American people."[8] Moreover, he appeared to blame the American people; he argued that "too many [people] now tend to worship self-indulgence and consumption," and that capitalistic individualism weakened Americans' ability to come together to solve national problems.[9] The speech soon drew serious negative reactions from listeners, who began to question Carter's ability as a leader because he, as the *Chicago Tribune* reported, "deplored the prevailing lack of confidence in government, but did little to restore it."[10] Carter could not conceal his own negative emotional responses to what he believed were serious problems, failing to instill optimism or confidence in his listeners. Carter did not treat speeches as performances, and his tendency to make statements without attending to political considerations hurt his chances of reelection.

Carter did not make efforts to conceal his anger toward people he disliked, and this was evident in his 1980 campaign against Ronald Reagan. Peter Bourne, a former special assistant to Carter, notes that Carter derided Reagan's lack of knowledge on issues, and he made attacks that "[implied that Reagan] was a racist" and did not pass laws to help voters of color.[11] Voters did not respond well; the *Boston Globe* reported that "the president [seemed] bent on discarding his last ace, his reputation as a decent and compassionate man."[12] His advisors urged him to stop going after Reagan so intensely, but Carter continued to attack the challenger as someone unfit to be president.[13]

Carter's attacks on Reagan, which involved him talking about "his daughter Amy's fears of nuclear war" as the basis for his concern, "seemed silly"; Reagan, by contrast, looked "confident and restrained" by calmly and simply reiterating his vision for the United States.[14] An Indiana University study of people who watched the debate found that, while Carter appeared to be the more honest candidate, Reagan appeared to be the stronger one.[15]

A second aspect of high self-monitoring is social stage presence, or the ability to draw attention to oneself in social situations. Here again, Carter does not show the traits of a high self-monitor. During his 1976 campaign for president, for example, the "oft-repeated question" was, "Who is Jimmy Carter?"[16] When voters learned that he was governor of Georgia from very humble beginnings, the common follow-up question was, "How can such a man expect to lead a pluralistic American society, and the rest of the Western World as well?"[17] They asked this question in spite of Carter's experience with foreign policy; he had traveled much of the world as a naval officer and, as governor, had dealt with various international bodies, visiting Israel, Japan, and other countries to negotiate trade deals.[18] Moreover, Carter's tenure as governor was extremely productive: he had passed "a comprehensive package of prison reform legislation" and "environmental protection laws, generally conceded to be among the toughest in the nation at the time."[19] In spite of these accomplishments, Carter had entered the race virtually unknown.

The beginning of Carter's campaign was remarkably inauspicious because of his seeming inability to draw voters' notice. Even after he became president, few Americans believed they knew much about Jimmy Carter, and his weak social and stage presence remained difficult for him to overcome. Indeed, many people who voted for Carter did not have "an ideological connection to [him]."[20] His pollster, Pat Caddell, found that after the election "fifty percent of the public still [did] not know where Carter [stood] on the issues," not because he had changed policy positions, but because he was ineffective in conveying his message.[21]

Finally, high self-monitors tend to exhibit other-directed self-presentation, or the tendency to present the most appropriate parts of one's personality for social advantages. Contrastingly, Carter was brutally honest and did not change his message even slightly to appeal to his audiences. A prime example of this was his first speech after being elected governor of Georgia in 1970. Despite having the support of many Southern Democrat segregationists during the campaign, he declared in his oath of office that "the time for racial discrimination is over," much to the chagrin of those supporters.[22]

Consistent with being a low self-monitor, Carter was more concerned about honesty. In a campaign interview on PBS, when Bill Moyers asked Carter what he wanted his legacy to be, he stated that he "[hoped] people [would] say, 'You know, Jimmy Carter made a lot of mistakes, but he never told me a lie.'"[23] Carter believed that the best way to have a strong foreign policy was to have "the high moral character of the American people . . . mirrored" in transparent and direct diplomacy.[24] Carter rarely gave speeches that were inconsistent with his values or beliefs, and his advisors often chided him for not altering his messages to have a useful political impact. For example, in March 1976, in a television interview on *Face the Nation*, discussing defense and the quality of US officials, especially diplomats, Carter was especially critical and candid. In response, Zbigniew Brzezinski argued that public, direct criticism "ought to be couched in political terms" of reform.[25]

Scholars portray Carter as a notoriously stubborn leader who "found compromise very difficult" because of "his commitment to the truth."[26] As governor, Carter conceded that he chose "not to compromise [on policy decisions] until it [was] absolutely necessary" but claimed that there was no situation in which "an adamant position on [his] part doomed a desirable goal."[27] Indeed, as Julian Zelizer explains, this affected Carter's relationship with the legislative branch even before he had become president, and certainly during his tenure. To that effect, Carter's advisor and White House Chief of Staff Hamilton Jordan noted that his boss simply did not "understand the personal element in politics."[28]

Carter's success in politics may seem surprising in light of these low self-monitor traits. However, in the wake of the Watergate scandal, the American public had lost trust in their elected officials, both for the crimes they committed and the lies they told about them. In those turbulent times, Carter's perception as honest and moral had a distinct advantage with the electorate. Jordan noted that "the desire and thirst for strong moral leadership in this nation was not satisfied with the election of Richard Nixon."[29] This is perhaps why congressional liaison Frank Moore stated that "the President's greatest strength perceived by the people . . . was that he was *not* an ordinary politician."[30] Although he failed to be reelected, Carter's determination to pursue policies that truly reflected his beliefs meant that he had few regrets after his four years in office. In his interview with the Miller Center following the end of his presidency, Carter said, "We thought our agenda was proper. We thought we were all honest and serving in a pleasant attitude, but in a self-sacrificial way in that we were dedicated to what we were doing. We were idealistic, maybe to a fault."[31]

In his postpresidential career, Carter continued to exhibit the qualities of a low self-monitor. Detailing Carter's statements and positions since leaving the presidency, Zelizer notes that "Carter defiantly took unpopular stands about foreign affairs, but stands that he fervently believed in, displaying almost no concern about who would dislike him as a result.... He was seemingly unafraid to issue tough statements against government leaders whom he did not like, even if they were American allies."[32]

CARTER'S MILITARY ASSERTIVENESS

Although general beliefs in the efficacy of the use of force are not embedded personality traits in the way that self-monitoring is, we still see a remarkable consistency: Carter's belief that the military should be used only to protect vital national interests was expressed repeatedly in his speeches and policy preferences. Chapter 4 has shown that Carter was a significantly more dovish speaker than most Cold War presidents. In the online appendix, I further show that Carter's public rhetoric during noncrisis periods was more dovish compared to other presidents.

The idea that the military should serve only to defend the country manifested itself in Carter's campaign promises to reduce the military budget. Carter decried the "unbelievable bureaucratic hierarchy" that the military had established and proposed "a roughly five-to-seven-billion-dollar decrease" in defense spending, and a reduction in the numbers of high-ranking officers and other noncombat troops.[33] During his term as governor and in his presidential campaign, Carter denounced military expansion, consistently indicated his dovishness in campaign rhetoric and gubernatorial policies, and took this ideology with him to the Oval Office. Even as governor, Carter generally opposed leveraging the country's foreign military presence to influence other nations. Although Carter supported the military as a useful institution, he disagreed with using it overseas, asserting that "young Americans should never again be sent to die in battle unless our own nation is endangered"; the United States should take this lesson from "the unhappy experience in Vietnam and Cambodia."[34] Carter's desire to bring troops home and to slash the military budget is typical of individuals with low military assertiveness.

After taking office, Carter immediately set out to fulfill his campaign promises, beginning with reducing the military budget and seeking to restructure the military as a primarily defensive force. While Carter did not achieve enormous defense budget cuts, he did propose to Congress a $2.7 billion cut, with the advice of his defense secretary, Harold Brown.[35] Some of these spending cuts targeted weapons systems the Ford administration had commissioned for military modernization, but the majority of cuts focused on gradual budgetary reductions through better management. Furthermore, extra drills to assure combat readiness meant that defense spending actually increased each year of Carter's presidency.[36] Although Carter overestimated his ability to reduce the military budget, he was committed to reorganizing and downsizing the military so it could serve as an exclusively defensive force. Carter did carry out his campaign promise to begin withdrawing troops and nuclear weapons from South Korea in 1977, and he fired Major General John Singlaub after Singlaub publicly warned that the troop withdrawal would lead to war between North and South Korea.[37] Carter limited the troop reduction after resistance from the South Korean regime, and more importantly, significant backlash from Congress, the Joint Chiefs of Staff, and the US intelligence community. These actions wholly conform to the predicted behavior of reputation critics.

In spite of Carter's firm belief that the military must be downsized, his approach to defense spending changed in 1979. Following the Comprehensive Net Assessment of 1978, which revealed important strategic deficiencies, Carter realized that a smaller military would not be able to defend vital national interests adequately. In January 1979, the Carter administration requested a modest increase of 3 percent in the administration defense budget for fiscal year 1980.[38] However, Carter proposed "significant increases in the resources necessary to assure our national security" for the 1981 fiscal year budget, which was submitted following the Soviet invasion of Afghanistan.[39] Indeed, Soviet actions in Afghanistan, coupled with new knowledge of American strategic deficiencies, pushed Carter to increase the defense budget in order to block further Soviet expansionism and to maintain strategic equivalence with the USSR. Increased defense spending was a reaction to changing circumstances that convinced Carter that the Soviet Union was an immediate threat to US allies and interests.

The second indicator is the president's attitude toward covert military action. Carter had little interest in using covert military operations; before his election, he stated "we must move away from making policies in secret; without the knowledge and approval of the American people."[40] On a different occasion he stated, "We must not use the CIA or other covert means to effect violent change in any government or government policy."[41] In the 1978 State of the Union address, Carter made a clear commitment to openness: "Foreign policy decisions must be able to stand the test of public examination and public debate. If we make a mistake in this administration, it will be on the side of frankness and openness with the American people."[42] This is not to argue that Carter completely refrained from covert activities. For example, in the months prior to and following the Soviet invasion of Afghanistan, Carter engaged in covert action whose purpose was to mainly "harass" Soviet forces. But, overall, the frequency of covert action probably reached a lower point under the Carter administration than at any time since the Truman administration. Compared to his successor, Carter scores much lower in terms of money expended and levels of force involved in covert activity. A deputy director for the CIA stated, "Covert actions in the Reagan administration have been fewer, but 'noisier' and more expensive."[43] Furthermore, the Reagan administration would also expand the authority of the CIA to conduct domestic covert operations and collect intelligence in ways that Carter's executive order restricted.[44]

The third qualitative indicator involves the president's use of diplomacy and international institutions to solve international crises. I examine evidence of the president's belief in the utility of back-channel diplomacy, multilateral negotiations, and conflict resolution through international institutions, rather than using force to address threats posed by external forces. Carter certainly favored diplomacy over military force to resolve conflicts, much more so than most presidents before him. Even as governor, Carter was unusually active in establishing ties directly with Latin American nations, as well as through the Organization of American States. He was also active in other international organizations, such as the Trilateral Commission, through which he met his future national security advisor, Zbigniew Brzezinski. In his 1976 campaign, Carter repeatedly mentioned the important role of multilateralism in resolving international crises, asserting, for example, the use of UN Resolution 242 to implement "bilateral discussions between Israel and its neighbors" for peace as the basis for potential settlement of the Arab-Israeli conflict.[45] From his pursuit of arms reduction treaties with the Soviet Union to cuts in defense spending and covert action, Carter's actions clearly show a low level of military assertiveness.

That Carter was skeptical of the efficacy of the use of military force is supported by interviews with his staff. For example, Stuart Eizenstat, the assistant to the president for domestic affairs and policy, stated that Carter's dovishness continued throughout his administration:

> I think that the Christian thing had an effect on him . . . that it had some real impact on his sense of unwillingness to use American military force, which is in some respects a positive. . . . There was, I think, more than simply a political reluctance to do it. . . . He used to say time and time and time again that he was the first President who had never had a man die in combat in his term in office since—I don't know, 1920, or whatever it was.
>
> And it was said so many times that I remember Hamilton [Jordan] or [press secretary] Jody [Powell] or both on one or two occasions said, "Mr. President, this is not ending up being a plus, because it's giving the

perception that you're not willing to stand up for American interests. Somehow it's being interpreted by people as being a sign of weakness rather than a sign of strength." And yet he continued to repeat it. It was something he felt very deeply about.[46]

This commitment to diplomacy and to negotiations with adversaries, and rejection of the use of force, also manifested itself in his statements and actions after his tenure. For example, during the lead-up to the first Gulf War, Carter publicly urged President Bush to give economic sanctions more time to work and to engage in diplomacy. Feeling he was unsuccessful in slowing down the drive toward military intervention, he even sent a letter to the leaders of the other governments on the UN Security Council, urging them to pursue negotiations and not to follow the United States but instead to support the Arab League efforts.[47]

In sum, both quantitative evidence and qualitative indicators support the characterization of Carter as a marked example of a low self-monitor dove.

Self-Monitoring and Carter's Main Advisors

It has long been established that Jimmy Carter's two principal foreign policy advisors, Secretary of State Cyrus Vance and National Security Advisor Zbigniew Brzezinski, had conflicting worldviews about the Soviet Union and how US foreign policy ought to be conducted. While both were more dovish overall than some Republicans at the time, Brzezinski was relatively more hawkish than Vance.[48] I argue that the two also differed in their level of self-monitoring. Specifically, Vance demonstrated low self-monitoring tendencies, whereas Brzezinski seems to be a high self-monitor. According to my theory, we should see differences in the willingness of these individuals to fight for face. Before proceeding, however, I should emphasize that my conclusions as to Carter's advisors' self-monitoring dispositions are based on my behavioral assessment of limited historical evidence.[49]

Cyrus Vance, like President Carter, was a low self-monitor who did little to manage his own image for social gain. As White House Chief of Staff Hamilton Jordan summarized, "Vance didn't have an ounce of the self-promoter in him. He wasn't concerned with his image: he was there to serve," not to build a reputation.[50] Vance's motivations came from his belief that he "had the responsibility to return to the community some of the benefits and blessings [he] had" from his wealthy upbringing in the form of "government service."[51]

This sense of obligation did not come with a tendency to draw attention to himself or his accomplishments; indeed, it was remarkable that Vance's work did not draw more attention given its high quality. While Philip Habib, a US diplomat who worked with many famous foreign policy makers like

Henry Kissinger, called Vance "probably the finest public servant [he] ever worked with,"[52] other observers, including Vance's State Department Director of Politico-Military Affairs Leslie Gelb, characterized him as someone "who shunned publicity" and was "a man who left no footprints" in spite of his talents.[53] Henry Kissinger similarly remarked that "if he had any weakness, it was that he was not sufficiently assertive"[54] and often could not bring attention to his work and ideas. This inability to attract attention, described in the literature as low social stage presence, is typical of low self-monitors.

In addition, Vance did not show the tendency to present different self-images to different people strategically; instead, he was, according to Hamilton Jordan, "solid as a rock and completely predictable."[55] Vance himself stated that he wanted his legacy to be that of a "reasonably decent, honest person who tried to do some things for the country that might have lasting effect,"[56] not necessarily as a great or well-known diplomat. Vance's brother observed that "he was known for his integrity,"[57] and colleagues frequently described him as "Mr. Integrity [and] Mr. Honesty."[58] He was known to take positions that could potentially damage his social standing just to defend his fundamental values. A prime example of this is Vance's decision to resign after Carter ordered a military rescue of the hostages being held in Iran, even before the mission occurred and failed, because he considered the measure counterproductive following months of diplomacy.

Cyrus Vance was only the second secretary of state in US history to resign over policy disagreements, but, in Jordan's words, staying on to support of Carter's decision to intervene "would have meant lying—and this was not possible for him."[59] Vance's strict adherence to his principles regardless of his social situation, combined with his inability to draw attention to himself, suggest that he was a low self-monitor.

In contrast to Vance, biographical evidence suggests that Carter's other principal advisor, Zbigniew ("Zbig") Brzezinski, was a high self-monitor. As Jordan summarized, "if Cy Vance didn't have an ounce of the self-promoter in him, Zbig had several pounds" of that trait.[60] Long before becoming national security advisor, Brzezinski closely monitored his image; he successfully gained widespread recognition and a reputation as a competent and charismatic professor whose high-profile and theatrical lectures were "events."[61] Carter writes that Brzezinski was "a natural center of public attention"[62] not just because of his ideas, but also how he presented them. Brzezinski understood that "the media were becoming increasingly important in the discussion of foreign affairs."[63] Accordingly, he used print and televised media to build notoriety. Brzezinski's actions indicate a strong social stage presence and a tendency toward image management that high self-monitors are more likely to show.

Another hallmark trait of high self-monitors Brzezinski exhibited throughout his political career was his ability to present different sides of himself to others to improve his social position. For example, Brzezinski created a working environment in which, as Carter observed, he could "work harmoniously"[64] with his staff while at the same time putting out more aggressive public statements to which Vance's State Department would (ineffectively) object.[65]

The difference between Vance and Brzezinski in their levels of self-monitoring should be reflected in their positions regarding the importance of fighting for reputation for resolve. If my theory is correct, we should observe Brzezinski and Vance clashing over whether Carter should care about this reputation in crises over issues that had little material interests. The two advisors, to be sure, differed significantly in their beliefs about the nature of Soviet intentions, which exacerbated their policy disagreements. As I show elsewhere, Brzezinski had relatively more hawkish views about the USSR compared to Vance, although he was not as hawkish as Reagan or Weinberger.[66] Specifically, we should expect Brzezinski to be more concerned about reputation and credibility during crises with the Soviet Union, and to try to convince Carter of the importance of "face" during such conflicts. Vance's preferences, on the other hand, should be closer to those of low self-monitor Carter, and he should show much less concern about reputation for resolve.

Reputational Concerns and Carter's Crisis Decision Making

The dispositional theory offers a predictive model for a leader's behavior based on self-monitoring and military assertiveness. During Carter's presidency, Soviet actions during three international crises were perceived by some members of the Carter administration as posing challenges to America's reputation and standing. The first took place in 1977–78 over increased Soviet activities in the Horn of Africa. This crisis did not involve US vital interests by any means, but it was perceived as a challenge to America's reputation for resolve and standing in Africa. The second crisis took place in the summer and fall of 1979, when information about the presence of an alleged Soviet combat brigade in Cuba was discovered. Even though stationing Soviet troops in Cuba had a more direct effect on American security than Soviet actions in the Horn of Africa, the size of the Soviet unit as well information about its history meant that this discovery was not as much a major threat to US national security as it was another challenge to US "face." The third crisis started in December 1979 when the Soviets invaded Afghanistan. This action was perceived not just as posing a challenge to the US reputation for resolve, but even more critically, as having the potential to significantly affect vital US material interests in the Middle East and the Persian Gulf, by allowing the Soviets an opportunity to control oil resources and to reinforce their presence in the region. The invasion of Afghanistan was, unlike the other two crises examined, a crisis over vital interests as perceived by Carter, and not purely a reputational military interstate dispute. Overall, Carter's rhetoric and behavior during these crises matches the theory's predictions. The combination of Carter's dovishness and low self-monitoring affected both his reasoning—which downplayed the importance of image and emphasized the importance of honesty—and his policies, which demonstrated his reluctance to use military instruments to protect or salvage US reputation for resolve.

THE HORN OF AFRICA

In the summer of 1977, Somalia invaded neighboring Ethiopia in an attempt to conquer the Ogaden Desert, in which ethnic Somalis lived. This local ethnic conflict between two poor African states grew into a Cold War standoff. Members of the National Security Council (NSC), including Brzezinski, identified Soviet and Cuban support of Somalia in the Horn of Africa as posing a significant challenge to US reputation for resolve in the administration's first major crisis. However, none of the Carter administration saw this crisis as presenting a threat to American vital interests. Perhaps the biggest difference between Brzezinski and some NSC members on the one hand, and Carter and Vance on the other, revolved around the crucial issue of what the Horn of Africa crisis was really about. Brzezinski saw the crisis through the prism of a Soviet "test" of American willingness to stand firm, a clear challenge to US reputation for resolve. He and others sought to have the United States resist Soviet challenges through some limited use of coercive military means and threats to link Soviet actions to consequences for the future of détente and of arms control negotiations. Both Carter and Vance, by contrast, rejected that "reputation" prism and resisted Brzezinski's recommendations. Although Carter was closer to Brzezinski than any of his other advisors, even Brzezinski could not convince Carter of the importance of reputation in international politics.

Background
Intelligence reports during 1977 indicated that Ethiopia, a US ally, was forging closer ties with Communist regimes, including Cuba and the Soviet Union. This crisis in the "Horn" of east Africa increased worry for the Carter administration, already concerned by the Shaba I conflict in Zaire in early 1977. In that conflict, the Front for the National Liberation of the Congo (FNLC) had crossed the border from Angola into the Shaba province of Zaire. The president of Zaire, Mobutu Sese Seko, accused Angola, Cuba, and the Soviet Union of collaborating to sponsor the rebels. As a result, many anti-Communist states sent assistance to support the Mobutu regime. Carter refused to send any weapons or troops, even though "Shaba I" (as it became known) was one of the first conflicts faced by Carter in his first year in office, a time during which one would expect him to be most willing to show resolve.[67] The Carter

administration was disposed to see such an incident in regional terms; as a result, the United States kept its role to a minimum, allowing only civilian-chartered deliveries of nonlethal equipment. Carter also believed that there was no evidence of Cuban involvement, which the State Department supported (however, the role of the Cubans in Shaba remains uncertain).[68]

With the Shaba episode as backdrop, the United States witnessed the Soviet Union and Cuba increase their level of military support to Ethiopia during 1977, including Cuban advisors and troops. State Department reports indicated that the newly elected Ethiopian leader, Mengistu Haile Mariam, was likely to sever ties with the United States after seeking accommodation with the Soviets. Mohamed Siad Barre, the Somali dictator, had designs on the Ogaden region of Ethiopia and resented Ethiopia's growing closeness with the Soviet Union. Barre reached out to the United States in the hopes of securing military aid and eventually expelling the Soviets from Somalia.

An NSC Policy Review Committee was established to assess the crisis. It suggested in April 1977 that US policy should continue to seek closer Ethiopia-US ties, but relations continued to deteriorate, partly because the Carter administration, with its emphasis on human rights, refused to continue to supply military aid to the Ethiopian leader. Mengistu's turn to the Soviet Union was alarming to the administration as well as its allies, such as Saudi Arabia and Iran. Still, Carter was willing to explore closer relations with Somalia, which was in the process of loosening ties with its Soviet patron, but he remained cautious. Thus, consistently with his election pledges, Carter did not desire to intervene in the regional African crisis.

By the summer of 1977, the crisis had escalated into a full-scale war, deemed the "world's largest military conflict at the moment."[69] Barre had begun a campaign to merge the Ogaden into Somalia; in response, Ethiopia launched war in the Ogaden. Shortly before the Somali invasion, the Carter administration agreed to send Somalia defensive arms, and as a result, some US domestic actors accused Carter of encouraging Somalia's aggression. However, as soon as Somalia invaded the Ogaden, the offer of military assistance was withdrawn.

The Soviet Challenge to America's Reputation

On the night of November 28, 1977, the Soviet Union launched a major military airlift of arms and materiel bound for Ethiopia. In succeeding weeks, the USSR employed An-12 (NATO Cub) and An-22 (NATO Cock) transport aircraft along with seagoing cargo vessels to deliver an estimated $1 billion in fighter-bombers, tanks, artillery, and ammunition to Mengistu's regime. Ethiopia's armies were then faltering in the Ogaden under the attack of Somali-backed rebels who sought to capture territory claimed by the Mogadishu government as part of a "Greater Somalia." The Soviet resupply campaign was important for both the speed of the Soviet response and the morale boost it provided the beleaguered Ethiopian army. As a result of the weapons supplied by the USSR and the augmentation of Mengistu's forces by Cuban combat soldiers and Soviet technicians and advisors, Ethiopia mounted a successful counter-offensive and regained the Ogaden in early 1978.

These Soviet actions, as well as intelligence reports indicating growing direct Soviet involvement, led the members of the NSC to view this crisis as a challenge to US reputation for resolve. On January 12, 1978, in a memo to Brzezinski, NSC staff member Paul Henze noted, "I have become increasingly inclined to believe that the most basic reason the Soviets opted for Ethiopia over Somalia and moved in with tanks, MIGs and Cubans was the irresistible appeal of replacing the United States in a major country where we had been predominant since World War II. . . . The major attraction was to replace us in a key area at a time when, in the wake of Watergate and Angola, they estimate that we lack the will and the capacity to counteract what they are doing."[70] Henze saw the Horn of Africa as a repeat of the Soviet involvement in Angola earlier in 1977; he advised US pressure on the Soviets until they backed down.

The NSC staff was not alone in seeing Soviet actions as a challenge. On January 4, Carter met with President Valery Giscard d'Estaing in Paris, who was adamant that the US president must respond to the Soviet intervention. Giscard told Carter that the Americans were "a little naïve in an involuntary way."[71] He warned Carter that "what the Soviets were doing was incompatible with détente" and urged the president to issue a "strong warning" that "détente is global, and if they want détente then they cannot pursue a policy of destabilization in the Horn."[72]

Notwithstanding a growing sense within the administration that the Soviets were probing US resolve, a January 27, 1978 Special Coordination Committee (SCC) meeting on the Horn of Africa concluded that "there was a consensus of the group that the US government should be cautious about taking actions that would in themselves encourage a sense of crisis or confrontation with the Soviets or that would commit us prematurely to positions that could limit our flexibility."[73] Specifically, the SCC decided to be "cautious about encouraging those who are inclined to help the Somalis make commitments that they would expect us to back up."[74] Although the administration certainly wanted to make it costly for the Soviets to achieve its objectives, it was reluctant either to take military actions or to make any further commitments.

Brzezinski felt that if only he could convince Carter how crucial it was to project resolve, Carter would see the necessity of responding to Soviet involvement, even without US vital interests. On February 9, 1978, in a weekly report to Carter, Brzezinski urged the president to give more attention to the "political consequences of major Soviet/Cuban success."[75] Brzezinski argued that the cumulative effect of several trends, including growing political instability in Europe, the Horn of Africa, and triangular relations with China, could "be very serious internationally and then domestically. By the fall we could be under attack for having presided over a grave deterioration in the U.S. global position."[76] Brzezinski specifically warned Carter that "demonstrable Soviet success in the African Horn is likely to have a very direct psychological and political impact on Egypt, Sudan, Saudi Arabia and Iran. It will simply demonstrate to all concerned that the Soviet Union has the will and the capacity to assert itself."[77] This ripple effect appeared obvious and imminent to Brzezinski, who wrote: "This will encourage Libya and Algeria to act more aggressively; it will also make more likely increased Cuban involvement in the Rhodesian conflict. In effect, first through proxies (as in Angola) and now more directly (as in Ethiopia) the Soviet Union will be demonstrating that containment has now been fully breached."[78] In response to these concerns, Carter wrote, "Iran, SA, Egypt should stand firm in [defense] of Somali border."[79] Carter thought that protecting the border should be the task of regional actors, rather than the United States.

Determining How to Respond

In early February, the impact of Soviet assistance to Ethiopia became clear. The US intelligence community was predicting a more rapid advance by the Ethiopians and a more rapid defeat of the Somalis than expected. The administration was soon under pressure from close allies. On February 12, the foreign ministers of the five Western members of the UN Security Council—the United States, France, Britain, West Germany, and Canada—met secretly to discuss the events in the Horn of Africa. Vance declared that the United States would not deliver arms to Somalia as long as the Somali army was in the Ogaden. Vance's European counterparts demanded a more assertive US reaction, fearing the consequences of a Soviet success. For example, Britain's David Owen said that "he personally thought we [the United States] should have been tougher [toward the Soviets] over the Horn in the past."[80] Still, they advocated that the United States should demand that Siad Barre withdraw his troops from the Ogaden, which Carter did publicly on February 16.

Against this background, the NSC met several times during the critical month of February. A successful Soviet-backed Ethiopian invasion of Somalia would have major implications for the region as well as for US standing. The SCC meeting on February 21 was tense. Members of the SCC were divided over three related issues: first, whether to make a military defense commitment to US allies and regional actors if they were challenged by the Soviets while trying to help Somalia; second, whether to dispatch an aircraft carrier to the region; and third, whether to establish a linkage between Soviet actions and strategic bilateral relations.

The reports of the meeting reveal that Brzezinski favored "undertaking consultations with the Saudis, Iranians and Egyptians to encourage them to provide Somalis with non-US weapons (as transfer of US weapons was 'contrary to our arms sales agreements with the Saudis' and could 'have a seriously adverse impact on Congressional approval of the sale of F-15s to Saudi Arabia') and to provide air-cover for the Somalis in the event the Somali frontier is crossed."[81] Brzezinski suggested that the United States "would be willing to send a carrier task-force into the region to protect their [allies'] forces and arms transfers from Soviet attack or interference."[82] Brzezinski's recommendation to send the carrier was motivated by reputational concerns both regarding the Soviet Union and US allies in the region. He reasoned that "it is important that regional powers not see the United States as passive in the face of Soviet and Cuban intervention in the Horn and in the potential invasion of Somalia— even if our support is, in the final analysis, only for the record."[83]

In contrast, Secretary of Defense Harold Brown thought that sending a carrier would be of little help if Somalia were invaded, and that a failure to protect Somalia would be seen as a US failure. Brown did not believe that this signal would be seen as credible, saying: "[it] would be viewed as a failure of the US task force to do its job; and . . . failure in either event would impair the credibility of such task forces in future crises elsewhere—in short, [the] U.S. bluff would have been called."[84] Put differently, Brown objected to sending an aircraft carrier because he believed its ineffectiveness could result in a loss of face.

Meanwhile, Vance reported to Carter on February 22 that intelligence reports indicated that the Ethiopians, "with Soviet concurrence," were prepared to move into Somali territory if the Somalis did not withdraw from all Ethiopian territory.[85] Against this background, the Somalis asked for US weapons to be supplied through third parties and sought an invitation for the Somali leader to come to the United States "to show he had some moral support."[86] The Somalis, according to Vance, did not agree to discuss any Somali withdrawal from the Ogaden. The previous day, Deputy National Security Advisor David Aaron, recently returned from Ethiopia, reported to the SCC that "the Soviets are in Ethiopia deeply and pervasively and that we face a long term problem. . . . The Soviets will be there as long as it takes the Ethiopians to learn how to use modern military equipment."[87]

These reports reiterated the need to act more assertively; debates resurfaced in the previous day's SCC meeting about the best response to the Soviets. Specifically, the key question now was what the United States could, and should, do if Ethiopian and Cuban troops invaded Somalia.

Brown and Brzezinski were very concerned about US reputation and credibility, especially from the perspective of how US allies (Saudi Arabia in particular) might view a US reluctance to interfere. In contrast, Vance was more concerned about limiting escalation both regionally and globally. Vance suggested that "we should provide no help to Somalia until it has withdrawn from the Ogaden . . . and tell the Saudis to stop their arms transfers until the Somalis are out."[88] Brzezinski replied, "we and the Saudis should make the Soviets and others think that victory will be difficult for them. . . . We must not create the impression that we are isolating Somalia. . . . We should also say that if Somalia withdraws from the Ogaden, the U.S. would consider third country transfers to stabilize the situation. . . . This message . . . should also be conveyed to the Iranians, Egyptians and Pakistanis."[89]

At the same time, the advisors disagreed on how and for what purposes to employ US forces. These differences were most pronounced over whether to deploy an aircraft carrier to the region. Consistent with his low self-monitoring, Vance assessed the utility of the deployment in terms of its actual military effectiveness to compel the Ethiopians to stop an invasion, whereas the high self-monitor Brzezinski viewed it as a costly signal of support to US allies, and as a way to establish a positive image of US resolve in the face of Soviet challenge. Thus, Vance continued to oppose sending the carrier, saying that he "did not agree that the Ethiopians would not cross the frontier" and that "we would be playing a bluff we cannot carry through."[90] Brzezinski, on the other hand, took the position that the carrier would serve two purposes: first, it would "help Arab forces in Somalia," although such help in Somalia "would appear to be a non-starter." The second, more important consideration for Brzezinski was that "[the United States] could encourage Saudi Arabia to provide equipment, emphasizing their [concerns] and [shared] interests in not having Somalia overrun. They and others might deter the Ethiopians, once victorious in the Ogaden, from spilling over into Somalia. In these circumstances, a task force would be a confidence building measure, encouraging countries in the region that the U.S. is present, stands with them, will protect the flow of arms, and will provide protection from the Russians."[91]

These comments sparked a fierce debate in the SCC that reflected a clash in philosophies about the purpose of military coercion. Vance continued to push against sending the carrier on grounds that it would be ineffective in stopping the Ethiopians and that its presence could escalate tensions further with the Soviet Union, while Brzezinski (assuming that Carter would side with Vance) continued to be concerned about how US image would be affected by American inaction. The meeting's discussion of the aircraft carrier ended with Brzezinski reiterating his concerns about "the consequences both domestically and abroad of doing nothing." Vance said that he "disagreed" with Brzezinski and that, rather, the United States should take "each case [of Soviet challenge] on its own." He "would not put any US troops in Africa." Brzezinski, on the other hand, concluded that "he foresaw immediate regional and international consequences to an invasion of Somalia and that this action would contribute to uncertainty and destabilization in Egypt, Saudi Arabia, and Iran. The lesson they would learn is that if they are in a contest, they should not get caught relying on the United States." Brown's position was more nuanced: he was worried that the aircraft carrier would fail to prevent or prevail against an attack, which would reduce the credibility of this policy instrument against the Soviets in the future. He said that "he agreed with Dr. Brzezinski's analysis of the consequences in the short run [i.e., loss of reputation], but with Secretary Vance in the long run."[92]

Carter did not attend the February 21 SCC meeting, but secondary literature and memoirs reveal that the president sided with Vance, as stated very clearly in a June 1978 Annapolis speech. In his memoir, Carter annotated his speech with his reasons for choosing certain language. The purpose of the speech, he explained, was to telegraph to the Soviets his view of the US-Soviet relationship, so he included a clear assertion that increasing involvement outside the traditional US spheres of influence—in Asia and Africa—would lead to undesired and unconstrained military competition. In the speech, he said: "Détente must be broadly defined and truly reciprocal. Both nations must exercise restraint in troubled areas [he added, in his memoir, the phrase: "like Ethiopia, the Persian Gulf, Yemen, and Kampuchea"] and in troubled times.... Neither of us should entertain the notion that military supremacy can be attained, or that transient military advantage can be politically exploited."[93]

The February 23 NSC meeting, chaired by the president, began with a CIA assessment that the Ethiopians were likely to invade Somalia. Carter asked "whether there would be a shift in the region toward Ethiopia because of their military success."[94] Director of Central Intelligence (DCI) Stansfield Turner replied that "there is in the region a sense of coming to terms with the Ethiopians, particularly in view of US inaction. He noted that a Soviet General is directing the Ethiopians in battle and that the Ethiopians were even making progress in Eritrea."[95] Carter wanted to make this information public in order to arouse public opinion against the Soviet Union. Brzezinski, however, was worried that this information would only hurt US reputation because of the "passive role" of the United States.[96]

The record shows that Carter did not express concern about US "face." To the contrary, during the SCC meeting, after citing the congressional reaction to prior American military aid to Somalia as another reason not to act, Carter explained his view on US interests: "we want peace there, we want to get the Cubans and Soviets out, and we want the Somalis to withdraw from Ethiopia."[97] Still, Carter objected to asserting any linkage between this conflict and larger bilateral issues, and he continued to refuse sending an aircraft carrier to the region as a demonstration of US firmness. Carter supported that "in the event of an invasion of Somalia, should the countries of the region decide to deliver military equipment to Somalia, or to provide air cover or other units to counter Ethiopian or Cuban air capability, the US would be prepared to offset Soviet threats or actions directed at such assistance measures."[98] Still, he concluded the February 23 meeting with only a vague recommendation: "we should get our allies and the OAU [Organization of African Unity] to understand the situation and collectively deplore it."[99] The meeting ended without a clear decision: after Carter left the room, the rest of the participants struggled to understand what the president wanted.[100] However, Carter had no intention of escalating tensions with the Soviets, or using military coercion in this crisis. The February 26 SCC meeting concluded that "the US government should be cautious about taking actions that would in themselves encourage a sense of crisis or confrontation with the Soviets [or] that would commit us prematurely to positions that could limit our flexibility."[101]

"A President Must Not Only Be Loved and Respected; He Must Also Be Feared"

As the crisis escalated and the extent of Soviet involvement became known, the public criticized Carter's approach to the Soviets as too soft and costly for US reputation. Throughout the rest of this crisis, Brzezinski hammered the president with reports about the costs of appearing weak. Those memos were triggered by the scale of Soviet involvement—which he saw as a direct challenge to Carter's leadership, and by extension, to US leadership—and his growing frustration with the lack of interest on the part of the president to act assertively.

His campaign to make the president care about the US reputation for resolve is revealed in his weekly reports to Carter. Aptly titled "On the Psychology of the President," this memo begins: "a President must not only be loved and respected; he must also be feared."[102] It argues that the Middle East, the African Horn, and SALT require "very firm and decisive action."[103] Brzezinski lays out his case in this memo exactly as we would expect from a high self-monitor: he criticizes Carter for weakness in the areas of other-directedness and expressive self-control:

> I suspect that an impression has developed that the Administration (and you personally) operates very cerebrally, quite unemotionally. In most instances this is an advantage; however, occasionally emotion and even a touch of irrationality can be an asset. Those who wish to take advantage of us ought to fear that, at some point, we might act unpredictably, in anger, and decisively. If they do not feel this way, they will calculate that simply pressing, probing, or delaying will serve their ends. I see this quite clearly in Begin's behavior, and I suspect that Brezhnev is beginning to act similarly.[104]

When high self-monitors wish to cultivate a status-enhancing image, they often employ their acting skills, manipulation, and even deception. Brzezinski encourages exactly such behavior from President Carter in order to cultivate a reputation for toughness, when he writes:

I think the time may be right for you to pick some controversial subject on which you will deliberately choose to act with a degree of anger and even roughness, designed to have a shock effect. Obviously, the timing and the object ought to be calculated very deliberately; and Congressional support should be mobilized. The central point is to demonstrate clearly that at some point obstructing the United States means picking a fight with the United States in which the President is prepared, and willing, to hit the opponent squarely on the head and to knock him down decisively. If we do not do this soon to somebody, we will increasingly find Begin, Brezhnev, Vorster, Schmidt, Castro, Qadhafi, and a host of others thumbing their noses at us.

Carter initialed the top of the memo, indicating that he had read it, but he did not comment.

Brzezinski and other members of the NSC were growing increasingly concerned. On March 3, Brzezinski wrote to Carter that recent Soviet military activities in sub-Saharan Africa indicated the possibility of significant Soviet military initiatives elsewhere, including Angola, Guinea-Mali, Nigeria, the Rhodesian Patriotic Front, and Tanzania.[105] The same day, Brzezinski wrote Carter another memo, titled "The Soviet Union and Ethiopia: Implications for U.S.-Soviet Relations." Brzezinski begins that, in his judgment, the recommendations from the last SCC meeting did not go "far enough" and were "not responsive to the real problem." The risk was that "in promoting their influence the Soviets [were] becoming bolder. There is thus a striking contrast between the Angolan operation—conducted entirely by proxies—and the Ethiopian affair—in which the proxies still carry the major burden but the Soviet presence is more self-evident."[106]

Soviet actions in Africa had regional, international, and domestic implications, Brzezinski warned. Regionally, "Soviet success in Ethiopia . . . will have a significant demonstration effect elsewhere in Africa. It will encourage radical African states to act more assertively; it will also free the Cubans, perhaps even with more overt Soviet support, to become engaged in the struggle against Rhodesia."[107] Brzezinski raised the alarm about the international ramifications of Soviet involvement in the Horn of Africa: "the impact on Saudi Arabia and Iran will be significant." Moreover, he cautioned, "no one in the region will fail to notice that the Soviet Union acted assertively, energetically, and had its own way. This will have a significant effect on Soviet neighbors; I do not think anyone here appreciates the degree to which the neighbors of the Soviet Union are fearful of it and see themselves as entirely dependent on American resolution."[108] Brzezinski also warned that "in the longer run there will be a ripple-effect in Europe as well."[109] Brzezinski pointed to the reaction of domestic audiences: "it is only a question of time before the right wing begins to argue that the above demonstrates our incompetence as well as weakness. This will also complicate any attempt at a reasonable negotiation with the Soviet Union on matters of mutual importance, such as SALT."[110]

Brzezinski took another crack at making his case for sending an aircraft carrier to the region. First, he argued that without the carrier, the United States did not have the capability to keep its promise to prevent the Soviets from interfering with aid to Somalia. Second, "such military presence in the area would provide such an assurance [that a Somali withdrawal from the Ogaden would not be followed by an invasion]. . . . An aircraft carrier would have a pacifying effect on the Kenyans, provide reassurance to the Somalis, and some deterrent to the Soviet and Cubans in Ethiopia. If they don't cross the frontier, we could later assert that it was thanks to our presence and resolution."[111] He concluded this memo by warning that détente must be reciprocal and that "our limited actions in regard to the specific conflict [in the Horn of Africa] must be designed to convey our determination, while our broader response must be designed to make the Soviets weigh to a greater extent the consequences of their assertiveness for détente as a whole."[112]

Carter did not share Brzezinski's level of concern for appearing more resolved in this crisis. He wrote at the top of Brzezinski's memo: "I am concerned but we mustn't overreact."[113] In this way, Carter acknowledged Brzezinski's concerns about Soviet behavior but disagreed with Brzezinski's conclusions. Vance's memos to the president, and his statements during various SCC meetings, indicate that he shared Carter's approached and saw Soviet actions in the Horn of Africa as problematic but that he did not agree that reputation should guide US actions. From his perspective, and consistent with his low self-monitoring tendencies, Vance saw the horn crisis as a regional and minor one, and the possibility of linking the horn crisis to SALT as the "worst thing that could happen."[114]

The US intelligence community also feared a ripple effect from a perception of US weakness. A March 6 intelligence memorandum indicates that Iran, Kenya, and Sudan also felt threatened by Soviet presence in the Horn of Africa. The analysis reached conclusions consistent with Brzezinski's presentations to Carter about Soviet responses to potential US actions. The memo stated that the Soviets "have seen signs of U.S. concern mount in recent weeks, but probably perceive it as lacking focus, expressing frustration more than a determination to act. They see the U.S. as divided on the extent to which pressures should be brought to bear on the USSR outside the Horn of Africa. They probably believe the U.S. has for several weeks accepted a Soviet/Cuban backed Ethiopian victory as a fait accompli and that Washington now regards a possible invasion of Somalia as a watershed event. They are almost certainly persuaded the U.S. will not take action itself or mobilize others to act locally if there is no invasion of Somalia, and even if there is an invasion, they probably doubt that the U.S. could put together a countervailing effort in timely fashion."[115] In conclusion, the Soviets "will look upon their Ethiopian achievement as advertising to revolutionary forces in southern Africa their readiness and capability to act, and as providing a springboard from which to seize other opportunities to expand their role in arms struggles should they appear."[116]

Carter's unwillingness to adopt a tougher stance toward the Soviets made him a target of congressional criticism, even from Democrats. For example, Representative Robert Sike (D-Florida) told the House, "I find it exceedingly hard to comprehend an action of the U.S. Government which virtually gives the green light for the conquest of Somalia and Eritrea by Cuban forces under Russian control. . . . Arms for Somalia could have forced a negotiated settlement and kept the strategic Horn of Africa out of communist hands."[117] Similarly, Senator Thomas Eagleton (D-Missouri) argued that, without US assistance, "Somalia's relatively small and now-depleted military forces could not meet the military might of Ethiopia's Soviet-backed forces, thus assuring a Soviet takeover in the Horn of Africa."[118] During Carter's first six months in office, most of the public criticism came from Democrats. Carter recognized his unpopularity among his fellow Democrats, even going as far as to describe the Democratic Party as an albatross around his neck.[119]

Opinion polls suggest that Carter's soft approach toward the Soviets was unpopular with the public. Most Americans (71 percent) opposed sending troops to the Horn of Africa to stop the enemy forces but demanded a tougher stance against Russia and Cuba for their regional intervention.[120] A March 1978 Harris Survey found that 43 percent of respondents favored sending military supplies to the non-Communist Somali forces, and 69 percent favored threatening to halt SALT negotiations unless the Soviets left Africa.[121] Even some members of Carter's Democratic party believed that continued attempts to sign a SALT treaty were bad for US reputation for resolve. Notwithstanding Brzezinski's repeated calls for linkage, Carter ultimately refused to let the horn crisis derail the SALT II Treaty. Instead, Carter proposed sending military advisors to help Somalia, which only 23 percent of Americans favored.[122] In June 1978, when asked "how would you rate Jimmy Carter on handling the problem of Russian and Cuban military activity in Africa?" only 24 percent responded "positive," while 62 percent said "negative," and 14 percent said "not sure."[123]

Public opinion reflected a general perception that the Carter administration was weak. For example, people perceived that "he didn't know how to deal with the Congress, that he was not successful in getting things through the Congress, that he was surrounded by too many people from Georgia who were in over their heads, and that he was overwhelmed by all the details of issues in his Presidency."[124]

"Like Mayaguez???" . . . "Lying??"

Brzezinski and Carter's exchanges during the Horn of Africa crisis demonstrate two poles of self-monitoring. Brzezinski's memos indicated great concern with appearance, reputation, and image, consistent with his high self-monitoring inclinations; Carter's replies and statements suggested, as the theory would predict, very little concern with appearance, reputation, or image. The clashes between Carter's and Brzezinski's philosophies (or self-monitoring inclinations) demonstrate that even the president's closest advisor, having the same access to sensitive information as the president, can read a crisis situation in a totally different way.

The clash between Brzezinski's assertive foreign policy on reputational grounds and Carter's skepticism is reflected in Brzezinski's NSC weekly report from April 21, 1978. This memo reflects Brzezinski's frustration with Soviet behavior in Africa, and Carter's "contractual" approach to foreign policy thus far.[125] This memo is, significantly, written soon after Carter's Wake Forest speech of March 1978, considered his harshest speech on US-Soviet relations to date. Perhaps believing that he had won the battle for Carter's ear, Brzezinski suggests how Carter could restore US credibility following the Soviet success in the horn:

> Yes foreign policy . . . also involves the need to influence attitudes and to shape political events. This requires a combination of additional steps, none of which we have yet truly employed. In some cases what is needed is a demonstration of force, to establish credibility and determination and even to infuse fear; in some cases it requires saying publicly one thing and quietly negotiating something else; in many cases what is needed is prolonged and sustained exchange of political views, so that even our enemies share or at least understand our perspectives. Often it does not require solving problems but striking the right posture and sometimes letting problems fester until they are ripe for action.[126]

Brzezinski offered examples of what he had in mind, including:

> quiet efforts *to manipulate* African leaders to obtain desired results; a willingness to back some friendly country very strongly, so that it in turn is prepared *to use its force* on our behalf (for example, I think there is a good chance that by tangibly backing Morocco with arms we could get Hassan to use his troops for us the way Castro is using his on behalf of the Soviets); readiness *to use black propaganda* to stimulate difficulties for our opponents, for example by encouraging national sentiments among the non-Russian Soviet peoples or by using deception to divide the Soviets and Cubans on African policy.[127]

Carter's comments in the margins show that he was incredulous of Brzezinski's insistence on credibility and resolve. In one paragraph, where Brzezinski discusses the importance of a demonstration of force to establish credibility, Carter wrote, "Like Mayaguez???" This comment refers to the 1975 crisis in which President Ford authorized the use of force against a Cambodian ship in order to demonstrate US resolve at the end of the Vietnam War. Next to Brzezinski's suggestion to pursue a more deceptive foreign policy, Carter wrote, "Lying??" Carter's use of multiple question marks next to these comments suggests that he found Brzezinski's approach offensive, or unappealing, to say the least. Next to Brzezinski's recommendation to have another country use force on behalf of the United States, Carter wrote "Proxy war??" After setting forth his views, Brzezinski noted that he would be "developing some ideas for [Carter] regarding the above." Next to this sentence, Carter wrote, "You'll be wasting your time," indicating he was not interested in pursuing this line any further.

Carter resisted pressure not only from Brzezinski, but also from the intelligence community, which voiced concerns about foreign perceptions of US credibility, resolve, and standing. DCI Turner indicated that Politburo member Andrei Kirilenko said, "The Soviet Government was using the Somali-Ethiopian situation to prove its hypothesis that the US has now become a 'paper tiger.' "[128] The USSR would "continue testing the US in Africa, next in the Moroccan-Algerian context, picking up whatever gains it could until it meets effective US-backed resistance, after which it would reconsider its hypothesis."[129] But neither Carter's closest advisor, nor the collective wisdom of the US intelligence community, could convince Carter, even during his darkest views of the Soviets, that he should react to the Soviets for the sake of US reputation and that the Soviets were exploiting the perceived weakness of his failure to do so.

Summary
Soviet and Cuban involvement on the side of Ethiopia forced Somalia to withdraw its forces from the occupied areas of the Ogaden in mid-March. The conflict between Somalia and Ethiopia did not end with the Somali withdrawal, but the conflict received much less attention from the administration during the summer of 1978. The United States was not ultimately able to expel the Soviets or force them to withdraw by increasing the costs of their continued involvement.

The Horn of Africa crisis was the first major international crisis of the Carter administration. Although some members advocated a tougher stance, none viewed the horn as putting a vital US interest at risk. Rather, it was understood as almost purely a crisis of face. Consistent with his beliefs about the efficacy of military force, Carter deemphasized American power and strove to find a peaceful resolution. It is unclear whether Carter's lack of concern with reputational considerations throughout this crisis, and his reluctance to show a tougher stance, actually served to embolden the USSR. From Brzezinski's perspective, however, there is little doubt that Carter's refusal to deploy an aircraft carrier emboldened the Soviets and that it left the door open for the invasion of Afghanistan less than two years later. The successes of SALT II, and of détente writ large, Brzezinski later declared, were "buried in the sands of the Ogaden."[130]

The essence of Carter's response to the horn crisis can be seen in his reaction to Brzezinski's weekly report of April 21, 1978, described above. Rather than seeing increased deception and aggression as a potential foreign policy option, Carter reacted indignantly and immediately linked Brzezinski's suggestion to the Mayaguez crisis. Carter thus displayed the typical reaction of a reputation critic in refusing to frame the horn crisis as a challenge to reputation for resolve.

Finally, although it is beyond the scope of this book to assess whether Carter was right to dismiss reputational considerations, it should be noted that there is some evidence to suggest that the Kremlin's successful intervention in the horn did enlarge its self-confidence. Soviet documents reportedly reveal that, "to many Soviet leaders of the World War II generation, it was the successful intervention in the Horn of Africa that established the Soviet Union as a global power—a power that could intervene at will throughout the world with decisive consequences."[131]

THE SOVIET BRIGADE IN CUBA

When the US intelligence community analyzed the Soviet-Cuban military relationship in 1979, it discovered a Soviet ground combat unit had been present in Cuba since at least 1976. This finding and its potential implications for US reputation for resolve presented another crisis.[132] During this crisis, Brzezinski and other members of the administration (including Secretary of Defense Harold Brown) repeatedly urged the president to think about the reputational consequences of appearing weak in responding to this Soviet challenge. Unlike events in the Horn of Africa, the Soviet brigade in Cuba was considered an alteration of the status quo in America's backyard.

"A Crisis of Confidence among Our Friends"
In the midst of the SALT II negotiations, and in anticipation of the signing of SALT II at a June 1979 summit in Vienna, concerns grew about a possible Soviet-Cuban offensive extending into the Western Hemisphere.[133] In late October 1978, Brzezinski reported to the president that the Soviets had deployed nuclear-capable MiG 23-D (MiG-27) fighter-bomber aircraft to Cuba, a violation of the 1962 understanding reached after the Cuban Missile Crisis. The Soviets had also improved Cuban air defenses by deploying modern air-defense missiles; begun construction of a military airfield; and delivered a squadron of medium-range An-26 transport planes. In November, although there was clearly an increase in Soviet support to Cuba, Brzezinski complained that the

intelligence community had not provided any analysis on "the possible reasons why the Russians have put the planes in there and what this says about their view of relations with the United States."

The existence of the Soviet brigade in Cuba was first brought to the president's attention in Brzezinski's May 7, 1979 report to Carter, which noted that the Soviets were expanding their military activities in Cuba in a different pattern than in the mid-1960s. Brzezinski was concerned that these activities "represent a sophisticated attempt by the Soviets to fulfill the letter of agreements on 'what is a [submarine] base' reached with Kissinger while nonetheless developing an offensive military base in Cuba under the guise of joint basing and training arrangement."[134] On May 25, Brzezinski followed up that "this Soviet activity comes very close but does not unambiguously violate earlier assurances and promises given since 1962."[135]

By the end of June, however, Brzezinski grew concerned about the Soviet Union's objectives. He stated with alarm, "On rereading the Vienna protocols, I was struck by how intransigent Brezhnev was on regional issues. In spite of your forceful statement, the Soviets simply gave us no reason to believe that they will desist from using the Cubans as their proxies. . . . Accordingly, in the months ahead, I think we have every reason to believe that the Soviets will continue to transform Cuba into the strongest Caribbean and Central American military power, thereby further enhancing the revolutionary dynamism of a region close to us; that they will continue to supply and politically exploit the Cuban proxies in Africa; and that they will step up their pressure on Saudi Arabia (and we have evidence of South Yemen becoming a Soviet regional military warehouse)."[136]

A Soviet "Combat" Brigade

The nature of the Soviet brigade in Cuba was hotly contested within the administration during the spring and summer of 1979. On July 12, the intelligence community issued a coordinated interim report stating that "a Soviet force was present as a separate unit not part of an advisory group. But there was no agreement within the U.S. intelligence community on the size, organization or mission of the Soviet force."[137] Immediately after this report, Carter ordered stepped-up surveillance to collect more information about the brigade.

Soon after, several senators sent a July 27, 1979 letter to the president expressing concern about Carter's reluctance to resist the Soviets' increased presence in Cuba. In response, Vance sent a letter to Stone: "I wish to reaffirm the President's statement to you that it is the policy of the United States to oppose any efforts, direct or indirect, of the Soviet Union to establish military bases in the Western Hemisphere. However, there is no evidence of any substantial increase of the Soviet military presence in Cuba over the past several years or of a Soviet military base. Apart from a military group that has been advising the Cuban Armed Forces for fifteen years or more our intelligence does not warrant the conclusion that there are any other significant Soviet forces in Cuba."[138] Regardless, the president had raised the issue of the Soviet presence in Cuba with President Leonid Brezhnev at the Vienna summit, stating that a Soviet buildup "would adversely affect our relationship."[139] Still, as Vance noted, the intelligence analysts could not yet say whether it was "a combat force, a training structure for Cuban forces, or a facility for Soviet Development and testing of tropical combat tactics." Vance believed that neither the 1962 understanding banning offensive nuclear weapons, nor the 1970 prohibition on submarine bases, covered Soviet ground forces. Faced with mounting pressure, Carter promised to increase intelligence efforts. He also instructed his administration to pursue a public campaign intended to demonstrate the similarity of Cuban and Soviet foreign policies, and that Cuba was dependent on the USSR.[140]

The crisis took a dramatic turn in August, when US intelligence confirmed that "there was an actual brigade in Cuba, with headquarters and regular organization and that in fact it is scheduled to hold firing exercises within a week."[141] A few days later, the CIA's National Foreign Assessment Center confirmed for the first time the presence of a Soviet "combat brigade," not simply a training outfit. Further intelligence gathering suggested that this brigade included between twenty-six hundred and three thousand personnel, and it was composed of a brigade headquarters, three motorized rifle battalions, one tank battalion, one artillery battalion, and other noncombat support elements. The Soviets maintained that the brigade was engaged in training Cuban military personnel. Still, members of the administration and the intelligence community concluded that the available intelligence could neither exclude nor confirm a training function. Rather, they believed the brigade had a combat capability maintained by field combat exercise.[142]

Meanwhile, the CIA's report was leaked, most importantly to Florida Democratic Senator Richard Stone, a member of the Senate Foreign Relations Committee. Given Stone's well-known reservations about the SALT II Treaty, coupled with his skepticism about Soviet intentions in the Western Hemisphere, there was little surprise that he, in turn, chose to leak information about the brigade to the media. These findings created a public crisis.[143]

Congress's role in the brigade crisis largely revolved around Democratic Senator Frank Church, chairman of the Foreign Relations Committee and a steadfast supporter of the SALT II Treaty. The initial plan was for the State Department, after informing congressional leaders, to issue a short announcement that would downplay the brigade's significance. Church was the first senator to be notified; he was concerned about his own reelection because he had recently publicly defended the administration's statements that no new Soviet forces were present in Cuba. Vance allowed Church to make the announcement and salvage his reputation: after announcing the presence of the Soviet combat brigade in Cuba, Church insisted on immediate withdrawal of those "combat troops." Church also declared, "Russian combat units do not belong in Cuba. The president must make it clear we draw the line on Russian penetration of this hemisphere." Several other Senate Democrats conveyed similar remarks, some demanding that the president directly link the Soviet response on the brigade issue to US willingness to continue SALT II negotiations.[144]

By allowing Church this podium, the administration effectively allowed· the brigade to become the focal point of the Senate Foreign Relations Committee hearings on SALT II, and to be a "lightning rod" for SALT critics. Fen Hampson argues that, without the press leak, the Carter administration would have been able to pursue a more comprehensive and thorough intelligence assessment in order to dispel rumors of a Soviet buildup, or Vance could have persuaded Church to downplay the importance of the brigade.[145] Hampson argues that, without the weight given to Church's announcement, other senators who attempted to use the brigade as a smokescreen for their dislike of SALT would have been just "whistling in the wind."[146] The crux of Hampson's argument is that the Carter administration refused to confront the Soviets and link ratification of SALT II to the brigade because Carter and Vance were trying to appease Church. However, the documents show that Carter's refusal to make the linkage was not because of the discontent of one senator; in fact, many members of Congress sought linkage as a means of leverage over the Soviets. Instead, Carter was following his personal philosophy that the SALT treaty was more important than standing up to the Soviets.

The presence of a Soviet brigade in Cuba, and the public demand for a policy of "total linkage," could have driven Carter to threaten the Soviets that he would end détente if they refused to pull out of Cuba. However, Carter vetoed those options and rejected arguments that inaction could potentially harm America's reputation. Instead, on September 5, he affirmed the existence of a combat brigade in Cuba but continued in a softer tone that "this is a time for firm diplomacy, not panic, and not exaggeration," because the brigade was not an assault force that threatened the security of the US homeland.[147]

Meanwhile, members of the SCC viewed the stationing of the brigade as "unacceptable." Even Vance saw the presence of a Soviet brigade in Cuba as an issue that must be addressed in US-Soviet bilateral relations. But he also thought that, if the issue were made public, it was unlikely that the Soviets would agree to a withdrawal. Furthermore, the United States might be seen as disingenuous in claiming the brigade violated the understandings on Cuba, because those understandings did not unambiguously cover Soviet ground forces.[148] Carter approved of Vance's proposal to discuss the issue quietly with Soviet Ambassador Dobrynin. Vance and Dobrynin met several times during

September. The protocols of their discussions show that the Soviets had no intention of moving the brigade out of Cuba, or of apologizing for its presence. In fact, the Soviets launched both a public and private diplomatic offensive, taking a tough line against Carter's accusations and making clear they would not back down. For example, the Communist Party newspaper *Pravda* claimed in a story on September 10 that the brigade had been in Cuba since 1962 as a training unit, and that Carter's allegation of a combat brigade was "totally groundless."[149]

"Every Poll Shows That the Country Wants You to Be Tougher"

Soviet refusal to negotiate or apologize for the brigade placed the administration in a difficult position, especially because Carter, Vance, and other members of the administration had made public declarations threatening to link the episode to SALT II ratification if the Soviets refused to compromise. During a September 5 press conference, Vance stated that he would "not be satisfied with maintenance of the status quo," and the brigade posed a serious concern "affecting our relations with the Soviet Union."[150] On September 7, Carter linked the issue to the future of SALT, in a defensive response: "We do have the right to insist that the Soviet Union respect our interests and our concerns. Otherwise, relations between our two countries will inevitably be adversely affected."[151] The brigade did not seem to threaten vital American interests, but this time, the US reputation for resolve was engaged.

Congress also pushed the administration to link the fate of the brigade to SALT II. Republican Senator Robert Dole of Kansas attempted to force Carter's hand by saying that he would ensure that the Senate would refuse to consider the SALT II Treaty until the Soviet troops were out of Cuba.[152] Even congressional Democrats took a stand in favor of linkage: for example, senior Democratic Senator Russell Long changed his vote to oppose SALT II, asserting that the brigade was a clear indicator of Soviet "bad faith."[153]

In the midst of this push, on September 13, 1979, Brzezinski expressed his views to Carter in a weekly report entitled "Acquiescence vs. Assertiveness." Brzezinski explained that the Soviets were becoming more assertive and the US more acquiescent, especially in contentious regions like Afghanistan, Africa, and Latin America. Brzezinski indicated that his interpretation of Soviet behavior was not "designed to suggest that we somehow adopt a reckless policy of confrontationalism, nor is it meant to hint that our policy has been one of appeasement."[154] Rather, he believed that "the country craves, and our national policy needs . . . a more assertive substance to our foreign policy. I believe that both for international reasons as well as domestic political reasons you ought to deliberately toughen both the tone and the substance of our foreign policy."[155] Indeed, both types of audiences were salient in Brzezinski's view that "the country associates assertiveness with leadership, and [so does] the world at large."[156]

At the same time, Brzezinski did not believe that the brigade was a repeat of the Cuban Missile Crisis of 1962. "The situation is not really analogous; we face a political challenge and we cannot fully undo the reality we don't like, whereas in 1962 we faced a direct military pressure, and we could—through direct military pressure—undo it. . . . In fact, you [referring to Carter] are facing a situation much more like that faced by Kennedy in 1961, when the Soviets suddenly put up the Berlin wall. That situation was 'unacceptable,' but we had no choice except to live with it. Kennedy was not prepared to knock it down. Neither are we prepared to create a military situation in order to get the Soviets to remove their troops from Cuba."[157] Brzezinski stressed that he was not in favor of sending more troops to Guantanamo. Instead, he recommended taking "at least one" step that "genuinely hurts the Soviets," as well as maintaining a tough posture for a few months on the Soviets in public pronouncements.[158] As for SALT, Brzezinski suggested the president would "not get SALT ratified if the public thinks we were timid on this issue," and that a tougher posture would include: "1) more defense; 2) SALT ratification; 3) assertive competition."[159]

From the very beginning, Brzezinski was concerned with how Carter was managing others' impressions of the brigade. In an undated memo to Carter, Brzezinski noted that the president had to decide whether to "treat the matter primarily as a domestic public relations issue, which should not be allowed to impinge significantly on US-Soviet relations; or treat it as a fundamental strategic issue, dictating a reassessment of US-Soviet relations."[160] Brzezinski saw many reasons why Carter should not give exaggerated public significance to the brigade, namely, "its consequences for SALT, the hardening of the Soviets against withdrawal, and confusion of U.S. allies and domestic audiences."[161] Moreover, as Brzezinski correctly pointed out, the brigade had become a crisis only because of US intelligence failure, not because of Soviet escalation. At the same time, Brzezinski believed the crisis would have long-term implications for US "national policy" and not just "public policy." As he explained to Carter, "it is obvious to me that at some point we will have to draw a line with the Soviets and that we ought to be using this occasion, at the very least, to start building our case. Otherwise, we will have damaged our credibility severely when we are faced with the predicated crisis [in the Caribbean]."[162] The problem, as Brzezinski saw it, was how to convince the Soviets of American credibility in future crises, given that there were strong incentives for the United States to downplay Soviet behavior in this crisis. "Our problem, then, is *not* to allow a rather low-key public response to convince the Soviets that we are in a situation which we find uncomfortable but bearable."[163]

US credibility, however, was already suffering, Brzezinski asserted: the United States had protested several Soviet actions with démarches but without follow-up sanctions. For example, the United States had complained about the Soviet presence in Cuba several times, and Carter had raised this in his discussions with Brezhnev at the Vienna summit. "The fact that we complain repeatedly and fail to respond when the Soviets do not deal adequately with our complaints, gives rise to the danger that the Soviets will regard them as primarily meant to set the record straight by assuaging US Congressional and public opinion." Ultimately, Brzezinski warned, actions rather than words were required to convince the Soviets that the United States would be resolute. He acknowledged that there was no clear path forward in the Cuban or Caribbean context: "the only really effective means at our disposal to make Moscow sit up and take notice is to explain to the Soviets that if they insist on messing around in our backyard, we will have much less compunction than has been the case until now about messing around in theirs."

Carter was urged by Brzezinski to think about US standing, both in the eyes of the Soviets and in the eyes of the American public. As Brzezinski explained to the president in a memo from mid-September, "A cosmetic outcome will not wash. The country will see through it; SALT will be jeopardized; you will be seen as zigzagging ('the status quo is not acceptable'—except cosmetically . . . !) the world will see it as U.S. acquiescence. . . . A gradual but steady toughening up in our policy is therefore the preferable alternative. It will require telling the country quite frankly that we cannot get the brigade out, short of a head-on military confrontation. Instead there are other things that you are prepared to do in order to confront the Soviet Union with the fact that détente must be a two-way street."[164]

There was also the fear that Carter would appear too passive with the Soviets, thereby losing domestic support. "The direct political benefit" of such a course of action would be to put Senator Ted Kennedy, running against Carter in the Democratic primaries, on the spot: "By toughening up our posture vis-à-vis the Soviets, you will either force Kennedy to back you, or to oppose you. . . . If he backs you, he is backing an assertive and tough President; if he opposes you, he can easily be stamped as a latter-day McGovernite."[165] Brzezinski also monitored public opinion, explaining to Carter that "the country does not care about the brigade—but it does care about the Soviets. Every poll shows that the country wants you to be tougher. Unless you convey credibly the message that you will not let the Russians push us around (in addition to blasting Castro personally) you will lose SALT."[166]

Indeed, public opinion polls from that time mostly confirm Brzezinski's interpretation. Specifically, just before the crisis, when asked in July 1979 "How would you rate Carter on foreign policy?" 38 percent answered "positive," while 58 percent said "negative."[167] In September 1979, in the midst of the crisis, a majority of the sample showed concern about Soviet behavior. Asked, "How worried are you about the Soviet combat troops stationed in Cuba?," 19 percent answered "very worried," and 44 percent were "somewhat worried," while 36 percent said, "not worried at all."[168] The public also wanted to see more linkage between the brigade and the SALT negotiations than Carter was willing to consider. In September 1979, asked, "Do you think the Senate should delay ratification of SALT II until the Soviet troops are removed from Cuba?," 67 percent answered "yes," while 22 percent said "no."[169]

Refusing to Link

Despite voices from all sides encouraging harshness with the Soviets by linking the fate of SALT II to the brigade, Carter resisted using the diplomatic coercive tool of linkage. This tension can be seen in the NSC meeting on September 17. The president opened by saying that "he believes that the Soviet presence in Cuba is of growing importance. . . . It adversely affects SALT. . . . How we handle the issue, therefore, will have enormous consequences."[170] The NSC meeting soon grew heated over possible options if the Soviets did not remove their equipment from Cuba. The NSC's assessment was that the Soviets were unlikely to settle the issue, whether by withdrawing the brigade, by satisfactorily altering its characteristics, or by committing to a future that might damage Soviet relations with Cuba. "The Soviets have made what they consider to be a concession and offered a way out of the impasse by reiterating both publicly and privately that the unit is attached to a 17-year-old training center," thereby making any allegations regarding the "arrival" of Soviet combat units totally baseless.[171] The Carter administration was presented with a lose-lose situation, leaving itself open to criticism from the left (for blowing the brigade issue out of proportion) and the right (for not being tough on the Soviets and for appeasing them for the sake of SALT).

In order to break this deadlock, Brzezinski recommended that the United States look outside of Cuba, adding that "the worst outcome for us will be to get caught somewhere between the two positions, left with a cosmetic solution which is picked apart not only in the Congress but also within our own party." Taking added steps in Cuba would only make the Soviets more self-confident, rather than restrained. Brzezinski assessed that, first, the Soviets would not allow for a repeat of the Cuban Missile Crisis resulting in a clear US political victory. Second, if the United States responded only in Cuba, that small-scale response would give the Soviets no real reason for restraint. Third, if the US response was more generalized, utilizing coercive means outside of Cuba, then the Soviet negotiators would be forced to worry because the implications were more serious for them. Vance disagreed, because the United States was already tilting toward China, thereby adding to Soviet sense of insecurity.

Carter, however, was most worried about SALT. Based on conversations with certain senators, Carter was led to believe that "all are still open about their vote on SALT, but they all insist that we must forcefully resolve the Cuban problem first." Later in the meeting he added, "If there is no satisfactory answer today from Dobrynin, Vance should ask for a meeting with Gromyko. This issue is like a cancer under the American skin. Gromyko should know this and realize that we cannot accept it." Then came the punch line: "Thus far, we have bent over backward to accommodate Soviet sensitivities. . . . If they are not forthcoming, we will 'bust the hell out of them.' This is what the American people are demanding." Carter had come to accept that, although the United States did not formally link the fate of SALT to the situation in Cuba, the reality was that the two were linked in the minds of the American electorate. He thus said that there were a few steps the United States could take, but expressed caution: "I don't want to drive the Soviets into a war-like attitude if that is not necessary. After . . . Vance has met with Dobrynin, I would like to discuss the next steps."[172]

Carter rejected further attempts by Brzezinski, the following day, to convince him to dismiss Vance's proposals. Brzezinski again pressed for treating this issue as part of the larger question of Soviet misconduct. Carter rebuffed him, responding to his memo by writing at the bottom: "Zbig, don't discount the probability/possibility of a false statement re the present mission of the brigade. It *is* a factor, & we should not shift just to the 'larger question' (which has long been apparent to us & to the world.) In my opinion, they are *not* using the brigade [just] to train Cubans." While the "false statement" to which Carter was referring is unclear, it is clear that the president did not believe the Soviets were in Cuba simply to train.[173]

When Vance returned from his meetings with the Soviets with no diplomatic solution in sight, he proposed, and Carter accepted, an alternative. First, Carter sent a letter to Brezhnev in which he stated that the existence of the brigade caused "deep and serious concern." He urged Brezhnev toward mutual agreement, warning that "it would be a tragedy for our countries if this work for peace [SALT] would be today put under threat as result of the fact that both our governments could not resolve the problem which has caused on one side a feeling of deep concern."[174] The second component of the plan was to seek the advice of sixteen former US officials, both Democrats and Republicans, regarding the brigade issue. Brzezinski at first vehemently objected to the idea, but he chaired such an "alumni panel" on September 28. In a memorandum to the president, Brzezinski explained that the majority of the participants concluded that the Soviet brigade did not pose a threat, that it had probably been there since 1962, that any US response should be "measured," and that this issue should not be linked to SALT.[175]

The discussions of the alumni group expressed a wide range of options for US responses to the Soviets and the Cubans. In a memo from Deputy National Security Advisor David Aaron to Carter on September 28, "the discussion divided unpredictable lines between those who felt we should minimize the importance of the combat brigade so as to protect a far more important possibility of SALT ratification and those who felt it was part of a broader pattern of Soviet activity which required a firm U.S. response—again for the sake of SALT."[176]

"No Reason for a Return to the Cold War"

In the following days, Carter was under continued pressure from Brzezinski and Vance.[177] While both advisors agreed that the brigade was not a major threat to US security, Brzezinski continued to try to persuade Carter to view the crisis through the lens of reputation and credibility. Vance continued to argue that the real vital interest was saving SALT II.

On October 1, Carter held a major televised address to the nation on "peace and national security," in which he discussed the brigade. Carter's speech made it clear that he shared Vance's view that his top priority was keeping SALT alive. Carter mainly sought to defuse the crisis and return to normal relations with the Soviets. For example, although Carter stated, "the presence of Soviet combat troops in Cuba is of serious concern to us," he also said that the Soviets had guaranteed that they would not change the brigade's "function or status."[178] Carter interpreted this statement to mean that "they do not intend to enlarge the unit or to give it additional capabilities" and that these reassurances were given at "the highest level of the Soviet government."[179] He did not mention the importance of saving face in light of Soviet adventurism. Instead, he reassured the public that the brigade did not pose a threat to US security interests and advocated ratifying the SALT II arms control agreement.

The policies Carter eventually chose were narrow and related almost entirely to Cuba, not to Soviet interventionist activities. For example, he pledged to increase intelligence and surveillance related to Cuba. Carter did not demand a withdrawal of the brigade (even the NSC saw that this was an unrealistic objective); he accepted the Soviet purpose for the troops; and he recognized there was no real threat to the United States and no need to return to the Cold War.

Brzezinski was so disheartened by Carter's chosen approach that he contemplated resigning. He then confronted Carter about his choices. Brzezinski challenged Carter that the United States "had told the Russians on several different occasions that it took great exception to their action in Vietnam, Iran, the Middle East and Africa, and more recently in Cuba . . . but then we do nothing about it." The way this matter was handled, Brzezinski continued, "could be dangerous for the future because the Russians could miscalculate, and that is exactly what happened with Khrushchev and Kennedy." According to Brzezinski, Carter was "quite furious" and told Brzezinski he "had no intention of going to war over the Soviet brigade in Cuba." Brzezinski insisted he was not advocating war, but felt the United States needed to be more forceful in dealing with "Soviet adventurism."[180]

Carter also faced pressure from allies to show more assertiveness. On October 2, Prime Minister Margaret Thatcher sent Carter a secret communiqué in which she stated that while she and her government wished to see SALT II ratified, "after what has happened in Angola, Ethiopia and elsewhere, there is an imperative need to demonstrate to the Russians that the West will not tolerate further action of this kind by them and their allies." Thatcher also urged the president that it was "essential that the Soviet Union should recognize your resolve in this matter."[181]

The public viewed Carter's response to the brigade crisis as weak. At best, the public was evenly split. Forty-four percent of respondents to a Gallup poll in October 1979 said that they disapproved of the way Carter was dealing with the Cuban situation, while 40 percent said they approved.[182] There was a similar split on the issue of linkage to SALT. For example, in November 1979, polls asked, "Do you think the Senate should delay voting on SALT until the troops are removed?," 38 percent said yes, while 39 percent said no (23 percent had no opinion).[183] At the same time, there were also clear indications that the public was increasingly unhappy with Carter's soft approach. In November 1979, asked, "How would you rate Carter's foreign policy?" 59 percent said negative, while only 38 percent said positive.[184] In December, just days before the Soviet invasion of Afghanistan, a poll asked, "Did Carter go too far, not far enough, or just far enough with his plan to address the Russian combat troops in Cuba?" A mere 8 percent said he went too far but 38 percent said that he did not go far enough.[185]

Summary

The discovery of the Soviet brigade in Cuba was the discovery of an intelligence failure. Concerns for US reputation for resolve and credibility were significant in this crisis for three reasons: first, the discovery of the brigade came at a time when the United States was perceived to have acquiesced to Soviet actions abroad. Second, after several members of the Carter administration demanded publicly that the Soviets remove the brigade, the Soviets' refusal to give any concessions led to a further decline in US public standing. Finally, US credibility was engaged because domestic actors from the left and the right began to doubt the ability of the United States to enforce potential Soviet violations of SALT II. A tougher stance toward the Soviets could have made Carter appear more resolute at home and might have allowed him to gain momentum in selling SALT II to the otherwise reluctant American public and conservative elites. Yet, notwithstanding these incentives to act, Carter once again underplayed reputational considerations and resisted Brzezinski's calls to examine how the appearance of weakness could affect Soviet behavior, as well as US domestic and international standing. Carter held adamantly to his positions, even entering into a serious argument with his closest advisor because of his nonresponsiveness to Brzezinski's reputational concerns.

Importantly, my argument is impartial as to whether Carter should have accepted Brzezinski's recommendations. Rather, this analysis merely suggests that image-type considerations about demonstrating resolve were not important in Carter's overall calculus. Carter's approach was grounded in different calculations—specifically, whether escalation would affect SALT II.

THE SOVIET INVASION OF AFGHANISTAN AND ITS AFTERMATH

The Soviet invasion of Afghanistan, starting in December 1979, was a further blow to US credibility and reputation for resolve during the Carter administration. This was so, not only because of the past histories of Soviet crises, but also because the fall of the shah of Iran, a US ally, and the capture of the American hostages in Teheran had further shaken the stability of the region and the faith of the American people in the competency of their leaders. Moreover, unlike the previous crises, the invasion of Afghanistan was perceived as posing a more direct threat to US vital interests in the Middle East.

Given that the material stakes involved in the Soviet invasion were higher, compared to the previous episodes, it is natural to expect the president, even a low self-monitor dove like Carter, to react assertively to the Soviet challenge. The theory predicts that Carter would refuse to use a reputation prism to consider potential policies in this crisis. Rather the theory would expect Carter to view the crisis as posing a risk to US material (and possibly vital) interests, and Carter would contemplate actions that would make it harder for the Soviets to make further gains.

High self-monitoring, I posit, would have led Carter to be concerned about potential adverse effects on US reputation for resolve among US allies and adversaries. We see this evidence in Brzezinski's memos, but such reputation-guided discourse is absent from Carter's statements. While Carter responded harshly to the Afghanistan invasion, his response was not guided by concern for appearing "tough" or "resolved," but rather out of fear that the Soviets could launch an attack against other vital US interests in the Middle East unless they were resisted in Afghanistan. Carter came to see a Soviet move into the Persian Gulf as a genuine threat, because Afghanistan changed his beliefs about the intentions of the Soviet Union and to recognize its expansionist aims. Carter's military moves were intended to guard against an unlimited revisionist Soviet Union that would continue to assert its influence in the gulf.

"A Blatant Violation of Accepted International Rules of Behavior"

On Christmas morning 1979, reports arrived in Washington that Moscow had begun to airlift soldiers to Kabul, Afghanistan.[186] By December 29, there were an estimated thirty thousand Soviet soldiers in Afghanistan. Communists had taken power in a 1978 coup, installing their own president, who was later assassinated. As the country became even more destabilized, the USSR intervened to prop up its client state. The Soviets justified their invasion as a response to an Afghan government request, under the terms of a twenty-year friendship treaty signed in 1978 for economic and military assistance.

The magnitude and timing of the Soviet invasion caught US decision makers by surprise. The day following the invasion, Brzezinski wrote Carter a memo entitled, "Reflections on Soviet Intervention in Afghanistan." Brzezinski stated, "US is facing *a regional crisis*. Both Iran and Afghanistan are in turmoil, and Pakistan is both unstable internally and extremely apprehensive externally. If the Soviets succeed in Afghanistan, and if Pakistan acquiesces, the long-term dream of Moscow to have direct access to the Indian Ocean will be been fulfilled."[187] Brzezinski warned that "Soviet 'decisiveness' will be contrasted with our restraint, which will no longer be labeled as prudent but increasingly as timid; B. At the same time, regional instability may make a resolution of the Iranian problem more difficult for us, and it could bring us into a head to head confrontation with the Soviets."[188] Finally, he said, "Unless we tell the Soviets directly and very clearly that our relations will suffer, I fear the Soviets will not take our expressions of concern very seriously."[189]

Soon after, it became clear that the Soviet presence in Afghanistan could pose a risk to US interests in the Middle East. In the December 27 Policy Review Committee meeting, Brzezinski warned, "We also have to keep in mind the Soviet sponsorship of aggression in Cambodia and perhaps Angola and now Afghanistan—and we may also encounter increasing bad Soviet behavior in Iran." Domestic ramifications were also evident, as Brzezinski further warned: "this is all going to result in us receiving intense domestic pressure from both the right and the left. We have to get this message across to the Soviets most forcefully."

But Brzezinski's basic problem with Moscow was "maintaining our credibility," as reflected in a memo entitled, "Our Response to Soviet Intervention in Afghanistan."[190] In order to do that, the United States should seek to achieve three goals with respect to the Soviets: "The first is punitive: we want them to pay the price for infringing fundamental principles of international behavior. The second is coercive: we want them to withdraw their troops and allow Afghanistan to return to the semblance of sovereignty and neutrality. The third is deterrence: we want to prevent the Soviets from crossing further thresholds, such as hot pursuit of rebels across international frontiers or escalation of the fighting with the rebels to a massive scale."[191]

Next to this, Carter wrote: "1+3 interrelated; 2 unlikely. Maximum initiative & action by others." Although these comments can be interpreted in several ways, it is clear that, from the very beginning of the crisis, Carter did not think it likely that the United States could compel the Soviets to leave Afghanistan. Perhaps Carter made this judgment because he felt that it was out of the question to use military means to coerce the Soviets to leave. His other comment regarding "action by others" suggests that, even early on, Carter wanted some of the burden for addressing the invasion to be borne by allies. Carter stressed these effects in a press conference on December 28. He called the invasion a "blatant violation of accepted international rules of behavior," representing "a grave threat to peace."[192]

During the December 27 NSC meeting, Carter drew a parallel between the Soviet Union's invasion of Afghanistan and its invasion of Czechoslovakia in 1968. Brzezinski picked up on that theme in a December 29 memo, in which he reminded Carter that President Lyndon B. Johnson had cancelled the first scheduled round of SALT talks immediately after the invasion of Czechoslovakia. Brzezinski thought that it would be a mistake to freeze the current round of SALT II talks, but he also believed "it would be a mistake to confine our response to this Soviet intervention in Afghanistan to words. . . . I do think something definite in our bilateral relationship with Moscow should follow this extraordinary act of Soviet arrogance and brutality. . . . In my judgment, such resolve on our part would have significant benefits for us, both domestically and internationally."[193] The issue of credibility arose again on January 2, in a memo entitled, "Possible Steps in Reactions to Soviet Intervention in Afghanistan." Brzezinski reiterated that, without a US response, "our international credibility and prestige will be seriously eroded, particularly in the eyes of those countries most vulnerable to Soviet intervention, either directly or indirectly. Without firm US actions, some of these countries may draw the conclusion that they have no choice over the long run except to accommodate themselves to Soviet power."[194]

"We Must Assume the Worst of Each Other"

The Soviet invasion of Afghanistan differed from past Soviet actions in driving Carter to shift his views about Soviet expansionist intentions and the threat to US interests in the Middle East.[195] Before the invasion, Carter had viewed Soviet intentions as opportunistic in nature. Afterward, Carter declared that the invasion had fundamentally altered his views on the nature of the Soviet threat. In his memoir, the president stated, "the brutality of the act was bad enough, but the threat of this invasion to the rest of the region was very clear—and [would have] had grave consequences."[196] Carter conceded during an NSC meeting that "he and President Brezhnev do not understand one another. The president said he does not know what Brezhnev's next step is and what he is aiming to accomplish. Perhaps Brezhnev is in the same position. Both of us, he said, must assume the worst of each other."[197]

Carter expressed his heightened distrust of Soviet intentions during his January 4 address. He announced a set of policies meant to demonstrate that the United States would no longer "continue to do business as usual with the Soviet Union" because "the Soviets must understand our deep concern."[198]

Carter stated that the "invasion is an extremely serious threat to peace because of the threat of further Soviet expansion into neighboring countries."[199] On January 20, only a few days before the State of the Union address, *Meet the Press* asked Carter why it took him three years to reach these conclusions about the Soviet leadership's intentions. The president answered:

> I've never doubted the long-range policy or the long-range ambitions of the Soviet Union. . . . But it is obvious that the Soviets' actual invasion of a previously nonaligned country, an independent, freedom-loving country, a deeply religious country, with their own massive troops is a radical departure from the policy or actions that the Soviets have pursued since the Second World War. *It is a direct threat because Afghanistan, formerly a buffer state between the Soviet Union and Iran and the world's oil suppliers and the Hormuz Straits and the Persian Gulf, has now become kind of an arrow aiming at those crucial strategic regions of the world.*[200]

As I have argued elsewhere, Carter's response to Soviet actions in Afghanistan is directly tied to his changing view of Soviet intentions.[201] He became willing to pursue harsher policies when he saw that the Soviets had expansionist intentions and were better positioned to attack US vital interests in the Persian Gulf. Thus, rather than being persuaded to "fight for face," Carter's response to the invasion should be understood within the context of a more fundamental shift in his perceptions of Soviet intentions and capabilities.

Soviet intentions became a major topic of debate within the administration, "not merely an intellectual exercise."[202] Brzezinski emphasized to Carter that this debate had significant policy implications: How long should present policy be maintained? To what extent should US allies be pressured to recognize the wider strategic character of the Soviet challenge? How energetically should the United States reinforce the Western presence in the Persian Gulf and Indian Ocean area? To what extent should the United States reinforce the situation in Pakistan? Carter's acceptance that the Soviets were pursuing a grand expansionist design also meant that Carter became more willing to accept Brzezinski's warnings that the United States needed to stop Soviet expansion to protect American vital interests.[203]

The Soviet invasion, however, did not induce such a fundamental shift in Vance's perception. Vance felt "that the primary motive for the Soviet action was defensive, [and] that the Soviets do not have longer-term regional ambitions beyond Afghanistan." Indeed, Vance saw Afghanistan "largely as an expedient reaction to opportunities rather than as a manifestation of a more sustained trend." Therefore, Vance continued to "nurture hopes of a relatively early return to more normal East-West relations."[204] Carter's interpretation of Soviet intentions this time was more consistent with that of Brzezinski than

Vance's. As I explain elsewhere, this was primarily because Carter took the invasion as a betrayal of the Soviet premier's personal assurances to Carter during their meetings at the 1979 Vienna summit.[205]

Carter's newfound beliefs led Carter to change his policy choices as well, including a greater acceptance of the use of covert action. One of the few instances in which Carter ordered covert action took place just prior to and following the invasion of Afghanistan. Carter offered covert assistance in Afghanistan six months before the March 1979 invasion, providing nonlethal aid to rebel groups. Following the invasion, Carter approved covert lethal assistance, including the delivery of rifles and rocket-propelled grenades from former Soviet allies. Carter wanted to make Soviet actions in Afghanistan costlier, and his presidential finding for this action specifically called for harassment of Soviet forces.[206] These weapons were channeled through a network of suppliers, with the supply chain remaining secret throughout the program. However, there was great risk of Soviet retaliation against Pakistan, the main staging area for the weapons program, if US assistance grew too large. Two months before the invasion, an NSC memo cautioned that proposed covert aid should be supplied carefully lest it "evoke a more direct Soviet threat to Pakistan."[207] Weeks after lethal aid was approved, CIA analysts in January 1980 urged that covert aid by the United States, Pakistan, and China might provoke Soviet retaliation against Pakistan in the form of support for tribal separatism.[208] Despite the change in Carter's views of Soviet intentions, he kept covert action in Afghanistan limited both in scope and in goal.[209]

"The Most Serious Threat to World Peace since WWII"

The invasion of Afghanistan, unlike Soviet involvement in Angola, the Horn of Africa, Yemen, or Nicaragua, pushed the United States to take action to protect its vital interests in the Persian Gulf. Given these fears, Carter came to believe that a threat of military force was necessary to dissuade what he had come to perceive as an expansionist Soviet Union from entering neighboring countries.[210] Still, with regard to Afghanistan, Carter refrained from making a compelling threat that would risk direct US involvement.

Following several Presidential Review Committee (PRC) discussions in late December 1979, Carter concluded on January 2, 1980 that "our ultimate goal is the withdrawal of Soviet troops from Afghanistan. Even if this is not attainable, we should make the Soviet involvement as costly as possible and should use the events in Afghanistan as a rallying point for our policies in the area." Although Carter would "not permit our interest in SALT to deter us from speaking and acting forcefully," he was reluctant to declare that SALT was dead. He also refused to entertain the possibility of sending ground forces to Afghanistan.

Carter's approach to the crisis was thus based on calculations of material interests rather than reputational ones. Put differently, the rationale for being resolute, as the transcript of the NSC meeting on January 2 reveals, was that the Soviets would gain control of neighboring countries in which US vital interests were at stake. Thus, Carter summarized, the purpose of acting in Afghanistan was to "deter the Soviets from going into Pakistan and into Iran," now seen as more likely because of the Soviet capabilities and intentions revealed by the invasion.[211]

Brzezinski's approach to the crisis was different. Unlike Carter, he saw the invasion as a significant blow to US reputation and credibility and was therefore willing to go further than Carter in punishing the Soviets, because "our response will determine how several key states will adjust their foreign policy and particularly whether they will accommodate themselves to the projection of Soviet military powers." At the same time, like Carter, he also saw the crisis as affecting US interests. He stated in a memo to Carter, "We will never know whether any of this could have been averted, but we do know one thing: if we do not respond in a timely fashion, the consequences of an inadequate response will be even more horrendous because our vital interest in the Middle East will soon be directly affected."[212] The January 8 SCC meeting reiterated this theme: Brzezinski warned that Soviet actions "in Afghanistan ... created an objective threat and a dynamic development in the area as serious for our security and vital interests as Soviet actions in Greece in 1947."[213]

Notwithstanding the realization that US vital interests were at risk, Carter's policies in response to the invasion were largely political, economic, or symbolic in nature. Not all of them were popular domestically (or with US allies). Indeed, the public considered the embargo on exports of US grain to the USSR to be more punitive toward American farmers, and the US boycott of the Moscow Olympic Games to be more punitive toward US athletes than Soviet leaders.[214] These responses reinforced Carter's weak image and encouraged Republican Bob Dole to claim, "Carter took a poke at the Soviet Bear and knocked out the American farmer."[215]

Some military steps were taken in response to the invasion, but only through Pakistan as a proxy, and only covert in nature. To keep Pakistan out of Soviet reach, Carter reaffirmed the 1954 security guarantee to Pakistan, pledging that the United States would intervene against a threat from the north. The United States also began to provide defensive arms to Pakistan. Additionally, because of the threat that the Soviets posed to US allies in the Persian Gulf, the United States believed that improved Rapid Deployment Force (RDF) and air projection capabilities, as well as prepositioning heavy equipment and supply, were critically needed in the Middle East. Carter also implemented some coercive military instruments although those did not include the actual use of military force. In particular, he issued a public deterrent threat, which reflected his fear of further expansion into vitally important areas in the region. He asserted in the January 23, 1980 State of the Union address: "The implications of the Soviet invasion of Afghanistan could pose the most serious threat to world peace since the Second World War."[216] Carter warned the Soviets against further encroachment by proclaiming the Carter Doctrine: "an attempt by any outside force to gain control of the Persian Gulf region will be regarded as an assault on the vital interests of the United States. It will be repelled by the use of any means necessary, including military force."[217]

Losing Momentum Domestically and Abroad

The public initially viewed Carter's policies in response to the Afghanistan invasion favorably. In January 1980, a poll asked the following: "Do you think any of the other candidates running for President could handle the situation in Afghanistan better than Jimmy Carter?" The results showed that 50 percent answered "No," while only 27 percent said "Yes" (23 percent said they had no opinion).[218] The same month, another poll asked whether "Jimmy Carter's actions against the Soviet Union [are] strong enough, too strong, or not strong enough?" Those results showed that 49 percent saw Carter's actions as strong enough and 5 percent said they were too strong, while 36 percent thought they were not strong enough (9 percent had no opinion).[219]

However, as Carter's policies failed to elicit a visible reaction from the Soviets, approval of Carter began to diminish. In January 1980, when asked, "How would you rate Carter on his handling of the Afghanistan crisis?," the public was split: 48 percent said positive, while 43 percent said negative.[220] Similarly, the same month a poll asked, "How effective do you feel President Carter's policies will be in getting the Russians to pull out of Afghanistan?" The public was once again split: 49 percent thought the policies were either somewhat effective (40 percent) or very effective (9 percent), while 47 percent thought they were not very effective.[221] Two months later, the trend was more negative, as 62 percent said that they would rate "Carter's handling of the Afghanistan situation" negatively, compared to only 33 percent whose rating was positive.[222]

Despite the public's lackluster support, we see very little criticism by Congress of Carter's handling of the Afghanistan crisis. As Congress had advocated in the two earlier crises, Carter responded to the Soviets' actions with firmness and a concern for the greater geopolitical implications of the invasion, so we would not expect Congress to criticize Carter's concern about Soviet expansionism or the administration's increased firmness.[223] However, the invasion of Afghanistan was the death knell for SALT, as Carter understood very well.[224] By late 1979, conservatives in Congress capitalizing on the brigade crisis eliminated any substantial chance of SALT II being ratified by the Senate. After the invasion, on January 3, the president asked the Senate to postpone further consideration of SALT II; however, he did not altogether withdraw the treaty, allowing for ratification to be raised once the crisis had passed (although the treaty was, in the end, never ratified).[225]

By March, Carter's policies were losing momentum both domestically and internationally. The majority of US allies resisted shouldering any of the economic burden associated with US reactions to the invasion. According to Brzezinski, the allies' reluctance stemmed from a sense of fear and uncertainty: the Europeans certainly understood the strategic threat, but they were trying to preserve détente out of fear. The allies' second concern, according to Brzezinski, was that the Europeans saw the United States as inconsistent, "so they do not want to go along with us and then ultimately see us reverse our position." In response to these concerns, Brzezinski advocated a constant, measured, and assertive posture. The United States could also put pressure on these governments privately; as Brzezinski put it, "a major public dispute with the Allies would shift the emphasis on Afghanistan from an East-West to a West-West conflict and would surely lead your domestic critics to charge that the problem is not with the Europeans but with the failure of this Administration's credibility, policies and leadership."[226]

Carter sensed that he was not successfully altering Soviet behavior in Afghanistan. In a March 18 memo to Carter, Brzezinski reiterated the need to establish a "more assertive tone."[227] Brzezinski's major concern was, "How will a Soviet success affect our regional and global position? How can we avoid having this look like a U.S. defeat?"[228] Concerned about US standing, Brzezinski said, "the major danger is that every single effort we have undertaken regarding Afghanistan might appear, by June or July, to have been a total or at least partial failure. This will be a disaster: (a) in Southwest Asia itself, where we will be perceived as a pitiful, helpless giant; (b) among our Allies and supporters, who will be castigating us for our vacillation, lack of leadership, and well known tendency to speak with two voices; (c) in the Kremlin, which will perceive us as a paper tiger and an unworthy partner; and (d) domestically. . . . In the long run, our task is to restore our strength and the credibility on the part of others that we are willing to use that strength to defend our vital interests."[229]

Carter accepted some of Brzezinski's policy suggestions and rejected others. But more importantly, there is no evidence that Carter ever subscribed to the reputational logic for why those policies were necessary. Rather, Carter focused narrowly on preventing the Soviets from expanding into neighboring countries. Consistent with the record from previous crises, here too Carter's private statements and writings during the 1980s lacked reference to reputational concerns or image-based considerations as primary motivating factors. In Carter's memoir, he refers to Afghanistan as "the first time they [the Soviets] had used their troops to expand their sphere of influence since they had overthrown the government of Czechoslovakia in February 1948 and established a Soviet puppet government there."[230] Carter did not mention US reputation for resolve or US credibility as the foundation for his policy responses to the invasion but rather focused on the fact that "[if] the Soviets could consolidate their hold on Afghanistan, the balance of power in the entire region would be drastically modified in their favor, and they might be tempted toward further aggression. We were resolved to do everything feasible to prevent such a turn of events."[231]

The perception that Carter was weak ultimately contributed to his defeat in the 1980 presidential race. Exit polls indicated that 31 percent of voters disliked his foreign policy, especially his reaction to Soviet adventurism and the Iran hostage crisis.[232] Both crises contributed to perceptions that Carter was weak and could not effectively leverage US power in the international system. Indeed, exit polls indicated that 48 percent of voters believed he was a "weak leader," and 32 percent believed that he was unable to "get things done."[233]

Summary

The invasion of Afghanistan forced President Carter to reevaluate his view of Soviet intentions. He became convinced that Afghanistan was just the first step in Soviet expansion in the Middle East, and that it threatened American allies and vital interests in the Persian Gulf. The president stated, in his oral history with the Miller Institute, "I thought then and think now it was a very serious threat to our country's security and to international stability for the Soviets to invade Afghanistan. . . . We presumed that the Soviets might very well be successful and quickly consolidate their hold on Afghanistan and use Afghanistan as a launching pad to go directly to the Persian Gulf through Iran . . . and perhaps even through Pakistan. . . . So I reacted strongly because I wanted Brezhnev to know that if they did thrust toward the Persian Gulf, it would be the same as an attack on our country."[234]

Despite these concerns, Carter's response was not overly militarily assertive. The president did not use military force against the Soviets; did not issue an explicit compelling threat that warned the Soviets to get out of Afghanistan; and offered only limited and indirect covert military support for local allies to harass the Soviets. (As we see in the following chapter, Ronald Reagan would, while president, significantly escalate US involvement in Afghanistan.) Nevertheless, Carter did issue a public deterrent threat intended to dissuade the Soviets from further expansion and instituted several costly political, economic, and symbolic policies aimed to punish the Soviets for their betrayal of his trust.

In this crisis, Carter's policies were more hawkish, but Carter's discourse shows that he did not accept Brzezinski's reputational rationale for those policies. Rather, it was Carter's newfound belief in Soviet expansionism that made him more protective of US material interests; he became more assertive with the Soviets when materials interests were clearly at stake.

Alternative and Additional Contextual Explanations

While the dispositional theory provides a cogent explanation for Carter's crisis discourse and policies, other explanations might explain other components of Carter's decision-making process. As this section shows, however, none of these alternative explanations offers a compelling account for Carter's behaviors across these crises.

MATERIALIST EXPLANATIONS

Historians and political scientists have long attempted to explain leaders' behaviors in terms of the structure of the international system, while disregarding individual leader characteristics. Specifically, in the context of the Cold War, the international system was organized around the threat of nuclear war and the resulting need to maintain the nuclear balance between the United States and the Soviet Union.[235] Under these assumptions, as I explain in chapter 5, US leaders should care more about reputation for resolve in a bipolar system and should also care more during times where the nuclear balance is perceived as shifting in favor of the USSR.

If those systemic explanations were valid, concerns about reputation for resolve should have been especially pronounced during the Carter administration. During the 1970s, there were no signs of a Soviet collapse, and the nuclear balance was perceived to favor the USSR. As I detail elsewhere, during early 1978, the administration conducted a comprehensive net assessment that concluded that for the most part the trends in "the military component of national power" would "favor the Soviet Union."[236] The comprehensive net assessment further concluded that this strategic balance was expected to affect the United States adversely within less than a decade.[237] Later projections from 1978 predicted a steady US decline on most key indicators into the 1990s.[238]

The US-Soviet nuclear balance continued to have great importance in Central Europe, the superpowers' traditional realm of competition. In January 1978, a CIA report entitled "The Balance of Nuclear Forces in Central Europe" concluded that "[improvements] that have been made in Soviet tactical nuclear forces in Central Europe over the past several years have eroded much of NATO's longstanding nuclear advantage there."[239] This destabilization of NATO's dominance in Central Europe had implications for deterrence, as well. "If present trends continue and Soviet forces over the next few years attain a general nuclear parity in Central Europe, the basis of deterrence there will shift more to the conventional forces of both sides."[240] Parity would also undermine the effectiveness of NATO's existing nuclear weapons: "the growth of the Pact's tactical nuclear forces has reduced the credibility—and therefore the utility—of NATO's theater nuclear weapons as a counter to the Pact's conventional strength."[241]

The deliberations in the May 17, 1979 NSC meeting further reveal that the strategic nuclear balance was perceived to be deteriorating faster than had been expected in 1977, and that it would continue to do so into the early 1980s. Intelligence reports further highlighted the adverse trends in the nuclear balance.[242] While the nuclear trend might have been part of the reason that Brzezinski cared more about reputation for resolve in repeated interactions with the Soviets, even over nonvital issues, the same cannot be said of Carter. Carter's crisis decision making reveals that trends in the nuclear balance did not lead him to attach significance to reputational considerations, contrary to systemic-level explanations espoused by structural realists.

Next, I probe whether materialist cost-benefit calculations can better explain Carter's crisis decision making. The historical record shows mixed support for this explanation. On the one hand, the interplay of the Carter administration officials directly contradicts this hypothesis. The main players in the Carter foreign policy establishment—Brzezinski, Vance, and Brown—were exposed to the same information regarding the material benefits and costs involved in using military instruments in each of these international crises, but each reached different policy recommendations. Further, it seems that Carter was against reputation-based policies even when not very costly, such as with sending an aircraft carrier to the Horn of Africa.

At the same time, Carter's calculus for whether to use military instruments does appear to rely on material cost-benefit calculations, rather than reputational considerations. Because escalating tensions with the Soviets over their interventions in the Horn of Africa or the brigade in Cuba would have been disastrous for SALT II, Carter (and Vance) probably judged that the United States was better off refraining from using military coercion. In Afghanistan, the material cost-benefit balance was different because US vital interests were at stake, leading Carter to resort to military instruments he had rejected in the past. In Carter's thinking, however, reputational considerations were not part of the decision-making calculus in any of these crises.

In stark contrast is Brzezinski who, throughout these crises, focused on the reputational costs and benefits of failing to react to the Soviets. Concerned about the inferences audiences would draw, Brzezinski was focused on the reputational costs of US responses to Soviet aggression, and he largely ignored the outcome of the materialist calculus. As a result, Brzezinski reached different conclusions from Carter about the need to use military coercion against the Soviets and Cubans in Africa. These different calculations reflect differences in individual philosophies on the role of reputation in decisions whether, and where, to use military force.

DOMESTIC POLITICAL EXPLANATIONS

As chapter 5 explains, scholars have outlined several domestic political explanations that can affect crisis foreign policies: some explanations focus on public opinion, while others highlight the president's core constituency, or domestic actors like members of the US Congress. The theory I posit, on the other hand, predicts that a low self-monitor president would pursue policies that reflect his inner beliefs, not because they would appease domestic audiences.

Domestic pressures from elites and public opinion would have pushed Carter toward more concern about reputation for resolve. Therefore, Carter could have been expected to take a more coercive approach toward the Soviets during the horn crisis and the brigade crisis. But instead, Carter chose policies that were very unpopular domestically. The American people were expecting more toughness against the Soviets; indeed, his national security advisor repeatedly highlighted this point. Public opinion polls, as well as the preferences of Carter's core constituency, repeatedly showed a desire for more resolve in the face of Soviet challenges. If anything, domestic political considerations should have pushed Carter to be more concerned about reputation for resolve during the horn and the Soviet brigade crises.

Carter's presidency was marked by fluctuations in public opinion, with an overall negative trend. Public support for Carter's foreign policy spiked during periods of success, such as at the Camp David Accords and the beginning of the Soviet invasion of Afghanistan, but the public generally did not support Carter's foreign policies. Approval was at its lowest (below 20 percent) in August 1980, just before Carter lost the election.[243] Carter was not winning over voters with consistent policies, and the administration did not respond with policy changes. The unpopularity of his foreign policy cost him the 1980 election. Carter would not necessarily have been reelected by showing more resolve or more sensitivity to image considerations; he was seen as weak because of the Iran hostage debacle and US economic downturn of the 1970s, in addition to tensions with the Soviets. Still, as public opinion polls suggest, his policies to address the Soviet threat significantly contributed to perceptions of him as a weak leader.

The public was not the only domestic actor exerting pressure on Carter to make more resolute policy choices. Congress and other domestic elites also pushed Carter to do more to demonstrate resolve. For example, conservative members of Congress linked their votes on the SALT II Treaty explicitly to the presence of the Soviet brigade in Cuba, which led to growing opposition to the treaty.[244] Even Democrats in Congress criticized Carter's stance toward the Soviets in the Horn of Africa as being too weak, stating that Carter was allowing the conquest of Somalia and Eritrea by Soviet-backed Ethiopian forces, which would lead to an eventual takeover in the horn.[245] The brigade crisis contributed to the erosion of support for SALT II, as more members of Congress became worried that the Soviets were exploiting détente. However, the biggest blow to SALT was undoubtedly the Soviet invasion of Afghanistan. Even though Carter was initially determined not to let the invasion affect SALT II, he quickly realized that he could not get a majority in the Senate to ratify the treaty.[246]

In sum, the available evidence does not support the theory that domestic political considerations played an important role in shaping Carter's crisis decision making. While the president's advisors continued to monitor the preferences of the electorate and Carter's core constituency, the president's policies were not in line with the preferences of the American public or domestic elites before Afghanistan. Some of the policies he chose to punish the Soviets in response to the invasion were also unpopular with the American public and Congress.

OTHER INDIVIDUAL-LEVEL EXPLANATIONS

Other individual-level explanations also fail to account for the limited role that reputation for resolve played in Carter's decision making. First, Carter was a southern president through and through: born and raised in Georgia, he was always proud of his southern upbringing and of much of southern culture. According to Dafoe and Caughey, such presidents should exhibit more, not less, concern for reputation for resolve.[247] Yet this was not true of Carter.

Second, Carter's resistance to acting to shore up the US reputation for resolve, especially with regard to the Horn of Africa crisis, occurred at the end of his first year in office. The conventional wisdom would expect Carter to want to establish a reputation for resolve, in the expectation of an ongoing relationship with the Soviets. According to Dafoe, reputational concerns should be more acute earlier in a leader's tenure.[248] But Carter, although a new and relatively inexperienced president, followed neither course; rather, from the beginning of his presidency, Carter pushed back against advisors who sought to emphasize US reputation for resolve in crisis responses to the Soviet Union in the Third World. His policies became, if anything, more hawkish toward the Soviets at the end of his presidency.

———

As a low self-monitor dove, Carter had neither the personality typical of successful politicians nor the strategic beliefs consistent with American concerns at the time. The exceptional nature of his term provides both a hard test and an important case for the dispositional theory. There is strong support for the theory that Carter was not concerned with reputation for resolve in foreign policy, despite being repeatedly reminded by his national security advisor of its importance; that his crisis policies repeatedly favored restraint and reluctance—even distaste—for military coercion; and that he did not change his crisis policies even when unpopular with the public or Congress.

7

Ronald Reagan and the Fight against Communism

"If the United States cannot respond to a threat near our own borders, why should Europeans or Asians believe that we are seriously concerned about threats to them? If the Soviets can assume that nothing short of an actual attack on the United States will provoke an American response, which ally, which friend, will trust us then?"
—RONALD REAGAN, ADDRESS TO A JOINT SESSION OF CONGRESS, APRIL 28, 1983

President Ronald Reagan left a popular legacy of toughness against Communist foes in furtherance of American security. During his time in office, Reagan and his advisors confronted a host of international crises. This chapter focuses on four of them: the escalation in Afghanistan, the intervention in Lebanon, the invasion of Grenada, and the air strikes against Libya. Each posed a challenge, real or perceived, to US reputation for resolve and so are good tests of the dispositional theory. This chapter examines the extent to which reputational concerns shaped President Reagan's discourse, decision making, and policies during these crises. A review of Reagan's self-monitoring tendencies and beliefs about the use of force place him closest to the ideal-type high self-monitor hawk, of the eleven presidents studied, and thus, we should expect his behavior to consistent with that of a reputation crusader. Reagan's advisors pulled him in different directions than Brzezinski and Vance pulled Carter: Secretary of Defense Caspar Weinberger, although also a hawk, was a low self-monitor that recommended restraint in the use of military force for the sake of demonstrating credibility and an image of resolve. Secretary of State George Shultz, on the other hand, while relatively less hawkish than Weinberger, displayed high self-monitoring tendencies and was largely concerned with the reputational fall-out of, especially, backing down. As for Reagan, his behavior and discourse during the crises covered cannot be convincingly explained simply by highlighting his hawkish tendencies. In order to fully appreciate Reagan's policies, rhetoric, and state of mind, we must look at how these hawkish tendencies interacted with his high self-monitoring disposition.

The rest of the chapter proceeds as follows. I begin with a brief discussion of Reagan's self-monitoring and his beliefs about the effectiveness of military force. In the online appendix, I provide some background on the circumstances surrounding Reagan's presidency. Most of this chapter, however, is dedicated to analyzing Reagan's discourse and policies during the selected crises. I end this chapter with a discussion of a number of potential alternative explanations, and I argue that none offers a compelling account of Reagan's discourse and behavior.

Classifying Reagan: Self-Monitoring and Military Assertiveness

REAGAN AS A HIGH SELF-MONITOR

Perhaps unsurprisingly given his background as a successful actor, Ronald Reagan scores as a high-self monitor. Based on the self-monitoring surveys completed for Reagan, as reported in chapter 4, Reagan is a statistically significant high self-monitor.[1] As discussed previously, high self-monitors adjust one's expressive behavior to match one's social situation. High self-monitors are thus able to present themselves differently to suit the desires of their audience, while low self-monitors tend to act more consistently, regardless of with whom they interact. Again, self-monitoring has three major components: expressive self-control, social stage presence, and other-directed self-presentation. While Reagan exhibited high expressive self-control and strong social presence, his other-directedness tendencies were perhaps less pronounced than high self-monitor dove Clinton (as shown in chapter 8). Still, Reagan displayed all three components of high self-monitoring in a manner that distinguishes him from low self-monitors.

First, Reagan possessed high expressive self-control. Ronald Reagan was a professional actor, and his training played a very large role in his political career, especially given that he did not enter politics until his fifties. When Reagan was asked during his first political campaign to become governor of California how he would govern, he replied, "I don't know, I've never played a governor."[2]

Even before he started campaigning, Reagan used his acting skills to convince other people to trust his authority and accept his point of view. Reagan had worked as a political spokesman for General Electric (GE). The company's public relations executive, Earl Dunckel, claimed that Reagan had "an almost mystical ability to achieve an empathy with almost any audience. . . . Reagan was able to talk on any subject, for example education, and persuade a group of educators that he must have had training in that area."[3] Reagan had a natural ability to appeal to people. In his question-and-answer sessions, Reagan was funny and friendly, with the ability to make his audience feel close to him.[4] In situations where Reagan needed only common sense rather than recall of data, he "had tremendous instincts for saying the right thing at the right time," recalled his press spokesman Larry Speakes.[5]

Throughout his political career, Reagan was capable of giving people the impression that he was well-informed about most political issues and knowl-edgeable enough to address them effectively. Nowhere was this skill more evident than in the 1980 presidential debate with Jimmy Carter. While political analysts such as Burton Kaufman concluded that Carter was better at addressing the issues themselves, Reagan appeared more "relaxed, reasonable, and informed . . . [and] also came across as warmer . . . and more intimate with the voters" than did then-President Carter, who focused more on presenting the issues than on tailoring his message for the debate or the audience.[6]

Reagan's success in the debate, and, indeed, in his entire political career, came in no small part from his inclination to make others believe that he was more informed than he was, while also appearing charming and likeable. This level of acting ability and expressive self-control is typical of high self-monitors. Biographer Lou Cannon saw Reagan's expressive self-control as so integral to his success in office that Cannon referred to him as "the 'acting' president."[7] Cannon observed that "to those who took a more traditional approach to the pres-idency, Reagan almost never seemed prepared. He had a handful of bedrock convictions and a knack of charming people of any rank or station. . . . But Reagan lacked a technical grasp of any issue, and he was usually bored by briefings."[8]

Playing these roles successfully was not solely attributable to Reagan's in-nate talent, but also to his extensive preparation. Reagan and his staff spent considerable time preparing and rehearsing speeches well in advance. On speak-ing tours, before running for governor, Reagan was already known for being extremely prepared; he would not "appear before an audience, write a speech, deliver a paper or even have a discussion with a very small group unless he . . . researched and reviewed the subject before the group for consideration."[9] In his first campaign for governor, Reagan's "ability to take direction and follow a script . . . endeared him to campaign strategists" that wanted to help get him elected.[10] As a result, Reagan's speeches to the press and to the country were much more calculated than they appeared. The Reagan presidency thus con-sisted of a series of public performances, with Reagan playing the role that his advisors and speechwriters crafted.

The second aspect of Reagan's self-monitoring involves his social stage pres-ence. Reagan could quickly ingratiate himself with people, even those who had preconceived negative opinions of him. In his speaking campaign for GE, Reagan spoke to assembly-line workers about politics. Political analysts such as Gerard DeGroot note that "he had the knack of making every one of them feel like the most important person on earth" and that Reagan "projected a genuine sensitivity."[11] Lou Cannon claimed that Reagan liked being in the spotlight from a young age, and his choice to go into Hollywood came from a desire "to be seen as well as heard,"[12] something he could not do as a radio broadcaster.

Reagan no doubt possessed a natural charisma that made people pay attention to him. Political scientist Richard Melanson remarks that Reagan's "mellifluous baritone, craggy good looks, and easy affability thrived behind microphone and camera,"[13] and this added to his ability to "deliver lines sincerely, narrate poignant stories, and publicly evince an impressive range of emotions" as an actor.[14] This seemingly innate ability to draw attention to himself and to gain the support of others based on his personality is typical of high self-monitors.

The third major aspect of self-monitoring—other-directed self-presentation— is a measure of one's willingness to alter one's behavior in order to increase one's social status. Unlike Carter, Reagan was careful not to mention certain issues on the campaign trail that would cause him to lose support. For instance, when attempting to win over southern GE workers to the conservative cause, Reagan avoided mentioning the Tennessee Valley Authority as an example of a wasteful program, because of its popularity in the region and GE's involvement.[15] When campaigning for president, Reagan mentioned issues such as "school prayer, abortion, law and order, and 'reverse discrimination'" only to his most conservative audiences.[16] Changing the nature of his speeches in order to match the sensibilities of the listeners is a behavior typical of many politicians, but it is a particular hallmark of high self-monitors.

Moreover, Reagan's other-directedness manifested in his cordial, even meaningful, interactions with his opponents. For example, at the dedication of the Carter presidential library in Atlanta in 1986, Reagan knew that Rosalynn Carter remained bitter at her husband's loss to Reagan. Reagan then delivered a speech directly to Carter "that picked Carter's best traits and praised them,"[17] along with Carter's efforts to bring peace to the Middle East. After hearing the speech, Carter stated to Reagan, "I think I now understand more clearly than I ever had before why you won in November 1980, and I lost."[18]

Reagan's other-directedness was especially clear in his dealings with congressional leaders, about whom Reagan "had strong opinions, which he kept within the White House."[19] Although he disliked certain opponents—especially Representative Thomas P. "Tip" O'Neill, who frequently attacked Reagan and his policies in the press—he spoke to opponents cordially and attempted to be seen as understanding their viewpoints. Moreover, Reagan was adept at controlling how he looked to other people. Indeed, his entire persona as an actor belied a man who was very much a loner in his private life. When working for

Reagan, press spokesman Larry Speakes noted the stark contrast between "the public Ronald Reagan, an outgoing, friendly, personable man, and the private Reagan, who . . . tends to be a loner, content to spend his time with his wife and no one else."[20] Whether joking his way through a cabinet meeting, choreographing a summit with Mikhail Gorbachev, or delivering a folksy presidential address, Reagan had a knack for putting on a good show.[21]

In sum, Reagan exhibited the characteristics of a high self-monitor. H. W. Brands writes: "Reagan was the most compelling communicator in American politics since Franklin Roosevelt, and he knew it. His mastery of the rhetorical art reflected his long experience as an actor and public speaker. His years with General Electric taught him how to read a room; his time before the camera trained him to see an audience beyond the camera. He mixed humor and pathos, philosophy and anecdote. But his greatest strength was the focus he brought to his task."[22]

REAGAN'S MILITARY ASSERTIVENESS

I classify Reagan as a hawk, based on qualitative and quantitative indicators of his military assertiveness. First, text analysis of Reagan's foreign policy speeches, shown in chapter 4, shows that Reagan was more hawkish than Presidents George H. W. Bush, Kennedy, and Carter. In the online appendix I depict Reagan's hawkishness based on the full spectrum of his public speeches on foreign policy (figure 7A.1), and based solely on foreign policy speeches during noncrisis periods (figure 7A.2).[23] Overall, Reagan's speeches through 1986 tended to be mostly hawkish, which supports his categorization as a reputation crusader, especially during the 1981–86 period covered in this chapter.

As for qualitative indicators, Reagan's attitudes toward defense spending, covert actions, and international organizations all reflect a president who scores high for military assertiveness. Reagan's general political ideology, outlined in a 1964 speech titled "A Time for Choosing," also known as "The Speech," focused on limiting the power of the federal government. Reagan also mentioned the threat of Communism and what he believed the United States needed to do in order to respond to it.[24]

This outlook explains Reagan's approach to defense spending. The Reagan administration's first proposed five-year defense plan "[required] an average real budget increase of 8.1 percent per year from 1981 to 1987, for a net real increase of 59 percent,"[25] which would have been the biggest military buildup since the Korean War. While Reagan wanted the government to limit spending in other areas and to avoid wasteful programs, defense was clearly an exception, and Reagan drove up national deficits in order to build up the military. Reagan believed that his predecessors had been "unilaterally disarming" while the USSR had been expanding the size of its military,[26] and in order to remain competitive with the enemy, Reagan was in favor of spending more on both conventional and nuclear forces.

The primary reason Reagan increased military spending to such an enormous degree was to repurpose the military to engage in offensive operations against the Soviet Union if necessary. In a leaked "Defense Guidance" paper, the Reagan administration's Department of Defense stated that it wanted to have the option to "render ineffective the total Soviet (and Soviet allied) military and political power structure" by attacking "political and military leadership and associated control facilities, nuclear and conventional military forces, and industry critical to military power."[27] One advisor, Thomas Reed, claimed that "that the United States [focused under Reagan] on prevailing over the Soviets,"[28] not merely following earlier policies of containment. Reagan strongly preferred offensive and preemptive action against what he believed was an unrelenting Communist enemy, and he believed that expanding military operations was the best way to improve US position.[29]

Reagan followed through on his promises to increase defense spending. In 1980, the last year of Carter's presidency, the military budget had been approximately $144 billion in 1981. By 1984, the budget was $265 billion, and it peaked at $294 billion in 1985 before leveling off.[30]

A second qualitative indicator I use to assess Reagan's military assertiveness is his attitude toward covert military action. A key element of Reagan's foreign policy as president was his use of covert operations, especially in Afghanistan and Latin America, to exert his will and fight Communism wherever it appeared. With Executive Order 12333, Reagan gave the CIA primary responsibility over covert action except in cases where the president decided otherwise. During the Reagan presidency, the CIA provided aid to anti-Communist movements, seeking to slow or reverse the spread of Soviet influence. Reagan approved covert actions that touched all areas of the globe: arming CIA-trained mujahedeen forces in Afghanistan and Pakistan, aiding anti-Communist forces in Angola and El Salvador, destabilizing Communist regimes in Cambodia and, of course, in Nicaragua. Reagan used covert action in Iraq, Libya, and most prominently, in an arms deal with Iran that would be used to fund the Nicaraguan Contras.

The Reagan administration often used proxy forces, most notably the Contras, to carry out these covert missions. "Between 1984 and 1986, National Security Council officials not only provided specialized military advice to the Contras, but also helped raise millions of dollars from private U.S. sources to compensate for what the administration saw as insufficient congressional funding ($38 million in 1984–1985)."[31] His administration refused to sign treaties with the Central American republics that would include "bans on military exercises, foreign military bases and advisors, and an arms freeze" that would have impeded the overthrow of Nicaragua's Sandinista government, for example.[32]

As the Iran-Contra affair revealed, Reagan (intentionally or not) ignored both domestic and international law to fund the Contras, as "Congress had banned U.S. contact with the Contras and prohibited CIA funding of those groups either directly or indirectly" for their repeated human rights violations.[33] Promoting the fight against the Sandinistas also involved mining Nicaragua's harbors, in spite of a "May 1984 International Court of Justice (World Court) meeting that ruled the United States should immediately halt attempts to blockade or mine Nicaragua's ports."[34]

A third qualitative indicator to determine a president's level of hawkishness is his approach to diplomacy through multilateral organizations. While Reagan wanted to improve US reputation around the world using the military, he was much less willing to do so using the United Nations and other international organizations. In "The Speech," Reagan criticized the UN and claimed that it was "an organization that [had] become so structurally unsound that [one could] muster a two-thirds vote on the floor of the General Assembly among nations that represent less than 10 percent of the world's population."[35] Reagan also believed that the use of the US military to fight Communism and establish freedom was a better way of ensuring the safety of the United States and its allies than "vainly trying to win friends through agreements like the Law of the Sea and the Panama Canal treaties."[36] Reagan did not trust the work of international organizations for helping US allies or for effectively resolving tensions between existential enemies, and so he preferred the use of the military in foreign affairs.

Reagan made it clear that he would not allow the UN to constrain US policy and diplomacy, especially with regard to authoritarian regimes. Reagan believed that the admission of new countries to the UN had disadvantaged the United States, stating during the 1960s: "We cannot safely rest the case of freedom with the United Nations as it is presently constructed. Not until reconstruction of this organization puts realistic power in the hands of those nations which must, through size and strength, be ultimately responsible for world order, can we submit questions affecting our national interest to the U.N. and be confident of a fair hearing."[37]

Upon becoming president, Reagan selected Jeane Kirkpatrick as ambassador to the United Nations.[38] Kirkpatrick described her diplomatic strategy as "[taking] down [America's] 'kick me' sign" and using the UN to negotiate from the position of strength created through Reagan's military buildup.[39] Reagan never intended to use the UN as a means of speaking to allies and enemies on a level playing field. Instead, Reagan's diplomacy was accompanied by military coercion or demonstrations of force, and his administration's activity in the United Nations reflected that he did not believe in negotiation without it. Reagan also succeeded in pulling the United States out of UNESCO, stopped US contributions to UN funds, and encouraged Congress to withhold America's

United Nations dues as a means to force UN budget reform. The Senate also voted to cut $500 million from US contributions to the UN.

In sum, prior to becoming president, through Reagan's first term, and at least until 1986, Reagan's military assertiveness supports his classification as a hawk. One might wonder whether Reagan's nuclear arms control negotiations with the Soviet Union during his second administration indicate that Reagan's beliefs about the efficacy of military force had changed. And if so, what is the significance of this change on Reagan's classification as a "hawk" for the period in question?

As some scholars have noted, the idea of Reagan making any compromise with the USSR for arms control or for positive diplomacy was unthinkable during his first administration. Robert Dallek confidently predicted that "it [seemed] unlikely that the Reagan administration [would] desist from [its] approach and try to reach meaningful arms control agreements with Moscow."[40] But in early 1984, Reagan's public speeches began to stress negotiation and dialogue, rather than confrontation.[41] Several events may have contributed to a moderation in Reagan's tone. First, the USSR accidentally shot down a Korean passenger plane in 1983 that strayed into Soviet airspace, which made it clear to Reagan how quickly unintentional acts could escalate. The second event, perhaps more importantly, was the Soviet response (including issuing of a nuclear alert) to NATO military exercise Able Archer in late 1983. This exercise tested procedures for using nuclear weapons in the event of war. The Soviets' reaction drove home to Reagan the idea that the Soviets were sincerely fearful of an American nuclear attack. Third, by 1984 Reagan felt confident about the strength of the American military as a result of the massive buildup he had undertaken, which allowed him to negotiate with the Soviets from a position of strength.[42]

At the same time, other scholars have shown that notwithstanding Reagan's beliefs about the utility of military force, he always embodied two conflicting approaches about the Soviet Union. As Keith Shimko explains, "Reading Reagan's comments is like listening to two people, Reagan the optimist and Reagan the pessimist. Reagan the optimist believed that the Cold War and the arms race were built on misunderstandings and misperceptions which stood in the way of a realization of genuine common interests; Reagan the pessimist viewed the Cold War as the inevitable and enduring outcome of conflicting ideologies and inherently antagonistic forms of government."[43] Thus, the dramatic reversal in the tenor of Reagan's Soviet policy toward the end of his presidency might not have been facilitated solely by the rise of Gorbachev, but also due to Reagan's long-standing liberal and optimistic beliefs about the illusory nature of the US-Soviet conflict that always coexisted with his hard-line attitude toward the USSR.[44]

Regardless of which interpretation of Reagan's views regarding the Soviet Union and arms control one chooses to adopt, all of Reagan's beliefs about the efficacy of military force, as revealed through the other indicators of military assertiveness mentioned above, had not changed in any fundamental way. Reagan was by no means a "dove" by 1986, and probably not even when he left office: his beliefs about the efficacy of conventional military force remained consistent with that of a hawk.

Self-Monitoring and Reagan's Main Advisors

Although Reagan wanted his administration to avoid the squabbles and bureaucratic paralysis that the Carter administration experienced with Brzezinski and Vance, his principal foreign policy advisors also clashed over a variety of foreign policy issues.[45] Secretary of Defense Caspar Weinberger, who was willing to promote his vision of fighting the Soviets uncompromisingly, battled with Secretary of State George Shultz, who held relatively more pragmatic views of the USSR. As I show below, the two disagreed about the need to fight for reputation for resolve. Interestingly, it was the more hawkish Weinberger who was reluctant to use military force in places like Lebanon, Grenada, and Libya, whereas the more pragmatic Shultz warned of the risks of backing down. The two advisors differed significantly in their self-monitoring inclinations: Weinberger's personality is more consistent with that of a low self-monitor, while Shultz's tendencies seem more like a high self-monitor. These differences, I argue, contributed to their different positions about whether military force should be used in places with little material value at stake in order to project a reputation for resolve.

From what we can glean from biographical accounts, Weinberger was on the lower side of the self-monitoring scale. Weinberger had a clearly defined ideology but was unable to modify his message to persuade others to take his side, often leading him to fight to implement his vision. This ideology was deeply Republican and hawkish, favoring limited domestic spending and a strong military posture against the Soviet Union. Weinberger espoused this view from an early age and did not change during his college years at Harvard.[46] Rather than adjusting his self-presentation to fit in with the less conservative campus environment, Weinberger called himself the "lone conservative" in his social circles and found that his professors "taught with a liberal bias."[47]

These traits remained unchanged well into Weinberger's political career. He became known for being "totally unyielding in defense of principles he [considered] important,"[48] but this was often frustrating, rather than impressive, to those around him. Weinberger's response to criticism was not persuasion or compromise, but to fight even harder for his preferred policies. For example, his stance on slashing funding for Nixon's domestic agenda made him so unpopular within his own organization that "he was denied access to the president and could not even get White House policy aide John Ehrlichman to return his phone calls."[49] Later, as secretary of defense, "Weinberger's abrasive personality left him convinced that his policy was the only valid option," and as a result he worked even harder to increase defense spending.[50] His single-mindedness, monotonic, and unflinching tendencies earned him the nickname, "Caspar One-Note."

Weinberger lacked political finesse, and his low self-monitoring tendencies made him both unable and unwilling to convince others of his beliefs even as defense secretary. When he believed that his agenda would not be implemented, he left his position in 1987. Consistent with having low expressive self-control, Weinberger rarely if ever used emotions to achieve his goals and inspire others. As reporter Dolly Langdon noted, Weinberger remained the "gentle, soft-spoken and courtly" individual throughout difficult defense budget fights and was often "genuinely baffled to find himself in the eye of a political storm" when presented with opposition.[51] Weinberger did not use emotions strategically, as even his memoirs were criticized for being "generally devoid of emotion" and focused primarily on the facts, not his feelings.[52] This lack of emotional expression extended to his dealings with others: while he was "invariably polite,"[53] he often butted heads with top officials. As one former Reagan official put it, "you can't understand the frustration of dealing with Cap until you sit down and try to reach some kind of accommodation. He keeps saying the same thing over and over again. It's like water dripping on a stone."[54]

Unlike Weinberger, biographical evidence suggests that Reagan's secretary of state, George Shultz, is higher on the self-monitoring scale. Taubman described him as "by nature and training a . . . mediator" who preferred "conciliation to confrontation."[55] Those who worked with Shultz noted that when faced with a dispute, he had a tendency to "sit for hours or days if necessary, listening carefully, interrupting only for clarification, until an acceptable compromise could be reached" with those who opposed him.[56] Indeed, as General James Mattis once remarked, Shultz was capable of "bringing together" myriad opposed groups and working to find a solution to their issues, from "blacks and whites [and] management and labor" to "Israelis and Russians and the United States and the USSR."[57] This ability to work well with opposed groups of people and to present many persuasive sides of an argument shows a strong level of other-directed self-presentation, a key component of high self-monitoring. During tough negotiations, Shultz was a master at giving credit to others for his own work for more productive results. Lonsdale describes this tactic as "[making] it their idea, and [working] behind the scenes."[58]

Shultz also appears to have possessed strong expressive self-control. He was seen as "inscrutable . . . reserved, [and] self-contained" and "spoke with deliberation" to control precisely what he conveyed to others.[59] Those who tried to discern what he was feeling at any given time "got few easy clues from Shultz himself. More often than not, his only tell-all response in a conversation would be an arched brow, a mild frown, an angry scowl or a stare, or an occasional smile."[60] Attempting to seek compromise, Shultz was especially hesitant to show his anger: "So rare is a sighting of Shultz visibly angry that people talk about the red-faced variant as though they had just seen a passenger pigeon, extinct since 1914, on the wing."[61] Yet Robert Gates, the former deputy director of Central Intelligence, recalls that Shultz cultivated a public image that was starkly different from the one that colleagues and friends held. Thus, according to Gates, Shultz could be "confident and bold" in public settings but was "excessively thin-skinned, sensitive even to implied criticism."[62] In addition, Shultz showed a very different personality on weekends. Outside the aloof image he cultivated in the workplace, Shultz was "engaging, humorous, interesting . . . and would show up at his Saturday seminars or Sunday meetings in really outrageous golf clothes totally at odds with his usual businesslike mien."[63]

Perhaps one of the largest differences between Weinberger and Shultz was the latter's ability to choose when and how to modify his outward behavior to achieve desired outcomes. Thus, Shultz "chose" when to be rigid and when to cooperate, both inside and outside his department. Weinberger, on the other hand, was consistently rigid and did not readily change or compromise, which rarely resulted in the outcomes he sought. When Shultz faced disagreements, "he knew when to speak up, when to keep his powder dry, when to draw the line, when to blur distinctions, when to confront the Congress, and when to hold out his hand."[64] Shultz skillfully "knew how to maneuver in Washington's bureaucratic labyrinth":[65] when he had to work across departments on specific projects, such as arms control negotiations, he could even set aside some differences with his enemies. As Robert Gates found, when he worked with the Department of Defense and the Central Intelligence Agency (CIA), Shultz did so "with a harmony that was unique in the administration," and disputes "were fought out above the table with everyone having a chance to be heard."[66] This behavior "won him allies in both Defense and CIA, and eased his path considerably" when he had to manage future interagency issues.[67]

We expect Weinberger's and Shultz's differing self-monitoring dispositions to manifest in deliberations over reputational crises. Contrary to the Carter case, here we would expect the more hawkish advisor—Weinberger—to be more reluctant to fight for reputation owing to his low self-monitoring tendencies, and to observe the less hawkish advisor, Shultz, to be more concerned about saving face in crises that did not involve major material stakes owing to his higher self-monitoring tendencies.

Reputational Concerns and Crisis Decision Making

Given that Reagan was a hawk, it is not surprising that he would want to use military force. But my theory uniquely predicts that, because Reagan was a reputation crusader, we should see reputational considerations play a significant role in his crisis decision making. We should observe evidence that credibility concerns, appearing tough, and saving face are critical both in Reagan's personal decision making and in accompanying policy debates. Unlike Clinton, whose dovishness made him more reluctant to initiate and escalate reputational contests, I expect Reagan to actively seek out opportunities to demonstrate resolve through the application of military force for the sake of enhancing US reputation for resolve, doing so in geographic areas that do not involve important material interests. The evidence I present is highly consistent with these predictions.

Moreover, my theory does not predict that all decision makers care equally about reputation for resolve, even if they are all exposed to identical information. While Reagan and his advisors shared hawkish views to some degree, Reagan and his closest advisors varied significantly in their concerns about reputation for resolve, and thus, in the policies they advocated. Consistent with the theory, Secretary Weinberger—highly hawkish but exhibiting lower self-monitoring tendencies—advocated more restraint and voiced less concern about reputational fallout than did the more dovish Secretary Shultz, who had high self-monitoring tendencies. Thus, we see that hawkishness is not determinative of concerns about reputation for resolve, or the selection of policies to enhance US reputation through the use of military instruments.

REAGAN'S ESCALATION IN AFGHANISTAN

Consistent with his classification as a reputation crusader, Ronald Reagan viewed delivery of military assistance to the Afghan rebels, known as the mujahedeen, as crucial to demonstrating resolve. To that end, Reagan took several steps that Carter had rejected. First, Reagan significantly increased aid to the mujahedeen. While this assistance was officially provided through a covert CIA program called Operation Cyclone, the Soviet Union, the United States' allies, and the American public were fully aware of the rapidly increasing military aid to the Afghan rebels, if not always informed of the details. Second, Reagan also authorized better equipment for the mujahedeen in 1982 and in 1985 provided them with Stinger missiles. The Stinger missiles were intended to reverse the mujahedeen's deteriorating odds of victory and also had the benefit of showing American resolve and commitment to its cause in Afghanistan. Third, as the dispositional theory would predict, one of the major objectives of Reagan's policy toward Afghanistan (besides defeating the Soviets) was to "show firmness" and "demonstrate our commitment" to assist those around the world who were fighting Soviet encroachment.[68] Fourth, Reagan's National Security Decision Directives (NSDDs) caution that nothing should be done that would indicate a willingness to soften American policy on Afghanistan. Even as the

United States entered arms control talks with Moscow and bilateral relations began to improve, Reagan made clear that he was unfalteringly committed to removing the Soviets from Afghanistan.

Reagan's willingness to use his foreign policy to impress on world leaders the level of American resolve differs markedly from Carter's relative lack of concern for appearing resolved. This difference affected the actions each took with respect to the Soviet invasion of Afghanistan.

Carter "Lowered the Credibility of the United States"

Even before assuming office, Reagan exhibited dissatisfaction with Carter's foreign policy. At a debate leading up to the Republican primary election in 1980, then-Governor Reagan said:

> [President Carter] lowered the credibility of the United States when he made, in diplomatic language, what was an extremely serious warning to the Soviets not to invade Afghanistan, indeed, he even used the term that serious consequences would follow. Now, he knew we had no way to back that up there. There wasn't anything we could do. We weren't going to put in troops and try to chase them out. So they invaded, and the world saw us once again still standing here, just as we are still standing after he made the speech that he wouldn't accept the Soviet brigade in Cuba. But we accepted it.[69]

In Reagan's view, Carter's unwillingness to follow through weakened America's reputation for resolve. Later, in a presidential debate with Carter, Reagan closed by asking the audience if "America [is] as respected throughout the world as it was? Do you feel that our security is as safe, that we're as strong as we were four years ago?"[70] Of course, the unstated answer to Reagan's rhetorical questions was no.

Even though Reagan gave priority and preeminence to reputational concerns, his critique of Carter's foreign policy went further, to include what Reagan saw as a general inability to confront the USSR. To Reagan and many members of his cabinet, there existed no greater threat to US security than the Soviet Union and its Communist ideology.[71] Reagan believed the Soviet leadership was working tirelessly toward a "one-world Socialist or Communist state"[72] and that the Soviet Union's sociopolitical system made the country naturally aggressive.[73] The Soviet Union's expansionist tendencies had been enhanced by Carter's unwillingness to take a firm stance against the proliferation of Communist regimes in the Third World.[74] This Soviet aggression proved most glaring in Afghanistan. That isolated Central Asian country provided the Reagan administration an opportunity to weaken the Soviet Union and to rebuild America's damaged reputation for resolve.

Stepping Up the Heat

Over the course of the 1980s, Reagan showed US resolve by increasing assistance to the mujahedeen, through Operation Cyclone,[75] by both monetary means—$30 million in 1981 increasing to $450 million in 1985 to $500 million by 1987—and nonmonetary means, such as increased intelligence and access to more advanced weapons.[76] A "qualitative" improvement in the type of weapons the administration furnished to the mujahedeen in 1982 accompanied the significant growth in assistance.[77] This initial increase was resisted by career members of the CIA and Defense Department. But, in the end, Reagan sided with those who wanted to increase aid, most notably Director of the CIA William Casey and Under Secretary of Defense for Policy Fred Iklé.[78] The expansion of the CIA's Afghanistan program helped realize the administration's goal of "keep[ing] maximum pressure on Moscow for withdrawal and . . . ensur[ing] that the Soviets' political, military, and other costs remain[ed] high while the occupation continue[d]."[79] The early expansion in aid to the rebels suggests that Reagan was willing to do much more than Carter to defeat the Soviets in Afghanistan.

In tandem with the Reagan administration's evident desire to back the Afghan rebels, Congress lent strong support. Members of the legislative branch even pushed some aid increases. Representative Charles Wilson in particular played an outsized role in increasing the aid budget for the Afghan resistance. In 1983, Wilson agreed to support a host of unrelated measures important to his colleagues on the House Appropriations Committee in exchange for their approval of an additional $40 million for the mujahedeen. Later, in 1984, Wilson set aside a further $50 million for Operation Cyclone, bringing total aid to about $130 million.[80] This increase dovetailed nicely with the administration's own preferred strategy.

Still, the Reagan administration waited almost a year, until 1985, before expanding the CIA's program for three reasons. First and foremost, it feared that an increase in aid could antagonize the Soviet Union into attacking Pakistan.[81] This fear was particularly strongly held by Zia Ul-Haq, the president of Pakistan. Because Zia's government played a key role in the distribution of American-supplied weapons in Afghanistan, it was nearly impossible for Reagan to offer the mujahedeen more and better weapons without Pakistani consent. Second, some administration officials expressed concern that if the United States increased the flow of weapons to Afghanistan, some of those weapons would eventually reach America's enemies in the Middle East.[82] Lastly, members of the intelligence community, including CIA Deputy Director John McMahon, did not think the mujahedeen could win against the Soviets, and they therefore questioned the merits of sinking ever-greater resources into the Afghan conflict.[83] Based on these three considerations, Reagan at first held off expanding the Afghan program. Eventually, in December 1982, Reagan sided with Casey and Iklé, who both advocated sending better weapons, and he authorized the CIA to deliver "bazookas, mortars, grenade launchers, mines, and recoilless rifles . . . of Soviet manufacture."[84] Thereafter, in 1985, the Reagan administration asked Congress to double funding for Operation Cyclone to $250 million; Congress responded by appropriating $450 million for the Afghan rebels.[85]

"A $250- Million 'Covert' Aid Program Can't Really Be Covert"

Even though Reagan approved the dramatic growth in American assistance to the Afghan rebels, he initially chose to preserve the "plausible deniability" of the CIA's involvement with the mujahedeen.[86] At first glance it may seem strange for Reagan to keep the CIA's activities in Afghanistan covert. But, as discussed above, there were concerns of Soviet retaliation against Pakistan for overt US assistance, and Pakistan's President Zia objected to an overt program. The idea that the Soviets might attack Pakistan if provoked was propagated by John McMahon, CIA deputy director for operations (1978–81) and deputy director of central intelligence (1982–86), as well as Edward Juchniewicz, CIA assistant deputy director of operations, who both felt that if the United States publicly admitted to implementing a policy that resulted in the deaths of Soviet soldiers, a Soviet military response looked probable.[87]

Like McMahon, Zia believed that to openly acknowledge the CIA's role in Afghanistan would be to risk a Soviet attack. But besides the specter of Soviet aggression, President Zia had two additional reasons for wanting Operation Cyclone to remain covert. First, the Pakistani public harbored deeply anti-American views at the time, creating a likelihood of domestic political consequences if Zia worked publicly with the CIA.[88] Second, the Soviets portrayed their intervention in Afghanistan as an effort to save the country from turmoil created by capitalist countries.[89] Pakistani officials thought it unwise to give this propaganda any kind of credibility. In 1986, at which point the program's "plausible deniability" had virtually disappeared,[90] Zia allowed the program to become overt with the introduction of Stinger missiles.

But covert action could still improve America's reputation for resolve vis-à-vis the Soviet Union because Moscow and regional American allies would draw inferences about US resolve from the ever-greater resources expended on Operation Cyclone. Hence, the covert operation still allowed Reagan to signal resolve to both Middle East allies and the USSR.[91] Such inferences naturally resulted because American assistance to the mujahedeen was an open secret on the international stage. Early in Reagan's term, Egypt's President Anwar Sadat had stated in a television interview that the United States had purchased Egyptian arms to send to rebels in Afghanistan. Sadat's revelation confirmed Soviet accusations that Washington was helping the mujahedeen.[92]

The news of Reagan's 1982 decision to provide the mujahedeen with more advanced weaponry broke in the *New York Times* in 1983.[93] By 1984, several newspaper articles noted American assistance to Afghan rebels had reached $280 million.[94] Although this figure may be an overestimate, it illustrates that the escalation of American efforts against the Soviets in Afghanistan had become, for all intents and purposes, public knowledge.[95] By 1985, more stories chronicled the "skyrocket[ing]" aid offered to the mujahedeen.[96] It was also in 1985 that, according to the *Chicago Tribune*, Richard Armitage and William Schneider Jr. told Congress that the Reagan administration had "shifted its policy and will now openly support Moslem insurgents in Afghanistan."[97] Mohammed Nabi Salehi, an Afghan mujahedeen representative, at the same time testified to Congress about how the United States was supplying weapons to the Afghan rebels.[98] The introduction of Stingers in 1986 may have been the end of plausible US deniability, but in reality the ever-growing American assistance to the mujahedeen was common knowledge.[99] The media also openly debated American aid to the mujahedeen. Some journalists also called for a program of overt aid.[100] Given the level of information about the CIA's work in Afghanistan that had become public, it would be unimaginable that the Soviets were not aware of Reagan's support for the mujahedeen. Indeed, a 1984 CIA report noted that Soviet intelligence frequently used American media reports to learn about covert aid to the Afghan rebels.[101]

Domestically, at least, Reagan paid a price for not previously publicizing the full scale of his efforts in Afghanistan. In a September 1981 poll conducted by *Time* magazine of a national sample of registered voters, 42 percent of respondents believed that Reagan was "too soft" on the Soviets for their invasion of Afghanistan, only 4 percent believed he was "too hard," while 28 percent believed he was "just right" on the issue.[102] Both Reagan and the American people wanted to do more to fight against the Soviet Union and to provide military aid to the rebel forces for expanded operations.[103]

NSDD 75: "Rebuild[ing] the Credibility"

National Security Decision Directives (NSDDs) enumerate policies, policy objectives, and, most importantly, the rationale behind America's national security strategy.[104] These documents evidence how, as the dispositional theory would predict, Reagan chose to offer considerable assistance to the mujahedeen in order to improve America's reputation for resolve. One of the earliest NSDDs addressing Afghanistan, NSDD 75, was signed on January 17, 1983. It says American policy should keep maximum pressure on Moscow for withdrawal and ensure that the Soviets' political, military, and other costs remain high while the occupation continues.[105]

Reagan's directive radically altered American policy. No longer would the United States seek to simply "harass" Soviet forces in Afghanistan as under

Carter;[106] instead it would endeavor to compel withdrawal from Afghanistan. In light of the ideological underpinnings of the Reagan Doctrine and the Cold War rivalry between the United States and the Soviet Union, the desire to evict Soviet forces from Afghanistan might have been expected regardless of Reagan's concern for America's reputation for resolve.[107] However, other sections of NSDD 75 indicate that Reagan found reputational reasons for engaging in Afghanistan.

In NSDD 75's section "The Third World," Reagan expresses his desire to create a strong reputation for steadfastness:

> The U.S. must rebuild the credibility of its commitment to resist Soviet encroachment on U.S. interests and those of its Allies and friends, and to support effectively those Third World states that are willing to resist Soviet pressures or oppose Soviet initiatives hostile to the United States, or are special targets of Soviet policy. The U.S. effort in the Third World must involve an important role for security assistance and foreign military sales, as well as readiness to use U.S. military forces where necessary to protect vital interests and support endangered Allies and friends.[108]

The section begins by establishing the restoration of American credibility as a policy priority. This first sentence leaves no doubt that Reagan sought to use conflicts in Asia, Africa, Latin America, and elsewhere to strengthen America's reputation for steadfastness. The document then explains that, to bolster "the credibility of its commitments" to states in the developing world, Washington must provide "security assistance and [conduct] foreign military sales" to demonstrate that the United States would not cede the so-called periphery to the Soviet Union.[109]

NSDD 75 demonstrates Reagan's thinking regarding the status of America's reputation for resolve: First, Reagan thought Carter had damaged the United States' reputation, as evidenced by his choice of the word "rebuild" instead of a word like "strengthen" to describe the administration's policy objective. Second, the NSDD intimates that Reagan thought America should rebuild its reputation by effectively "support[ing] those Third World states that are willing to resist Soviet pressure."[110] Put simply, the way to rebuild America's reputation for resolve was to show resolve in Third World conflicts. To this end, NSDD 75 called for transferring weapons and material assistance in order to enhance the ability of Third World states to defend against Soviet pressure, and to use force directly where vital interests were endangered. Overall, NSDD 75 reveals that Reagan was concerned about building a strong reputation for resolve in Third World disputes.

Although the directive refers to "rebuild[ing] the credibility of [US] commitments" to support "Third World states," it does not mention Afghanistan. The paragraph immediately following this does, however, in its discussion of the "weaknesses and vulnerabilities" in the "Soviet Empire." This paragraph instructs the United States to "keep maximum pressure on Moscow"[111] to withdraw from Afghanistan, thus implying that pressuring Afghanistan was important to affirming America's steadfastness in Third World conflicts and in "maximizing restraining leverage over Soviet behavior."[112]

NSDD 166: From "Harass[ment]" to "Defeat"

Reagan stepped up pressure on the Soviet forces in Afghanistan on March 27, 1985, when he signed NSDD 166. This directive was part of a massive expansion of Operation Cyclone, which grew out of a policy review that started in late 1984.[113] That same year, Casey visited Pakistan to talk to officials about a significant increase in aid to the mujahedeen. Having received Pakistan's consent to the new aid, Casey advocated during the review process that the administration escalate the conflict in Afghanistan.[114]

In January 1985, the National Security Planning Group (NSPG) received intelligence reports from Moscow that the Politburo was worried that Soviet forces had become less effective, and that key officials in the Soviet government wanted to withdraw. However, hard-liners in the Politburo carried out a final intensification of the conflict in an effort to attain victory within two years. To ensure the Soviets did not succeed, Reagan administration officials persuaded him to offer more weapons to the rebels. With the strong encouragement of both Shultz and Casey, Reagan signed NSDD 166 in March 1985.

The directive affirmed the principles of NSDD 75, stating, "The ultimate goal of [American] policy is the removal of Soviet forces from Afghanistan and the restoration of its independent status."[115] However, acknowledging this was not a goal to be easily attained, the directive therefore elaborated a number of "interim objectives."[116] One was to "show firmness of purpose in deterring Soviet aggression in the Third World."[117] The directive says, "Our support of the Afghanistan resistance demonstrates our commitment to resisting Soviet aggression." Reagan thus indicated his belief that the United States could gain a stronger reputation for resolve through firmness in Afghanistan. He explained that the United States could not withhold support to the rebels because it could damage the US reputation for resolve, among other reasons. The directive indicates Reagan's belief that Afghanistan would affect how America was perceived in other Third World conflicts: "Withdrawal of that support for the Afghan resistance would send a signal to the Soviets and to anti-Soviet insurgencies in Central America, Africa, and Asia that our purpose in standing up to Soviet imperialism was not firm."[118]

Reagan believed that maintaining a reputation for resolve would become even more crucial as arms control negotiations resumed. As he explains in the NSDD: "Our support [to the Afghan rebels] demonstrates to the Soviets that we will continue to resist low-level Soviet aggression while pursuing arms control. With the resumption of arms control talks in Geneva, it is important to signal to the Soviets that we will continue to oppose unacceptable Soviet behavior in other fields."[119]

The contrast between Reagan's policy toward Afghanistan, as described by NSDD 166, and Carter's approach was noted by Milt Bearden, a career CIA official who, in 1985, became deputy director of the CIA's Soviet–East European Division: "The CIA's covert action role in Afghanistan dating back to the Carter administration called for 'harassing' the Soviets, not driving them out." According to Bearden, with this NSDD, Reagan was "upping the ante," as he had just "rewritten the ground rules." Similarly, Reagan administration State Department official Peter W. Rodman argues that NSDD 166 was "a clear policy of seeking to defeat the Soviet Union . . . and [to] force a Soviet withdrawal."[120]

NSDD 166 proved a turning point in administration policy. Funding for the mujahedeen significantly increased thereafter, as the Reagan administration asked for amounts in excess of $450 million in 1986 and "reprogram[med] more than $200 million from an unspent Defense Department account."[121] The CIA also began to share intelligence with local allies, including Pakistan.[122]

Sending the Stingers

The final reformulation of the CIA's program occurred in April 1986, when Reagan authorized the supply of American Stinger missiles to the rebels in Afghanistan. At the time, Stingers were America's most advanced surface-to-air missile and were well suited for shooting down Soviet helicopters.[123] This was a significant decision for the administration, in part because it would remove the last pretense of plausible deniability—an inability for Moscow to verify that America was supplying the mujahedeen.[124] Since the United States was the only country that could supply a large number of Stingers to the Afghan rebels, American involvement would become undeniable.[125] The timing of Reagan's decision to introduce Stingers can be understood by the evolution of the conflict during the period starting when Mikhail Gorbachev became general secretary of the Central Committee of the Communist Party of the Soviet Union in March 1985, through spring 1986.

When Gorbachev came to power, some in the Reagan foreign policy team hoped the new general secretary would change course in Afghanistan and withdraw. Those hopes were dampened when Gorbachev agreed with hard-liners in the Politburo to escalate the conflict in a final effort to win the war.[126] The Soviet decision to escalate made the mujahedeen's prospects appear bleak. Beginning in 1984 the Soviet Union deployed an increasing number of Spetsnaz soldiers—Soviet Special Forces—to Afghanistan.[127] So extreme was the effect on the mujahedeen's prospects in 1985 that a Pentagon intelligence study questioned the viability of the Afghan resistance.[128] However, even as the Soviets appeared increasingly successful to Washington, it became doubtful that

Gorbachev's Moscow would ever attack Pakistan.[129] The changes in the conflict in Afghanistan, Lundberg argues, put the rebels at risk of defeat and persuaded members in the Reagan administration, like Iklé, to advocate for supplying the Stingers.

On February 26, 1986, the Planning and Coordination Group unanimously recommended to Reagan that the United States supply Stinger missiles to the mujahedeen.[130] In March, Reagan formally approved the proposal and directed that missiles be sent.[131] The US public welcomed the decision. As opinion polls consistently showed, the American people, unaware of the full scope of covert operations in Afghanistan, wished to see the president place more pressure on the Soviets. For instance, on the eve of the decision to supply the Stingers, in April 1986, a poll by the *Roper Report* using a national sample of adults found that 40 percent of Americans believed that Reagan was "too soft" on the Soviets for their invasion of Afghanistan, while only 2 percent believed he was "too tough," and 32 percent believed he was "just right."

Because many documents pertaining to Afghanistan are still classified, it remains unclear what role Reagan played in the initiation of the Stinger idea or the subsequent debate. However, there exists some evidence to suggest that Reagan was partial to the idea to send Stingers. In his autobiography, Shultz recalls discussing Stinger missiles with Reagan and Casey and that Reagan raised no objections.[132] Reagan may have had no objections because, even prior to becoming president, Reagan considered sending American-made missiles to Afghanistan. Two weeks after the Soviet invasion of Afghanistan on January 9, 1980, Reagan gave a campaign speech in Pensacola, Florida, in which he argued that America should supply anti-aircraft missiles to rebels in Afghanistan.[133] That same week, Reagan told the Exchange Club in Charleston, South Carolina, "with our treaty with Pakistan, I feel we ought to be funneling weapons through there that can be delivered to those freedom fighters in Afghanistan to fight for their own freedom. That would include those shoulder-launched, heat-seeking missiles that could knock down helicopter gunships that the Soviets are using against [the rebels]."[134] During the same speech Reagan criticized Carter for a "lack of any contingency plan, of ways for sending signals to the Soviet Union" and continues by saying "I think it's time for the free world to put up some signs that would make [Moscow] take another look at the speedometer as to how fast they're going."[135] Reagan's remarks in Pensacola and Charleston suggest that, even before becoming president, Reagan thought it necessary to signal American resolve by stepping up US assistance to the Afghan rebels.[136]

Afghanistan, Resolve, and Arms Control Negotiations

As clearly revealed from NSDD 166, for Reagan, disputes over regional issues like Afghanistan could not be sidelined just because the United States was engaged in arms control talks with the Soviet Union. Despite progress with Gorbachev in arms control negotiations, Reagan never took Afghanistan off of the negotiating table or out of the public eye. Transcripts from the historic Geneva Summit on November 19 and 20, 1985 illustrate the linkage between Afghanistan, concerns about resolve, and arms negotiations. This summit, and the language of NSDD 166, demonstrate that despite the importance of arms control negotiations, it was even more important to Reagan to continue to show resolve against Soviet activity.

Instead of entering into immediate discussions about nuclear weapons, Reagan chose to discuss the sources of mistrust between the United States and the USSR, citing Soviet expansionism and the Soviet Union's declared interest in creating a "one world communist state"[137] as the "basis"[138] of Washington's mistrust. Reagan then directly linked Soviet behavior in the Third World to arms control by saying "if we can go on the basis of trust, then those mountains of weapons will disappear."[139] By clearly connecting Soviet activity in the Third World with the arms race, Reagan showed that the United States remained resolved to challenge Moscow in Afghanistan.

Gorbachev responded that he did not want to spend much time debating these issues with Reagan, as that would only breed further mistrust between the two countries.[140] But the general secretary nonetheless tried to assure Reagan that the Soviet Union did no more than support progressive movements with indigenous origins.[141] He said it would be absurd to think that Moscow had the power to topple governments in so many countries.[142] Reagan, instead of moving on as Gorbachev requested, brought up Afghanistan specifically. The president effectively said the Soviets were not supporting, but imposing, Communism. Specifically, Reagan noted, "Their 'leader' was supplied by the Soviet Union. Actually he was their second choice, since the first one did not work out as they wished. The Soviet invasion has created three million refugees."[143] While Reagan walked away from Geneva with agreement on some points, the Afghanistan issue stood unresolved. Reagan remained unyielding and, with these comments, made clear the United States had no intention of changing its stance.

Reagan's public statements during 1985 and 1986 further suggest that his strong desire for an arms control treaty with Moscow would not soften his tone on Afghanistan. For example, Reagan issued statements every year acknowledging the anniversary of the Soviet invasion of Afghanistan. In the 1985 statement, Reagan said, "To demoralize and defeat the Afghans, the Soviets have unleashed the full force of their modern weaponry. Poison gas has been razed down from the air upon Afghan settlements. Massive attack helicopters have been used against mere villages. Hundreds of thousands of innocent civilians have been injured or killed, and countless tiny mines have been strewn across the countryside to maim and blind Afghan children."[144] Similarly, soon after the arms control summit in Reykjavik in October 1986, Reagan issued another statement that gave no hints of softening the administration's policy. Reagan accused the Soviets of engaging in a "brutal onslaught" and said, "The Afghan people did not invite the Soviets to bomb and burn their villages, to maim and orphan their children, to rewrite their history, and to spurn their religion and culture. They did not invite the Soviets to destroy their fields and lay waste to vast portions of their country."[145] Even as the personal relations between the two leaders thawed, Reagan made clear that Moscow should not interpret the new détente as a softening of America's position.

In September 1987, Gorbachev communicated to Shultz that the Soviets would be withdrawing from Afghanistan within five months to a year. The USSR signed the Geneva Accords on April 14, 1988, formalizing its withdrawal.

Summary

There is a stark difference in how Reagan and Carter approached the Soviet crisis in Afghanistan. Carter did not give much weight to reputational concerns, and he furnished the mujahedeen with limited assistance as a means to "harass" the Soviets. Reagan, on the other hand, made it a policy priority to improve America's reputation for resolve through challenging the Soviets. He escalated the conflict significantly, providing advanced American weaponry and a more than sixteen-fold increase in annual assistance to the rebels. Furthermore, as stated in the NSDDs, withdrawing aid from the mujahedeen was considered unacceptable on the basis that doing so would cause America's allies to doubt Reagan's willingness to help Third World resistance movements.[146] Instead, NSDDs 75 and 166 laid out a strategy for using the war in Afghanistan to enhance America's reputation for resolve in the region.

THE INTERVENTION IN LEBANON AND THE INVASION OF GRENADA

Reagan saw both the intervention in Lebanon and the invasion of Grenada through a prism of US credibility. The documents reveal that, while the invasion of Grenada was already in motion by the time the US Marines in Lebanon were attacked, Reagan considered both episodes to be tests of US reputation for resolve. Moreover, the conventional wisdom that Reagan willingly withdrew from Lebanon is inaccurate. Despite calls to pull the Marines back from Lebanon, and to abort the Grenada invasion, Reagan continued to cite concerns about the need for the United States to demonstrate its determination to use military force, even in places that did not affect vital interests. Finally, throughout the crisis, Reagan was under conflicting pressures from his top two advisors. Weinberger was against keeping the Marines in Lebanon, consistent with his low self-monitor disposition, and was also not enthusiastic about invading Grenada. In contrast, the high self-monitor Shultz saw reputation for resolve as critical in both crises.

"We Are More Resolved Than Ever"

American involvement in Lebanon was related to a US-brokered ceasefire in the Lebanese Civil War.[147] The Marines were initially deployed into Lebanon as part of a multinational force (MNF), created in August 1982 to help implement the agreement between the Palestinian Liberation Organization (PLO) and Israel that ended their involvement with the progovernment and pro-Syrian sides of the Lebanese Civil War. The MNF was to aid the Lebanese military in evacuating the PLO, Syrian forces, and other foreign combatants; to assist in establishing a sovereign independent Lebanon; and to aid in securing Israel's northern border. The first deployment lasted less than a month, as the Marines successfully completed the evacuation of PLO militants in the summer of 1983. Shortly thereafter, the prospect for peace in Lebanon took a significant blow when Bashir Gemayel, president-elect of Lebanon (and an ally of Israel and the United States) was assassinated. This prompted the Israel Defense Forces (IDF) to move into Lebanon. The situation deteriorated quickly, and when Bashir's brother, Amin, was elected president on September 21, he requested that the MNF be redeployed into Beirut.

The Marines were redeployed on September 29 as part of the MNF, under orders to "establish a presence" and to "establish [an] environment that will permit the Lebanese Armed Forces [LAF] to carry out its responsibilities in the Beirut area, and be prepared to protect U.S. forces and conduct retrograde and withdrawal operations from the area."[148] The US public was divided on whether to support Israel and whether to send troops to Lebanon to quell the unrest there. Before the multinational intervention, 40 percent of the public approved of Israel's invasion of the country, while 35 percent disapproved.[149] The public's response to Reagan's decision to send the Marines was also somewhat inconsistent. A month after the Marines had been sent, 41 percent of the public approved keeping them in Lebanon, while 50 percent wanted them withdrawn.[150] Nevertheless, 74 percent of the public believed that the United States had a vital interest in keeping Lebanon out of Communist hands.[151]

The risks to the Marines in Beirut became obvious when, on April 18, 1983, a suicide bomber drove a pickup truck loaded with explosives into the US embassy. The bombing killed sixty-three people, including seventeen Americans. Reagan responded to the embassy bombing with "stiffened resolve and a renewed urgency to see the peace process move forward. Following the attack he declared, 'Because of this latest crime, we're more resolved than even to help achieve the urgent and total withdrawal of all . . . foreign forces.' "[152]

Nevertheless, it soon became clear to Reagan and his advisors that the prospects for peace in Lebanon were remote, and that Syria would be willing to pull its forces out of Lebanon only in response to a considerable show of American force. The IDF decision in July to withdraw some of its forces and redeploy southward allowed Syrian and PLO forces to gain momentum and power. These events left Reagan with a tough choice, as he put it in his diary on September 10, between "getting out or enlarging our mission."[153]

"Lebanon: A Litmus Test for U.S. Credibility and Commitment"

Reagan's concerns about US credibility and resolve motivated many of his actions related to Lebanon, it appears, and were shared by Reagan's national security advisor, Robert "Bud" McFarland, and Secretary of State Shultz, but not by Secretary of Defense Weinberger, which is consistent with the theory's prediction. The memoranda prior to the intervention indicated that the United States sought greater opportunities in Lebanon through a military rather than a diplomatic campaign. Reagan and Shultz saw Lebanon as providing an important opportunity for the United States to signal its presence and establish its credibility with Middle East allies. In the language of NSDD 64, "Next Steps in Lebanon," Reagan notes:

> By taking the lead in obtaining the withdrawal of Israeli and other foreign forces from Lebanon and tangibly demonstrating our willingness to promote the security of that troubled country, we will earn the respect of the Arab world and show that U.S. leadership can make a decisive difference in promoting peace and security in the Middle East.[154]

Indeed, the notion of Lebanon as a test case can be gleaned most directly from a paper prepared by Reagan's NSC staff, titled "Lebanon: A Litmus Test for U.S. Credibility and Commitment."[155] The document is dedicated to outlining the "current problem of U.S. credibility" and how US actions in Lebanon posed a clear test of US resolve. Specifically, the memo explains that "since our disengagement from Vietnam, there has been a steady and perceptible erosion of U.S. credibility in the Middle East." These perceptions, the memo continues, were intensified by the Soviet invasion of Afghanistan and the failed Iranian hostage crisis. "The effect of this erosion has been repeatedly manifested in the private statements of moderate leaders in the region to U.S. leaders." The memo further claims that "the extent of Syrian intransigence in withdrawing its forces from Lebanon and the degree of Syrian intervention on the Lebanese crisis are directly proportional to the *perceived credibility of the United States as it seeks to obtain its stated objectives in Lebanon*."[156]

The rest of the memo makes the case for what the United States should do to counter Soviet actions in Syria. The memo concludes, "If we are to maintain our credibility in Lebanon and with the important Arab states in the Middle East beyond the Levant, we need to stand up to Syrian intervention in Lebanon and underscore our willingness to use military power in support of the President's stated objectives." The NSC memo further states that it does not advocate a large-scale military intervention in Lebanon. Rather, "the Syrians must be persuaded by a clear demonstration of our military power that we will support the GOL [government of Lebanon] in the face of Syrian subversion and intervention." The NSC was aware of the risks of a signal of resolve: "The risk with this 'signalling,' or what may become incremental demonstrations of power, is that it will not be understood or that it will be discounted by the Syrians and Soviets. There are at least even odds that the SARG [government of Syria] will show more flexibility in a negotiated settlement if they are persuaded that the U.S. will defend its stated interests in Lebanon."[157]

The NSC raised another possibility of "using major military force to compel Syrian disengagement from the current crisis and force the withdrawal of all foreign forces from Lebanon. . . . Were we to succeed in forcing Syrian withdrawal—and in obtaining a simultaneous Israeli withdrawal—we would be seen as having scored a major success in restoring U.S. credibility." Yet, the memo deemed this course of action unlikely, because the United States was "not ready to take such a major step owing to Congressional opposition and the reluctance of our MNF partners to join such an undertaking."[158]

Indeed, Congress pressed Reagan to pull the Marines out of Lebanon, or at a minimum, limit the time that the Marines could be deployed there. To appease congressional leaders, on September 20, 1983, Reagan agreed to permit the Marines to stay for another eighteen months. This time limit was suggested by O'Neill, whose support for the mission guaranteed the resolution's passage in the House. Still, in exchange for the extension, the Democrats had forced Reagan to promise that he would not try to expand the Marines' role, relocate them, or otherwise change their mission without congressional approval.[159]

Nevertheless, Reagan understood that the decision to stay was not a popular one. On September 21, 1983, a mere month before the Beirut bombing, Reagan's chief strategist, Richard Wirthlin, sent a memo to Reagan's top advisors briefing them on public support for keeping troops in Lebanon. Wirthlin noted that since early September, "approval of the president's handing of the situation in Lebanon has remained stable with 32% approving. A majority of Americans disapprove (56%) while the remaining 12% express 'no opinion.' These attitudes, he noted, are nearly identical to those toward the situation in El Salvador. Wirthlin also warned that over the past week, there had been a "gradual loss of support" for the mission. Specifically, "almost all Americans do not like our troops taking hostile fire without recourse. Either they want to pull them out (45%) or they want them reinforced (42%)." Importantly, however, Wirthlin noted, "when faced with the prospect of Soviet-allied Syria taking control of Lebanon slightly less than half of those who initially wanted the Marines withdrawn change their mind. This translates into 24% of adult Americans who want the Marines out of Lebanon regardless of the ramifications." This suggested to Reagan and his advisors that if Lebanon were seen through the prism of a global contest between the United States and the Soviet

Union over influence in the region, the American public would be willing to keep the Marines in Lebanon.

In addition to sending the Marines to Lebanon to demonstrate US resolve, on September 20, 1983, Reagan sent National Security Advisor MacFarlane to Beirut to inform Assad that the battleship *New Jersey* would soon reach Lebanese waters. All three men—Reagan, Shultz, and McFarlane—saw a tight connection between the decision to send the USS *New Jersey* and, two days later, the warring factions' agreement to a negotiated cease-fire in Geneva. Indeed, in a public statement, Reagan noted: "We ordered the battleship *New Jersey* to join our naval forces offshore. Without even firing them, the threat of its 16-inch guns silenced those who once fired down on our marines from the hills, and they're a good part of the reason we suddenly had a cease-fire."[160]

Notwithstanding this progress, the situation was a morass, and Reagan was forced to decide whether to continue to risk further costs by remaining in Lebanon. As Shultz soberly stated in a memo to the president dated October 5, 1983, titled "Our Middle East Policy," Reagan's options amounted to putting US reputation on the line by engaging with the Syrians in the hope of achieving a limited but meaningful success (i.e., preventing the Syrians from dominating the outcome of the Lebanese Civil War), or rejecting these costs and accepting a Syria-controlled Lebanon. Consistent with my theory's predictions, Reagan chose the first option—engaging US reputation for resolve in the process.

Reagan's key advisors were in significant disagreement over whether the Marines should stay in Lebanon. On October 18, in a NSC meeting, Weinberger raised concern about the presence of the Marines in Lebanon and made a strong case to "redeploy" them to ships offshore. Shultz and McFarlane objected; Shultz's objections can be found in a detailed memo he wrote to the president on October 13, titled "Our Strategy in Lebanon and the Middle East," in which he detailed the adverse consequences of pulling out of Lebanon, including to US reputation for resolve and credibility. It begins by noting that the cease-fire in Lebanon, while a "major achievement of our diplomacy," would result in "the struggle in Lebanon . . . shift[ing] to the political arena. This phase will be as difficult and as potentially dangerous to our interests as the situation before the ceasefire." The memo makes it clear that Shultz was advocating for the Marines to stay, arguing that "[a] satisfactory outcome to the Lebanese political negotiations should be our priority objective, since so much depends on it—our standing in the Middle East and our prospects for bringing the Marines home in honorable circumstances."[161]

President Reagan endorsed Shultz's views; contrary to the advice of Weinberger, he decided to keep the Marines in Lebanon, supported by the USS *New Jersey*. Similarly, in a letter to the governor of New Hampshire, Reagan asked rhetorically whether there is any way "the U.S. or the Western World for that matter can stand by & see the Middle East becomes part of the Communist bloc? Without it our West Europe neighbors would inevitably become Finlandized and we'd be alone in the world."[162]

On October 23, 1983, a suicide bomber detonated a hijacked truck containing explosives near the Marines' barracks in Beirut, killing 231 Americans. In the NSPG meeting the day following, Reagan observed, "This is an obvious attempt to run us out of Lebanon.... The first thing I want to do is to find out who did it and go after them with everything we've got."[163] Similarly, in his memoirs, McFarlane recalls, "What the President did not want to do [after the bombing], above all, was to pull out of Lebanon immediately, to be seen as running away as a result of the tragedy that had taken place. To the contrary, the barracks bombing seemed to strengthen his resolve to stay."[164] By the end of October, Reagan ordered the MNF to "harden" militarily, which meant significant US troop reinforcements. At a press conference on October 24, 1983, Reagan declared that his administration would remain steadfast in its belief that the MNF's near-term withdrawal was not an option, as this would negatively affect US credibility and lead to the mission's unnecessary failure. However, by October 1983, the possibility of completing the mission's objectives had diminished. Still, Reagan continued to argue that US "actions in Lebanon are in the cause of world peace," reminding Congress and the public of the administration's commitment to Lebanon.[165]

By 1983, the public was completely divided: 45 percent believed that sending the Marines into Lebanon was a mistake, 45 percent did not believe so, and the rest had no opinion.[166] Reagan thus met with skeptical but not entirely coherent public opinion about the issue. Given this inconsistency, he continued to use the military to deter Communist aggression and to maintain America's international reputation for resolve. But as the situation in Lebanon proved to be a quagmire, the more the public grew tired of the deployment. By October 1983, only 28 percent of the public approved of the way Reagan had been handling the situation, while 59 percent disapproved.[167] The October 23 bombing caused a rallying effect that allowed Reagan's approval ratings to rise in November and December.[168] However, the bombing did not influence the public's perceptions of performance in Lebanon; in November, only 34 percent approved of Reagan's handling of the situation,[169] and by January approval had fallen back down to 28 percent.[170] The rallying effect that Reagan had gained from the bombing and from the invasion of Grenada (more on this below) had disappeared by February 1984.

Reagan's public refusal to remove the Marines from Lebanon continued until the MNF's final days. In the months after the bombing, Reagan tried to maintain the mission in Lebanon because he viewed it as an important signal of US resolve. But with the collapse of the Gemayel government and the chaos that followed, Reagan was under pressure from his advisors and Republican congressional leaders to agree to a withdrawal. In the words of Pemberton, "Reagan's Lebanon policy had as much to do with his self-image of 'standing tall' and not 'cutting and running' as it did with a close analysis of the United States national interest."[171]

"The Events in Lebanon and Grenada, though Oceans Apart, Are Closely Related"

On October 19, 1983, a radical Marxist group inside Grenada murdered Prime Minister Maurice Bishop in a Cuba-inspired coup. A violent Marxist military council trained by Cuba put itself in charge, shot and jailed Bishop's supporters, enacted its own martial law, and imposed a shoot-on-sight, twenty-four-hour curfew. Those events also threatened about a thousand Americans present in Grenada, many of whom were students at St. George's School of Medicine. Two days after the Beirut barracks attack, on October 25, some five thousand American troops charged the shores of Grenada in Operation Urgent Fury, the largest US military operation since Vietnam.[172] In a NSPG meeting on Grenada and Lebanon on October 23, the NSC staff described for McFarlane the mission of the Joint Special Operation Command "to secure the Governor General, prison, and air fields." The operation was a decisive military victory, although nineteen Americans were killed during the invasion, along with over one hundred people from Cuba and Grenada. Beyond a rescue of American students, the invasion of Grenada was intended to be a costly signal that America was resolved against Communism, as well as a means of restoring American confidence in the military's ability to conduct successful military missions post-Vietnam.

The close proximity—two days—between the Lebanon bombing and Reagan's decision to invade Grenada raises the question whether the invasion of Grenada was a face-saving countermove to the tragedy in Beirut. There is some evidence to suggest, however, that preparations for the invasion of Grenada preceded the Lebanon bombing: Reagan's diary of Friday, October 21, contains the following passage: "About 4 A.M. or so I was awakened by Bud McFarlane. I joined him & George S. [Shultz] in the living room. We were on the phone with Wash. about the Grenada situation. I've OK'd an outright invasion in response to a request by 6 other Caribbean nations including Jamaica & Barbados." The next day, Reagan wrote, "about 2:30 in the morning awakened again: this time with the tragic news."[173] This suggests that Reagan had authorized the invasion prior to the Lebanon bombing.

There is also evidence to suggest that the events in Lebanon pushed Reagan to rush the Grenada invasion plans. Put differently, Reagan had planned to invade Grenada prior to the bombing in Beirut, but the timing of the invasion, and Reagan's determination to act sooner rather than later, changed as a result of the Beirut bombing. First, immediately following the bombing, NSC staff stated, "At the NSPG, we should also seek to point out that last night's events in Lebanon increase the need to take action [in Grenada]."[174] This suggests that the NSC felt a sense of urgency to take military action to demonstrate American resolve. Second, the Joint Chiefs of Staff believed that the invasion plans were put together too hastily. According to Shultz and McFarlane, in the NSPG meetings on Lebanon and Grenada, Weinberger continued to resist the invasion plan, arguing that there had to be far greater preparation and a much larger force before an operation could begin. Weinberger, backed by the Joint Chiefs, pushed hard on Reagan, making clear his preference to delay the invasion in favor of an ultimatum, and for the president to reconsider his decision to proceed with the rescue mission. "The debate was intense," Shultz recalls, but "President Reagan held firm."[175]

Weinberger's memoirs, however, indicate that military planning with regard to Grenada had already started before the Lebanon bombing. After the bombing, Reagan rushed to put these plans into action, and his final decision to invade took place following the attack. As Weinberger explains, "The practical requirements and logistics of such an action are very large, and the planning time required is normally far longer than the few days we had. . . . But all these [military] considerations were presented to the President, together with the risks involved."[176] Weinberger and Chairman of the Joint Chiefs of Staff John W. Vessey discussed the plans with Reagan on October 22, noting the small window of time to gather intelligence. According to Weinberger, "The president was aware of the difficulties, but generally seemed to me to be willing to accept the risks."[177] The following day, Weinberger writes, the president "polled each Chief of Staff and each told him the plan would work; but each said he was concerned about the lack of time to get intelligence, and to rehearse and practice several of the more difficult aspects of the operation." Still, Weinberger continues, "by now, it was clear to me from comments and questions that the President had decided to move into Grenada."[178] That same day, Reagan gave the green light for the invasion. Weinberger gave a similar account: "We were planning that very weekend for the actions in Grenada to overcome the anarchy that was down there and the potential seizure of American students, and all the memories of the Iranian hostages. We had planned that for Monday morning, and this terrible event [in Lebanon] occurred on Saturday night."[179]

Reagan's public speeches following the invasion also establish a linkage between the events in Lebanon and the Grenada invasion. The link, in Reagan's mind, was the Soviet Union, hence he viewed the two events as an opportunity to signal resolve to the Soviets. Thus, his October 27 speech noted: "The events in Lebanon and Grenada, though oceans apart, are closely related. Not only has Moscow assisted and encouraged the violence in both countries, but it provides direct support through a network of surrogates and terrorists."[180]

"Our Days of Weakness Are Over"

The Grenada operation was a clear signal to the Soviets and to Communist governments of Latin America that the United States was willing to send troops even to small and strategically insignificant places like the island of Grenada in order to oppose Communism in Latin America.[181] Soviet and Cuban activities in Grenada concerned Reagan long before the invasion, however.

Even prior to the invasion, the theme of restoring America's image as a strong nation willing to demonstrate resolve through military force dominated Reagan's speeches:

> You can all remember the days of national malaise and international humiliation. Everywhere in the world freedom was in retreat and America's prestige and influence were a low ebb. . . . All this is changing. While we cannot end decades of decay in only 1000 days, we have fundamentally reversed the ominous trends of a few years ago.

Reagan's private and public reasoning following the invasion suggest that he did not view it as just a liberation mission: the US reputation for resolve was a significant factor in his decision. For example, in a phone conversation with the Australian prime minister, Reagan raised his reputational concerns:

> And the next thing I knew over the weekend—I was awakened in the middle of the night—they [the Organization of Eastern Caribbean States] had sent an urgent plea that they were going to contribute whatever military they had. They didn't have enough to do the job and they wanted our help to go in there and straighten this out and reinstitute a democratic government there. . . . I could not see how we could turn down these countries right here that we're trying to help in the Caribbean, and have any credibility left any place in the world. I think anyone, whether it's in America or the Middle East or where, would say, "Well, what the hell, if they turned down a request like that, how can we depend on the United States?" So, I said, "All signals go."[182]

Similarly, in public statements, Reagan explains how reputational concerns motivated him to use force in Grenada:

> We couldn't say no to those six small countries [Caribbean neighbors of Grenada]. We'd have no credibility or standing in the Americas if we did. If it ever became known, which I knew it would, that we had turned them down, few of our friends around the world would trust us completely as an ally again.[183]

A few weeks later, Reagan gave an emotional speech to the Congressional Medal of Honor Society in New York. Aides took pains to tell reporters that he had written it himself. "Our days of weakness are over!" Reagan declared. "Our military forces are back on their feet, and standing tall."[184]

The invasion of Grenada was not announced to the public until after US forces landed. Secrecy allowed US troops the advantage of surprise, and, as Reagan made clear, it also enabled the demonstration of resolve to outside audiences without being constrained by domestic actors (or US allies) who would have objected. As Reagan later explained:

> Frankly, there was another reason I wanted secrecy [for the Grenada invasion]. It was what I call the "post-Vietnam syndrome," the resistance of many in Congress to the use of military force abroad for any reason, because of our nation's experience in Vietnam. . . . We were already running into this phenomenon in our efforts to halt the spread of communism in Central America, and some congressmen were raising the issue of "another Vietnam" in Lebanon while fighting to restrict the president's constitutional powers as commander in chief.[185]

Regardless of whether the invasion was calculated to signal America's resolve, there is little doubt that its success helped Reagan deflect the political consequences of the unpopular Lebanon policy. Wirthlin had been conducting monthly polls when the Beirut bombing occurred and continued to track public opinion during and after the Grenada invasion a few days later. His polls show that Reagan's approval rating dropped dramatically during the forty-eight hours following the Beirut attacks, but it significantly rebounded after the invasion. Most other polls took place only after the Grenada invasion and were thus unable to capture any effect on Reagan's approval ratings.[186] Reagan was aware of this dramatic shift in public opinion. His diary entry from October 27 says, "Success seems to shine on us. . . . The speech must have hit a few nerves. . . . ABC polled 250 people before the speech, the majority were against us. They polled the same people right after the speech & there had been a complete turn-around."[187]

Global public opinion was, however, far from positive. UN member states sought to pass a resolution "deeply deploring" the invasion as a "flagrant violation of international law." More than one hundred member states, and eleven members of the Security Council, voted in favor of the resolution, but it was vetoed by the United States.[188] Reagan was unmoved: "One hundred nations in the United Nations have not agreed with us on just about everything that's come before them where we're involved, and it didn't upset my breakfast at all."

In contrast with Lebanon, Grenada was a domestic public opinion success: 55 percent approved the invasion, while only 34 percent disapproved.[189] By December, 59 percent of the public approved the way Reagan had handled the situation.[190] Ironically, much of the public understood that Reagan had invaded the island nation to show American strength after the bombing in Lebanon had showed weakness; 47 percent of the public believed that the invasion was intended to "show military strength," and 40 percent believed that the invasion was only to show strength and not because it was "really necessary" to go in at that time.[191]

Nevertheless, to manage the concerns of US allies, George Shultz traveled to Europe on October 27 to meet with the British, French, and Italian foreign ministers. All three nations expressed criticism, as did many Latin American countries. On October 28, the United States vetoed the UN Security Council resolution "deeply deploring" the invasion.[192] Shultz writes, "we took a lot of heat over the Grenada operation. We were opposed by the British and the French and many others around Europe and by Congress, particularly before they heard from the folks back home."[193]

In sum, as Hayward contends, "The significance of the Grenada invasion cannot be overstated. . . . The military operation ranked alongside Reagan's firing of the air traffic controllers in 1981 for its sobering effect on world perception of Reagan's toughness. It removed the last lingering doubts in Europe about America's staying power, which, despite Reagan's rhetoric and defense buildup, [had] persisted."[194] Shultz similarly praised the president: "the president was decisive, despite the distraction of our tragedy in Lebanon. He held firm against the Pentagon's desire for more time to prepare. His firmness probably was bolstered by the fact that, by chance, he had been in Augusta with McFarlane and me, two strong supporters of the action."[195]

"The Status Quo Won't Do It"

The invasion of Grenada boosted Reagan's popularity and US reputation for resolve, but the situation in Lebanon continued to deteriorate. Reagan wanted to escalate military operations there and change the rules of engagement. For example, in his diary entry for December 1, 1983, Reagan noted that a portion of the NSC meeting that day was spent on "whether to step up our artillery fire on Druze batteries lobbing shells in the direction of our Marines. So far we haven't done anything. We're a divided group. I happen to believe taking out a few batteries might give them pause to think. Joint Chiefs believe it might drastically alter our mission & lead to major increase in troops in Lebanon."[196]

In preparing for the NSPG meeting on Lebanon on December 1, McFarlane laid it out bluntly to the president. If the United States chose to stick to the May 17 agreement, "we are left with either: doing more of the same and making no progress; being more assertive in both our diplomatic and military moves; or quitting." Moreover, he stated, "your advisors have a basic disagreement on how we should use military power in Lebanon." His talking points to the president laid out three alternatives: first, a gradual withdrawal to offshore positions; second, "to complement our proposed hand-nosed diplomatic initiatives, we can take a more aggressive and assertive stance and use measured military force to convince the Syrians and their surrogates that force will be met with force, if necessary"; or third, "we can rely much more heavily on our military power together with the Israelis and try to force the Syrians out of Lebanon in a military solution." McFarlane argued that, "to make progress on Lebanon toward the objectives you have set and if we are committed to the May 17 agreement . . . the status quo won't do it."[197]

In an attempt to signal US determination, Reagan stepped up the military operations in Lebanon. On December 3, he approved air strikes against Syrian SAM batteries in retaliation for Syrian attacks on US F-14s conducting a reconnaissance mission over Lebanon. McFarlane wrote, "the operation was a failure. . . . Two of our aircraft were shot down," resulting in one death and the capture of another pilot. "It was an embarrassing demonstration of American military ineptitude. . . . The sense of defiance was palpable," McFarlane notes. "I knew it was time to step back and take a hard, rigorous look at the realities of our very ability to forge viable strategy in the Middle East—so determined was Secretary Weinberger's resistance to any use of force at all."[198]

On December 21, 1983, McFarlane gave the president a memo titled "Putting the Marines Back Aboard Ship," explaining that Weinberger wanted to pull the Marines back for safety concerns, while Shultz objected, because "to do this would provide a pretext for the other MNF countries to reduce or withdraw their contingent." McFarlane suggested that Reagan meet separately with Weinberger and with Shultz to figure out how to "minimize the vulnerability of the Marines until the political climate justifies their withdrawal." Then, on December 30, Weinberger sent the president a report by the Joint Chiefs of Staff, recommending a reexamination of alternative means of achieving US objectives in Lebanon, as well as "develop[ing] alternative military recommendations for accomplishing the mission of the USMNF while reducing the risk to the force." The paper noted that the other MNF contributors would likely want to restructure their positions during 1984, and it recommended that the United States should move the US MNF aboard amphibious ships and work to strengthen the Lebanese Armed Forces.[199]

In the meantime, President Reagan had instituted the Long Commission, which investigated the 1983 Beirut barracks bombing. Its report, released on December 20, 1983, blamed the attack on the commanders in Lebanon, and it recommended the immediate withdrawal of the Marines. As a result, the US public and congressional opponents expected that, by the end of 1983, Reagan would announce the MNF's withdrawal. Instead, on December 10, Reagan had said that the Marines would leave only when "internal stability is established and withdrawal of all foreign forces is assured."[200] Moreover, on December 27, the president announced that he would take personal responsibility for the faults listed in the report and any failures resulting from the US intervention in Lebanon, saying: "I do not believe, therefore, that the local commanders on the ground, men who have already suffered quite enough, should be punished for not fully comprehending the nature of today's terrorist threat. If there is to be blame, it properly rests here in this Office and with this President. And I accept responsibility for the bad as well as the good."[201]

Reagan had not given up on success in Lebanon; he further instructed the US MNF contingent to actively defend its position in Beirut militarily and gave no sign that the administration's resolve to remain in Lebanon was weakening. In order to appear resolute in the face of these threats, Rumsfeld proposed a strategy of "leaning somewhat forward." Thus, by December 14, the administration had resumed its military campaign against Syria, which allowed the United States to appear to be advancing in Lebanon, rather than retreating. Carefully orchestrated public visits by US generals and CENTCOM commanders, and increased public training cooperation between the LAF and US military, were geared toward pressuring Syria to enter into negotiations with the implied threat of a near-term offensive or direct conflict with the United States.

This policy also failed to win support from Weinberger and Vessey, who loudly voiced their objections to the provocative move. Weinberger believed that further additions to the rules of engagement would push the United States to the frontline of the dispute between the Syrian and Lebanese factional militias:

> Beirut was an absolutely inevitable outcome of doing what we did, of putting troops in with no mission that could be carried out. There was no agreement on either side of the pullback. You didn't need a buffer force. There's nothing more dangerous than in the middle of a furious prize-fight, inserting a referee in range of both the fighters, both the contestants. That's what we did.[202]

While recognizing the opposition within the administration, Reagan nonetheless signed NSDD 117, which reflected Shultz's plan. It stated, "The decisions directed in NSDD 111 bearing on our diplomatic and military measures for Lebanon [increasing involvement in the civil war and establishing strategic cooperation between Israel and Arab opponents of Syria] are reaffirmed. This specifically includes measures to assure the Rules of Engagement provide for an effective self-defense against the range of foreseeable threats." The NSDD continued, "The U.S. contingent of the MNF supported by naval surface and tactical air forces will pursue a policy of vigorous self-defense against all attacks from any hostile quarter."[203]

Reagan was frustrated about how public debate was affecting decision making regarding Lebanon. Thus, during a NSPG meeting, he commented: "I have to say I am pretty mad about the way we have backed into a situation so that we are reduced to considering the redeployment of our forces in Lebanon in response to the public debate stimulated by leaks from within our government."[204]

"He May Be Ready to Surrender, But I'm Not"

As Congress returned to work in January 1984, the Democrats immediately began pressing resolutions to withdraw the Marines. Even Republican loyalists were backing away from Reagan's policy.[205] For example, Senator Paul Laxalt (R-Nevada) warned Reagan that "Republican support was fragile," while House Minority Leader Robert Michel (R-Illinois) said that "something will have to give."[206] Congress was reflecting the public mood at the time. The polls showed that in December, 48 percent of the public favored withdrawing the Marines from Lebanon; by January, 59 percent believed the United States should leave.[207]

On January 11, Shultz reported to the president that Rumsfeld's efforts at achieving a security arrangement with the Syrians were "unraveling," and that he believed that "Syrian views on Lebanon appear to have hardened in response to domestic criticism of the MNF here and in Europe." Shultz believed that demonstrating resolve was affecting Syria's willingness to negotiate. In a memo, he observed that "the Syrians welcomed Rumsfeld when the *New Jersey* was firing and scorned him when the firing stopped—and [Shultz] noted that our forces in general were scaling down their action."[208] Shultz was convinced that Syria and the Lebanese opposition believed that Congress would eventually force a US pullout and that this had been a primary factor in Syrian intransigence during December.

Pressure on Reagan to withdraw did not stem only from Congress or the public. During the NSPG meeting on January 9, 1984, Weinberger and the Joint Chiefs found a new ally in their calls for redeployment, as Vice President George H. W. Bush was also ready to withdraw the troops. Consistent with his status as a low self-monitor, Bush "gave a short shrift to Lawrence Eagleburger's final pleas that abandoning the Lebanese government would undercut America's credibility all around the world."[209]

Indeed, Weinberger—one of the most hawkish members of the administration with regard to the Soviets, who believed strongly that they were expansionist in nature—was extremely reluctant to commit US military forces in Lebanon and Grenada. His low self-monitoring inclinations might help explain why he exerted a lot of pressure on Reagan to withdraw and was not worried about the implications for US reputation for resolve. Consistent with being a low self-monitor hawk, Weinberger laid out in a major public speech in November 1984 his objections to the use of force in Lebanon and Grenada as a means to signal US resolve when vital issues are not at stake. In this speech Weinberger argued that the use of combat forces should be approved only when either the United States' or its close allies' vital national interests were at risk; that the war had to be fought "wholeheartedly, with the clear intention of winning"; that decisive force should be employed in the pursuit of clearly defined political and military objectives; that US leaders must constantly reassess whether the use of force is necessary and appropriate; that there must be a "reasonable assurance" of Congressional and public support; and that force should be used only as a last resort.[210]

Secretary Shultz, on the other hand—who was far less of a hard-liner on Soviet relations than either Weinberger or Reagan but who, like Reagan, had high self-monitoring inclinations—was "more inclined to believe that the presence of American forces on the ground was important in demonstrating the nation's resolve and lent credibility and strength to its diplomatic efforts." Consistent with being a high self-monitor hawk, Shultz's memoir reflects that reputation for resolve is required for successful bargaining: "the use of force, and the credible threat of the use of force, are legitimate instruments of national policy and should be viewed as such."[211] Shultz recalls a 1982 argument with the Soviets and Nicaraguans about MIGs coming to Nicaragua: "When I told Gromyko that such a development was unacceptable to us, the threat was credible: the president had agreed on a plan to take them out. The Soviets, the Cubans, and the Nicaraguans sensed that we meant it."[212]

These conflicting views about the use of force were fully on display during the deliberations regarding Lebanon. Yet, notwithstanding pressure from Weinberger, the military commanders, Congress, and the American public, Reagan sought a way to keep the United States in Lebanon. According to Shultz, Reagan was willing to embark only on a modified plan that included a deployment of "an antiterrorist force that would have mobility and a more active mission than the marines." The new deployment, Shultz argued, "would maintain U.S. presence, show U.S. staying power, and address the emerging issue of terrorism. . . . Expanded rules of engagement would allow naval and air firepower to strengthen the Lebanese armed forces."[213] Similarly, Reagan notes in his diary that on January 26, "we took up the business again & came up with a plan for deployment of the Marines but only after sending in Army training units who specialize in anti-terrorist measures."[214]

Indeed, even as late as early February, Reagan's public statements indicated that he was committed to staying in Lebanon. When asked about Tip O'Neill's campaign of pressure to remove the Marines, Reagan replied, "He may be ready to surrender, but I'm not." Similarly, in his weekly radio address on Saturday, February 4, Reagan maintained that "our efforts to strengthen the Lebanese Army . . . are making sure and steady progress," and that there were "no reasons to turn our backs on friends and cut and run."[215]

In agreement with Shultz's plan to protect US reputation by only partially withdrawing from Lebanon, Reagan left for California in early February. However, by the time Shultz returned from Central America later that month, he sensed that the president was no longer committed to staying in Lebanon, where the situation was rapidly deteriorating. "Vice President Bush, with Cap Weinberger at his side, convened a series of crisis-management meetings out of which came decisions to move up and condense the schedule for departure of the marines with no compensating deployment."[216]

In addition to pressure from some of his advisors, several other events in February pushed Reagan to surrender to withdrawal. On February 1, the House of Representatives passed a nonbinding resolution calling for the "prompt and orderly" withdrawal of the Marines. In a final plea, Reagan conceded that "the situation in Lebanon is difficult, frustrating, and dangerous. But that is no reason to turn our backs on friends and to cut and run. If we do we will be sending a signal to terrorists everywhere: They can gain by waging war against innocent people."[217]

Events in Lebanon deteriorated quickly during February, leaving little hope that US forces could make a difference. The LAF and the Gemayel government collapsed, leaving the Marines without a government to support.[218] Reagan was under pressure from MNF allies to withdraw. Reagan notes in his diary on February 13, "a hush hush cable from Geo. B. [George Bush] re Lebanon. [British Prime Minister] Margaret T. [Thatcher] feels strongly we should tell Gemayel to abrogate the May 17 agreement with Israel. Geo. wanted to know if he could tell her we wouldn't object. That's all we can say—we won't oppose but won't urge either."[219]

The decision to pull out of Lebanon was not easy for Reagan to make or for Shultz to accept. In his memoirs, Shultz notes, "Our troops left in a rush amid ridicule from the French and utter disappointment and despair from the Lebanese," and he lamented that the "precipitous departure made an impact.... I knew then that our staying power under pressure would come into question time and again—and not just in the Middle East."[220] Similarly, just weeks after withdrawing from Lebanon, Reagan publicly denounced Congress for "second guessing about whether to keep our men [in Beirut]," arguing that it severely weakened his ability to "negotiate and encouraged more intransigence from the Syrians and prolonged the violence."[221]

Reagan understood quite well that the redeployment of the Marines from Lebanon signified a critical blow to US reputation for resolve and credibility. This realization is stated very clearly in NSDD 128, which Reagan signed on February 26. It concluded, "In view of the serious developments in Lebanon and the perceived erosion of U.S. credibility ... we have lost credibility in the wake of state sponsored terrorism and we need to review on an urgent basis steps we can take to effectively counter state sponsored terrorism and bolster confidence in US commitments to Israel and our Arab friends."[222]

Summary

The use of military force in Lebanon and Grenada demonstrates the importance to Reagan of demonstrating resolve, even in the face of strong and persistent domestic and international opposition. But this analysis also reveals a deep divide within his administration on the issue of reputation for resolve. Just as Carter was caught between his two main advisors—Brzezinski and Vance—so was Reagan subjected to conflicting advice by his two main advisors, Weinberger and Shultz. As shown in the Carter chapter, the more hawkish Brzezinski cared more about reputation for resolve and primed Carter with those concerns, although Carter ultimately rejected Brzezinski's reputational policy rationales. Weinberger was the more hawkish of Reagan's advisors, but in contrast to Brzezinski, he was a low self-monitor. Consistent with the theory's prediction, we see that he was against military interventions motivated by demonstrating resolve. Shultz, who was seen as more moderate but with high self-monitoring tendencies, primed Reagan with reputational concerns and resisted pressure to withdraw from Lebanon. The contrast between these two presidents and their advisors shows that hawkishness does not necessarily result in more support for international intervention to show resolve. Ultimately, not all hawks push for credibility, and differences in self-monitoring disposition play a key role in this variation.[223]

AIR STRIKES IN LIBYA

Reagan's decision to order an air raid in Libya, to thwart ongoing incidents of state-sponsored terrorism by Libyan dictator Muammar Qaddafi, shows that Reagan viewed a strong response as critical to restoring and reinforcing US reputation for resolve in the Middle East. Following the complications of American intervention in Lebanon and the subsequent withdrawal, allies like Egypt began to question US credibility as a regional player, limiting the feasibility of a multilateral response to Qaddafi. Documents related to planning provocative naval maneuvers in the Gulf of Sidra and the air raid against multiple targets in and around Tripoli reveal that among the primary objectives was the Reagan administration's desire to signal resolve, both to adversaries and allies. Consistent with theoretical predictions, Reagan's desire to pursue this objective led him to order an extensive air raid despite potential repercussions from European allies, the Soviet Union, and domestic audiences.

From Diplomacy to Carrier Groups in the Gulf of Sidra

When Reagan first took office, he inherited over a decade of strained relations with Libya. After Muammar Qaddafi overthrew the pro-Western leader of Libya, King Idris, in a 1969 military coup, the Nixon administration moved quickly to stem the flow of US military aid, blocking the sale of twelve C-130 cargo planes to Libya. Qaddafi's relationship with the United States continued to sour under Ford and Carter, and Libya pivoted to the Soviet Union to fill the gap in military aid. By 1979, the State Department placed Libya on the list of countries supporting terrorism; Qaddafi then allowed the US Embassy in Tripoli to be attacked and burned.

Breaking with the Carter administration's Libya policy, Reagan moved beyond purely diplomatic measures to push back against Qaddafi's growing adventurism. In June 1981, Reagan directed the NSC to increase pressure on Qaddafi, and he reauthorized naval maneuvers in the Gulf of Sidra.[224] On August 19, after American planes had patrolled the Gulf of Sidra for twenty-four hours, Qaddafi ordered a response to the American show of force: two Libyan fighter planes fired on two American F-14s launched from the USS *Nimitz*. The two Libyan planes were shot down. Qaddafi then publicly vowed to assassinate Reagan in retaliation. Qaddafi's threat made it clear that the Gulf of Sidra incident would not end Libya's threat to security of US interests. In a message sent to Qaddafi through the Belgians, Reagan drew a clear line in the sand:

> Any acts of violence directed by Libya or its agents against officials of the US, at home or abroad, will be regarded by the US government as an armed attack upon the US and will be met by every means necessary to defend this nation in accordance with Article 51 of the United Nations Charter.[225]

Concurrently, in NSDD 16, entitled "Economic and Security Decisions for Libya," Reagan ordered sanctions on Libyan oil, preparations for the voluntary withdrawal of US nationals from Libya, and the exploration of proportional military response to future attacks on US interests.

"The American People Are Not—I Repeat—Not Going to Tolerate Intimidation"

After a notable decrease in Libyan adventurism in 1982–83, the US intelligence community detected resurgence in subversive activity by Libya on the African continent. Reports showed that Qaddafi was orchestrating an intervention in Sudan in pursuit of his regional goals for Pan-Arabism, and he had ordered an aerial bombing of a CIA-backed radio station in Omdurman, from which Libyan exiles had been broadcasting anti-Qaddafi messages. Although Libya publicly denied responsibility for the bombing, Qaddafi openly proclaimed his hostility toward Sudanese President Ghafar el-Nimeiry and attributed his position in Sudan to his broader fight against the United States: "The peoples will march forward and will develop a people's war of liberation in Sudan, and tomorrow in Egypt and in every area that America seeks to dominate. . . . We must force America to fight on a hundred fronts all over the earth."[226]

Following Qaddafi's renewed incursions into Sudan and growing evidence that the Libyan dictator was engaging in state-sponsored terrorism, Reagan issued NSDD 138, "Combatting Terrorism." The directive did not mention Libya explicitly, but it noted that "U.S. Citizens and installations, especially abroad, are increasingly being targeted for terrorist acts . . . by state-sponsored terrorist movements."[227] It called on the defense and intelligence communities to develop the necessary capabilities "to conduct military operations to counter terrorism directed against US citizens" and to "develop a military strategy that is supported by an active, preventative program to combat state sponsored terrorism before the terrorists can initiate hostile acts."[228] With the language of the directive, Reagan indicated that US counterterrorism policy would leverage the support and capabilities of regional allies.

A potential military intervention in Libya, particularly one that involved overt action, was seen as risky by some in the administration. In January 1985, Donald Fortier, NSC director for politico-military affairs, and Vincent Cannistraro, a CIA officer on rotation at the NSC, wrote a white paper highlighting the potential risks of a more aggressive policy in Libya. Fortier and Cannistraro were particularly concerned about the possibility that increased US pressure on Qaddafi would be counterproductive to the objectives established in NSDD 138, to ultimately prevent or deter future terrorist attacks on US interests. "Active American participation in anti-Qaddafi activity by the Libyan opposition may result in the removal of the last restraints against Libya-sponsored terrorism directed at American citizens and officials."[229] But Fortier and Cannistraro argued that a broad approach in Libya ought to include active reassurances to regional allies, particularly President Mubarak in Egypt, that the US would maintain a role in anti-Qaddafi operations.[230]

As the Reagan administration was developing its response strategy to the increasingly hostile Libyan regime, on June 14, 1985, TWA flight 847 was hijacked soon after departing from Athens. In a three-day hostage situation, the hijackers demanded the release of seven hundred Shi'ite Muslims from Israeli custody. After touching down in Beirut International Airport for the second time, the hijackers approached one of the passengers, US Navy diver Robert Stethem, shot him in the head, threw his body onto the tarmac, and shot him again. This shocking murder of a US service member brought state-sponsored terrorism to the attention of the American public and to the forefront of the discussions surrounding Libya within the Reagan administration.

The TWA 847 hijacking marked a turning point in Reagan's rhetoric surrounding the threat posed by Libya, because it led him to frame the ensuing fight as a test of US resolve in the face of a multilateral affront to American influence abroad. In a speech to the American Bar Association on July 8, Reagan described the threat of state-sponsored terrorism against the United States as an international campaign by several rogue state governments, including Libya, Iran, Cuba, North Korea, and Nicaragua, to "remove American influence from those areas of the world where we're working to bring stable and democratic government" and "to expel America from the world."[231] These attacks on the United States and its allies would not be ignored:

So, the American people are not—I repeat—not going to tolerate intimidation, terror, and outright acts of war against this nation and its people. And we're especially not going to tolerate these attacks from outlaw states run by the strangest collection of misfits, loony-tunes, and squalid criminals since the advent of the Third Reich.... There can be no place on Earth left where it is safe for these monsters to rest or train or practice their cruel and deadly skills. We must act together, or unilaterally if necessary, to ensure that terrorists have no sanctuary anywhere.[232]

This marked shift in rhetoric about the need to counter the threat posed by terrorism indicates that Reagan viewed US policy toward Libya within the broader context, that of a rogue state's challenge to America's willingness to respond. Through the lens of US reputation for resolve, a failure to directly respond to governments supporting terrorism, particularly by destroying their capabilities to launch terrorist attacks, would be perceived as weakness and, in Reagan's words, "intimidation." Following the hijacking, Reagan convened a meeting of the NSPG on July 13 to discuss Libya policy and to begin planning actions against Qaddafi. Operation Rose, conceived as the overt component part of Operation Flower, was proposed as a preemptive military strike, executed in coordination with the Egyptian military, to remove Qaddafi from power.

The state sponsors of terrorism would not be the only audience to whom Reagan demonstrated resolve in light of escalating attacks on US interests abroad. Following the NSPG meeting, National Security Advisor John Poindexter flew to Cairo with American Ambassador to Egypt Nick Veloites to present Operation Rose to Egypt's President Hosni Mubarak and to secure the necessary military support. Once Poindexter dove into his talking points about the military intervention, Mubarak quickly ended the meeting, saying that if Egypt were to take any military actions against Qaddafi, it would do so on its own schedule. This outcome was largely unsurprising to Veloites, who was more familiar with Mubarak and his current view of US resolve, that "American resolve and staying power in the region had already been found wanting in Lebanon, and Mubarak believed that the US would retreat again when American blood was spilled, leaving Egypt to face Qaddafi's forces alone."[233] Mubarak's concerns were shared by many in the Pentagon; Defense Secretary Weinberger and the Joint Chiefs feared a protracted ground war in the Libyan desert. As Joseph Stanik explains, if anything kept the Egyptian military from quickly pushing back Qaddafi's forces, this would require a major resource commitment by the United States. "U.S. Logistical support of an Egyptian invasion of Libya could develop into a major ground operation—requiring as many as six divisions, or about ninety thousand troops—if the Egyptians ran into serious trouble."[234] Overt military action through Operation Rose was stymied by concerns of US resolve both inside the administration and from regional allies. Covert operations against Qaddafi were launched in October under Operation Tulip, as Reagan secured funds for the CIA to train Libyan opposition groups.

On December 27, 1985, members of the Abu Nidal terrorist network launched tandem attacks in the passenger terminals of Leonardo da Vinci Airport in Rome and Schwechat International Airport in Vienna. The attackers threw hand grenades into the crowded areas surrounding the El-Al ticket counters and opened fire on the crowds. Rome police killed three of the four attackers, and the fourth was subsequently captured; all three Vienna attackers led police on a car chase before they were arrested. In total, eighteen people were killed, including five Americans. In a televised address, he directly implicated Qaddafi in the attacks:

> Qaddafi and other Libyan officials have publicly admitted that the Libyan Government has abetted and supported the notorious Abu Nidal terrorist group, which was directly responsible for the Rome and Vienna attacks. Qaddafi called them heroic actions, and I call them criminal outrages by an outlaw regime. Qaddafi deserves to be treated as a pariah in the world community.[235]

The attacks fit squarely into Reagan's conception of state-sponsored terrorism, and his response to the tragedy would again serve as a signal of US resolve. Reagan called a meeting of the NSPG on January 3, 1986 to begin planning a direct response to Qaddafi's aggression and to review the available military options. During the meeting, Reagan, Shultz, Chief of Staff Donald Regan, and Poindexter reviewed the many costs of a direct military intervention. First, despite previous attempts to evacuate US nationals and businesses voluntarily from Libya, a significant number of Americans were still living in the country, and military strikes would likely endanger them. Second, the presence of Soviet military advisors on the ground in Libya raised the risk of entangling the USSR in a broader international conflict. Third, the recurring leaks of military planning to the press limited the administration's ability to surprise Qaddafi, which fortified the arguments against military intervention. Despite these significant costs, the January 3 meeting closed with Reagan's authorization of a three-phase naval maneuver in the Gulf of Sidra, with all naval vessels instructed to use aggressive self-defense if they faced Libyan targets that had not yet fired but appeared hostile. Reagan's diary entry on January 7 reveal his thinking in authorizing the maneuvers:

> We beefed up the Sixth Fleet in the Mediterranean Sea. If Mr. Qaddafi decides not to push another terrorist act, okay, we've been successful with our implied threat. If on the other hand he takes this for weakness and does loose another one, we will have targets in mind and instantly respond with a hell of a punch.[236]

From Reagan's perspective, the maneuvers were meant to send a clear threat to Qaddafi and to remove doubts about American reputation for resolve by putting intervention-ready naval assets on Libya's doorstep. Reagan's language regarding Qaddafi's perceptions of US "weakness" mirrors his rhetoric in the counterterrorism speech delivered after the TWA 847 hijacking, framing the maneuvers as a direct message about US willingness to use military force. Talking points used during the following NSPG meeting on January 6 reaffirm that reinforcing US reputation for resolve was a key objective of the naval maneuvers; they reveal that Reagan's view of the conflict through the lens of US credibility was gaining adherents among the NSC staff. A memo to Poindexter uses this lens to analyze Qaddafi's logic for continuing to sponsor terrorist attacks against US interests in the region:

> He [Qaddafi] is more inclined to risk direct attacks because he perceives that our response will be a limited one as was the case following the terrorist attacks on US facilities in Lebanon and the TWA hijacking.... Specifically US objectives should be to: reverse the perception of US passivity in the face of mounting terrorist activity.[237]

By benchmarking the naval maneuvers against the previously unsuccessful attempts to signal US credibility, the memo echoes Reagan's language on the intervention in Libya: it would serve as a test for the credibility of US threats against state sponsors of terrorism and would counter increasing perceptions of American passivity. The memo posits that a successful show of resolve and willingness to use force would deter future attacks against Americans: "Operations in the Gulf of Sidra . . . indicate that we are prepared to back our actions with military force, and may reduce the likelihood of a move by Qaddafi against US citizens seeking to depart Libya."[238]

Attack on La Belle Discotheque and Operation El Dorado Canyon

Despite the presence of the Sixth Fleet off the coast of Libya, Qaddafi unleashed another terrorist attack, this time targeting US service members stationed in Germany. On April 5, 1986, La Belle Discotheque in West Berlin, known to be frequented by US soldiers, was bombed. Two of the three killed were US soldiers, as were seventy-nine of more than two hundred injured. US intelligence was able to intercept communications from Libya to the Libyan Peoples' Bureau in East Berlin congratulating them on the successful attack, directly implicating the Qaddafi regime in targeting Americans abroad. This was the precise challenge to US resolve for which Reagan had prepared by increasing naval presence in the Gulf of Sidra.

That initial threat was codified in the operation's mission statement: the purpose of the operation was to "demonstrate U.S. resolve and capability against Libya . . . [and] to keep Libyan armed forces uncertain as to US intentions, and to signal Libyan, European and Arab observers that the US has the capability and the will to conduct military strikes if necessary."[239] Failure to follow through on this demonstration of willingness to use force would be an insurmountable blow to US reputation for resolve, and as the mission statement acknowledges, Qaddafi, US allies, and the world were watching.

During the planning of the air raid on Libya, President Reagan demonstrated a notable willingness to accept the military and diplomatic costs of a strong show of force in the name of asserting American resolve. On April 7, the NSPG met to discuss a direct strike on Qaddafi's key military and terrorist assets in Libya. During the meeting, Reagan advocated a precision strike to minimize civilian casualties. This prompted Chairman of the Joint Chiefs of Staff William Crowe to voice JCS opposition to attacking the Azizayyah Barracks, Qaddafi's command center and his likely location, because its location posed a danger to nearby civilians. However, this target proved to be too important to Reagan, who wanted to erase any doubts of US resolve and send a clear message to Qaddafi that he was willing to bear the costs of hitting the Libyan dictator in his home. Reagan overrode the JCS objection: the Azizayyah Barracks stayed on the list. Reagan also faced significant pushback on the operation from his European allies. Since the advent of American sanctions on Libya, the Europeans had rejected close cooperation with US efforts to isolate and undermine the Qaddafi regime. This time, Reagan hoped to secure the support of the United Kingdom for the operation, but this posed a significant challenge: Prime Minister Thatcher had, in the weeks leading up to the operation, publicly argued that an American retaliatory strike on Libya would violate international law. After Reagan personally guaranteed to Thatcher that the air raid would focus only on terrorist support facilities, she agreed to the operation and permitted the United States to use British bases and the American F-111s based there.[240]

On Tuesday, April 15, at 2:00 a.m. Libyan time, the US Air Force, Navy, and Marine Corps carried out coordinated air strikes on several targets in Tripoli and Benghazi, code-named El Dorado Canyon. Over the course of the twelve-minute strike, sixty tons of munitions were dropped on the Libyan targets, resulting in their near-total destruction and forty Libyan casualties. As ordered by Reagan, the air raid hit Qaddafi's command center in the Azizayyah Barracks, but the Libyan dictator survived the attack. In his memoirs, Reagan underscores the intended message of the raid:

> The attack was not intended to kill Qaddafi; that would have violated our prohibition against assassination [of foreign leaders]. The objective was to let him know that we weren't going to accept his terrorism anymore, and that if he did it [engage in terrorism] again, he could expect to hear from us.[241]

A memorandum prepared the day of the air raid by Tom Gibson, entitled "Talking Points on US Action in Libya," echoes Reagan's intentions and reveals that the target audience of the operation included more countries than just Libya. Concern for US reputation for resolve is evident: "This necessary move by the President is supported by the American people, and established a dramatic marker by which Libya and the rest of the world can assess future US responses to terrorism against Americans."[242] If the international community saw US actions in Lebanon as the previous benchmark of waning US resolve, the Libyan air raid would rectify the world's view and restore American credibility.

Public Opinion

Reagan's decision to order the air raid on Libya in 1986 was not driven by a desire to pander to public opinion. Reagan's advisors, particularly those on the NSC, were actively engaged in tracking public sentiment throughout the operation's planning phase. However, the nature of the final operation far exceeded what public opinion polling revealed was desired by the electorate; Reagan was willing to risk exceeding his mandate in order to signal US resolve against Qaddafi and state-sponsored terrorism.

Reagan's advisors on the NSC, and Oliver North in particular, were especially concerned about the potential public response to an overt military intervention in Libya. The White House commissioned a secret poll by Richard Wirthlin and Ronald Hinckley to gauge public support for a possible US strike.[243] According to a memo sent to North on March 25, 1986, entitled "US Public Opinion on Terrorism," the polls showed that the public was generally supportive of some sort of military response to state sponsored terrorism:

> As can be seen from the response statistics, about half the public (49 percent) favor a military response to state-supported terrorism. However, it is clear that most of these people support a military response if it is directed against terrorist facilities, and not aimed at non-terrorist targets. The other half of the population (48 percent) looks to non-military options, either in terms of economic or diplomatic sanctions or taking no action at all.[244]

The secret poll also showed that a very small part of the population (10 percent) favored a military intervention on the scale of Operation El Dorado Canyon.

Alternative and Other Contextual Explanations

MATERIALIST EXPLANATIONS

Did Reagan use Third World conflicts to build a strong reputation for resolve in order to compensate for the unfavorable shifts in the balance of nuclear forces during the 1960s and 1970s? As we saw in chapter 6, the nuclear superiority the United States had once enjoyed was perceived to have evaporated during the 1970s.[245] Caspar Weinberger said:

> We had campaigned on the fact that we had had inadequate resources for defense and that we were falling behind a steady Soviet buildup, and that we needed to restore our deterrent capability. After he [Reagan] was elected, before he took office, we were given formal classified briefings, and saw it was infinitely worse than we had thought. The Soviet expansion had been taking place at a very rapid rate, and they were actually ahead of us in practically every category—planes and submarines and surface vessels, artillery pieces, infantry division, and small arms, everything. . . . So the gap was growing.[246]

At the time of Reagan's presidency, policy makers in Washington widely believed that the shift in the nuclear balance would lead Moscow to "challenge U.S. interests in a crisis . . . mainly because [Soviet decision makers] now expect[ed] [the United States] to be more inclined to play it safe and avoid risks."[247] Robert Jervis remarked that if the Soviets believed America would not stand firm, then Moscow would "gain a bargaining advantage" in future crises.[248] Accordingly, Reagan's actions to demonstrate America's willingness to stand firm in crises in order to overcome the negotiating handicap created by the Soviet Union's sense of nuclear superiority could serve as evidence against the dispositional theory presented in this book.[249]

The available evidence, however, casts doubt on this interpretation for three reasons. First, the theory that adverse shifts in the balance of nuclear forces lead policy makers to pursue a greater reputation for resolve would lead one to expect Carter to be as committed as Reagan, or more so, to building a reputation for standing firm. Not much changed in the overall balance of forces between the Carter presidency and the first term of the Reagan administration. In fact, Reagan's intense investment in defense, coupled with other developments, made the strategic balance appear to favor the United States during the Reagan years.[250] Thus, this alternative would predict that Reagan would care equally, or even less, about reputation for resolve, compared to Carter. Clearly, however, that was not the case. Therefore, some other variable must account for Reagan's greater drive to build credibility.

Second, although one could argue that Reagan's behavior was influenced by his perceptions of the strategic balance, the evidence indicates that the strategic balance was actually moving in America's favor as a result of Reagan's nuclear modernization. NSDD 12 declared that the modernization program was to "help redress the deteriorated strategic balance with the Soviet Union."[251] Casper Weinberger wrote in his Annual Report to Congress that Reagan's program "revitalize[s] our strategic nuclear deterrent [and] end[s] the decline of U.S. strategic capabilities relative to Soviet forces."[252] The CIA and Defense Department's Joint Net Assessment recorded in 1983 that "the Soviets show signs already of being concerned about our turnaround and the possibility that their gains of the past two decades may be eroded in the future."[253] It also predicted that the Soviets would be "overly" concerned by the modernization program's effects on the strategic balance.[254] Shultz discussed the deployment of the Pershing II missiles in a later interview, stating, "Once of the things I tried to do, and I think successfully, with the President, was to put into the strategic context that 1983 was going to be the year of the missile. This was a year when we were either going to have an agreement or we were going to deploy missiles, and that was going to be very hard to do in Europe."[255] Given the findings of the Joint Net Assessment and the stated goals of the modernization program, it seems that Reagan should not have needed to bolster the US reputation for resolve by intervening in Third World conflicts solely to improve America's bargaining position relative to that of the USSR.

Contrary to what would be predicted based solely on perceptions of the nuclear balance, Reagan continued to seek improved credibility through Third World interventions with as much, if not more, vigor than at the start of his presidency. The invasion of Grenada took place after the Joint Net Assessment predicted that the Soviets had become concerned about the strategic balance. Reagan continued to intensify the conflict in Afghanistan after his reelection. Reagan approved action in Grenada and Afghanistan in part because, as described above, he wanted to use the conflicts to strengthen American credibility. It appears Reagan did not become less concerned with demonstrating resolve simply because the Soviets perceived the strategic balance as becoming less favorable to Moscow. The dispositional theory may offer a stronger explanation of why Reagan focused so intently on resolve and credibility, even as America's nuclear capabilities were modernized.

Third, we do not see a correlation between beliefs about the nuclear balance and concerns about reputation for resolve. In his work *Images and Arm Control*, Keith Shimko traces the statements made by Reagan and his top advisors about the strategic balance. While the public nature of those statements may lead one to question their sincerity, they do provide more direct evidence about individual perceptions. Shultz most often described the nuclear balance in terms of Soviet advantage or imbalance (ten times), followed by parity or balance (four times), but he never claimed the Soviets enjoyed strategic superiority. Weinberger also referred to the nuclear balance most often in terms of advantage or imbalance (180 times). Such statements, however, decreased dramatically during the second administration (specifically, 150 in the first term compared to thirty during the second). Weinberger at times also described the balance as providing the Soviets with nuclear superiority (nineteen times). Yet, as Shimko argues, those were rare and all appeared in 1984 or earlier.

Far more common were Weinberger's vague references to the need to "restore" or "regain" a sufficient nuclear deterrence. Unlike Shultz, Weinberger flatly rejected the idea of parity between the two superpowers.[256] Interestingly, however, the evidence in this chapter suggests that it was Shultz, rather than Weinberger, who favored taking military action in Lebanon and Grenada to demonstrate US resolve. Weinberger, who saw the nuclear balance as more dire, opposed these military operations and urged the president to reconsider them.

A review of Reagan's public statements on the nuclear balance shows during his first term, he most often referred to the strategic balance as one of Soviet advantage or imbalance (twenty-one times), while during his second term this number dropped significantly (six times). On five occasions during his first term, and twice during his second term, Reagan referred to the strategic balance in terms of Soviet superiority. Reagan never referred to the nuclear balance in terms of parity during his entire tenure. Still, when pressed to explain his views on the strategic balance, Reagan often stumbled, providing incoherent answers about what a window of vulnerability actually meant, or how he operationalized "superiority" in nuclear weapons. Nevertheless, given Reagan's statements, the evidence suggests that Reagan's concerns about reputation for resolve were at least partially driven by his assessments of the nuclear balance. But that Reagan continued to express concern about reputation for resolve during his second term—when the Soviets were no longer perceived to have a nuclear advantage and when the notion of a window of vulnerability had been debunked—casts doubt on this interpretation.[257]

Next, I question whether materialist cost-benefit calculations drove Reagan to use military instruments, rather than reputational considerations. As we have seen in the previous chapter, Carter's main foreign policy advisors reached different conclusions based on the same foreign policy information about the material values at stake. Weinberger and Shultz never disagreed about whether Grenada, Lebanon, or Libya had more or less material importance. But they did argue about the importance of demonstrating resolve in those cases precisely because the material value at stake was low.

Part of the reason for their disagreement, I argue, is that Weinberger and Shultz differed in their self-monitoring dispositions. Thus, the lower self-monitor, Weinberger, comparing himself to Shultz said, "Oddly enough, I was generally on the side of more caution and more concern about the safety of the troops."[258] Weinberger was less convinced by reputational logic. The higher self-monitor, Shultz, however, strongly believed that the use of US forces on the ground or a threat to use force was a key component of demonstrating resolve and exercising effective coercive diplomacy. That these two advisors were able to reach such starkly different conclusions based on essentially the same information highlights their individual differences in dispositional beliefs about the importance of reputation in international relations. During the crises studied here, Reagan repeatedly accepted Shultz's logic and policy recommendations. The only time that he favored Weinberger was in the last phase of his fight to keep the forces in Lebanon, where it became clear Congress would not allow him to continue the mission.

DOMESTIC POLITICS

The evidence seems to suggest that Reagan was to some extent mindful of public opinion and closely monitored public reactions to his policies and public speeches, as we would expect from a high-self monitor. At the same time, however, contrary public opinion did not dissuade Reagan from pursuing reputation-guided policies of resolve.

In the case of Lebanon, for example, the public was divided on how to respond to the Israeli invasion and resulting unrest. Reagan was willing to send troops despite skeptical public opinion, and he pulled out long after public opinion turned negative; he remained in the country even after public opinion fell drastically following the October bombing. The primary actor that constrained Reagan in Lebanon, and eventually pushed him to withdraw, was Congress. Reagan capitulated, and did so reluctantly, only when it was clear that congressional opposition threatened his mandate and would not allow him to continue the operation. Indeed, Congress's opposition undermined US reputation for resolve in Reagan's eyes, forcing him to pursue a face-saving exit strategy that he later regretted. Howell and Pevehouse postulate that "if Republicans had ruled both the Senate and the House, congressional dissent would have softened, and Reagan might have held firm through the spring and summer of 1984, as he plainly preferred."[259]

Similarly, the military operation in Grenada, which was clearly intended to signal resolve to both international and domestic audiences, was undertaken in secret precisely because Reagan knew Congress and the American people would not support it out of fear of another Vietnam; indeed, he faced opposition even from Weinberger and the Joint Chiefs. Ultimately, the operation was successful and resulted in a significant surge in public support, but when Reagan had undertaken the operation, there was great uncertainty about its results. Public opinion did not indicate support for using military force in Libya either, which Reagan took nonetheless.

Overall, Reagan's responses to international crises show that neither domestic public opinion nor elite opinion was the driving factor behind his decisions to use military instruments to show America's resolve. This pattern of ignoring or circumventing domestic impediments in order to demonstrate resolve to outside actors is also consistent with Reagan's policy in Nicaragua and El Salvador.[260] The evidence suggests that there, too, left to his own devices, Reagan would have introduced American military forces into the region, probably in significant numbers. Reagan was significantly constrained by Congress from sending troops or legally providing the kind of military assistance he envisioned. Unable to assist the Nicaraguan Contras legally, he resorted to selling arms to Iran—a country on the State Department terrorist list—and diverting the profits to fund the Contra rebels. This episode shows that Congress was somewhat effective in constraining Reagan, but also that Reagan was very determined to signal resolve to the Communists. That determination led him take actions that were highly risky and unpopular.[261]

OTHER INDIVIDUAL-LEVEL EXPLANATIONS

Dafoe and Caughey predict that southern presidents should emphasize reputational concerns more than nonsouthern presidents.[262] Just as this theory did not hold for the southerner Jimmy Carter of Georgia, it also does not hold true for Reagan. Although born in Illinois, Reagan spent most of his life in California. Contrary to Dafoe and Caughey's predictions, Reagan sought to demonstrate strength with the Soviets and took actions in Afghanistan, Nicaragua, Lebanon, Grenada, and Libya, among others, in order to shore up America's reputation for resolve.

Scholars have also argued that reputational concerns should be more prominent for newer leaders.[263] Carter rejected reputational concerns from the very beginning of his presidency, while Reagan demonstrated that he cared deeply for the US reputation for resolve even following his reelection. For example, Reagan's strongest policies with regard to Afghanistan, as well as the greatest US involvement in Nicaragua, and the strongest US showing of resolve in Libya, all took place after Reagan's reelection in 1984, when Dafoe's theory would predict that reputational concerns would no longer be at the forefront of a second-term president who no longer had to concern himself with reelection.

Conclusion

Reagan's crisis decision making matches the predictions of an ideal-type "reputation crusader." That Reagan was eager to use military instruments is not surprising given his hawkishness. But the rationale he provided for fighting, both in public and in internal documents, was remarkable in that it consistently emphasized the importance of demonstrating credibility, resolve, and toughness in the eyes of adversaries and allies. My theory attributes Reagan's concern for US reputation for resolve to his high self-monitoring disposition. Like Carter, Reagan was informed by advisors who held very different philosophies about the importance of reputation in world politics, and about how to best demonstrate resolve. But the dynamic between Reagan and his advisors was different. While Carter's more hawkish advisor, Brzezinski, was a high self-monitor and the low self-monitor was the more moderate Vance, in this case, the roles were opposite. Weinberger comes close to an ideal-type low self-monitor hawk, with his focus on building up the military and crushing the Soviet Union in an arms race, but he was far more reluctant to commit to use force for the sake of demonstrating to the Soviets that the United States was tough and willing to initiate and escalate conflicts that did not involve crucial material interests. Shultz, as we have seen, comes closer to an ideal-type high self-monitor hawk, who like Reagan, advocated using military power to demonstrate US resolve.

8

Bill Clinton and America's Credibility after the Cold War

This chapter tests the dispositional theory against the crisis decision making of President Bill Clinton. Of all the presidents studied in this book, Clinton comes closest to an ideal-type high self-monitor. A review of both quantitative and qualitative indicators of military assertiveness from before and during his presidency indicates that his beliefs about the efficacy of military force leaned toward the dovish side of the military assertiveness scale. Taken together, we should expect Clinton's crisis behavior to be consistent with what I term a "reputation believer." Because of his more dovish tendencies, Clinton, unlike Reagan, did not seek out opportunities to show resolve and was at first reluctant to use force to demonstrate resolve; but once he sensed a loss of reputation, he was prepared to escalate with military force as the theory predicts.

President Clinton faced several international crises that challenged US reputation for resolve. I focus on three: the intervention in, and subsequent withdrawal from, Somalia; the invasion of Haiti; and the third Taiwan Strait crisis. These crises took place at different times during his administration, involved different parts of the world, had different material stakes, and varied in their outcomes.

In the rest of the chapter, first, I briefly evaluate several indicators in order to characterize Clinton's self-monitoring and his beliefs about military force. In the online appendix I review the circumstances that led to Clinton's election in 1992 and his reelection in 1996. The third section details Clinton's crisis decision making in Somalia, Haiti, and Taiwan. Finally, I assess the validity of alternative and other contextual explanations.

Classifying Clinton: Self-Monitoring and Military Assertiveness

Bill Clinton is an example of a reputation believer, with a high self-monitoring disposition and low military assertiveness. The following two sections further explore why Clinton should be classified as a high self-monitor dove (i.e., a reputation believer).

CLINTON AS A HIGH SELF-MONITOR

Clinton displayed all three main components of high self-monitors: expressive self-control, social stage presence, and other-directed self-presentation.

Although expressive self-control gauges an individual's talent for acting, it does not imply that one must be a professional actor (like Reagan) to have it. Rather, individuals with high expressive self-control show proclivities for all kinds of public performances. Clinton excelled at using expressive self-control to win over his peers from very early in life. For example, young Clinton was capable of debating positions passionately, even on a moment's notice, in the classroom. As biographer David Maraniss notes, in mock historical trials in Clinton's Latin classes, he "put up [vigorous defenses] and became enraptured with the courtroom, where he had a captive audience susceptible to his powers of persuasion, a focus group for his budding rhetorical and political skills."[1] In early life, his most successful performance was to get his teachers to believe he was "a model student," even as he and his friends "were more like fraternity brothers who knew how to impress elders with their manners and then have a good time out of view."[2]

Clinton quickly adapted his ability to his political career. In his 1978 campaign for governor, he used his emotional expressiveness to promote himself as the strongest candidate and win the support of the voters. A method that Clinton used with great success was to bring others to tears in order to win their sympathy and support. Biographer John Gartner notes that Clinton's tendency to cry for others who suffer "is so infectious that it can trigger tears in others"; the tears provide "the opportunity for powerful political theater, all the more powerful because [they are] genuinely felt."[3]

On the campaign trail and as president, Clinton was an expert at giving speeches that won the hearts and minds of the public. Journalist Joe Klein argued that the press understood as early as the second presidential debate in October that Clinton would defeat George H. W. Bush (a low self-monitor). When an African American woman asked the candidates how they would help common people escape poverty, Bush delivered a long-winded answer about what he heard in the White House, but Clinton "took three steps toward the woman and asked her, 'Tell me how it's affected you again?' . . . The three steps . . . spoke volumes about his ability to show empathy, his concern, his desire to respond to the needs of the public. . . . Bush, by contrast, was caught gazing at his wristwatch.' "[4]

One of the questions on the Self-Monitoring Scale pertains to one's ability to lie with a straight face. Clinton was able to control his emotional expressions to gain sympathy from his listeners, and sometimes to hide the fact that he was lying. An example of this occurred during the Monica Lewinsky scandal, where Clinton notoriously stated in a national address that he "did not have sexual relations with that woman." Clinton's response contained real emotional anger as he faced the cameras; it thus came as a surprise to many, even some people close to the president, that he had actually had an affair.[5]

Clinton also displayed a strong social stage presence; wherever he went, Clinton could immediately draw attention to himself. Before he entered national politics, journalist Philip Martin described Clinton as "the Sun King" because he had "a common touch [and] a dangerous charisma" that helped him win over others.[6] Clinton supplemented his social stage presence with his ability to win over almost everyone he met with his "kind, outgoing, and inquisitive" personality, combined with his tendency to speak to "everyone with whom he came in contact."[7] This allowed him to earn local fame and respect.

By the time Clinton entered politics, he learned to apply his charming, engaging demeanor in a successful campaign method. Meredith Oakley noted that this "personal, personable style" was a success from early in his career, allowing him to accomplish the rare feat of earning enough votes in the primary for the 1978 Arkansas gubernatorial election to avoid a runoff.[8] Oakley notes that Clinton's charisma earned him respect from so many people that it overshadowed questions related to his experience or policy positions.[9] The charming, popular Clinton won the gubernatorial election handily, and when he later spoke at the 1980 Democratic National Convention, "he and the Arkansans in that audience knew that he would someday return to be the convention's star attraction."[10]

When Clinton began his campaign for president, his popularity immediately shone through, and journalist Joe Klein observed that "the Clinton campaign appeared to exist entirely, and very comfortably, within the grammar of popular culture." Clinton bolstered his campaign speeches with television appearances playing the saxophone, and he earned the nickname "Elvis" from his staff for his ability to draw and appeal to crowds.[11] The general public "favor[ed] his policies, [was] impressed by his gifts, [and was] bemused by his personal indulgences,"[12] which made him seem at once a good leader, a charismatic individual, and a regular person. Clinton could draw crowds, and this aspect of his high self-monitoring disposition helped him politically.

Concerning the third component, one of Clinton's greatest political skills was his other-directed self-presentation: his capacity to show the best sides of himself to others strategically in order to win their favor. For Clinton, this manifested itself in his tendencies to change his style—and his apparent values and beliefs—to match those around him. Clinton's ability to be the person he needed to be in order to gain social advantages served him well in his campaigns.[13] Philip Martin observed that Clinton "was [more] willing to hedge his notion of virtue [than to] risk rejection by the voters."[14] This was evident early in his career, as his policy platforms and rhetoric differed tremendously between his first and second stints as governor of Arkansas. In his first campaign, Clinton was much more willing to take positions against the Arkansas Republican establishment: he attempted to limit the power of the timber and trucking industries, proposed raising taxes to fix infrastructure problems, and even "expressed misgivings about the state's death penalty."[15] Clinton could get away with actions because of his optimism and general power of persuasion. But in 1980, voters punished him for attempting to further what they perceived as an elitist agenda; they elected Republican Frank White. To win reelection in 1982, Clinton radically altered his positions to seek favor with voters. By 1990, when Clinton spoke at a Democratic Leadership Council meeting, he would argue that his fellow partisans would need to "get on the right side of issues" like the death penalty and flag burning in order to win in conservative areas.[16]

After being elected president, Clinton maintained what his former colleague Arkansas lawyer Cliff Jackson called "his malleability . . . his willingness to be anything to anyone"[17] in order to maintain popularity. This often meant that the president would initially support one side of an issue but then switch to the other side (or at least to a neutral position) in order to avoid conflict. One of the first examples of this was, in the first month of his presidency, his announcement that he would sign an executive order allowing gay people to serve openly in the military.[18] However, when the Joint Chiefs argued against lifting the ban, and many in Washington and elsewhere still showed opposition to the measure, Clinton chose instead to pursue the compromise known as "Don't ask, don't tell."[19] Although Clinton's personal beliefs did not change, he altered his public stance to win favor.

Preston reports that Clinton's network of friends is consistent with that of a high self-monitor. Rather than having a small group of friends who really know him, "for Clinton, friends are links in an ever-expanding network of contacts, useful for both future political support and as a source of advice." Clinton's self-monitoring was evident in his interactions with his network of friends, which some referred to as FOBs, for "friends of Bill." Clinton had "a way of making you feel you were the most important friend in his life and what happened to you was the most important thing that ever happened." Secretary of Labor Robert Reich described Clinton's "you-are-the-only-person-in-the-world-who-matters gaze."[20] He has been described as a "master of sustained eye-contact, haunting reactions in the eyes of an audience of one or a thousand."[21]

Like Reagan, Clinton generally avoided direct conflict with others. He would often use surrogates to present alternative ideas during Oval Office meetings or to make arguments he felt uncomfortable making.[22] As with Reagan, the president's desire to avoid conflict often left those "advocating positions before the president to come away believing (erroneously) that Clinton had agreed with them or adopted their position."[23]

In sum, Clinton's high self-monitoring was very evident to those working with him. He constantly probed the environment (through polls, questioning FOBs, etc.) for feedback regarding his performances and signals of popular policies.[24] Reflecting on Clinton's strong expressive control and "chameleon-like" behavior, George Stephanopoulos describes watching Clinton as like looking into a kaleidoscope: "what you see is where you stand and where you are looking at him. He will put one facet toward you but that is only one facet."[25]

CLINTON'S MILITARY ASSERTIVENESS

Clinton and Reagan were both high self-monitors, but they had fundamentally different beliefs about the international system and the US role in it. Using an adaptation of the military assertiveness scale created by Herrmann, Tetlock, and Visser, this section looks at elements of Clinton's noncrisis foreign policy to determine Clinton's beliefs about the use of force.[26] The scale uses three metrics: preference for higher defense spending, use of covert action, and involvement with international organizations to resolve conflicts.[27]

Military defense spending during the Cold War serves as a strong metric of a leader's military assertiveness. Clinton's case, however, is different: he was the first president since the end of World War II without a rival superpower. The fall of the Soviet Union had created an entirely new strategic environment, one where a large US military was not clearly necessary. Thus, this analysis of Clinton's defense spending looks not only at the changes to the defense budget but also at the military's new post–Cold War role.

Clinton significantly reduced the size of the military and wanted to repurpose a large share of military industries and forces for nonmilitary domestic roles. During his first term as president, Clinton oversaw a drastic reduction in the military budget. In a 1992 speech at the University of Pennsylvania's Wharton School of Business, Clinton pledged to "convert defense spending to domestic growth" by using the money saved from defense cuts to "provide displaced defense workers assistance in retraining, placement, and relocation," along with making new investments in domestic infrastructure.[28] In this he was true to his word: the 1992 defense budget had been $286.6 billion, while under the first Clinton administration, defense spending fell every year from 1993 to 1996, when it hit a low of $253.2 billion.[29] These reductions of the size of the military budget in favor of domestic spending were much lower than George H. W. Bush's proposals at the end of his presidency; Clinton's proposed 1994 budget of $263.4 billion was "$12 billion less" than the Bush estimates and was part of a reduction that cut $88 billion more over four years than Bush had recommended.[30]

Still, the reduction in spending cannot be attributed solely to dovishness. Secretary of Defense Les Aspin described the Clinton cuts as part of "the first truly post–Cold War budget," designed not to "merely [cut] forces . . . [but to buy] the right forces for the right missions in the future."[31] This meant that, alongside reducing the size of the military, the Clinton administration spent additional money on developing military technology. Defense budget analyst Michael O'Hanlon notes that Clinton's investments in technology were critical for the later implementation of "unmanned aerial vehicles (UAVs), missile defense systems, satellite-guided weapons, and improved rapid-targeting and radar technology" that helped give the US military "a stellar warfighting record" from the late 1990s to the early 2000s.[32]

The second indicator of a leader's level of military assertiveness is whether the leader favors the use of covert military action to pursue foreign policy goals. The use of covert action is a strong metric because it signals a leader's desire to influence international events irrespective of domestic political concerns. Clinton was notoriously unwilling to use the CIA to accomplish his foreign policy goals and did not maintain strong relationships with intelligence officials. Instead, he preferred to use more overt means with both friends and enemies.

While Clinton appreciated CIA intelligence, he did not seek to influence international events through the covert use of force but instead expected the intelligence community merely to "look for trouble, in order to warn the president and Congress about it."[33] In a 1994 report, the Senate Select Committee on Intelligence reported that "covert action funding represents a small and shrinking fraction of the intelligence budget."[34] Journalist James Risen observed that one of Clinton's few uses of covert action was in Haiti, when he asked the CIA to disseminate leaflets asking citizens "to remain calm and not resist" the US military invasion in 1994. However, when the administration found that the leaflets used "voodoo symbols to get the message across," it ordered the CIA to destroy the leaflets on the grounds that "the Clinton White House could not show support for one religion over another."[35] Clinton did not want the CIA to perform actions that ran counter to overt policy stances, instead relegating it to a more defensive and subdued role. However, the Clinton administration did engage in some covert military action: beginning in 1995, Clinton used the CIA to implement a rendition program, detaining terrorist suspects and handing them over to foreign governments for questioning, with the goal of disrupting terrorist plots developing abroad.

Clinton's dislike for covert military action showed in his relationships with CIA officials. Director of Central Intelligence R. James Woolsey notably joked that "I didn't have a bad relationship with the president. . . . I just didn't have one at all."[36] In fact, Woolsey met with Clinton only two times during his two-year tenure as DCI, an all-time low for the position.[37] The Clinton administration was very cautious to avoid any CIA involvement with the training and arming of Bosnian and Croatian armed forces in 1996.[38] Clinton valued building connections with others and did not approve of using the CIA to influence international affairs secretly or without US allies' consent, which puts him low on the scale of military assertiveness.

The third and final indicator of military assertiveness looks to whether the president disfavors the use of multilateral organizations to solve crises diplomatically. Clinton valued international organizations like the United Nations as means of building coalitions, creating friendliness internationally, and gaining approval for new foreign policies. From the time he took office in 1992, Bill Clinton supported the efforts of UN peacekeepers and their operations, citing these efforts as an expression of the "assertive multilateralism" that Clinton sought in his foreign policy.[39] Clinton backed the UN's creation of a "quick-deployment force" that could be used to intervene against rogue leaders.[40] This would allow the United States to project power as part of a multistate project, rather than through unilateral action. Clinton was also in favor of US participation in international legal bodies; for example, in 2000, Clinton signed the Rome Statute, which established the International Criminal Court.[41] While Clinton noted that "[the United States was] not abandoning [its] concerns about significant flaws in the treaty," he argued that the United States would "be in a position to influence the evolution of the court" by signing.[42] Clinton was committed to building international support for the United States through both military and nonmilitary means, and he favored use of international organizations to build cooperative partnerships, rather than acting without international support.

Public support for UN peacekeeping efforts waned, however, as many Americans blamed UN incompetence for the deaths of eighteen soldiers in the 1993 Battle of Mogadishu (described below).[43] While the United States still wanted to deploy peacekeepers to many other parts of the world, it was not willing to contribute its own troops. In the case of the Rwandan genocide, the United States delayed a Security Council resolution calling for a stop to the violence, and it failed to contribute significant resources for fear of getting embroiled in another African conflict.[44] When the Clinton administration later chose to involve itself militarily in Bosnia and Kosovo, it led NATO countries in aerial bombing campaigns of contested areas. Clinton valued international cooperation and did not want to use the US military to solve problems without consulting allies and the international system. In this regard, he ranks low on a scale of military assertiveness.

In sum, on all three categories of military assertiveness Clinton scores relatively low. Combined with his high self-monitoring, we can confidently classify Clinton as a high self-monitor dove, or what I call a reputation believer. Before I test the theory's predictions for a reputation believer against Clinton's record of crisis decision making, I examine Clinton's presidential elections to probe the role Clinton's self-monitoring and hawkishness played in them.

Reputational Concerns and Clinton's Crisis Decision Making

The dispositional theory predicts that, as a high self-monitor dove, Clinton will demonstrate reluctance to use military instruments in international crises. However, as a high self-monitor, Clinton should seek to resort to the use of military instruments when he senses that the US reputation for resolve is at stake. Indeed, reputational considerations—especially maintaining an image of a tough president who would not be humiliated or pushed around—played a major role in Clinton's crisis discourse and decision making. Clinton understood the limitations of military tools to accomplish certain political goals and realized that, without the support of the American public and Congress, he could not sustain military campaigns even if US reputation for resolve was at stake.

The evidence presented in the rest of this chapter provides strong support for the dispositional theory. I should caution, however, that the conclusions I reach in this chapter are tentative, mainly because the vast majority of primary sources on Clinton's foreign policy are still classified. The analysis here draws on a variety of secondary sources, oral histories, memoirs, and public statements by the president and his advisors.[45]

STRUGGLES IN SOMALIA

American involvement in Somalia began when President George H. W. Bush ordered US soldiers to land in Mogadishu on December 9, 1992, to facilitate a UN humanitarian relief mission to address starvation in Somalia. The mission was to be short, but after entering office, President Clinton agreed to prolong the US military presence in an effort to suppress rising violence and to support the UN operation.

Efforts to clamp down on violence were not totally successful. Forces loyal to a local warlord, the self-proclaimed president of Somalia Mohamed Farrah Aidid, killed twenty-three Pakistani UN peacekeepers. In response, the United States participated in a manhunt seeking to capture Aidid and bring him to justice. On October 3, a raid meant to capture several of Aidid's top aides turned into a two-day struggle, remembered in history books as the Battle of Mogadishu or "Black Hawk Down," resulting in the grisly deaths of eighteen Americans.[46]

Members of Congress and the public, enraged, demanded the immediate departure of US forces from Somalia. Clinton resisted these calls, fearing that American credibility would be badly damaged if the United States departed. He was ultimately forced to recall American troops but did so on a six-month timetable, which included a period of buildup of US forces. This buildup and the prolonged drawdown were the best Clinton could do to demonstrate resolve, given the intense domestic political pressure for American forces to return home. Clinton's reaction to the crisis matches the predictions of dispositional theory: once America's reputation for resolve became jeopardized, he resisted strong political pressure from Congress and the public to withdraw troops immediately and instead chose to stand firm as long as politically possible.

Background

United States involvement in Somalia had begun at the end of George H. W. Bush's presidency. Somalia had descended into civil war in 1991 after the regime of Mohamed Siad Barre fell and infighting began within opposition forces.[47] Civil war and anarchy resulted in the destruction of most of the country's agricultural industry. As a result, an estimated three hundred thousand Somalis had starved to death before the international community intervened.[48] In April 1992, under Bush's leadership, the United States and a number of other countries pushed the United Nations to organize a relief effort. As of August, the United States and western allies were assisting with the UN Operation in Somalia I (UNOSOM I) through Operation Provide Relief, delivering thousands of tons of food and medical aid. Despite these efforts, however, UNOSOM I largely failed to alleviate the humanitarian crisis because most aid was stolen or could not be distributed.[49] Local warlords and clan leaders seized food deliveries to ensure others' loyalty and obedience.[50] As the ineffectiveness of UNOSOM I became obvious, the United Nations Security Council approved the creation of an international coalition known as the Unified Task Force (UNITAF) on December 3, 1992, in UN Resolution 794. UNITAF's mission would be to establish a "secure environment" for international relief workers and to create "as soon as possible the necessary conditions for the delivery of humanitarian assistance."[51]

President George H. W. Bush offered to send twenty-five thousand American troops as part of UNITAF in December 1992.[52] At the time, Bush insisted on a highly limited role for US forces; a short US involvement was envisioned for a humanitarian mission—not to defend any vital interest of the United States.[53] In the discussions prior to the passage of UN Resolution 794, the Bush administration rejected proposals for state-building efforts and promised only to secure transport routes necessary for the safe distribution of food and medical supplies.[54] The circumscribed nature of the mission became a source of tension with the UN secretary-general, who wanted a much more ambitious assignment, including disarming landmines and creating a civilian police force.[55] Members of the Bush administration thought such an expansive operation excessive and firmly declined to commit the United States to any such state-building mission.[56] Brent Scowcroft, Bush's national security advisor, reportedly told the Clinton transition team that American soldiers would likely depart before Clinton's inauguration on January 20.[57]

It seems that Bush thought the operation would be worthwhile even if Clinton were to pull the troops out after entering office. When UN Secretary-General Boutros Boutros-Ghali asked if forces would remain after Clinton's inauguration, Secretary of State Lawrence Eagleburger replied that the Bush administration was ready to send troops and that, if Clinton objected, the United States would withdraw by January 19.[58] Later Scowcroft had Clinton's transition team briefed about the operation.[59] According to Anthony Lake (who would become national security advisor in Clinton's first term), the Bush administration "checked with [the Clinton transition team] . . . and we said fine, because people were starving and it was their watch and they knew what they were doing and all that."[60] Clinton essentially agreed to what was planned and expected to be a short and limited humanitarian intervention.[61] The Bush administration planned to end the US presence in Somalia within three to four months.[62]

After Clinton assumed the presidency, he and his team "came in and had a strategy of handing the operation over to the UN, but not trying to solve the underlying conflict in Somalia."[63] Early on, it was important to the Clinton administration that the United States be able to reduce its involvement. In February 1993, however, violence in Somalia greatly increased. The United States had planned to complete the transfer of responsibilities to the United Nations in March, but the spiraling violence caused some officials to question whether America should leave so quickly.[64]

Over the summer of 1993, American causalities began to mount. Four American service members died on August 8 when a bomb detonated under their vehicle, and six more Americans were injured on August 22 by a landmine.[65] Before long, Clinton changed course in Somalia and decided to prolong US involvement. He supported UNSC Resolution 814, passed on March 26, 1993, which allowed the United States to station eight thousand soldiers in Somalia and to create a Quick Reaction Force (QRF) of one thousand troops to help suppress the violence. Just weeks after Resolution 814 took effect, militants loyal to local warlord Mohamed Farrah Aidid attacked and killed twenty-three Pakistani soldiers assisting with the United Nations operations.[66]

The attack on the Pakistani forces forced Clinton to choose between backing down and escalation. Several officials believed that the United Nations and the United States had to respond or else it would signal that the peacekeeping missions were "not serious."[67] Colin Powell, who was then a member of the

Joint Chiefs of Staff and who had opposed US military intervention in Somalia, recommended the United States stand firm and try to capture Aidid. Clinton accepted Powell's advice "somewhat reluctantly" and "said, 'Yes, we'll send them in.'"[68]

With support from the Clinton administration, the United Nations Security Council responded to the attack with Resolution 837 on June 6, 1993. The resolution condemned the attack and authorized all "necessary measures . . . to secure . . . arrest and [detain] for prosecution, trial and punishment" those responsible for the killing of the twenty-three Pakistani soldiers.[69] Clinton was evidently not willing to back down in Somalia and forfeit the hard-fought gains US forces had made. His administration supported Resolution 837 and agreed to extend the stay of American forces to 1995; Clinton also gave Defense Secretary Les Aspin "clear direction to stay the course with other nations to help Somalia."[70] Rather than abandon Somalia in the face of Aidid's aggression, the United States and its allies stood firm and launched a campaign to arrest Aidid.

The Battle of Mogadishu

The efforts to capture Aidid were largely carried out by a joint special operations task force called Task Force Ranger.[71] During the summer of 1993, Task Force Ranger launched six raids to try to apprehend Aidid and his associates.[72] Some of Aidid's top aides were captured, but Aidid himself remained at large. These operations were not free of casualties: both American and foreign troops were injured or killed.[73]

The worst days came on October 3 and 4, when eighteen American servicemen were killed and a further seventy-three wounded.[74] The fateful clash, which became known as the Battle of Mogadishu or "Black Hawk Down," began as another attempt to capture two of Aidid's close supporters.[75] Things began to go wrong on October 3 when one soldier fell from a helicopter, which led to a series of events that resulted in two Black Hawk helicopters being brought down by enemy fire.[76] By October 4, the attempt to capture Aidid's lieutenants had become a mission to rescue members of the task force.[77] Video of a US soldier's body dragged through Mogadishu's streets was seen on major news channels by nearly 6 in 10 Americans.[78] The loss of American forces shocked the American public and would force Clinton to terminate US involvement in Somalia.

Clinton's Immediate Reaction

Clinton's early statements suggest that he wanted to continue with the operation. On October 4, he told reporters in San Francisco:

> The only thing I have done so far [in response to the situation in Mogadishu] is to authorize the Rangers that are there who are wounded or exhausted or done more than their fair share to be replaced, to roll over that group and

then to send some more people there with some armored support so that we can have some more protection on the ground for our people. None of this happened when we had 28,000 people there. And even though there are lots of U.N. forces there, not all of them are able to do what our forces did before. So I'm just not satisfied that the folks that are there now have the protection they need.[79]

This quotation reveals much about Clinton's initial reaction to Somalia. At no point does he allude to the possibility of a withdrawal. Instead, he announces his willingness to immediately deploy more personnel to continue the fight against Aidid. He approaches the problem from the perspective that American forces lack sufficient numbers to attain US objectives with an acceptable level of risk. The statement that no major disasters occurred when the United States had more soldiers on the ground strongly hints that Clinton thought that future incidents resembling the Battle of Mogadishu could be prevented by deploying more soldiers. While Clinton, like most leaders, wanted to reduce the casualties suffered by his own forces, he clearly had no desire to terminate America's involvement even after the losses already suffered. Instead, his immediate response was to say that he would bolster America's military presence to lower the cost of attaining America's objectives.

One could make the counterargument that the remarks in the immediate aftermath of the Battle of Mogadishu were made based on little information, prior to consultation with advisors, and so may be an imperfect reflection of Clinton's decision making. Clinton did preface his statement by saying, "I'll be doing a lot more work on this today."[80] However, even if he had not fully investigated all the options and digested all the information, Clinton obviously had discussed possible responses to the Battle of Mogadishu in enough depth prior to the press conference to be ready to state that he had ordered more soldiers to Somalia. It therefore seems reasonable to infer from his initial response to the press that Clinton wished to continue contributing to the UN operation, despite the loss of life.

Clinton further expressed unwillingness to abrogate America's commitments to Somalia or the United Nations when he said on October 4 that "I do not want to do anything which would imperil the fundamental success of one of the most successful humanitarian missions we've seen in a long time."[81] Just in case the press had any doubts about Clinton's position, an administration spokeswoman, Dee Dee Myers, stated that America's "commitment to the mission [in Somalia] has not changed."[82] In light of Clinton's declared desire to continue American involvement in Somalia, it seems clear that the casualties suffered were not enough to convince Clinton to withdraw. Just as dispositional theory would predict, Clinton preferred to stand firm and proceed with the mission, rather than back down after the United States had suffered relatively few casualties.

"Our Own Credibility with Friends and Allies Would
Be Severely Damaged"

Most members of Congress took a very different approach. Deputy National Security Advisor Samuel R. Berger recalled that on October 4 there was "a volcanic eruption from the Congress."[83] The next day, both Secretary of Defense Aspin (formerly a member of Congress) and Secretary of State Warren Christopher were ordered to appear before a joint session of Congress, where Aspin was "massacred by his former colleagues."[84] Virtually all the members at the joint session demanded a "clear road map for an exit from Somalia."[85]

Clinton also invited committee chairs and members of the congressional leadership for a meeting on Somalia. The message conveyed at that meeting could hardly have been clearer. Senator after senator said, "we want those troops out now."[86] Berger recalled that the powerful chairman of the Senate Appropriations Committee, Democratic Senator Robert Byrd, with a quiver in his voice, told the president "how we had to get our troops home tomorrow. We are going to act. When the Congress reconvenes, we're going to cut off the money for any continuation of American presence there."[87]

The position taken by most members of Congress, in both parties, was that America's commitment to the UN mission in Somalia had to end. Senator Robert Dole (R-Kansas) said, "If we had a vote today, we'd be out today." Dole later came to support a slower withdrawal but remained insistent that American forces must leave Somalia.[88] During the week after the incident in Mogadishu, a spokesperson noted that Senator John McCain (R-Arizona) had "received more than 2,000 calls on this issue, and only two dozen of them indicated any support for remaining in Somalia. . . . The overwhelming sentiment expressed has been 'to get out of there and get out of there now.' "[89] Representative Barney Frank (D-Massachusetts) told reporters that America needed to "get out of Somalia."[90] Representative Howard L. Berman (D-California) described his reaction to the situation in Mogadishu as "a sense of disgust and outrage."[91]

Public opinion had favored getting out of Somalia even before the Battle of Mogadishu.[92] Polling data from October 3–4, just before the firefight, showed that US citizens preferred to leave Somalia by a nearly two-to-one margin; there was an increase in this sentiment by the time of another poll on October 5, just after Mogadishu. The principal change between the two polls was an increase in the percentage that wanted to pull troops, from 58 to 64 percent. The same poll showed that only 28 percent of Americans wanted to keep troops in Somalia;[93] 37 percent of Americans wanted to leave immediately, 25 percent before the end of the year, and only 1 percent wanted to remain

TABLE 8.1. Public Support for President Clinton's Handling of Somalia Intervention, June–November 1993

Survey Date	Approve	Disapprove	Don't Know	Survey Organization
June 21–24	51%	21%	27%	CBS/*NYT*
September 9–15	41%	39%	19%	Times Mirror
October 5	33%	53%	14%	ABC
October 6	30%	49%	21%	NBC
October 6	21%	58%	21%	CBS
October 6–7	26%	56%	18%	CBS
October 7	36%	52%	12%	ABC
October 7	31%	58%	11%	*Time*/CNN
October 7–10	36%	58%	6%	*Washington Post*
October 8–10	32%	59%	9%	Gallup
October 12	34%	62%	4%	ABC
October 18–19	29%	58%	13%	CBS
October 21	29%	63%	8%	*Time*/CNN
October 21–24	33%	54%	13%	Times Mirror
November 11–14	35%	57%	8%	ABC/*Washington Post*

Source: Information from Mathew Baum, "How Public Opinion Constrains the Use of Force: The Case of Operation Restore Hope," *Presidential Studies Quarterly* 34, no. 2 (2004): 216.

until after December 31, 1993.[94] In other words, a strong majority of Americans preferred to pull out of Somalia within less than three months. Another poll by *USA Today* on October 5 showed that 43 percent of Americans thought troops should be withdrawn "right away," 26 percent wanted a "gradual" withdrawal, and only 7 percent said troop levels should be kept constant. The same *USA Today* poll found that just 18 percent of Americans wanted to escalate and send more soldiers.[95] Support for withdrawal also appears to have been bipartisan, just as it was in Congress: between 55 and 60 percent of Democrats, Independents, and Republicans polled even before the Battle of Mogadishu favored pulling troops out of Somalia.[96] Widespread and bipartisan opposition to Clinton's Somalia strategy put the president under pressure to pull out American forces (see table 8.1).

The pressure on Clinton from both Congress and the American public was immense, by all accounts.[97] Some in the administration took very seriously the threat that Congress would cancel funds for Somalia. Alphonso Maldon, the White House Military Office director, said he recommended that Christopher and Aspin try to talk Byrd out of offering an amendment to cancel funding because "otherwise . . . we can expect Byrd to heavily influence Members' opinions to withdraw troops."[98] As pressure from Congress and the public seemed to intensify, Clinton negotiated with legislators on a date for American forces to leave Somalia.[99]

On October 7, Clinton gave a speech announcing the recall of American forces by March 31, 1994. Some saw this as a "compromise" with legislators.[100] Others, such as Deputy Assistant to President Clinton for National Security Affairs Nancy Soderberg, argued that the president gave up very little and effectively resisted congressional demands:

> Clinton resisted putting an early date [on withdrawal]. Congress wanted us out right away, but we said, No, we're going to keep to the original timetable, and I think we maybe added a little to it. So it's frustrating that everyone says we cut and run from Somalia, when in fact we had always been on track to hand it over to the UN.[101]

Two days before the Mogadishu incident, a "Joint Staff team . . . completed [a report that] recommended withdrawing the majority of U.S. forces by 31 March 1994."[102] Based on the administration's planning, one could argue, as Soderberg did, that Clinton backed down from nothing in Somalia, but rather carried out the mission largely as planned. Of course it cannot be known for certain what would have happened if "Black Hawk Down" had never occurred. It does look as if Clinton wanted to leave Somalia at some point, even if his preferred departure date would not have been the one announced on October 7.

Anthony Lake recalls how, in negotiating with congressional leaders, Clinton steadfastly resisted calls for an immediate departure. An important reason was to avoid sending a message that others can "kill and humiliate our people and the United States will immediately retreat."[103] In the end, on October 7, Clinton announced that all American forces would leave Somalia by March 31, 1994.[104] His plan for withdrawal called for a large buildup in forces, followed by a gradual reduction in troop numbers over a six-month period. The administration intended to dispatch "1,700 Army troops with 104 armored vehicles" and to station the USS *Abraham Lincoln* with thirty-six hundred Marines offshore.[105]

Shortly after Clinton's announcement, the administration informed Congress that three thousand US Army soldiers, not the initially estimated seventeen hundred, would be stationed in Somalia.[106] As Lake says, one reason for the buildup was certainly to attempt to prevent the appearance that America had backed down. It was also not until May 1994 that the United Nations accepted full control and responsibility for the international humanitarian intervention in Somalia.[107] Clinton himself defended the buildup of American forces by claiming that if the United States were to retreat from Somalia just "when the job gets tough," the world would see America as irresolute. He said:

> I am proposing this plan because it will let us finish leaving Somalia on our own terms. . . . For, if we were to leave today, we know what would happen. . . . Our own credibility with friends and allies would be severely

damaged. Our leadership in world affairs would be undermined at the very time when people are looking to America to help promote peace and freedom in the post-cold-war world. And all around the world, aggressors, thugs, and terrorists will conclude that the best way to get us to change our policies is to kill our people. It would be open season on Americans.[108]

This constitutes clear evidence that Clinton rejected plans for a quick retreat from Somalia because he did not want the United States to look irresolute to allies and enemies. Instead of immediate departure, Clinton chose a large buildup of forces followed by a phased withdrawal because it was the best he could do politically to demonstrate America's steadfastness. He argued that the buildup would help demonstrate that, when Americans took on a challenge, they would do the job right.[109] In other words, Clinton's plan sought to illustrate US credibility, and to show that America fulfills the obligations it accepts, even when things get difficult. Clinton's address to the nation on October 7 provides particularly unmistakable evidence that Clinton resisted calls for immediate withdrawal because of credibility concerns and that he decided to increase troop numbers in Somalia largely to show American resolve.

The announcement of a timetable for removing US military personnel from Somalia allayed some anger in Congress. Senate Majority Leader George Mitchell (D-Maine), Senate Minority Leader Bob Dole (R-Kansas), and Chairman of the Senate Armed Services Committee Sam Nunn (D-Georgia) all supported the six-month pullout plan announced by Clinton.[110] Some legislators, however, remained intensely critical of Clinton and continued to insist on a much faster drawdown of forces. Senators John McCain (R-Arizona) and Phil Gramm (R-Texas) continued for some time to try to "[tie] a president's hands" through legislation.[111] Congressional leadership blocked efforts to legislate an early withdrawal date.[112] By the narrowest of margins (22–21), the House Foreign Affairs Committee adopted the timeline proposed by the president, and the House agreed that US forces would be out of Somalia by March 31, 1994. Clinton's plan for a departure from Somalia accomplished two tasks. First, it appeased congressional and public anger and, second, it attempted to save face by delaying the withdrawal.[113]

Summary

Clinton's decision to send more soldiers to Somalia first and then slowly withdraw completely, despite public and congressional pressure for a faster withdrawal, matches with the predictions of the dispositional theory. After the Battle of Mogadishu, Clinton initially wanted to continue the operation as planned. He ordered deployment of more troops to assist American forces in defending against attack. Only when confronted with extraordinary pressure from the public and Congress did Clinton decide to announce a date by which US soldiers would leave Somalia. Even after announcing the date for withdrawal, he first built up the US military presence to demonstrate resolve and to show that America would not back down because of the deaths of the eighteen service members. His public statements indicate that a major motivation behind his decision to delay the withdrawal was his concern about US credibility and overall reputation for resolve. The theory predicts that Clinton's high level of self-monitoring would lead him to be concerned about reputation for resolve. His dovish tendencies about the use of force would lead him to be reluctant about applying military instruments, but to be more willing to escalate to military coercion in order to protect reputation for resolve.

CREDIBILITY CONCERNS AND THE HAITI INVASION

Operation Uphold Democracy was launched on September 19, 1994 by President Clinton. It sought to enforce the removal of the military government of Haiti and to return the democratically elected President Jean-Bertrand Aristide to power. While most internal documents pertaining to the Haitian crisis remain classified, the available evidence suggests that, despite initial reluctance to use force in Haiti, Clinton ultimately decided on military action once he believed America's reputation for resolve was at stake.

Background

The Haiti situation, like many of the dilemmas Clinton faced, predated his term as president. After the country suffered the oppressive rule of the Duvalier family from 1957 to 1986 and subsequent political uncertainty and transition, Haiti eventually held presidential elections on December 16, 1990. Jean-Bertrand Aristide, a leftist and somewhat anti-American Catholic priest,[114] won 67 percent of the vote.[115] Upon assuming the presidency, Aristide introduced a series of domestic reforms.[116] The reforms proved controversial and quickly brought Aristide into conflict with Haiti's elite.[117] On September 29, 1991, Raoul Cédras, a lieutenant general appointed by Aristide, led a coup d'état. The coup succeeded, and a military junta was created. Forced out of Haiti, Aristide made his way to Washington, DC, where he remained until 1994.

Although the United States had backed Aristide's opponent in the 1990 election, President George H. W. Bush condemned the coup and imposed economic sanctions on Haiti's junta.[118] The Organization of American States (OAS) also organized an embargo.[119] Bush's economic sanctions blocked all assets of the Haitian government in the US and prevented Americans from making payments that would benefit the military regime. On October 28, 1991, American sanctions expanded to ban the import or export of specified goods and services.[120] The OAS embargo likewise expanded rapidly; originally covering only fuel and weapons, it soon included all goods other than medical supplies, food, and other essentials.[121] These economic measures did not convince the junta to step down. Rather, Cédras and his cronies continued to commit gross human rights violations. Many Haitians sought refugee status in the United States.[122]

The influx of refugees during the 1992 election prompted then-candidate Clinton to criticize the Bush administration's policy toward Haiti. Clinton argued against the practice of intercepting refugee boats and sending them back to Haiti.[123] Clinton instead promised to grant temporary asylum to those fleeing Haiti "in the absence of clear and compelling evidence that they weren't political refugees."[124] Once in office, however, he backtracked and continued the Bush interception policy, concerned about possible domestic political consequences of letting thousands of refugees into the United States.[125] Clinton conceded to a reporter in 1993 that "maybe I was too harsh in my criticism of [George H. W. Bush]."[126] Clinton had avoided any commitment during the campaign to use force against the military dictatorship in Port-au-Prince.[127] Thus, Clinton began his presidency by using economic sanctions and diplomacy in an effort to persuade the Cédras regime to restore power to Aristide.

Early Efforts to Restore Democracy

Clinton's reliance on nonmilitary tools of statecraft with respect to Haiti is consistent with the predictions of dispositional theory: as a high-self monitor dove, Clinton should have been reluctant initially to use force in Haiti. After all, Haiti was not a country of vital strategic importance to the United States and, at least initially, any crisis there did not threaten to jeopardize America's reputation for resolve.[128] America's reputation would not become tied to the successful resolution of the crisis in Haiti until 1994.

Comments from Clinton and his White House staff clearly indicate that, in 1993, the newly inaugurated president preferred a negotiated solution over the use of military force. In one of the administration's first statements on Haiti, the White House director of communications said on March 2, 1993 that the administration strongly supported the negotiating process undertaken by the UN and the OAS in Haiti.[129] This press release reveals that the administration's ideal policy would be negotiation and economic statecraft to secure the reinstallation of Aristide as president. The wish for a nonmilitary resolution also appears in Clinton's early public comments at a joint press conference on March 16, 1993 with Aristide:

> I want to make it clear in the strongest possible terms that we will not now or ever support the continuation of an illegal government in Haiti and that we want to step up dramatically the pace of negotiations to restore President Aristide.[130]

His language set out that America would refuse recognition of the junta and commit to continue its use of sanctions and diplomacy, but Clinton's statement promises nothing else: he makes no mention of the possible use of US forces. This indicates that, at the time, Clinton was disinclined to approve military intervention. No evidence could be found to suggest that, at the time these remarks were made, anyone believed that America's reputation for resolve needed defending by the use of force in Haiti. The initial reliance on economic statecraft and multilateral negotiations through the UN and OAS comports with dispositional theory.

Clinton's administration moved forward without using force; it tightened sanctions and accelerated the pace of negotiations. Secretary of State Christopher Warren appointed Lawrence Pezzullo as special representative in Haiti.[131] Pezzullo's mission was to work with UN Special Envoy Dante Caputo and the OAS to "push forward with the rapid settlement of [the Haiti] issue."[132] When Pezzullo's efforts were unavailing, Clinton approved new sanctions. On June 4, 1993, Clinton informed Congress that, because "the parties in Haiti have not been willing to . . . take the steps necessary to begin democracy's restoration," those who stood in the way of an agreement, and their immediate relatives, would be barred from entering the United States.[133] Furthermore, those who provided material support to the Haitian dictatorship would find their assets within US jurisdiction frozen. Earlier sanctions had dealt primarily with the property of the Haitian government and "unlicensed financial transactions with Haitian persons."[134] The new sanctions directly targeted Cédras's backers. It appeared the new sanctions might yield results when, on June 21, Cédras sent Caputo a letter desiring to resolve the Aristide dispute.[135]

Caputo and Aristide agreed to talks. On July 3, after less than a week of discussions, Aristide and Cédras signed an agreement that was intended to lay the groundwork for a "satisfactory solution to the Haitian crisis and the beginning of a process of national reconciliation."[136] The agreement provided that Cédras would "retire" and Aristide would resume the presidency on October 30, 1993. The UN and OAS would oversee implementation of the agreement.[137] Overall the deal looked, at least for a short while, like a diplomatic success.

The USS *Harlan County* Incident

To support the agreement, the United States and Canada sent the USS *Harlan County* with 218 military advisors to train the Haitian military. The *Harlan County* planned to dock in Port-au-Prince, but when it arrived on October 11, a Cuban tanker occupied the *Harlan*'s docking space. Had that been the only problem, the *Harlan*'s captain might have found another place to dock. Far more menacing, however, was a band of machete-wielding protesters on the dock. They had surrounded the car of American embassy attaché Vicky Hudleston, who had intended to greet the *Harlan County* when it came into port. Instead, the arriving American and Canadian service members faced a mob chanting "remember Somalia."[138] The Mogadishu tragedy had occurred only a few days earlier.

Fearful that the protesters might harm the service personnel on board the *Harlan County*, who were equipped only with light arms and "had no real combat capacity," the ship's captain stayed at sea.[139] The *Harlan County* did not land but waited for orders; finally, on October 12, it was instructed to withdraw. The captain had become concerned that the protesters could open fire and hit the *Harlan County*, preventing the advisors from arriving safely. After the Mogadishu debacle, the Clinton administration felt it could not afford any more casualties when conducting what were essentially humanitarian missions. The *Harlan County* never docked in Haiti.[140]

The withdrawal of the USS *Harlan County*, although a disappointment for the administration, did not affect the credibility of the United States in Clinton's view. On October 12, the same day the *Harlan* left Port-au-Prince, Clinton fielded questions from the press. One reporter asked "Do you have a message for the military leaders in Haiti who have . . . so far thwarted our mission?"[141] Clinton's response implied the United States had not backed down. He said:

> First of all, the objective of the United States is to restore democracy and President Aristide to Haiti. The instrument of that was the sanctions. . . .
>
> [The *Harlan County*'s mission] is different from the other missions we have been discussing. This is not peacekeeping. This is not peacemaking. This is an agreement that has been made, that if honored, would enable our people to come in and simply serve as trainers, 600 of them. So I have no intention of sending our people there until the agreement is honored.
>
> What I intend to do now is to press to re-impose the sanctions. I will not have our forces deposited on Haiti when they cannot serve as advisors, when they cannot do what they were asked to do.[142]

Clinton made two points in arguing that the United States had not been irresolute. First, he pointed out that the intended purpose of the military personnel on board the USS *Harlan County* was only to train the Haitian military. The United States had promised to provide trainers if the parties to the agreement, namely Aristide and the Cédras regime, honored their commitments. Since the junta, or at least its supporters, seemed to have violated the agreement, the American trainers could not do their job properly, and so the United States was not obliged to send its military advisors. The Clinton administration had not said it would use force to insert its military advisors in Haiti, and, for that reason, the United States had not backed down by withdrawing the *Harlan County*. Second, Clinton expressly noted that the goal of the *Harlan County* mission was not to restore Aristide to power; rather, the economic sanctions were intended to convince the junta to leave.

Prominent members of Congress began to express concerns about the administration's foreign policy and credibility. On October 17, the *Washington Post* reported that "most of those contacted for this article—and a dozen lawmakers, foreign diplomats and scholars interviewed—said they considered" that American foreign policy was no longer "strong," "sure-footed," or "unflinching."[143] Senator Sam Nunn, the chairman of the Senate Armed Services Committee, worried about the impact of the *Harlan County* incident on America's reputation for resolve. He characterized Clinton's Haiti policy as:

> "We are down here and, by golly, we are going to train you whether you want it or not, and we are going to kick your top man out. But there is one caveat. If you shoot one of us, we are going home." That is weird. . . . To those who do not want us, all you have got to do is shoot one of us, and we are out of here.[144]

This comment shows Senator Nunn's concern about Clinton's reluctance to use force and to accept casualties, even to attain objectives the administration had designated as important. Such unwillingness weakened the image of the United States as highly resolved. Other senators voiced similar concerns. Senator Tom Harkin (D-Iowa) criticized the administration, saying:

> The mightiest nation on Earth . . . [is] being faced down by a rag-tag element of no more than 100 drug traffickers, smugglers, and murderers, and we turned around and tucked our tail and ran. . . . If we cannot support duly elected democratic governments 800 miles from our shores, again what kind of message will we send to potential coup leaders?[145]

Cédras's behavior after the *Harlan County* incident strongly suggests that the dictator thought the United States would not use force to remove the junta. On multiple occasions, General John J. Sheeden, whose responsibilities included planning an invasion of Haiti, had warned Cédras that if he did not resign soon, the United States would send in troops and force Aristide's return to power.[146] Cédras, apparently doubting Sheeden's admonitions, declined to resign peacefully until he learned American forces were literally in the air on their way to Haiti.[147]

Officials in the administration soon became aware of the perceived damage to America's reputation. In October, Assistant Secretary of State for Inter-American Affairs Alexander Watson said before Congress that "demonstrating U.S. resolve in a region with strong historical, cultural, economic, and political ties to the U.S." could "enhance U.S. influence and credibility internationally."[148] Secretary of State Warren Christopher recalled in his autobiography how the members of the administration were becoming aware of the negative trends in world opinion of the United States: "Taken together with the re-verses we suffered in Somalia that fall, the *Harlan County* incident created a perception of lack of resolve that took us some time to shake off."[149] As we shall see, the perceived decline in America's reputation for resolve as a result of the *Harlan County* incident appears to have contributed to the changes in Clinton's policy toward Haiti over the next year.

"I'm Never Going to Wimp Out . . . Like I Did in Haiti Again"

Less than a year after the *Harlan County* incident, the Clinton administration shifted from avoiding the use of force in Haiti to a strategy that depended on a successful invasion with twenty thousand troops. This policy reversal seems to have been, in large part, the result of reputational concerns. The pace of the change, although quick, was not instantaneous. First, the transition grew out of many discussions and a detailed policy review process. Second, like most doves, Clinton continued to hope for a diplomatic solution. Thus, in the days immediately after the *Harlan County* left Haiti, the administration reverted to sanctions and multilateral diplomacy.

On October 13, the UN Security Council approved Resolution 873, which reinstated international sanctions against the Cédras regime because of its obstruction of the UN Mission in Haiti (UNMIH).[150] To comply with the UN resolution, the Treasury Department reintroduced all suspended sanctions on October 18, and Clinton ordered six US Navy ships to begin enforcement of the reinstituted embargo.[151] The administration soon found the sanctions to be insufficient, and it asked the Security Council to restrict economic in-tercourse with Haiti further. On May 6, 1994, the council agreed and passed Resolution 917. The new resolution required states to deny takeoff, overflight, and landing permission to all noncommercial flights to or from Haiti, and it urged governments around the world to freeze the assets of anyone employed by the Haitian military or police, and their immediate relatives.[152]

Even in the face of these economic sanctions, the military dictators in Haiti were not willing to leave power voluntarily. The intransigence of the Haitian junta put Clinton in a bind. He had promised to return Aristide to power and had been embarrassingly thwarted by a group of just a hundred or so protest-ers; he felt compelled to remove Cédras in order to defend America's foreign policy credibility.[153] At the same time, Clinton did not want to endanger the lives of American service members. Consistent with Clinton's dovish tenden-cies, diplomatic efforts continued right up until the invasion, but Clinton was aware that military force might be necessary to achieve the administration's objectives in Haiti.

Indeed, shortly after the *Harlan County* incident, Clinton would tell his aides "I'm never going to wimp out . . . like I did in Haiti again."[154] That incident and the Somalia fiasco left the president lacking confidence in his secretary of state and secretary of defense. He complained, "no one told me about the downside," referring to the humiliation he had suffered following their advice. Shortly thereafter, members of Clinton's foreign policy team began to hint that changes might occur in US policy. The *Washington Post* on October 15 reported that

> a senior official said last night that the naval enforcement was "the least" of the military options Clinton will discuss. . . . Asked if the president is ruling out the use of U.S. ground forces, the official said, "We will not rule out anything," a message clearly intended for Haitian military leaders.[155]

US Ambassador to the UN Madeleine Albright told an interviewer on October 17 that the administration had not "ruled out anything" and was still considering a whole range of possible responses to the situation in Haiti.[156]

As a high-self monitor dove, Clinton naturally preferred a peaceful resolution to the dispute with the Cédras regime. However, once Clinton exhausted all peaceful solutions, he became more willing to contemplate the use of force. This comports with the predictions of the dispositional theory. Despite early discussions, the military option did not gain traction until it became obvious in 1994 that economic sanctions were not working and that the situation in Haiti was worsening.[157] In the early part of 1994, Larry Rossin, staffer at the NSC, Deputy Secretary of State Strobe Talbott, National Security Advisor Anthony Lake, and Deputy National Security Advisor Sandy Berger agreed that no peaceful solution to the conflict with Cédras could be reached and urged the president to use force.[158] Clinton appears to have understood the need for a revamped policy toward Haiti, and by May he began to explore, but still declined to commit to, a military solution.[159]

By April, George Stephanopoulos, a close advisor to Clinton, had joined the group that supported the use of force. Those who favored a military intervention in Haiti voiced their views in a meeting held on May 7, 1994, at which General John M. Shalikashvili presented the reasons that the Joint Chiefs of Staff opposed such a course of action.[160] Clinton decided to postpone plans for an invasion for a little longer. Nonetheless, on May 2, 1994, he had for the first time expressly declined to rule out the use of force when speaking with the press.[161] On May 8, 1994, when asked by a reporter how long he would wait to see if sanctions could produce results, Clinton replied, "I think I have to let Mr. Gray [special advisor for Haiti] do a little work before I can answer that question."[162] It seems as though Clinton still had some hope that sanctions could produce results, but those hopes would be extinguished during the summer of 1994.[163]

Despite increased partiality of the president and many in the administration to the military option, some in Washington offered serious counterarguments against restoring Aristide's presidency. The most troubling information about Aristide came from CIA reports that questioned whether Aristide was fit to be president. One report intimated that Aristide suffered serious mental health problems and would be unable to effectively lead Haiti upon his return. Far more damning were reports that included evidence of Aristide committing violence and perpetrating serious human rights violations against his opponents.[164] Upon hearing these reports, many members of Congress expressed outrage and deep concern. Senator Bob Dole, the Senate minority leader, called the reports "very disturbing" and questioned whether the United States should help Aristide, saying the exiled president might not "believe in democracy with a small 'd,' and that he may not be very successful once he returns."[165] But Clinton remained unpersuaded; both Vice President Al Gore and President Clinton publicly denied the CIA's allegations.[166] Stephanopoulos recalled that Clinton said privately, in response to the CIA reports, that "you can make too much of normalcy . . . a lot of normal people are assholes."[167] Even if he did not like or trust Aristide, Clinton continued to lean toward military intervention in Haiti.

On September 15, 1994, Clinton declared his willingness to use military force to end Cédras's rule. At the speech announcing the invasion, Clinton also gave an ultimatum to the junta: "Your time is up. Leave now, or we will force you from power."[168] Prior to the invasion, Clinton engaged in coercive diplomacy; early in September, Clinton ordered a massive military buildup in the Caribbean, in part to intimidate the junta.[169] The administration also convened a number of closed-door meetings and issued a report that called the Haitian dictators some of the worst human rights violators in the hemisphere, in order to "beat . . . the war drums."[170] The administration's coercive diplomacy would also get some unexpected and not entirely welcome help from former President Jimmy Carter.

Charles David, the Haitian junta's foreign secretary, sent a letter to Carter, asking the former president to act as a mediator.[171] Clinton reluctantly agreed to allow Carter to go to Haiti to negotiate. The Haitian junta had also reached out to Colin Powell and Sam Nunn as potential mediators. Deputy National Security Advisor Berger later recalled that "President Carter called and said he was going to Haiti and taking Colin Powell and Sam Nunn with him. It was sort of a self-appointed delegation."[172] There existed some hope that Carter's diplomatic efforts would work, but the administration was unwilling to postpone the invasion.[173] American forces would land on September 19, whether or not Cédras surrendered. With his credibility on the line, Clinton's mind was made up. When Carter's negotiations came to a standstill, Clinton phoned Carter and told the former president that he needed to leave Haiti.[174] Only when Cédras learned "that the 82nd Airborne was on its way" did he agree to US demands and allow American forces to enter Haiti peacefully.[175] Warren Christopher, acknowledging the need for a credible threat of force to make negotiations work, believed that if American soldiers had not been in fast approach, diplomacy "would never have been successful."[176] Thus, twenty thousand American military personnel arrived in Haiti unopposed on September 19.[177]

The last-minute negotiations with Cédras reveal three things about Clinton's foreign policy. First, Clinton wanted to avoid casualties and was highly averse to the use of force. He agreed to let Carter, Powell, and Nunn go to Haiti in hopes of minimizing fighting. Second, if negotiations had failed and the Haitian military resisted, Clinton would still have authorized the invasion. Third, events had left him with no alternative but to introduce US troops into Haiti.[178] Clinton hoped coercive diplomacy would work. But Cédras's desire to make his rule last as long as possible meant the United States could not remove the junta without the use of force. Since Clinton felt he could not afford to back down, the US launched an invasion of Haiti.[179]

American forces, coupled with a small number of soldiers from fifteen other countries, began to arrive in Haiti on September 19, 1994. Thanks to Carter's efforts, the US military encountered minimal opposition.[180] Until the last minute, the Defense Department had expected the troops would need to force their way in to the country; they received news that they could change their entry plan only a few hours before they landed.[181] Upon arrival, the US military force was to oversee the restoration of Aristide to his presidency and to create an environment suitable for UN peacekeepers to replace the US military.[182] According to Defense Secretary William Perry, the general idea was to use "overwhelming force to bring the situation under immediate and complete control."[183] Plans called for completion of the handoff to the UN Mission in Haiti (UNMIH) by March 31, 1995.[184] After that date, the United States agreed to station only twenty-five hundred military personal in Haiti as part of UNMIH.[185] American forces would leave entirely not later than January 1996.[186] Before the transition, the United States military would have a lot of work to do. The timetable for complete withdrawal from UNMIH would later be moved up to April 15, 1996; the mission was formally dissolved on June 1996.[187]

The Role of Credibility in Clinton's Decision to Intervene

Most newspaper articles from the weeks prior to the start of Operation Uphold Democracy surmised that Clinton would go through with the military intervention, in part to prevent damage to the US reputation for resolve. Typical was the *Washington Post*: "Clinton has crossed the line of no return. Despite the risks, any retreat from his vow to oust Haiti's military government would be a devastating blow to the credibility of his presidency and of U.S. foreign policy."[188] Georges Fauirol, an affiliate of the Center for Strategic and International Studies, argued that Clinton "is in a peculiar and dangerous position on Haiti. . . . He has said the military regime must go. He has put his credibility on the line. But he doesn't have any way to make them go . . . unless he launches an invasion."[189] Scholars of America's foreign relations had difficulty identifying any good reason for the invasion other than to show resolve. Michael Mandelbaum argued that, "beyond the immediate issue of Clinton's credibility, invading Haiti doesn't have anything to do with U.S. vital interests as traditionally defined."[190] Given Haiti's low strategic importance, the desire to signal American resolve seems to have had a significant effect on the decision to undertake Operation Uphold Democracy.

Several foreign policy advisors from previous Democratic administrations agreed that preserving the credibility of America's commitments drove Clinton's new and more aggressive policy on Haiti, but they publicly urged the president to forgo an invasion. As the *Washington Post* reported, "In the last few days, veterans of the Kennedy, Johnson and Carter administration found themselves troubled by . . . the step Clinton seems poised to take."[191] They were almost all bothered by the belief that Clinton had prepared an invasion to stem a decline in American credibility. Theodore C. Sorensen, one of Kennedy's senior advisors, recalled that the primary reason Kennedy had authorized the Bay of Pigs operation, ultimately a failure, was to show resolve. Now, Sorensen said, "they are saying that Clinton cannot afford to back down. I think Clinton must have misgivings about it. I hope he rises to them and doesn't repress them. If his heart is not in it, he should not do it."[192]

Several high-ranking members of Clinton's own administration also discussed credibility as a motive for invasion. On August 1, the *Los Angeles Times* quoted Anthony Lake, then national security advisor, as saying: "I do not believe that any President of the United States should ever put American lives at risk simply for the purpose of sending some sort of wider message."[193] Lake also argued that "Clinton does not want to risk U.S. troops in a military adventure just to prove his toughness."[194] This was not the first time Lake had publicly opposed the use of force to demonstrate resolve; he had resigned from Nixon's National Security Council because he believed the invasion of Laos occurred solely out of reputational concerns.[195]

Despite Lake's initial reservations about using force in Haiti to demonstrate resolve, however, less than a month later he would do an about-face. In a September 12 speech to the Council of Foreign Relations, Lake cited the need to protect US credibility as the first of four reasons for the invasion of Haiti.[196] "Lake argues that the president's credibility cannot afford another retreat or more delay on Haiti."[197] The other three justifications offered by Lake for an invasion were that "Haiti is . . . a test of U.S. commitments to defend democracy," that the United States must "prevent further destabilization in the region resulting [in] flights of refugees," and that it must curb "gross abuses of human rights."[198] Lake's second point addressed the perceived need to demonstrate US resolve to support fledgling democracies. Thus Lake's case in favor of military intervention rested in substantial part on arguments about the importance of strengthening America's reputation for resolve.

Without access to currently classified internal documents, it cannot be determined for certain why Lake changed his mind on the importance of resolve. Two possible answers exist. First, perhaps Lake had a change of heart and came to believe that Clinton could not back down because of the damage it would cause to US credibility. Second, it could be that Clinton and other administration officials wanted to go into Haiti for reputational reasons, and they asked the national security advisor to present their reasons for the use of military force. It follows that Lake's speech might indicate his own thinking, or it might reflect the views of the president and the administration. Even if the speech represented his own position, Lake, as one of Clinton's closest counselors on foreign policy, would almost certainly have discussed issues of credibility with the president. Whether the first or second story better explains his apparent change of position, Lake's words and actions indicate that Clinton knew and understood the reputational implications of the decision to use force and thus that he may have authorized the invasion in part to bolster the view of America as a resolute state. Indeed, Clinton expressly mentioned in his address to the nation on Haiti, prior to the start of Operation Uphold Democracy, the same reasons that Lake gave for the invasion in his speech to the Council on Foreign Relations.[199]

Accounts from members of the Senate suggest that Clinton cared greatly about credibility and about America's reputation for resolve. "Senators who have met with Mr. Clinton report that the president knows an invasion is unpopular but feels he has no choice but to make good on his vow to topple the Haitian Junta. Thus our . . . president's slide toward the most politically unpopular use of military force since the Vietnam War."[200] This gives insight into Clinton's reasoning, and, assuming the senators reported honestly, the fact the decision to invade was likely made in part for reasons of credibility despite Clinton's wish to forgo the military option if at all possible coincides with the predictions of the dispositional theory.

It thus seems that Clinton threw domestic political considerations to the wind and decided to intervene for reasons of credibility. The *Wall Street Journal*'s C. A. Robbins wrote:

> [W]hat apparently clinched the deal was the president's belief that despite the strong opposition of the Congress and the American public, he couldn't afford to be seen backing down again. So strong was that belief, Mr. Clinton barred his domestic political advisers—who were certain to argue against an invasion—from his last meetings on Haiti.[201]

The strong domestic opposition to Operation Uphold Democracy, discussed below, is evidence of how much Clinton cared about a strong reputation for resolve.

Domestic and International Audiences

The domestic political opposition to the military intervention in Haiti was fierce. Nearly all Republicans and most Democrats opposed the invasion. Only the Congressional Black Caucus—joined by Florida lawmakers, who were concerned about the continued influx of refugees—supported a military solution. By September 1994, even some members of the Congressional Black Caucus spoke out against the plan to use force in Haiti.[202] Before the invasion, senators and members of Congress raced to go on record opposing the intervention. In the days before Operation Uphold Democracy was launched, "many Representatives used the period at the beginning of the [congressional] day reserved for one-minute speeches to denounce plans for an invasion."[203] Objection to the invasion was just as strong in the Senate. Senators of both parties held a series of discussions about Haiti; nearly "everyone who spoke publicly expressed opposition to an invasion."[204] Virtually every Republican and dozens of Democrats clamored for a vote "in which they [could] register their opposition to an invasion."[205] The tremendous resistance from Congress may have contributed to Clinton's choice not to ask for congressional authorization for Operation Uphold Democracy, as Congress would in all likelihood have denied such authorization by a "wide margin."[206]

Operation Uphold Democracy entailed considerable political risks for Clinton. Midterm elections were scheduled for November; if the operation in Haiti went badly, as Somalia had, the Democrats would almost certainly suffer "a debacle at the polls."[207] To risk losing a midterm election to invade Haiti means that something very important to Clinton must have been at stake. In all likelihood, as noted above, the matters of most importance to Clinton were his and the US reputations for resolve. The risk of considerable casualties was perceived as not trivial. Senator Richard Lugar and other Republicans opposed the intervention precisely because they did not expect the costs to be minimal and worried that a "failure might sour Americans on using force abroad when our interests really are at stake."[208] In the end, Operation Uphold Democracy would result in extremely few American casualties, but ahead of time most members of Congress were not at all certain of the administration's ability to prevent the loss of life. The likelihood of casualties being so uncertain, the military intervention had real domestic political risks, and, therefore, the decision for invasion almost certainly was not meant to advance Clinton's domestic political ambitions.

The views of Congress reflected the feelings of the American public. As the *New York Times* said, shortly after Clinton's address to the nation, "the

fact remains that a Haiti invasion is a mission the country does not believe in"
or support.[209] Prior to the invasion, support for "the use of force in Haiti measured only 37 percent."[210] No other US military operation since 1980 has had
such low levels of support.[211] Anthony Lake confirms that Clinton ordered
the invasion of Haiti despite public opposition; the former national security
advisor wrote:

> [Clinton's] political advisors, reading the polls and worried about the up-
> coming congressional elections, were opposed. The President, to his great
> credit, disagreed with them and made the decision to go ahead.[212]

While public support for the use of force did rise after the invasion, it did
not exceed 50 percent. After Aristide returned to power, the percentage of
Americans who approved of the use of force in Haiti rose to 48 percent, but
another 48 percent disapproved.[213] In the days immediately after the invasion,
support ranged from 40 to 46 percent.[214] One poll in November 1994 showed
that "64 percent of those [asked] took the position that the next Congress
should give a high priority to pulling American troops out of Haiti."[215] All
in all, the evidence suggests Clinton did not base his policy toward Haiti on
public opinion polls; if he had, Operation Uphold Democracy would never
have happened.

Since domestic political factors discouraged the decision to invade Haiti,
one might wonder what role homeland security concerns played. However,
given the limited strategic importance of Haiti to the United States and the
almost nonexistent threat posed by Cédras, it would be improbable that wor-
ries about America's security led to the invasion. Members of the administration categorized Haiti a "nonstrategic area," according to Nancy Soderberg, a
member of the NSC at the time.[216] Christopher said, in a later interview, "Haiti
is . . . not a vital American interest."[217] The public shared this perception; in
one poll, less than a quarter of Americans thought Haiti's fate was important
to the United States.[218]

The international community and many of America's partners in the Western Hemisphere were certainly concerned by the situation in Haiti. Shortly
after the coup that ousted Aristide, the OAS voted for sanctions.[219] But this
concern did not translate into support for a military intervention. Venezuela,
for example, lent critical assistance during the negotiation of the agreement
but later criticized the American-led invasion.[220] Brazil, Mexico, Uruguay,
and Cuba also opposed the use of force in Haiti.[221] Other countries around
the world were not happy with Clinton's decision to send troops, leading the
United States to give large sums in aid to various members of the UN Security
Council for their support of the intervention in Haiti. In addition, it agreed
not to oppose Russian "peacekeepers" in Georgia if Moscow would vote for
a resolution empowering the United States to intervene militarily in Haiti.[222]

Available sources indicate that the invasion was largely an American initiative. American military planners had long prepared plans for possible military intervention in Haiti but first contemplated multilateral participation only in July 1994.[223] It appears that the administration wanted international participation only to make it look like the US actions were part of a broader international effort to bring democracy back to Haiti, to add legitimacy to Operation Uphold Democracy.[224] The United States put together a coalition of fifteen countries; the Netherlands and Argentina, among others, contributed small numbers of forces. Still, US soldiers accounted for 95.7 percent of all those deployed. Washington sought allies and token support, but at no point had the United States faced pressure from other states to use force in Haiti. If one wishes to explain the military intervention in Haiti, one must look to factors other than domestic politics, security, and international pressure.

Summary

Clinton's actions with respect to Haiti comport with the predictions of the dispositional theory. Prior to the *Harlan County* incident, Clinton never discussed the use of force as a possible solution to the crisis in Haiti. Instead, economic sanctions were the administration's primary tool to pressure the junta to allow the restoration of Aristide. The reluctance to use force until after the failure of diplomatic or other nonmilitary attempts is consistent with the theory's predictions for a high self-monitor dove, like Clinton. However, after the *Harlan County* incident, the credibility of the United States was on the line. If Clinton still failed to convince the junta to leave, America's reputation for resolve would badly suffer. True to his dovish nature, only when that diplomacy failed did Clinton opt for a military invasion. However, negotiations with the junta allowed the US military to enter Haiti without much of a fight and restore Aristide to power with extremely few casualties. The available evidence fits with the predictions of dispositional theory for a high self-monitor dove: only when reputation became a serious issue did Clinton overcome his resistance to the use of force and opt for an invasion.

CRISIS ESCALATION IN TAIWAN

Clinton's strategic deployment of two naval battle groups during the 1995–96 Taiwan Strait crisis demonstrates his commitment to protecting American credibility abroad. Throughout the early 1990s, the American-Taiwanese relationship tightened alongside a strengthening Taiwanese independence movement. The People's Republic of China (PRC) engaged in a series of military demonstrations near the Taiwanese coast between July 1995 and March 1996, attempting simultaneously to intimidate the liberation effort and to coerce the United States into abandoning its support for Taiwan. True to his dovish tendencies, Clinton initially sought to counter Chinese aggression with diplomatic rather than military means. But when diplomacy was unsuccessful, Clinton understood that a failure to exercise military coercion would hurt US credibility in the eyes of its Asian allies, and so Clinton deployed two naval battle groups near Taiwan. Although the United States had no binding commitment to defend Taiwan against military action, Clinton refused to be "bullied" on the international stage,[225] resorting to the use of force as "reassurance" to American allies despite the risk of violent conflict with China.[226] Clinton's decision making during this crisis is thus consistent with the predictions of the dispositional theory regarding the behavior of a dovish high self-monitor president.

Background

When Clinton took office in 1993, he inherited a tangled web of diplomatic and strategic commitments in Asia. After the end of the Cold War, the United States and China were no longer bound together by mutual fear of Soviet expansionism, although new concerns partially filled the vacuum.[227] As Clinton's advisor Anthony Lake noted in 1993, the American relationship with China was still "one of the most important in the world" and would "strongly shape both our security and economic interests."[228] China was a key player in the ballooning Asian economy, which by 1992 consumed a greater share of American exports than Europe.[229]

Taiwanese democratization further complicated American allegiances across the strait. Although not fully democratized, the island held multiparty competitive elections and permitted a degree of political expression not tolerated on the mainland.[230] Well-publicized US interventions elsewhere to protect democracy seemed to imply a de facto US obligation to promote—and perhaps even facilitate—democratization abroad.[231] Thus, the Clinton administration faced a complicated diplomatic situation surrounding the Taiwan Strait, in terms of both the formal diplomatic agreements and new concerns following the end of the Cold War.

Tensions Escalate

Throughout the early 1990s, American policy drifted toward Taiwan.[232] Technological transfers from the United States to the "renegade province" increased more than fifteen-fold between 1985 and 1991. These transfers, although not explicitly prohibited under the 1982 communiqué, covered military technology ranging from computer chips to helicopters.[233] In September 1992, pressured on one side by a declining US defense industry and on the other by Clinton's harsh anti-China campaign rhetoric,[234] President George H. W. Bush approved the sale of 150 F-16 warplanes to Taiwan for $6 billion. Incensed, the PRC accelerated its own weapons sales; by the end of the year, M-11 Chinese missiles appeared in Pakistan for the first time.[235]

As the Taiwanese-American relationship tightened, Taiwan's flourishing independence movement further antagonized China. Taiwan's democratization led to greater freedom of expression than the mainland would tolerate, and mainstream Taiwanese political leaders began to disavow reunification while seeking global diplomatic recognition of the ROC.[236]

Clinton's Asia policy was at first marked by a series of reversals that alternately reassured and antagonized the PRC.[237] His administration's early policy bore little resemblance to his fiery anti-China campaign rhetoric, which had threatened to make China's Most Favored Nation (MFN) trade status dependent on its progress on human rights. The conditional MFN initiative was largely abandoned by 1994,[238] indicating early on that Clinton would be reluctant to allow disagreements over human rights issues to corrupt valuable trade relationships.[239] Still, Clinton continued to strengthen the Taiwanese-American diplomatic relationship and even upgraded Taiwan's diplomatic status: among other improvements, Taiwan's politicians could now transit (although not visit) the United States, and its high-level economic officials could meet those of the United States in official settings.[240]

Yet it was a symbolic gesture, rather than a meaningful policy change, that ultimately brought tensions between China and the United States to a boil. In May 1995, Taiwan's President Lee requested a visa to speak at his alma mater, Cornell University. While Clinton and his administration initially opposed granting the permission, Congress voted heavily in favor of it, with only one "nay" vote in the House and Senate combined.[241] Eventually, the Clinton administration approved the visa but emphasized that it was an exception to Taiwan's revised diplomatic status.[242]

The decision came, however, only months before a pivotal Taiwanese presidential election in which China hoped to depose Lee in favor of a candidate with more conciliatory tendencies toward the PRC. Lee himself exacerbated tensions when, during his visit to Cornell, he claimed publicly that the ROC would rejoin the mainland only under conditions of democracy—a concept antithetical to the PRC—and said privately that Taiwan was "definitely" not a part of the PRC.[243] The American invitation seemed to contradict both its public "one-China" stance and its official visitation policy in an act that, to the PRC, reeked of political interventionism. Fissures in the Sino-American relationship would quickly expand into outright cracks.

Crisis Breaks Out

Outraged by Lee's visit and remarks, China was engaging in what Todd Hall calls a "diplomacy of anger."[244] Beginning in July 1995, China's People's

Liberation Army (PLA) commenced a series of missile and naval tests that were intended to demonstrate China's anger; intimidate Taiwanese voters; and pressure the US government into disavowing its informal relationship with the increasingly recalcitrant ROC.[245] In an accompanying diplomatic protest, the PRC also temporarily withdrew its ambassador from the United States and suspended Sino-American talks over nuclear nonproliferation and missile technologies.[246]

Consistent with Clinton's dovish inclinations and recognizing China's genuine outrage, his administration initially attempted to pacify the PRC through diplomatic negotiation.[247] Over the next seven months, however, it became clear that Clinton was unable or unwilling to offer China the additional assurances it demanded before it would scale down its military exercises around the Taiwan Strait. This rift first emerged in early August 1995, when Secretary of State Warren Christopher met with Chinese Foreign Minister Qian Qichen in Brunei, tasked with "finding a way to soothe the hurt national pride of an economic superpower without being accused of a sellout" on human rights.[248] Complicating Christopher's mission was the fact that the PRC had recently detained and arrested human rights activist Harry Wu, a US citizen.[249] Christopher privately reassured Qian that the United States continued to support a one-China policy. He refused, however, to make any new public commitments or take any additional concrete actions to oppose Taiwanese independence.[250] As he exited the talks, Qian stated that "the situation [remained] the same as before the meeting," indicating that China required positive action to complement America's verbal reassurances.[251]

Undersecretary of State Peter Tarnoff's visit to China later that month followed a similar pattern. The PRC continued to escalate its military activities and missile tests near Taiwan, while demanding a fourth Sino-American joint communiqué that would rule out the possibility of any future US visits by Taiwanese leaders.[252] The United States held firm in its refusal. Tarnoff noted that the Taiwan issue was "not an area in which [he and Chinese officials] bridged many differences." The United States did, however, agree to host an October presidential summit in New York City, so long as discussions centered on security and human rights issues.[253] Despite wanting to focus on Washington's relationship with Taipei, China agreed to the talks with an eye toward the December Taiwanese legislative elections: Chinese officials hoped that the appearance of a strong Sino-American bond would force Taiwanese candidates to soften their rhetoric toward Beijing.[254] Throughout September, the PRC attempted to mollify Washington with a number of important concessions, first and foremost the announcement that it would suspend nuclear assistance to Iran.[255]

In October, however, the PRC amplified its coercive show of force with new rounds of military maneuvers just north of Taiwan in the South China Sea:[256]

China's television broadcast of President Jiang Zemin, surrounded by the new military leadership and watching naval exercises that included amphibious landings . . . was another reminder for Taiwan of the possible consequences of moves towards independence. And when the Chinese media highlights Mr. Jiang and his recent naval maneuvers only days before China's President is due to meet President Bill Clinton in New York, these are signals for the United States.[257]

Nevertheless, at the presidential summit on October 25, 1995, Clinton reaffirmed his commitment to a standing ambiguous policy regarding Taiwan but refused to issue a fourth Sino-American communiqué or to prohibit future visits from Taiwanese officials, conceding only that these visits would be "unofficial and private and rare."[258] While the meeting renewed Sino-American dialogue over such high-profile issues as nuclear nonproliferation and China's international trade status, tensions over the Taiwan issue continued to fester.[259] Even so, Secretary of Defense William Perry declared on October 30 that "the overarching premise" of Clinton's China strategy was that "whatever our differences with China we also have important common interests and that these interests make dialogue more rational than confrontation."[260]

The Situation Heats Up

Despite Perry's optimistic vision of Sino-American relations in October, the winter of 1995–96 saw China become increasingly bellicose. It appeared simultaneously emboldened by Clinton's failure to confront the PLA militarily and irritated by his refusal to distance the United States from Taiwan or to tighten Sino-American relations. Realizing that the Clinton administration placed a high priority on protecting its stake in the Chinese economy, one high-ranking PLA military official expressed the belief that the United States would risk only "limited intervention" on behalf of Taiwan because outright war would "seriously impair U.S. economic interests."[261] Xiong Guangkai, the PLA's chief of military intelligence, asserted that the United States would "not sacrifice Los Angeles to protect Taiwan," simultaneously questioning American resolve and insinuating that China would willingly enter a nuclear exchange to prevent Taiwanese independence.[262]

Chinese militancy was more than cheap talk. The most alarming and aggressive demonstration yet came in November, as the PLA simulated an amphibious invasion of Taiwan and an attack on its largest airport with the announced intention of discouraging pro-independence rhetoric.[263] Similar exercises continued through February of 1996. At this time, global faith in the American commitment to Asia was at a relative low. One professor at China's National Defense University had predicted that the United States would fail to intervene on behalf of Taiwan because "Americans can never take a beating, not even a light one."[264] The Clinton administration was relatively silent and gave only a few limited signs that the president had grown exasperated with Beijing. In December, an American aircraft carrier traversed the Taiwan Strait for the first time in over twenty-five years (although the detour ostensibly stemmed from adverse weather conditions).[265] In February, Clinton granted a visa to another high-ranking Taiwanese official. While far from overtly antagonistic, neither move could be expected to elicit favor from the PRC, nor did it indicate that the American relationship with Taiwan was being disavowed.

On March 5, the PLA announced it would conduct "ground-to-ground missile launching training" in the Taiwan straits. It specified two areas of the Taiwan port cities of Chilung and Kaohsiung and advised that foreign ships and aircrafts should not enter those areas from March 8 through March 15."[266] Defense Secretary William Perry informed Chinese Vice Foreign Minister Liu Huaqiu in a "very clear and very straight forward" manner that the planned exercises were "reckless" and "could only be viewed as an act of coercion."[267] In a March 8 interview, Perry reminded China that the United States "always" maintained a "substantial naval presence in the western Pacific," specifically pointing out that it had, "within a few hundred miles of Taiwan, a carrier, *Independence*," as well as "a guided missile cruiser and guided missile destroyer also nearby."[268] Through Perry's comments, America had now publicly and vehemently condemned the PLA's activity around the Taiwan Strait.

As the 1996 Taiwanese presidential election approached, in a final attempt to alter the course of the election, the PLA commenced its most aggressive and targeted war games yet. Between March 8 and 25, it launched four DF-15 missiles aimed only fifteen miles from the Taiwanese coast, followed north and south of the strait by "amphibious landing exercises [and] aerial bombing [that] involved some 40 naval vessels, 260 aircraft, and an estimated 150,000 troops."[269] The exercise was a clear signal that President Clinton could no longer ignore if he were to protect the credibility of US international commitments.

Clinton's Coercive Military Signaling

Despite Perry's warnings, the PRC announced on March 9 that it would begin another round of naval and air force demonstrations in the Taiwan Strait, lasting until March 20, just three days prior to the ROC's democratic presidential election.[270] Clinton's response was swift: the aircraft carrier *Independence* would close in on the strait, while the aircraft carrier *Nimitz* and its battle group would arrive in the general vicinity of Taiwan prior to the March 23 election. In total, the force deployed included "between 110–130 carrier-based strike aircraft, over 200 Tomahawk cruise missiles and at least three nuclear-powered attack submarines," in addition to four destroyers, two frigates, an oiler, and two replenishment ships."[271] It was, by any measure, a substantial show of force. The move "raise[d] the stakes" for the PLA's war games, indicating that the

United States was prepared for military confrontation should China assault Taiwan.[272]

Although the PRC continued with its demonstrations through March 20,[273] a confrontation proved unnecessary. The Taiwanese election on March 23 proceeded without other PRC intervention, and, despite the PLA's demonstrations, Lee won handily.[274] Tensions over Taiwan's status persisted, but violent conflict was averted. The American naval forces deployed to the region departed peacefully after the PLA's demonstrations had concluded on March 20.[275]

Clinton's response, one of the clearest examples of military signaling in modern American history, was consistent with the temperament of a high self-monitor president. It was a message designed to restore national credibility. By deploying the *Nimitz* and *Independence* battle groups, Clinton risked the possibility of a violent military confrontation even if China had not intended an immediate invasion of Taiwan. One Asian diplomat warned weeks before the election that if the United States got "into a direct confrontation with China, [it would] probably be alone. . . . No one expect[ed] a war, but everyone [was] worried that given the political, domestic situation in America, Taiwan, and China, it could somehow get out of hand."[276] A former Taiwanese defense minister had similarly cautioned that Beijing was "not that rational" and that he "would advise [the United States] not to" intervene militarily.[277] Moreover, high-ranking PLA officials had implied that China might go to nuclear war with the United States if it sided with Taiwan in an armed confrontation. In positioning the two aircraft carriers near the strait, Clinton had taken a decisive step toward committing American forces to Taiwan's defense, which was seen as a "judicious show of resolve" by a president who could not "afford to look soft" on China.[278]

One might argue that Clinton's actions reflected domestic political concerns: the president cared more about placating his constituents than protecting America's reputation on the global stage. With the 1996 presidential election approaching, Clinton had, by the winter of 1995, largely failed to act on his vehemently anti-China campaign rhetoric despite approving public opinion. A Gallup poll conducted in January 1996 revealed China's lowest favorability rating in the United States since the 1989 Tiananmen Square Massacre. A February EPIC/MRA survey showed that a majority of American voters wanted Clinton to use trade as political leverage against China. An EPIC/MRA representative further observed that Americans felt like "China [wasn't] playing by the rules."[279] Crucially, however, public opinion clearly indicated that a majority of Americans rejected the use of military means to coerce China. A Harris poll conducted before the United States announced it was sending naval forces to the strait found that about two-thirds of Americans opposed sending a US aircraft carrier to the Taiwan Strait to counter China's efforts at military intimidation (68 percent opposed) or using US military forces to defend Taiwan if mainland China actually tried to invade it (65 percent opposed). On both questions, the poll found no difference between Democrats and Republicans.[280]

Whereas public opinion does not appear to explain Clinton's decision making, there was congressional pressure from Republican members to act more assertively. Under the leadership of Speaker Newt Gingrich, House Republicans had long viewed Clinton's reluctance to confront China as the "Achilles' heel of the Clinton presidency,"[281] going so far as to argue that Taiwan should receive a seat at the UN.[282] As summarized by Congressman Steve Horn (R-California) in February 1996, Republicans believed that the president's "weakness encourage[ed] the PRC's bellicosity" and that "the Clinton administration [had] squandered American credibility through a dizzying series of policy flip-flops and retreats in the region."[283]

Clinton's decision to showcase American resolve was not mere domestic political calculation, but a strategic move designed to reassure America's allies in Asia. Along with National Security Advisor Anthony Lake and Secretary of State Warren Christopher, Secretary of Defense Perry said that the president believed that "a show of U.S. military resolve was needed to calm anxieties elsewhere in the region and demonstrated that the United States would not be bullied."[284] Another security advisor who sat in on Pentagon deliberations described the deployment as "a signal to our partners that we [were] there for the long haul, and not a transitory presence in the region."[285]

Summary

Although Clinton initially attempted to manage Chinese aggression toward Taiwan through diplomatic channels, he ultimately deployed two carrier groups near the Taiwan Strait as a demonstration of American resolve, a decision consistent with the temperament of a high self-monitor president. In the words of his secretary of defense, Clinton's actions around the Taiwan Strait were "reassurance to tell everyone in the area that we maintain[ed] a large stake in their peace and stability."[286] State Department spokesperson Nicholas Burns described the move as a "signal" that the United States had a "very great interest" in deterring Chinese aggression toward Taiwan.[287] At a time when the American commitment to allies in Asia had come into question, Clinton chose to risk violent conflict with the PRC—a growing superpower—in order to protect his nation's credibility abroad by bolstering its reputation for resolve.

Alternative and Other Contextual Explanations

MATERIALIST EXPLANATIONS

The nuclear balance, or other systemic variables, can hardly explain the pattern we observe. Clinton came to power when the United States was the sole remaining superpower and arguably the unipole of the international system. Militarily, the United States enjoyed unparalleled military advantage, nuclear and conventional, over all other major powers. Thus, the argument that a perceived decline in the nuclear (or conventional) balance of power leads leaders to fight for reputation cannot explain why Clinton decided repeatedly to risk escalation. Indeed, in a situation of nuclear superiority, this systemic explanation would predict that the United States would have little need for coercive military instruments to project a reputation for resolve. And yet, the United States under President Clinton did engage in reputation-guided policies, such as deploying two aircraft carriers near the Taiwan Strait, in spite of threats that China might escalate to nuclear war if the United States sided with Taiwan in an armed confrontation. Thus, concerns about credibility in a nuclear exchange cannot explain Clinton's crisis behavior and his concerns about reputation for resolve.

Another potential systemic explanation points to the unipolar structure of the international system. As discussed in chapter 5, scholars are split about how unipolarity should affect concerns about reputation for resolve. What is clear is that Clinton's behavior is inconsistent with claims that reputation for resolve should be significantly less salient in the post–Cold War era crisis decision making of US presidents. Still, as discussed in the introduction and conclusion of this book, the post–Cold War period exhibits variation in leaders' concern for reputation for resolve. Systemic theories seem inadequate to explain this variation among post–Cold War American presidents.

The evidence also clearly indicates that material cost-benefit analyses did not drive Clinton's decision-making process: Somalia and Haiti did not constitute vital US interests and had little to no material value to the United States, especially following the Cold War. Neither was the public convinced that the United States should intervene in Haiti. Haiti's low strategic value and nonexistent ability to threaten the United States militarily meant that America's security would be unaffected by the continuation of the Cédras government.

Taiwan presents a harder case because of its continual strategic importance to the United States in East Asia. Taiwan presumably had more strategic value to the United States for its technologically advanced economy and its proximity to the entrance of the South China Sea. However, the escalation of the threats in the Taiwan Strait crisis meant that US moves might come at an extremely high cost. It is difficult to say that Taiwan's strategic benefit, or reassurance to US allies with the continued enforcement of the Taiwan Relations Act, outweighed the risks of a costly direct military confrontation with China.

At the present time, our ability to refute this alternative is limited. Because primary documents are not yet available, it is not entirely clear whether and how much Clinton and his advisors disagreed about the material interests that were at stake in Somalia, Haiti, and Taiwan, and about the use of force to protect reputation. It seems clear from what we do know, though, that there was no serious threat to the US mainland in any of these crises.

DOMESTIC POLITICAL EXPLANATIONS

The evidence indicates that, although public opinion and congressional pressures played a role in pushing Clinton to get out of Somalia (as they did for Reagan in Lebanon), such concerns cannot explain Clinton's decision to intervene militarily in Haiti or to send aircraft carriers to the Taiwan Strait. Public opinion was against using military force in all these crises; no other military operation has had such low support as the invasion of Haiti since 1980.[288] However, even in the presence of domestic pressures and threats to cut support from Somalia, Clinton (like Reagan) took steps, such as pushing back the withdrawal time, that allowed him to save face and to mitigate a blow to US reputation for resolve.

Concerns about the reaction from Clinton's core constituency also cannot convincingly explain Clinton's crisis decision making. Democratic supporters, both among the public and in Congress, wanted Clinton to pull out of Somalia long before the Battle of Mogadishu and before the withdrawal deadline announced on October 7, 1993. Thus, while Congress played an important role in forcing Clinton to withdraw, it cannot explain Clinton's motivation to fight for reputation. Before the invasion of Haiti, Democratic Congress members raced to oppose the intervention. Clinton ignored these domestic political considerations in favor of shoring up US reputation for resolve. To be sure, Operation Uphold Democracy would result in extremely few American casualties, which helped Clinton in the midterm election. But at the time, Clinton decided to invade in spite of the fact that most members of Congress and his own constituency were not at all certain of the administration's ability to avoid loss of life.

Finally, unlike the cases of Somalia and Haiti, Congress showed strong bipartisan support for showing resolve in the Taiwan Strait. House Resolution 148, passed on March 18, 1996, by a vote of 369 to 14, expressed the sense that the United States should help defend Taiwan in the event of an invasion, a missile attack, or a blockade by China, although it stopped short of detailing what action the United States should pursue. Regardless, this resolution passed only after Clinton had publicly announced that the United States was deploying the *Independence* carrier battle group, and after the United States had already dispatched the *Nimitz*.

This is not to argue that Clinton ignored public opinion or did not care about domestic political consequences.[289] Public opinion may have constrained Clinton from using the military instruments at the best time to deploy them. Moreover, throughout those crises, it was important for Clinton, consistent with being a high self-monitor, to frame the policies for the public in a manner consistent with their beliefs and attitudes.

Clinton's attitudes toward domestic considerations in the reputational crises covered here also appear consistent with his decision making during another crisis not discussed in this chapter: the decision to use military troops in Bosnia in 1995. During that crisis, reputational considerations were front and center for Clinton. On July 17, 1995, during a meeting with his advisors, Clinton had complained, "I don't like where we are now. . . . This policy is doing enormous damage to the United States and to our standing in the world. We look weak. . . . And it can only get worse down the road. The only time we've ever made any progress is when we geared up NATO to pose a real threat to the Serbs. . . . Our position is unsustainable; it's killing the U.S. position of strength in the world." Similarly, Stephanopoulos writes, Clinton repeatedly said that the policy in Serbia "made everyone look weak and unprincipled."[290] Alongside these explicit concerns about reputation for resolve, Clinton was also made aware by his longtime political consultant Dick Morris that he "ought to take care of Bosnia before the 1996 elections," but that the American people would not support the use of American troops in any combat in Bosnia.[291] Those domestic political concerns prompted Clinton to instruct his team to "bust our ass to get a settlement in the next few months."[292] American negotiators were immediately dispatched to the Balkans.

On August 28, 1996, in a direct challenge to the negotiating efforts, the Bosnian Serbs launched a mortar attack on Sarajevo, killing thirty-seven civilians. Concerned that US and NATO credibility was on the line, NATO launched a massive air campaign against the Bosnian Serbs that lasted until mid-September. The threat of a sustained military action eventually got the Bosnian, Serbian, and Croatian foreign ministers to agree to a cease-fire on October 5; a final settlement agreement was reached just after the US election on November 21. Clinton then dispatched twenty thousand American troops to join the forty thousand NATO soldiers who were there to enforce the peace, despite public opposition to using US forces and a hostile Congress.

In making his case to the American people, Clinton relied on polls that suggested that the public would be more open to sending troops as part of a peacekeeping operation intended to stop genocide and to protect women and children. And indeed, in his public statements just before the bombing, Clinton had highlighted those themes, stressing the importance of US action to stop the "senseless slaughter of so many innocent people that our fellow citizens had to watch night after night." Although Congress remained divided, Clinton went ahead with the deployment, and public approval of his foreign policy climbed after he acted.[293] This episode suggests that, as with the crises in Somalia and Haiti, Clinton wanted to maintain reputation for resolve, but public opinion shaped policy contours to a larger degree than in the Carter or Reagan administrations.

OTHER INDIVIDUAL-LEVEL EXPLANATIONS

Finally, scholars have pointed that new leaders are more likely to fight for reputation early in their tenure. We find, however, that Clinton's pattern of behavior is the opposite. Only after US humiliation in Somalia and Haiti (his first two international crises as president) did Clinton truly escalate and order the invasion of Haiti. Clinton's behavior also fails to fit that predicted by Dafoe and Caughey that southern presidents are more averse than nonsouthern presidents to backing down from violent conflict as a result of a multigenerational culture of honor.[294]

Clinton was born and raised in the South, and to the extent he cared about reputation for resolve, this would be consistent with their theory. However, he was extremely reluctant to resort to the use of force in Haiti and invaded only after years of diplomacy had failed. Clinton was also reluctant to expend military force in Somalia after what was originally intended as a humanitarian mission declined into a challenge to US reputation for resolve. Given the time it took Clinton to justify the use of military force in the crises discussed here, it cannot be said that he reacted with greater concern for reputation for resolve than his nonsouthern counterparts, such as Reagan, nor that he resorted more quickly to force when that reputation was at stake.

Furthermore, Clinton does not seem drawn to military force based on historical precedents and analogical reasoning. The available record suggests that Clinton's humiliation during the *Harlan County* incident led him to invoke Reagan's reaction to Lebanon and his attempt to save face by invading Grenada. The record is still unclear, however, whether this analogy shaped Clinton's decision to invade Haiti. Even if this were the case, it is interesting that Clinton was taking his cue from a Republican president, one who also shared his high self-monitoring inclinations and thus his concerns about reputation for resolve. Overall, as more documents become available, we will be better able to assess the degree to which Clinton relied on analogical reasoning, and the extent to which analogies may have had an independent causal effect on his decision making.

Conclusion

Clinton's crisis discourse and policies appear to provide strong support for the dispositional theory. Unlike Reagan, Clinton's initial responses to international crises often included diplomacy and negotiations. His inclination was not to use military force if it could be avoided. But as an extremely high self-monitor, Clinton cared a lot about reputation, and US reputation for re-solve in particular. Thus, when he sensed that policies made him look weak in the eyes of adversaries or allies, he was willing to take risks and use military instruments to save face. Unlike Carter, reputational considerations were front and center for Clinton; unlike Reagan, Clinton had to believe there was a "reputation-for-resolve deficit" to overcome his innate reluctance to use military force.

Notwithstanding Clinton's high self-monitoring inclinations and the fact that his base comprised people who were extremely reluctant to use military force, he was willing to fight for reputation even without domestic political support. This reinforces my argument that, in the specific context of an international crisis, high self-monitor leaders see reputation for resolve as an especially important status-enhancing asset. This likely stems from the fact that they see their performance as more important to international audiences than domestic ones.

9

Conclusion

Why are some leaders willing to pay the costs of using of military force—even risking war—over nonvital issues, in order to be seen as resolved in the eyes of "others"? This book advances a simple theory to answer this important question. To understand which leaders are willing to fight for face, we must closely consider the individual psychology of those decision makers.

This is not to argue that the structure of the strategic environment, the preferences of domestic actors, or public opinion do not play a role in shaping policies. Rather, beliefs about the importance of reputation, I argue, are intimately linked to an integral feature of our personalities. As such, they are prepolitical, constructed from the bottom up. Some of us are born with the tendency to self-monitor, to strategically adjust our behavior in order to advance social status; some of us are low self-monitors, born with the inclination to insulate our behavior from the perceived demands of others and instead act according to our true inner beliefs. This personality trait affects the extent to which each of us cares about our country's reputation on the international stage.

Summary of Findings

The book leverages several methodologies to test my theory. In chapter 2, I developed the causal mechanisms that link self-monitoring to concerns about reputation for resolve in international relations. I offered a simple typology of four ideal-type leaders, based on each leader's self-monitoring disposition and military assertiveness, in order to explain variation in leaders' concerns about reputation for resolve, and when those leaders will be more likely to use military instruments to protect that reputation.

In chapter 3, I presented results from survey experiments that consistently and robustly demonstrate that the high self-monitors among us—and especially those who are more dovish—are significantly more likely to care about appearing resolved in the international arena. They are also more likely than their low self-monitor counterparts to use force to defend that reputation. My findings show that the hawk/dove dichotomy is insufficient to explain variation in willingness to fight for reputation. Rather, high self-monitor doves—but not low self-monitor doves—are willing to act against their dovish "type" by seeking to use force when it appears to be justified on reputational grounds. At the same time, high self-monitor and low self-monitor hawks differ in *why* they want to fight: high self-monitor hawks are motivated by image-related concerns, such as overall standing and public perception, while low self-monitor hawks are motivated by nonreputational concerns, such as domestic politics and deterrence. Importantly, the survey experiments also find that high self-monitors see reputation for *resolve* as the dominant social currency during international crises, shown by the result that high self-monitor doves want to fight more when they are told the international community is watching. Moreover, the evidence also suggests that high self-monitors see reputation for resolve as important because of the intrinsic benefits it offers to their country's standing, and not because of instrumental strategic benefits such a reputation could offer. Overall, the evidence in chapter 3 offers powerful microfoundational support for the theory.

Leaders are, at the end of the day, humans. When they occupy the office of the presidency, there is a radical shift in their responsibilities, knowledge, and priorities. But fundamentally, personality does not change; in particular, the self-monitoring trait is stable among adults. Based on a unique survey of sixty-eight presidential experts, as shown in chapter 4, most of the men who have come to occupy the US presidency since 1945 were high self-monitors. A minority of US presidents during that period were low self-monitors. This skewed distribution makes sense when one considers that candidates who are personable, adaptable, with some level of acting skill and political shrewdness—that is, fitting the profile of a high self-monitor—are more likely to win a US election. It can also explain why scholars believe that US presidents obsess about reputation for resolve, as I discuss later in this chapter.

The statistical analysis in chapter 4 confirms that high self-monitor US presidents not only care more about reputation for resolve but are significantly more likely than their low self-monitor counterparts to engage in and initiate the use of military instruments—including the display, threat, and actual use of force—to signal resolve during international crises. The statistical analysis further indicates that, consistent with the survey experiments, the effect of self-monitoring is even more pronounced among presidents who are low on military assertiveness (i.e., doves). I also uncover evidence suggesting that high self-monitor presidents are more likely to obtain a favorable outcome in international disputes, perhaps because they are more willing to demonstrate resolve.

I find further support for the theory when I zoom in on the crisis decision-making processes of Presidents Jimmy Carter (chapter 6), Ronald Reagan (chapter 7), and Bill Clinton (chapter 8), and Carter's and Reagan's main foreign policy advisors. Interestingly, the high self-monitor presidents, Reagan and Clinton, differed in their beliefs about the efficacy of military force, their degree of their ideological rigidity, and their attitudes toward public opinion. And yet, the high self-monitoring disposition they shared shaped their concerns about reputation for resolve, notwithstanding the very different strategic environments during which they served. Both presidents were obsessed with US credibility and were willing to use military force to enhance or salvage US "face." To be sure, Reagan's beliefs in the efficacy of force meant that he was far more eager to use military instruments to signal resolve, whereas the more dovish Clinton frequently attempted to use multilateral institutions during the crisis process. Ultimately, both presidents used military force repeatedly—even in the absence of support from domestic actors and advisors—to project reputation for resolve in areas far from US vital interests. The potential that international audiences perceived the United States as weak or irresolute concerned both leaders deeply, and they took significant political and military risks to avoid it.

Then consider President Carter, who might be the exception that proves the rule: he is the only clear-cut low self-monitor dove in our sample. His foreign policy was also unique in that he was unwilling to fight for reputation. Some will look at Carter's crisis decision making and conclude that his disregard for the reputational consequences of his actions invited Soviet challenges and made US allies question America's leadership. Others will disagree, claiming that Carter's approach saved the United States from fighting unnecessary wars. Regardless of the normative lens one places on Carter's foreign policy, the historical documents show that Carter was under great pressure from his advisors, Congress, and the American people to place a much higher value on US resolve and credibility. Carter's low self-monitoring pushed him to resist those pressures during these crises. Had the Soviets not invaded the strategically important Afghanistan—which Carter felt as a personal betrayal—it is fair to assume that Carter would have continued to resist pressure to make a deterrent threat to the Soviets in early 1980.

Interestingly, both Carter and Reagan were surrounded by foreign policy advisors who varied significantly in their self-monitoring dispositions. During the Carter administration, Brzezinski was a high self-monitor hawk and Vance was a low self-monitor dove. In the Reagan administration, it was the opposite: Weinberger was a low self-monitor hawk, whereas Shultz was a high self-monitor. Cross cutting variations in self-monitoring and hawkishness dispositions allowed me to test the theory on those advisors as well. Consistent with my theory, both high self-monitor advisors, Brzezinski and Shultz, were highly concerned about image and credibility (notwithstanding their differences in hawkishness) and urged Carter and Reagan respectively to demonstrate resolve in crises that involved little material value. On the other hand, the low self-monitors, Vance and Weinberger, repeatedly resisted demonstrating force for the sake of reputation. These findings show the applicability of the theory to lower-level decision makers; they also shed important light on how contention among the president's inner circle shapes crisis debates and policies, which current studies have largely missed.

Both the statistical analysis and the case studies further undercut several prominent alternative explanations for when and why leaders fight for reputation. I failed to find support for systemic or structural theories that emphasize the distribution of power in the international system, whether one considers the traditional balance of military capabilities or the nuclear balance. Further, I have shown that the length of a leader's tenure does not determine whether he or she is more willing to fight for reputation. High self-monitor leaders have, for example, fought for reputation both early in their tenure and during their second term. Moreover, I have uncovered significant variation among southern presidents in their concern for reputation, indicating that a cultural explanation linking concern for reputation to a unique aspect of southern heritage might be insufficient to explain these patterns.

On the other hand, domestic political explanations and materialist explanations receive mixed support. On the domestic side, I find that mass opinion rarely constrained high self-monitor leaders from pursuing reputation-guided policies. However, disapproval from the public combined with pressure from Congress did force high self-monitor leaders to modify their missions. Indeed, such pressures forced Reagan to withdraw from Lebanon, and Clinton from Somalia, because it became clear they would face a domestic backlash for pursuing policies, which would ultimately undermine their efforts to demonstrate resolve abroad. Finally, consistent with the theory's expectations, low self-monitor leaders are more likely to pursue materialist cost-benefit analysis in deciding to use force, whereas high self-monitors more explicitly incorporate reputation for resolve and image-based factors into their calculus. Still, across all cases we see more disagreement than consensus among key decision makers about whether force should be used to support reputation, thereby reinforcing that such concerns do not stem from features of the strategic environment or from access to information.

Lastly, this book focuses on *decision makers*, but the psychological underpinnings of this theory suggest that it can apply (with some adjustments) to ordinary citizens. Indeed, cross-national survey experiments on citizens in Israel and the United States shed light on how the public reacts to explicit, but also very subtle, reputational primes. The experimental results suggest that, when leaders pursue the use of force in furtherance of credibility and reputation for resolve, a segment of the population that typically disfavors using force—high self-monitor doves—may become more supportive of that conflict behavior. Accordingly, reputational concerns become a rational way in which leaders can publicly justify their military interventions in order to secure greater public support. However, the case studies also reveal that crisis behavior cannot be attributed solely to public pressure. The dispositions of individual leaders play a crucial role in shaping US foreign policy, with or without public support.

In sum, cross-national survey experiments, large-N statistical analysis, and historical case studies all offer support for the theory's observable implications as part of a layered methodology. Each methodology has allowed me to test a different aspect of the theory's observable implications. Taken together, these layered methods provide a powerful statement about the need to take leaders' characteristics seriously in the study of foreign policy decision making and reputation.

Broadening the Scope

This study has limitations brought about by its focus on US foreign policy decision making. First, the study offers a simple typology of four ideal-types of leaders: reputation crusaders, believers, skeptics, and critics. This theory should be taken as probabilistic rather than deterministic: I do not claim that high self-monitors will always be concerned about reputation, but rather that, on average, they are more likely to do so than low self-monitor presidents. Thus, even those presidents who do not fall neatly into the categories of high (or low) self-monitor should still display self-monitoring tendencies that push them to care more (or less) about reputation.

Second, this study focuses on the dispositions of heads of states, or more precisely, on US presidents and their foreign policy advisors. There is the potential to explain far more variation in crisis decision making by also testing the theory against lower-level foreign policy decision makers, even US senators or members of Congress. While the role of those individuals in shaping foreign policy might be less salient, this universe of cases could provide further evidence for the theory.

Third, this study has tested the theory on the United States. As I have explained in earlier chapters, the United States is an important and a hard test case for my theory. But the book should be seen as providing a template for implementing the theory to explain the behavior of nondemocratic leaders such as Russia's Vladimir Putin or the president of Turkey, Recep Tayyip

Erdogan. Nevertheless, I must be careful not to overstate the generalizability of the theory. As with any individual-level theory, leaders' dispositions are often affected by the institutional context. For example, a dictator's disposition likely has a stronger effect on crisis decision making, but there is probably less individual-level effect in parliamentary systems, where the prime minister's decision-making power is more diffuse. Moreover, the relationship between status and resolve may be less intimately linked as a result of other factors, such as culture or historical settings. Thus, cultures or periods in which honor, resolve, and overall strength on the international stage are not associated with greater social status might be less prone to the dynamics described in this book.

Finally, the focus on the United States also implies that leaders concerned about reputation for resolve had the military means to demonstrate that resolve if they desired. Other countries might not enjoy a similar power advantage over adversaries; put differently, the cost of fighting for reputation in some countries may be excessively high. Thus, high self-monitor leaders in weak countries might care about reputation for resolve but may not be able to act on those preferences with observable behavior.

Leaders, Psychology, and the Study of Reputation

For many decades, owing to the prominence of systemic approaches to the study of international politics, the field of international relations has resisted treating leaders as the central unit of analysis. There are important exceptions, and in many ways this study is built on the shoulders of these inspirational works.[1] Criticism has been leveled against individual-level theories, especially those employing psychological constructs, that such frameworks cannot offer systematic, parsimonious, generalizable, and externally valid theories. By employing a layered, multimethod research design and using more precise and less biased instrumentations to code the theory's main independent variables, I hope this study contributes to a resurgence in the study of leaders by offering a template for studying individual leaders and their psychology in ways that shed light on larger puzzles in international relations.

In recent years there has been a resurgence in the study of psychology in international relations. Scholars have convincingly demonstrated how leaders' emotions, causal beliefs, cognition, experience, and background shape the conduct of their foreign policy decision making. My study contributes to that literature by highlighting another way in which a leader's attributes play a critical role in intentional crises. Self-monitoring is unique in that it is not encompassed by any of the attributes listed above. Rather, it is a stable, genetically influenced trait.

At the same time, self-monitoring can shape leaders' other attributes in important ways. For example, self-monitoring is not an emotion, but it can explain whether reputation for resolve can become an emotional belief. According to Jonathan Mercer, while "reputation does not depend on emotion, the belief that one has a reputation often does. Emotion as evidence—a feeling that others view one as irresolute—explains why decision makers believe reputation matters independent of evidence that it does."[2] My theory can thus provide microfoundations for *why* a leader's fear of being perceived as irresolute can serve as evidence of reputation. High self-monitors, because of their disposition, are likely to be especially prone to displaying an emotional belief about the importance of reputation, and they are likely to do so without searching for evidence that it exists. High self-monitoring can similarly explain why these leaders have the emotional belief that reputation travels across time and space. But, importantly, I diverge from Mercer by showing that this tendency will be more pronounced among leaders who are high self-monitors than those who are low self-monitors. My study also highlights the role of emotions in a different way. Self-monitoring shapes leaders' emotional reactions to loss of status and reputation. As we saw in the discussion of Clinton's crisis decision making, the loss of face after the *Harlan County* incident led to an emotional outburst of anger that shocked even his closest advisors, while the evidence shows that Carter displayed no such emotional reaction to losing face. Thus, self-monitoring appears to condition when emotions will be activated.

Self-monitoring is not a causal belief in a cognitive sense either but critically shapes the beliefs of leaders about the importance of fighting for reputation, as well as makes these beliefs very resistant to change as the evidence in this book clearly suggests. High self-monitoring as a trait, in other words, leads individuals to develop a worldview that puts premium on cultivating a status-enhancing image. Those tendencies appear to be reinforced when such individuals occupy positions of power on the international stage and play a critical role in crisis decision making. Finally, self-monitoring is certainly distinct from experience or background—variables that scholars have argued shape leaders' crisis behavior. But as the discussion in the cases of Reagan and Clinton highlights, high self-monitoring can be instrumental in leaders' choice and ability to become successful politicians and leaders. Thus, self-monitoring explains both why most US presidents in the modern era are high self-monitors and features of their crisis behavior.

My findings also generate questions for future research in international relations, discussed below.

DISPOSITION VERSUS SITUATION

A focus on leaders' personality traits to explain foreign policy behavior requires some nontrivial assumptions. A first assumption is that, to the extent that leaders value reputation in private life, they also come to identify with their office (the presidency) and to value the reputation of the United States accordingly. Put differently, individual-level reputational concerns scale up to the state level through collective identification with the nation leaders lead. As a result, my theory allows us to move across different levels of analysis: while locating reputational concerns at the individual level, it explains behavior at the national level. Nevertheless, one should be open to the possibility that there may not be perfect correspondence between reputational concerns at the leader level and at the national level. For example, a leader from a foreign occupying power has no inherent connection with the state he or she governs, in which case the leader may not connect his or her personal reputational concerns to a greater concern with the reputation of the state. On the other hand, personalist regimes, such as that of North Korea under Kim Jong-Un, might display a high degree of congruence between the reputational concerns of the leader and that of the nation, because the fate of the state is directly linked to the dictator's personal fate.

Second, the dispositional theory does not argue that situational factors are unimportant. The long debate in the field of psychology on the relative importance of the person or the situation in explaining behavior has long concluded that both factors matter. More specifically, traits predict consistency in a wide distribution of behaviors over time, rather than governing only one behavior. The seminal work by William Fleeson on this topic has also proposed that individuals have a mean level of a trait, but the individual's behavior can vary around this mean based on the situation.[3] This distribution can explain the low cross situational consistency of single acts of behavior while also explaining the high consistency in behaviors over time. In the theory I advance, the trait of self-monitoring should be viewed similarly: while it cannot accurately predict leaders' behavior in any single moment or crisis, it can accurately predict and explain trends—the person's typical way of acting—over time.

But more fundamentally, I have presented evidence for the presence of person-situation interaction. Specifically, a decision maker's self-monitoring disposition is not determinative of the policies a leader will choose unless we also know the context, that is, the situation. This book focuses on militarized interstate crises. I have argued that in those situations, high self-monitor decision makers would likely view a display of resolve as increasing their social status. Put differently, high self-monitoring dispositions × situation of militarized interstate crisis = emphasis on reputation for resolve. As I note elsewhere in this book, the observable manifestation of high self-monitoring is likely to change when we are in the realm of noncrisis situations.

In addition, this book has also shown that high self-monitor individuals in the United States appear to be selected into the office of the presidency more frequently than low self-monitor individuals. Thus, high self-monitors tend to find themselves in situations of interstate crisis more frequently than low self-monitors, thereby bringing their concerns for reputation to the international stage. I posit that we might observe concern for reputation for resolve more frequently because of the interplay between high-self monitors and international crisis situations.

HAWKS VERSUS DOVES

My study shows that, in fact, hawks do not necessarily care more about reputation than doves, contrary to Snyder and Diesing.[4] The survey experiments, the statistical analysis, and the case studies debunk that proposition. Hawks might *want* to fight more than doves, but reputational considerations are not the hallmark of all hawks, and certainly not of hawks alone. Using the lens of hawks-doves thus masks important variation within each group, which can cause inaccurate predictions about which leaders are likely to fight for face.

At the same time, this study should not be taken to mean that low self-monitor hawks do not care about "deterrence." Indeed, some low self-monitor hawks, such as Caspar Weinberger, did not believe in sending troops to fight purely to demonstrate a reputation for resolve, but as secretary of defense, Weinberger was perhaps the strongest advocate within the Reagan cabinet for building US conventional and nuclear arsenals. He even pushed for counterforce doctrines, believing that those could increase US nuclear deterrence capabilities. Alternatively, there might be individuals who care about reputation for resolve not out of strategic concerns, but rather out of the desire to avoid appearing "weak," a label that could reduce his or her country's overall status. In sum, concerns about reputation for resolve and concerns about deterrence could be related but should not be conflated.

In this study I have left open the question of the origins of those beliefs about military assertiveness, and the extent to which they may change over time. Past informative experiences might affect leaders' attitudes both toward the efficacy of force, and toward the overall likelihood of success of military missions. I have tried to minimize some of this variation by examining in depth three post-Vietnam presidents, all of whom came to office with little foreign policy experience. Yet, the analysis I offer here is not intended to capture the deep causes of those leaders' beliefs about the utility of military force. To the extent that military assertiveness is an intervening variable in this theory, it is important to probe the importance of whether those beliefs are systematically shaped by a particular background condition.

LEARNING WHILE IN OFFICE

Just because self-monitoring remains stable in adulthood, does that mean that leaders' foreign policy is also static and cannot change while in office? The answer is no. That self-monitoring is a stable trait implies that leaders will not suddenly become obsessed with, or alternatively to cease to care about, reputation for resolve while in office. The presence or absence of concerns about image and the need to defend reputation for resolve is thus constant in my model. But at the same time, leaders learn and evolve their foreign policy over time (for a variety of reasons discussed in chapter 2).

First, the other key variable in this book, beliefs about the efficacy of force, is not constant. While in power, leaders can update and revise their beliefs about the usefulness of military force to solve problems. Thus, while some leaders may remain high self-monitors, their level of hawkishness can shift while in power. Put differently, reputation believers can turn into reputation crusaders (and vice versa), but they cannot turn into reputation critics or skeptics. Thus, their baseline propensity to use military force to fight for reputation might fluctuate. Second, leaders might shift their assessments about the nature of the strategic environment or the intentions of their adversary while in power. Such revisions in beliefs, as I show with Carter, can lead presidents to be more willing to use military instruments they had previously avoided. But this increased or decreased willingness to use force should not be accompanied by a "new" rationale that highlights the importance of face; rather we should see willingness to use force because the threat to the status quo now requires the use of military means or because material interests are now at risk.

Third, as I discuss at length in chapter 5, self-monitoring dispositions do not turn leaders into irrationally risk-accepting actors. While in power, even high self-monitor leaders often learn that military missions that can help bolster a reputation for resolve might be extremely risky and fail, resulting in a reputation loss. Indeed, Kennedy learned that very lesson with the failed Bay of Pigs operation, which he admitted was a sobering experience that led him to be more measured in his response to the Cuban Missile Crisis. Thus, high self-monitor leaders might become more reluctant to jump on subsequent opportunities to demonstrate resolve—or at the very least would be more selective and need reassurance that such missions will end successfully— even if they remain extremely concerned about appearing weak.

GENERAL REPUTATION VERSUS SIGNALING REPUTATION

My theory explains concerns about general reputation for *resolve*. But leaders may vary in their concern for other types of reputation beyond or in addition to resolve. For example, in recent years scholars have been especially focused on whether leaders pay a political cost, imposed by domestic audiences, for backing down from a threat during crises. One explanation for why the public might wish to punish such leaders is that backing down from a threat could jeopardize the country's reputation for resolve. But as many scholars have correctly pointed out, that particular crisis setup conflates general reputation for resolve with what Jervis terms "signaling reputation," a reputation for being consistent in carrying out threats.[5] This book, in contrast, has attempted to study reputation for resolve under a broader set of crisis conditions, which may or may not involve signaling reputation. These broader circumstances, including those without explicit threats, ground this study in the category of general reputation for resolve, which arguably has wider applicability than the typical "audience cost" models.

At the same time, this study also raises interesting questions about which leaders will be more likely to back down from a public threat. We could imagine that high self-monitor leaders will be less likely to back down out of a fear of reputational costs imposed by domestic and international audiences. Low self-monitor leaders might be less prone to make those threats at the outset when vital interests are not at stake, but once low self-monitor leaders choose to make a public threat, they might be more likely to follow up on it. This is because consistency in behavior is an important feature of low self-monitor individuals. Future work could further develop and test the implications that follow from this analysis.[6]

REPUTATION FOR RESOLVE IN DYADIC INTERACTIONS

In explaining the foreign policy of states I analyzed only one side of the strategic interaction, whether it was the initiator of the crisis or the respondent. Interstate crises, however, are dyadic (or k-adic) and are often governed by a strategic logic. Thus, one state's action is shaped by others' behavior (and anticipated future behavior). This raises a fundamental question not explored in this book: what does the interaction between leaders with similar (or different) self-monitoring levels during international crises look like? Indeed, if self-monitoring is a strong predictor of leaders' willingness to fight for reputation, then we could imagine that a crisis dynamic between two high self-monitor leaders during a crisis might be different from a conflict between two low self-monitor leaders, or within a mixed dyad. Given that high self-monitors are more likely to rise to top political positions, it might be fair to speculate that interactions between high self-monitor leaders will be more common than that between two low self-monitors.

The data required to empirically test a dyadic version of my theory is significant, and thus, it is outside of this book's scope. Nevertheless, it is worthwhile to consider some preliminary hypotheses about the observable implications if such an analysis were to be conducted. Because high self-monitor leaders (whether doves or hawks) are more likely to care about and fight for reputation, we can hypothesize that when two high self-monitors face off in a reputational crisis, the international situation would be especially volatile and potentially dangerous. Those kinds of reputational crises are likely to escalate, as both leaders are likely to care about reputation for resolve and would try to avoid humiliation, doubling down on their commitments rather than backing down. On the other extreme, two low self-monitor presidents might be least likely to escalate disputes that are purely reputational in nature. Realizing that vital interests are not at stake, two low self-monitors facing one another in a crisis could thus decide that acting tough on the international stage is too costly. In between these two extremes, we find mixed self-monitoring dyads. In such cases, we could imagine the high self-monitoring leader initiating (and escalating) more reputational disputes, while the low self-monitor may choose to back down if vital interests are not at stake.

High self-monitoring is a trait that is discernible to those observing the social interactions of their opponent.[7] Although categorization of a leader as a high or low self-monitor is a clinical construct, leaders' acts of self-monitoring are observable behavior revealed through these social interactions *outside of crises, and even before these leaders come to office.* As the literature indicates, and as I examined in the case studies, it is possible to assess a leader's level of self-monitoring by examining his or her propensity for adaptability, emotional control in social situations, or acting ability, for example.[8] In this way, opponents can determine whether a leader engages in a little or a lot of self-monitoring behavior. In a world in which leaders can gauge their opponent's level of self-monitoring before a crisis—and in which states understand the implications of a leader's self-monitoring on willingness to fight for reputation—leaders should be expected to strategically avoid selecting into reputational contests (i.e., conflicts over nonvital interests) with high self-monitor opponents, especially reputation crusaders. This is because such opponents are more likely to escalate and less likely to back down. Alternatively, low self-monitor leaders might find themselves more often challenged over nonvital issues, as others expect them to care less about reputation for resolve and therefore more likely to back down. Future studies could significantly enrich our understanding of these dyadic dynamics of reputational contests, both theoretically and empirically.

DO LEADERS INFER RESOLVE FROM OTHERS' REPUTATIONS?

In the analysis of this book I have attempted to avoid addressing the normative question of whether reputation for resolve *should* matter in international politics. I have studied this question elsewhere: Alex Weisiger and I showed that countries that back down in international crises are subsequently significantly more likely to be targeted than those countries that stand firm.[9] Nevertheless, the debate about whether leaders care about others' past actions is similar in one important respect to the debate about reputation building in international relations: both have neglected how leaders' characteristics shape beliefs about reputation.

Leaving aside the identity and self-monitoring of the opponent, I conjecture that leaders who are high self-monitors might be more likely than low self-monitors to take into consideration the past actions of the opposing state (i.e., its reputation for resolve) in their assessment of future behavior. Put differently, in estimating others' likelihood to stand firm in the future, high self-monitor observers are more likely than low self-monitor leaders to use reputation as evidence. This is because high self-monitors view the world through a lens in which images of resolve are desirable and can be shaped or controlled by the actor. Therefore, actors who do not show resolve in past interactions demonstrate to high self-monitor leaders that their state is dispositionally irresolute—either because it does not care about resolve or because it is unable to demonstrate resolve out of weakness. Either way, in the mind of a high self-monitor observer, past interactions offer a strong diagnostic indicator of the likely resistance of the other side. In contrast, low self-monitor observers believe that it is necessary to show resolve only when vital interests are at stake (and that actors cannot control their images). As a result, all else equal, low self-monitors might be more reluctant to use past actions to show future propensity when situational factors are dissimilar. That is, they are less likely to infer the other's disposition based on past actions.

Self-Monitoring and Foreign Policy: Avenues for Further Research

This book has introduced scholars of international relations to the psychological trait of self-monitoring. Although prominent in the field of psychology, self-monitoring has unfortunately remained largely unexplored to students of world politics. Self-monitoring should be of significant importance to international relations scholars who study signaling and perception in international politics, but there is also much to be gained by applying the concept of self-monitoring beyond studies of security. For example, international relations scholars could also consider foreign economic policies: are high self-monitor leaders more likely to employ coercive economic instruments, such as economic sanctions or trade wars, compared to low self-monitors? A second line of inquiry could exploit the other-directedness aspect of high self-monitors to explain and predict inconsistency (flip-flopping) in leaders' public discourse. Third, scholars could study the effect of self-monitoring on foreign policy issues that raise normative concerns, or that may be influenced by social desirability bias, such as humanitarian intervention, support of autocratic regimes, or the use of torture in violation of the laws of war. We may find that high self-monitor leaders are more likely to disguise their true beliefs on those issues, and be more prone to primes from advisors that emphasize status-enhancing social norms, compared to their low self-monitor counterparts.[10] Finally, in the context of face-to-face negotiations and bargaining styles, a high self-monitoring disposition might allow leaders to better control their expressive signals, and it might lead them to more accurately perceive interpersonal signals. Scholars might fruitfully study whether high self-monitor leaders are more effective than low self-monitors in achieving cooperation or desired bargaining outcomes.

———

At its core, this book has made the case for why leaders *should* matter to international relations, and also *how* they matter. Leaders' characteristics significantly shape their behavior on the international stage, but current scholarship lacks clear direction as to what characteristics are important and how those traits affect crisis decision making and international behavior more broadly. This book advances this research agenda by exploring the relationship between self-monitoring, military assertiveness, and contests of "face." I hope this book will infuse new ideas into the discussion of reputation in international relations by integrating the characteristics and psychology of leaders into our theories and empirics.

NOTES

Chapter 1: Introduction

1. Glenn Kessler, "Fact Checker: President Obama and the 'Red Line' on Syria's Chemical Weapons," *Washington Post*, September 6, 2013, https://www.washingtonpost.com/news/fact-checker/wp/2013/09/06/president-obama-and-the-red-line-on-syrias-chemical-weapons/?utm_term=.f318dabeab53.

2. Scott Pelley, "A Crime against Humanity," *60 Minutes*, April 19, 2015.

3. Patrice Taddonio, " 'The President Blinked': Why Obama Changed Course on the 'Red Line' in Syria," *Frontline*, May 25, 2015. The quote is from Andrew Bacevich.

4. Josh Rogin, "Syria Crosses Obama's New Red Line," *Bloomberg View*, March 19, 2015, https://www.bloomberg.com/view/articles/2015-03-19/syria-s-chemical-attacks-cross-obama-s-new-red-line.

5. "The Decline of Deterrence," *Economist*, May 1, 2014, 31–34.

6. This is regardless of whether these allegations (of American weakness, or of Obama's irresoluteness) are valid, which I treat as empirical questions beyond the scope of this book.

7. Jeffrey Goldberg, "The Obama Doctrine," *Atlantic*, April 2016, https://www.theatlantic.com/magazine/archive/2016/04/the-obama-doctrine/471525/.

8. William J. Clinton, "Address to the Nation on Somalia," *Weekly Compilation of Presidential Documents* 29, no. 40 (1993): 2023.

9. Ibid., 2024.

10. Ibid., 2025.

11. David C. Humphrey, Edward C. Keefer, and Louis J. Smith, eds., *Vietnam, June–December 1965*, vol. 3, *Foreign Relations of the United States, 1964–1968* (Washington, DC: Government Printing Office, 1996), 195.

12. Explanations involving cultures of honor and cults of reputation also make some dispositional arguments.

13. This is not to say that situational or structural factors do not shape the crisis behavior of leaders, but rather that there are individual-level sources of crisis behavior that have hitherto gone unacknowledged in the literature. Taking a first-image perspective is therefore necessary to show how two leaders facing similar structural factors might act differently.

14. I thank Josh Kertzer for this point. See Lloyd S. Etheredge, "Personality Effects on American Foreign Policy, 1898–1968: A Test of Interpersonal Generalization Theory," *American Political Science Review* 72, no. 2 (1978): 434–51; Brian C. Rathbun et al., "Taking Foreign Policy Personally: Personal Values and Foreign Policy Attitudes," *International Studies Quarterly* 60, no. 1 (2016): 124–37; Richard K. Herrmann, Philip E. Tetlock, and Penny S. Visser, "Mass Public Decisions to Go to War: A Cognitive-Interactionist Framework," *American Political Science Review* 93, no. 3 (1999): 553–73; Joshua D. Kertzer, *Resolve in International Relations* (Princeton, NJ: Princeton University Press, 2016).

15. Robert Jervis, *The Logic of Images in International Relations* (New York: Columbia University Press, 1970).

16. There are many different theories of personality in psychology. See Duane Schultz, *Theories of Personality* (Belmont, CA: Brooks/Cole, 1981). One strand includes psychoanalytic studies that seek to explain political behavior in terms of early childhood experiences, or of development later in adulthood. For example, see Walter Langer, *The Mind of Adolf Hitler: The Secret Wartime Report* (New York: Basic Books, [1943] 1972); or Alexander L. George and Juliette L. George, *Woodrow Wilson and Colonel House: A Personality Study* (New York: Dover, 1956); or Raymond J. Birt, "Personality and Foreign Policy: The Case of Stalin," *Political Psychology* 14, no. 4 (1993): 607–25; "Interest in psychobiographical approaches began to wane by the 1970s," wrote Levy in 2013; "however, with a shift in orientation toward more parsimonious and empirically testable theories and with the development of alternative psychological frameworks." Jack Levy, "Psychology and Foreign Policy Decision-Making," in the *Handbook of Political Psychology*, 2nd ed., ed. Leonie Huddy, David O. Sears, and Jack S. Levy (Oxford: Oxford University Press, 2013). Nevertheless, using more testable hypotheses, scholars continued to use models of personality to study foreign policy decision making. For example, Fred I. Greenstein, *Personality and Politics: Problems of Evidence, Inference, and Conceptualization* (New York: Norton, 1975); Lloyd Etheridge, *A World of Men: The Private Sources of American Foreign Policy* (Cambridge, MA: MIT Press, 1978); Margaret G. Hermann, "Explaining Foreign Policy Behavior Using Personal Characteristics of Political Leaders," *International Studies Quarterly* 24, no. 1 (1980): 7–46; David G. Winter, "Personality and Foreign Policy: Historical Overview of Research," in *Political Psychology and Foreign* Policy, ed. Eric Singer and Valerie Hudson (Boulder, CO: Westview, 1992), chapter 14; Alexander L. George and Juliette L. George, *Presidential Personality and Performance* (Boulder, CO: Westview, 1998); Jerrold M. Post, *The Psychological Assessment of Political Leaders* (Ann Arbor: University of Michigan Press, 2003). Another strand in the literature involves trait-based studies of presidential character. For example, James D. Barber, *The Presidential Character: Predicting Performance in the White House* (Englewood Cliffs, NJ: Prentice-Hall, 1972); Lloyd S. Etheredge, *Personality Effects on American Foreign Policy, 1898–1968*; Steven J. Rubenzer and Thomas R. Faschingbauer, *Personality, Character, and Leadership in the White House: Psychologists Assess the Presidents* (Washington, DC: Brassey's, 2004); Blema S. Steinberg, *Shame and Humiliation: Presidential Decision Making on Vietnam* (McGill-Queen's Press–MQUP, 1996); leader characteristics include need for power, cognitive complexity, integrative complexity, prior experience, locus of control, and leader decision-making style. For example, Margaret G. Hermann and Thomas Preston, "Presidents, Advisers, and Foreign Policy: The Effect of Leadership Style on Executive Arrangements," *Political Psychology* 15, no. 1 (1994): 75–96; Thomas Preston, *The President and His Inner Circle: Leadership Style and the Advisory Process in Foreign Policy Making* (New York: Columbia University Press, 2001); David G. Winter et al., "The Personalities of Bush and Gorbachev Measured at a Distance," *Political Psychology* 12, no. 2 (1991): 215–45; Philip E. Tetlock, "Cognitive Style and Political Ideology," *Journal of Personality and Social Psychology* 45, no. 1 (1983): 118–26; Margaret G. Hermann, "Assessing Leadership Style: A Trait Analysis," in *The Psychological Assessment of Political Leaders*, ed. Jerrold Post (Ann Arbor: University of Michigan Press, 2005), 178–214; Joseph S. Nye Jr., *Presidential Leadership and the Creation of the American Era* (Princeton, NJ: Princeton University Press, 2013), as well as operational code analysis of leaders. See, for example, Nathan Leites, *The Operational Code of the Politburo* (New York: McGraw-Hill, 1951); Alexander L. George, "Case Studies and Theory Development: The Method of Structured, Focused Comparison," in *Diplomacy: New Approaches in History, Theory, and Policy*, ed. Paul Gordon Lauren (New York: Free Press, 1979); Stephen B. Dyson, "Drawing Policy Implications from the 'Operation Code' of a 'New' Political Actor: Russian President Vladimir Putin," *Policy Sciences* 34, no. 3 (2001): 329–46; Jonathan Renshon,

"Stability and Change in Belief Systems: The Operational Code of George W. Bush," *Journal of Conflict Resolution* 52, no. 6 (2008): 820–46; and Mark Schafer and Stephen Walker, eds., *Beliefs and Leadership in World Politics: Methods and Applications of Operational Code Analysis* (New York: Palgrave Macmillan, 2006).

17. See, for example, Alexander L. George, "The Case for Multiple Advocacy in Making Foreign Policy," *American Political Science Review* 66, no. 3 (1972): 751–85; Robert Jervis, *Perception and Misperception in International Politics* (Princeton, NJ: Princeton University Press, 1976); Hermann, "Explaining Foreign Policy Behavior Using Personal Characteristics of Political Leaders"; Yuen Foong Khong, *Analogies at War: Korea, Munich, Dien Bien Phu, and the Vietnam Decisions of 1965* (Princeton, NJ: Princeton University Press, 1992); Richard J. Samuels, *Machiavelli's Children: Leaders and Their Legacies in Italy and Japan* (Ithaca, NY: Cornell University Press, 2003); Elizabeth N. Saunders, *Leaders at War: How Presidents Shape Military Interventions* (Ithaca, NY: Cornell University Press, 2011); Keren Yarhi-Milo, *Knowing the Adversary: Leaders, Intelligence, and Assessment of Intentions in International Relations* (Princeton, NJ: Princeton University Press, 2014); Brian C. Rathbun, *Diplomacy's Value: Creating Security in 1920s Europe and the Contemporary Middle East* (Ithaca, NY: Cornell University Press, 2014); Michael C. Horowitz, Allan Stam, and Cali M. Ellis, *Why Leaders Fight* (New York: Cambridge University Press, 2015).

18. More broadly, scholars have long contended that presidents have greater influence over foreign and defense policy compared to domestic and economic policies. See, for example, Robert A. Dahl, *Congress and Foreign Policy* (New York: Brace, 1950); Richard F. Fenno Jr., *Congressmen in Committees* (Boston: Little, Brown, 1973); Samuel P. Huntington, *The Common Defense: Strategic Programs in National Politics* (New York: Columbia University Press, 1961); Aaron Wildavsky, "The Two Presidencies," *TransAction* 4, no. 2 (1966), 162–73; Paul Peterson, "The President's Dominance in Foreign Policymaking," *Political Science Quarterly* 109, no. 2 (1994); Terry Sullivan, "A Matter of Fact: The 'Two Presidencies' Thesis Revitalized," in *The Two Presidencies: A Quarter Century Assessment*, ed. Steven A. Shull (Chicago: Nelson-Hall, 1991), 143–57; Brandice Canes-Wrone, *Who Leads Whom? Presidents, Policy, and the Public* (Chicago: University of Chicago Press, 2006). Especially in times of crisis, individuals are likely to have less knowledge, and thus be more likely to look to the president for leadership.

19. Lloyd Jensen, *Explaining Foreign Policy* (Englewood Cliffs, NJ: Prentice Hall, 1982); Fen O. Hampson, "The Divided Decision-Maker: American Domestic Politics and the Cuban Crises," *International Security* 9, no. 3 (1984): 130–65; Margaret G. Hermann and Charles W. Kegley, "Rethinking Democracy and International Peace: Perspectives from Political Psychology," *International Studies Quarterly* 39, no. 4 (1995): 511–33.

20. Bernard C. Cohen, *The Public's Impact on Foreign Policy* (Boston: Little, Brown, 1978).

21. Henry Kissinger, *Diplomacy* (New York: Simon and Schuster, 1994), cited in Hermann and Kegley, "Rethinking Democracy and International Peace," 515.

22. Paul Peterson, quoted in William G. Howell and Jon C. Pevehouse, *While Dangers Gather: Congressional Checks on Presidential War Powers* (Princeton, NJ: Princeton University Press, 2011), 8. This is not to argue that other actors are irrelevant. As I show in the book, Congress, for example, can affect presidents' decision to fight for reputation through legislative process and public appeals. Still, domestic actors are treated in this book as political players that are secondary to the president.

23. Kenneth Waltz, *Man, the State, and War* (New York: Columbia University Press, 1959); Kenneth Waltz, *Theory of International Politics* (New York: McGraw-Hill, 1979).

24. Robert Jervis, "Do Leaders Matter and How Would We Know?," *Security Studies* 22, no. 2 (2013): 153–79.

25. Daniel L. Byman and Kenneth M. Pollack, "Let Us Now Praise Great Men: Bringing the Statesman Back In," *International Security* 25, no. 4 (2001): 107–46, citation on 109.

26. Andrew Kennedy, *The International Ambitions of Mao and Nehru: National Efficacy Beliefs and the Making of Foreign Policy* (New York: Cambridge University Press, 2011), 12.

27. Saunders, *Leaders at War*.

28. Yarhi-Milo, *Knowing the Adversary*.

29. Horowitz et al., *Why Leaders Fight*; Jessica Weeks, *Dictators at War and Peace* (Ithaca, NY: Cornell University Press, 2014); Rathbun et al., "Taking Foreign Policy Personally"; Allen Dafoe and David Caughey, "Honor and War: Southern US Presidents and the Effects of Concern for Reputation," *World Politics* 68, no. 2 (2016): 341–81.

30. For example, Margaret G. Hermann et al., "Who Leads Matters: The Effects of Powerful Individuals," *International Studies Review* 3, no. 2 (2001): 83–131.

31. Goldgeier, for example, suggests that domestic political battles earlier in their careers shape the way leaders negotiate and bargain on the international stage. James M. Goldgeier, *Leadership Style and Soviet Foreign Policy: Stalin, Khrushchev, Brezhnev, Gorbachev* (Baltimore: Johns Hopkins University Press, 1994).

32. On the role of experience, see Richard Neustadt and Ernest May, "Thinking in Time," in *The Uses of History for Decision Makers* (New York: Free Press, 1986); Khong, *Analogies at War*; Jervis, *Perception and Misperception in International Politics*; Michael C. Horowitz and Allan C. Stam, "How Prior Military Experience Influences the Future Militarized Behavior of Leaders," *International Organization* 68, no. 3 (2014): 527–59. On how leaders learn, see, for example, Jack S. Levy, "Learning and Foreign Policy: Sweeping a Conceptual Minefield," *International Organization* 48, no. 2 (1994): 279–312.

33. Assessing the individual differences of 122 national leaders across the past two decades, Hermann and colleagues have uncovered a set of leadership styles that appear to guide how leaders interact with those they lead or with whom they share power. Seven traits have been found to be particularly useful in assessing leadership style: (1) the belief that one can influence or control what happens, (2) the need for power and influence, (3) conceptual complexity (the ability to differentiate things and people in one's environment), (4) self-confidence, (5) the tendency to focus on problem solving and accomplishing something versus maintenance of the group and dealing with others' ideas and sensitivities, (6) an individual's general distrust or suspiciousness of others, and (7) the intensity with which a person holds an in-group bias. See Margaret G. Hermann, "Explaining Foreign Policy Behavior Using the Personal Characteristics of Political Leaders"; Margaret G. Hermann, "Assessing the Personalities of Soviet Politburo Members," *Personality and Social Psychology Bulletin* 6, no. 3 (1980): 332–52; Margaret G. Hermann, "Personality and Foreign Policy Decision Making: A Study of 53 Heads of Government," in *Foreign Policy Decision Making: Perception, Cognition, and Artificial Intelligence*, ed. Donald A. Sylvan and Steve Chan (New York: Praeger, 1984), 53–80; Margaret G. Hermann, "Assessing the Foreign Policy Role Orientations of Sub-Saharan African Leaders," in *Role Theory and Foreign Policy Analysis*, ed. Stephen G. Walker (Durham, NC: Duke University Press 1987), 161–98; Margaret G. Hermann, "Syria's Hafez al-Assad," in *Leadership and Negotiation in the Middle East*, ed. B. Kellerman and J. Rubin (New York: Praeger, 1988), 70–95; Margaret G. Hermann, "Leaders and Foreign Policy Decision Making," in *Diplomacy, Force, and Leadership: Essays in Honor of Alexander George*, ed. Dan Caldwell and Timothy J. McKeown (Boulder, CO: Westview, 1993), 77–94; Margaret G. Hermann and Charles F. Hermann, "Who Makes Foreign Policy Decisions and How: An Empirical Inquiry," *International Studies Quarterly* 33, no. 4 (1989): 361–87; Juliet Kaarbo and Margaret G. Hermann, "Leadership Styles of Prime Ministers: How Individual Differences Affect the Foreign Policymaking Process," *Leadership Quarterly* 9, no. 3 (1998): 243–63.

34. Several studies have looked at the interaction between individual leader and type of advisory system that s/he sets up. For example, see Thomas Preston, "Following the Leader: The Impact of U.S. Presidential Style upon Advisory Group Dynamics, Structure, and Decision," in

Beyond Groupthink: Political Group Dynamics and Foreign Policy-Making, ed. Paul Hart, Eric K. Stern, and Bengt Sundelius (Ann Arbor: University of Michigan Press, 1997), chapter 7; Alexander L. George and Eric Stern, "President Management Styles and Models," in *Presidential Personality and Performance*, ed. Alexander L. George and Juliette George (Boulder, CO: Westview, 1998), 199–280.

35. Namely, many of those studies lacked clear separation between the measurement of the independent and dependent variables and were less clear about the effect of any particular trait on foreign policy behavior. Examples of previous research linking leaders' personal characteristics to their political behavior include Daniel Druckman, "Prenegotiation Experience and Dyadic Conflict Resolution in a Bargaining Situation," *Journal of Experimental Social Psychology* 4, no. 4 (1968): 367–83; Robert S. Byars, "Small-Group Theory and Shifting Styles of Political Leadership," *Comparative Political Studies* 5, no. 4 (1973): 443–69; David C. McClelland, *Power: The Inner Experience* (New York: Irvington, 1975); Herbert M. Lefcourt, *Locus of Control: Current Trends in Theory and Research*, 2nd ed. (Psychology Press, 2014); Michael J. Driver, "Individual Differences as Determinants of Aggression in the Inter-Nation Simulation," in *A Psychological Examination of Political Leaders*, ed. Margaret G. Hermann and Thomas W. Milburn (New York: Free Press, 1977), 337–53; Margaret G. Hermann and Nathan Kogan, "Effects of Negotiators' Personalities on Negotiating Behavior," in *Negotiations: Social-Psychological Perspectives*, ed. Daniel Druckman (Beverly Hills., CA: Sage, 1977), 247–74; Robert C. Ziller et al., "Self-Other Orientations and Political Behavior," in *A Psychological Examination of Political Leaders*, ed. Margaret G. Hermann (New York: Free Press, 1977); Hermann, "Assessing the Personalities of Soviet Politburo Members"; Margaret G. Hermann, "Personality and Foreign Policy Making," in *Perceptions, Beliefs, and Foreign Policy Decision Making*, ed. Donald Sylvan and Steve Chan (New York: Praeger, 1984); Hermann, "Assessing the Foreign Policy Role Orientations of Sub-Saharan African Leaders"; Bernard M. Bass, *The Bass Handbook of Leadership: Theory, Research, and Managerial Applications* (New York: Free Press, 2008); Stephen G. Walker, "The Motivational Foundations of Political Belief Systems: A Re-analysis of the Operational Code Construct," in *International Studies Quarterly* 27, no. 2 (1983): 179–202; Mark Snyder, *Public Appearances, Private Realities: The Psychology of Self-Monitoring* (W. H. Freeman/Times Books/Henry Holt, 1987); Hermann and Hermann, "Who Makes Foreign Policy Decisions and How"; Philip D. Stewart, Margaret G. Hermann, and Charles F. Hermann, "Modeling the 1973 Soviet Decision to Support Egypt," *American Political Science Review* 83 (1989): 35–59; Winter et al., "Personalities of Bush and Gorbachev Measured at a Distance"; Peter Suedfeld, "Cognitive Misers and Their Critics," *Political Psychology* 13 (1992): 435–53; Winter, "Personality and Foreign Policy"; Kaarbo and Hermann, "Leadership Styles of Prime Ministers"; Rubenzer and Faschingbauer, *Personality, Character, and Leadership in the White House*.

36. Jervis, "Do Leaders Matter and How Would We Know?"

37. For an excellent recent study on resolve in international relations, see Kertzer, *Resolve in International Relations*. Using a series of experiments, Kertzer argues that to understand what resolve is requires an interactionist approach that combines dispositional and situational factors.

38. Keren Yarhi-Milo, "After Credibility: American Foreign Policy in the Trump Era," *Foreign Affairs* 97, no. 1 (January/February 2018): 68–77.

39. Michael Tomz, *Reputation and International Cooperation: Sovereign Debt across Three Centuries* (Princeton, NJ: Princeton University Press, 2007), 821.

40. See Jack Snyder and Erica D. Borghard, "The Cost of Empty Threats: A Penny, Not a Pound," *American Political Science Review* 105, no. 3 (2011): 437–56; Marc Trachtenberg, "Audience Costs: An Historical Analysis," *Security Studies* 21, no. 1 (2012): 3–42. Also see Tomz, *Reputation and International Cooperation*. In Jack S. Levy, Michael K. McKoy, Paul Poast, and Geoffrey P. R. Wallace, "Backing Out or Backing In? Commitment and Consistency in Audience

Costs Theory," *American Journal of Political Science* 59, no. 4 (2015): 988–1001, the authors use a survey experiment to examine domestic responses to the president's decision to "back down" from public threats and "back into" foreign conflicts, finding that the president loses support in both cases, but suffers worse backlash for "backing out." Levendusky and Horowitz find, through the use of survey experiments, that a president's justification for why he backed down will have a large effect on audience costs. See Matthew S. Levendusky and Michael C. Horowitz, "When Backing Down Is the Right Decision: Partisanship, New Information, and Audience Costs," *Journal of Politics* 74, no. 2 (2012): 323–38. Furthermore, Kertzer and Brutger conclude that traditional audience cost experiments may overestimate how much people care about inconsistency, and that the logic of audience costs (and the implications for crisis bargaining) varies considerably with the leader's constituency. See Joshua D. Kertzer and Ryan Brutger, "Decomposing Audience Costs: Bringing the Audience Back into Audience Cost Theory," *American Journal of Political Science* 60, no. 1 (2016): 234–49. This recent scholarship shows that audience costs may vary by constituency. Therefore, the variations in experimental outcomes in the audience cost literature provide another set of alternative arguments for the variation in concern for reputation.

41. Thomas C. Schelling, *Arms and Influence* (New Haven, CT: Yale University Press, 1966), 124.

42. Ibid., 55–56.

43. Ibid., 124.

44. Barbara Walter, *Reputation and Civil War: Why Separatist Conflicts Are So Violent* (New York: Cambridge University Press, 2009).

45. On the conditions under which states can signal resolve during covert operations, see Austin Carson and Keren Yarhi-Milo, "Covert Communication: The Intelligibility and Credibility in Signaling in Secret," *Security Studies* 26, no. 1 (2017): 124–56.

46. This book focuses primarily on leaders, i.e., chief executives, and much less on their advisors. This is a conscious choice when studying crisis behavior in a democratic context, because although advisors do have agenda-setting power and can significantly shape policy choices, it is the chief executive in most democracies who has ultimate veto power over any particular course of action during a crisis. Therefore understanding how the dispositions and beliefs of these leaders shape their willingness to fight for reputation gives us a clearer picture of why they ultimately chose one policy over another. For the significant role of the power of the president relative to that of the bureaucracy in shaping crisis policies, see Krasner's and Art's critiques of Graham Allison. Stephen D. Krasner, "Are Bureaucracies Important? (Or Allison Wonderland)," *Foreign Policy* 7 (Summer 1971): 159–79; Robert J. Art, "Bureaucratic Politics and American Foreign Policy: A Critique," *Policy Sciences* 4 (December 1973): 467–90.

47. Shiping Tang, "Reputation, Cult of Reputation, and International Conflict," *Security Studies* 14, no. 1 (2005): 34–62, definition on 38; Jonathan Mercer, *Reputation and International Politics* (Ithaca, NY: Cornell University Press, 1996), 27.

48. This does not necessarily require the presence of an explicit commitment to defend a particular third party, or a threat to stand by a previously declared red line. See Robert Jervis's discussion in "Signaling and Perception: Drawing Inferences and Projecting Images," in *Political Psychology*, ed. Kristen Renwick Monroe (Mahwah, NJ: L. Erlbaum, 2002), 293–312, on the distinction between an actor's general reputation for resolve and his or her signaling reputation.

49. For example, see Hermann, "Explaining Foreign Policy Behavior Using the Personal Characteristics of Political Leaders," 7–46; Hermann et al., "Who Leads Matters," 83–131; Steinberg, *Shame and Humiliation*; Deborah Welch Larson, *Origins of Containment: A Psychological Explanation* (Princeton, NJ: Princeton University Press, 1985); Richard Ned Lebow and Janice Gross Stein, *We All Lost the Cold War* (Princeton, NJ: Princeton University Press, 1994); Robert Jervis, Richard Ned Lebow, and Janice Gross Stein, *Psychology and Deterrence* (Baltimore: Johns Hopkins University Press, 1985).

50. Thomas C. Schelling, *The Strategy of Conflict* (Cambridge, MA: Harvard University Press, 1960); Schelling, *Arms and Influence*; Robert Jervis, "Bargaining and Bargaining Tactics," in *Coercion*, ed. J. R. Pennock and J. W. Chapman (Chicago: Aldine Atherton, 1972), 272–88; Robert Jervis, *The Meaning of the Nuclear Revolution: Statecraft and the Prospect of Armageddon* (Ithaca, NY: Cornell University Press, 1989); Glenn H. Snyder and Paul Diesing, *Conflict among Nations: Bargaining, Decision Making, and System Structure in International Crises* (Princeton, NJ: Princeton University Press, 1977); Robert Powell, "Nuclear Deterrence Theory, Nuclear Proliferation, and National Missile Defense," *International Security* 27, no. 4 (2003): 86–118.

51. Theodore G. Hopf, *Peripheral Visions: Deterrence Theory and American Foreign Policy in the Third World, 1965–1990* (Ann Arbor: University of Michigan Press, 1996); Daryl Grayson Press, *Calculating Credibility: How Leaders Assess Military Threats* (Ithaca, NY: Cornell University Press, 2005); Mercer, *Reputation and International Politics*; Press argues that discussions of credibility and deterrence frequently conflate two issues. One is how other states view the reputation for resolve of State X, and the other is how State X's leaders themselves view the role of their actions in establishing their credibility (or not). See Press, *Calculating Credibility*, 10. In the context of deterrence theory, Mercer and Press study the first question, i.e., whether State X's reputation for resolve and credibility deters other states (and what metrics other states use to judge State X's resolve). In this book, I study the other side of the equation, i.e., the extent to which the leaders of State X value their reputation for resolve and are willing to use force to protect it. As Press puts it, "Do leaders believe that *their own* past actions affect *their own* credibility?" (Press, *Calculating Credibility*, 10). I argue below that there is important variation in the answer to this question, and therefore deterrence theory must be further qualified by incorporating variation in the willingness of a state's leaders to deter adversaries through threats or the use of force for the sake of generating a reputation for resolve rather than protection of a truly vital interest.

52. Fearon, "Domestic Political Audiences and the Escalation of International Disputes," 577–92; Fearon, "Selection Effects and Deterrence," 5–29; Paul K. Huth, "Reputations and Deterrence: A Theoretical and Empirical Assessment," *Security Studies* 7, no. 1 (1997): 72–99.

53. Allan Dafoe, Jonathan Renshon, and Paul Huth, "Reputation and Status as Motives for War," *Annual Review of Political Science* 17, no. 1 (2014): 371–93.

54. Remarkably, even those scholars who have criticized the importance of reputation for resolve acknowledge that, in real life, leaders and states do fight for reputation. See, for example, Press, *Calculating Credibility*, and G. Snyder and Diesing, *Conflict among Nations*.

55. Alex Weisiger and Keren Yarhi-Milo, "Revisiting Reputation: How Past Actions Matter in International Politics," *International Organization* 69, no. 2 (2015): 473–95.

56. Logan Grosenick, Tricia S. Clement, and Russell D. Fernald, "Fish Can Infer Social Rank by Observation Alone," *Nature* 445, no. 7126: 429–32; John Whitfield, *People Will Talk: The Surprising Science of Reputation* (Hoboken, NJ: Wiley, 2011). Apart from resolve, reputation appears to be important in other contexts such as honesty (Anne E. Sartori, *Deterrence by Diplomacy* [Princeton, NJ: Princeton University Press, 2005]), violence (Marc J. C. Crescenzi, "Reputation and Interstate Conflict," *American Journal of Political Science* 51, no. 2 [2007]: 382–96), alliance politics (Douglas M. Gibler, "The Cost of Reneging: Reputation and Alliance Formation," *Journal of Conflict Resolution* 52, no. 3 [2008]: 425–54; Gregory D. Miller, *The Shadow of the Past: Reputation and Military Alliances before the First World War* [Ithaca, NY: Cornell University Press, 2011]; Marc J. C. Crescenzi et al., "Reliability, Reputation, and Alliance Formation," *International Studies Quarterly* 56, no. 2 [2012]: 259–74), sovereign debt (Tomz, *Reputation and International Cooperation*), and economic sanctions (Timothy M. Peterson, "Sending a Message: The Reputation Effect of US Sanction Threat Behavior," *International Studies Quarterly* 57, no. 4 [2013]: 672–82). Certainly, political leaders and policy elites often refer to the

need to protect the country's reputation and status in national security matters and may describe opponents as "unreliable" or "weak" based on their past behavior (Robert J. McMahon, "Credibility and World Power: Exploring the Psychological Dimension in Postwar American Diplomacy," *Diplomatic History* 15, no. 4 (1991): 455–72; Dafoe et al., "Reputation and Status as Motives for War"; Jervis et al., *Psychology and Deterrence*; Press, *Calculating Credibility*). Tang calls this the "cult of reputation" (Tang, "Reputation, Cult of Reputation, and International Conflict"). Scholars frequently point to the importance of honor, prestige, and status in leading to the outbreak of wars: Donald Kagan, *On the Origins of War and the Preservation of Peace* (New York: Doubleday, 1995); Richard Ned Lebow, *A Cultural Theory of International Relations* (New York: Cambridge University Press, 2008); Barry O'Neill, *Honor, Symbols and War* (Ann Arbor: University of Michigan Press, 1999); Barry O'Neill, "Nuclear Weapons and National Prestige," Cowles Foundation discussion paper no. 1560 (New Haven, CT: Yale University, 2006). Alexander Lanoszka and Michael A. Hunzeker, "Rage of Honor: Entente Indignation and the Lost Chance for Peace in the First World War," *Security Studies* 24, no. 4 (2015): 662–95, argue that the pursuit of honor as an end to itself, most prevalent in wars of prevention and territorial occupation, better explains the prolonging of war than rational theories of information and commitment problems.

57. Paul Milgrom and John Roberts, "Limit Pricing and Entry under Incomplete Information: An Equilibrium Analysis," *Econometrica* 50, no. 2 (1982): 443–60; David M. Kreps and Robert Wilson, "Reputation and Imperfect Information," *Journal of Economic Theory* 27, no. 2 (1982): 253–79; see also Ross M. Miller and Charles R. Plott, "Product Quality signaling in Experimental Markets," *Econometrica* 53, no. 4 (1985): 837–72; Alvin E. Roth and Francoise Schoumaker, "Expectations and Reputations in Bargaining: An Experimental Study," *American Economic Review* 73, no. 3 (1983): 362–72.

58. Walter, *Reputation and Civil War*.

59. Todd S. Sechser, "Reputation and Signaling in Coercive Bargaining," *Journal of Conflict Resolution* (forthcoming).

60. Dustin Tingley and Barbara F. Walter, "The Effect of Repeated Play on Reputation Building: An Experimental Approach," *International Organization* 65, no. 2 (2011): 343–65.

61. Joe Clare and Vesna Danilovic, "Reputation for Resolve, Interests, and Conflict," *Conflict Management and Peace Science* 29, no. 1 (2012): 3–27; for showing that physiological reactivity mediated the relationship between anxiety and political attitudes, see Jonathan Renshon, Jooa Julia Lee, and Dustin Tingley, "Physiological Arousal and Political Beliefs," *Political Psychology* 36, no. 5 (2015): 569–85. On reputation as second-order beliefs, see O'Neill, *Honor, Symbols and War*; Dafoe et al., "Reputation and Status as Motives for War." Also see Kertzer and Brutger, "Decomposing Audience Costs."

62. Lebow, *Cultural Theory of International Relations*.

63. Patrick Morgan, "Saving Face for the Sake of Deterrence," in *Psychology and Deterrence*, ed. Robert Jervis, Richard Ned Lebow, and Janice Stein (Baltimore: Johns Hopkins University Press, 1985), citation from 134–36.

64. Allan Dafoe, "Resolve, Reputation, and War: Cultures of Honor and Leaders' Time-in-Office," PhD diss., University of California, Berkeley, 2012.

65. Dafoe and Caughey, "Honor and War."

66. Li Zhang, "Reputation and War," PhD diss., Harvard University, 2011.

67. Jonathan Renshon, Allan Dafoe, and Paul Huth, "Leader Influence and Reputation Formation in World Politics," *American Journal of Political Science* (forthcoming).

68. Jonathan Renshon, "Losing Face and Sinking Costs: Experimental Evidence on the Judgment of Political and Military Leaders," *International Organization* 69, no. 3 (2015): 659–95.

69. Tingley and Walter, "Effect of Repeated Play on Reputation Building."

70. Fearon, "Domestic Political Audiences and the Escalation of International Disputes"; Tomz, *Reputation and International Cooperation*; Robert Trager and Lynn Vavreck, "The Political Costs of Crisis Bargaining: Presidential Rhetoric and the Role of Party," *American Journal of Political Science* 55, no. 3 (2011): 526–45; Levendusky and Horowitz, "When Backing Down Is the Right Decision"; Kertzer and Brutger, "Decomposing Audience Costs."

71. Jervis, *Perception and Misperception in International Politics*; Mercer, *Reputation and International Politics*; Kertzer and Brutger, "Decomposing Audience Costs."

72. Mercer, *Reputation and International Politics*.

73. Tang, "Reputation, Cult of Reputation, and International Conflict."

74. G. Snyder and Diesing, *Conflict among Nations*.

75. High self-monitors could plausibly be motivated by different types of reputations in their everyday life. And indeed, as I show in chapter 2, the literature has examined how image considerations have shaped high self-monitors' consumption behavior, professions, and even life partners.

76. Mark Snyder, Self-Monitoring of Expressive Behavior," *Journal of Personality and Social Psychology*, no. 30 (1974): 526–37.

77. As I note in the next chapter, there has been some work in leadership style connecting self-monitoring of leaders with things such as openness to information and acceptance of constraints.

78. Herrmann, Tetlock, and Visser, "Mass Public Decisions on Go to War."

79. Tomz, *Reputation and International Cooperation*.

80. Jonathan M. Cheek, "Aggregation, Moderator Variables, and the Validity of Personality Tests: A Peer-Rating Study," *Journal of Personality and Social Psychology* 43, no. 6 (1982): 1254; William E. Wymer and Louis A. Penner, "Moderator Variables and Different Types of Predictability: Do You Have a Match?," *Journal of Personality and Social Psychology* 49, no. 4 (1985): 1002–15.

81. By excluding those speeches, I minimize the effect of external strategic circumstances and decision-making pressures on a leader's articulated preferences and also avoid conflating beliefs and behavior.

82. The foreign policy crises considered in this statistical analysis include those crises considered in depth in the case studies.

83. As I explain in chapter 6, I do not conduct case analysis of a low self-monitor hawk because none of the American presidents in my sample meet my selection criteria.

84. Most primary documents on Clinton's crisis decision making are still classified.

Chapter 2: What Types of Leaders Fight for "Face"?

1. Robert Jervis, *The Logic of Images in International Relations* (New York: Columbia University Press, 1970).

2. Mark R. Leary and Robin M. Kowalski, "Impression Management: A Literature Review and Two-Component Model," *Psychological Bulletin* 107, no. 1 (1990): 34–47; B. R. Schlenker, *Impression Management: The Self-Concept, Social Identity, and Interpersonal Relations* (Monterey, CA: Brooks/Cole, 1980).

3. Erving Goffman, *The Presentation of Self in Everyday Life* (Garden City, NY: Doubleday Anchor, 1959).

4. Jervis, *Logic of Images in International Relations*.

5. Michael N. Barnett, *Dialogues in Arab Politics* (New York: Columbia University Press, 1998).

6. Jennifer L. Erickson, *Dangerous Trade: Arms Exports, Human Rights, and International Reputation* (New York: Columbia University Press, 2015).

7. Austin Carson and Keren Yarhi-Milo, "Covert Communication: The Intelligibility and Credibility of Signaling in Secret," *Security Studies* 26, no. 1 (2017): 124–56; Austin Carson, "Facing Off and Saving Face: Covert Intervention and Escalation Management in the Korean War," *International Organization* 70, no. 1 (2016): 103–31.

8. Importantly, there are some types of impression management, such as those characterized as defensive, that high self-monitors are less likely to adopt. An example would be behaviors involving close attention and responsivity to others. People who engage in the latter type of impression management, Fuglestad and Snyder note, tend to be socially anxious and seek to appease others. The most important types of impression management engaged in by a high self-monitor involves "actively constructing public appearances that lead to favorable outcomes and social cachet," as well as expressive control and nonverbal decoding skills that are useful to image cultivation. Paul T. Fuglestad and Mark Snyder, "Self-Monitoring," in *Handbook of Individual Differences in Social Behavior*, ed. Mark R. Leary and Rick H. Hoyle (New York: Guilford, 2009), 585.

9. M. Snyder, "Self-Monitoring of Expressive Behavior," *Journal of Personality and Social Psychology*, no. 30 (1974): 526–37; M. Snyder, *Public Appearances, Private Realities: The Psychology of Self-Monitoring* (New York: W. H. Freeman, 1987); S. Gangestad and M. Snyder, "On the Nature of Self-Monitoring: An Examination of Latent Causal Structure," in *Review of Personality and Social Psychology* 6, ed. P. Shaver (Beverly Hills, CA: Sage, 1985); S. W. Gangestad and M. Snyder, "Taxonomic Analysis Redux: Some Statistical and Conceptual Considerations for Testing a Latent Class Model," *Journal of Personality and Social Psychology*, no. 61 (1991): 141–46.

10. M. Snyder, "Self-Monitoring of Expressive Behavior." This article has been cited 4,015 times since its publication.

11. Snyder and Gangestad published some studies in 1985 that indicated that monozygotic twins had very similar, if not identical, self-monitoring scores most of the time, and dizygotic twins had similar scores at better-than-chance frequency. This implies that self-monitoring is based on genetic traits, rather than nurture. Self-monitoring develops in early to middle childhood and is connected to the development of self-awareness. This would imply that self-monitoring stabilizes early in life and does not change easily.

12. E. L. Tobey and G. Tunnell, "Predicting Our Impressions on Others: Effects of Public Self-Consciousness and Acting, a Self-Monitoring Subscale," *Personality and Social Psychology Bulletin*, no. 7 (1981): 661–69. This does not mean that high self-monitor will not show cross situational consistency in some forms of self-presentations, such as those pertaining to background self-presentation or the overall ease with which they interact socially. At the same time, they will engage in situation-specific self-presentation that can enhance their status. Richard Lippa, "Expressive Control and the Leakage of Dispositional Introversion-Extraversion during Role-Played Teaching," *Journal of Personality* 44, no. 4 (1976): 541–59; Richard Lippa, "Expressive Control, Expressive Consistency, and the Correspondence between Expressive Behavior and Personality," *Journal of Personality* 46, no. 3 (1978): 438–61; Paul T. Fuglestad and Mark Snyder, "Status and the Motivational Foundations of Self-Monitoring," *Social and Personality Psychology Compass* 4, no. 11 (2010), 1031–41.

13. W. Ickes, R. Holloway, L. L. Stinson, and T. G. Hoodenpyle, "Self-Monitoring in Social Interaction: The Centrality of Self-Affect," *Journal of Personality*, no. 74 (2006): 681.

14. Fuglestad and Snyder, "Self-Monitoring," emphasis added. See also S. W. Gangestad and M. Snyder, "Self-Monitoring: Appraisal and Reappraisal," *Psychological Bulletin*, no. 126 (2000): 530–55.

15. M. Snyder, "Self-Monitoring of Expressive Behavior." M. Snyder, *Public Appearances, Private Realities*, 135, acknowledges that ability precedes motivation to self-monitor. However, the items on the Self-Monitoring Scale (Mark Snyder and Steve Gangestad, "On the Nature of

Self-Monitoring: Matters of Assessment, Matters of Validity," *Journal of Personality and Social Psychology* 51, no. 1 (1986): 125–39, are not meant to distinguish between the ability and motivation of an individual. "If motivation and ability go hand in hand, then there should not be any people with motivation who lack ability. Yet, such people clearly do exist, such as those with a high need for social approval.... Taken together ... the person with the extraverted disposition (who may possess some high self-monitoring abilities but lack high self-monitoring motivations) and the person with the high need for social approval (who may be motivated to engage in self-monitoring but lack the self-presentational abilities to do so) suggest that, with respect to self-monitoring, ability precedes motivation." M. Snyder, *Public Appearances, Private Realities*, 135.

16. M. Snyder, "Self-Monitoring of Expressive Behavior," 526–37. There is a lot of support in the literature for the relationship between self-monitoring and consumer behavior. For example, Kenneth G. DeBono and Karen Rubin, "Country of Origin and Perceptions of Product Quality: An Individual Difference Perspective," *Basic and Applied Social Psychology* 17, nos. 1–2 (1995): 239–47, found that high self-monitors bases their quality judgment of cheese solely based on an image-based advertising strategy, whereas low self-monitors based their judgment solely on performance-based strategy. See also, Kenneth G. DeBono, Amy Leavitt, Jennifer Backus, "Product Packaging and Product Evaluation: An Individual Difference Approach," *Journal of Applied Social Psychology* 33, no. 3 (2003): 513–21; DeBono and Snyder, "Understanding Consumer Decision-Making Processes: The Role of Form and Function in Product Evaluation."

17. W. Ickes and R. D. Barnes, "The Role of Sex and Self-Monitoring in Unstructured Dyadic Interactions," *Journal of Personality and Social Psychology*, no. 35 (1977): 315–30.

18. Sandor Czellar, "Self-Monitoring and Status Motivation: An Implicit Cognition Perspective," in *NA—Advances in Consumer Research*, vol. 34, ed. Gavan Fitzsimons and Vicki Morwitz (Duluth, MN: Association for Consumer Research, 2007), 333.

19. Clara Michelle Cheng and Tanya L. Chartrand, "Self-Monitoring without Awareness: Using Mimicry as a Nonconscious Affiliation Strategy," *Journal of Personality and Social Psychology* 85, no. 6 (2003): 1170–79.

20. M. Snyder and DeBono, "Appeals to Image and Claims about Quality"; Mark Snyder, Ellen Berscheid, and Alana Matwychuk, "Orientations toward Personnel Selection: Differential Reliance on Appearance and Personality," *Journal of Personality and Social Psychology* 54, no. 6 (1988): 972–29; Judith H. Langlois, Lisa Kalakanis, Adam J. Rubenstein, Andrea Larson, Monical Hallam, and Monica Smoot, "Maxims or Myths of Beauty? A Meta-analytic and Theoretical Review," *Psychological Bulletin* 126, no. 3 (2000): 390–423.

21. From an evidentiary perspective, it is important to distinguish between self-monitoring as ability and as motivation. Research suggests that self-monitoring is a phenomenon that has both an internal motivational component and an empirically observable behavioral component that makes it easy to measure across multiple individuals. To be clear, self-monitoring is primarily defined in terms of one's *capacity* to change the emotional messages one conveys, which translates into observable behavior that is measured by the Self-Monitoring Scale. It differs from purely motivational emotional factors (e.g., narcissism, the "need to belong," etc.). For example, subjects who had high "need-for-approval" scores on the Crowne and Marlowe Social Desirability Scale "were actually less able to communicate either positive or negative affects facially or vocally than were low need-for-approval subjects" (Susan F. Zaidel and Albert Mehrabian, "The Ability to Communicate and Infer Positive and Negative Attitudes Facially and Vocally," *Journal of Experimental Research in Personality* 3, no. 3 [1969]: 233–41, cited in M. Snyder, "Self-Monitoring of Expressive Behavior," 529). Self-monitoring is thus not merely a desire; it is rather a skill-based behavioral disposition that individuals use strategically to navigate social situations.

22. M. Snyder and B. H. Campbell, "Self-Monitoring: The Self in Action," in *Psychological Perspectives on the Self*, vol. 1, ed. J. Suls (Hillsdale, NJ: Erlbaum, 1982), 185–207.

23. Fuglestad and Snyder, "Self-Monitoring."

24. M. Snyder and N. Cantor, "Thinking about Ourselves and Others: Self-Monitoring and Social Knowledge," *Journal of Personality and Social Psychology*, no. 39 (1980): 222–34.

25. Importantly, this does not suggest that low self-monitors also necessarily attribute the behaviors of others to dispositional tendencies.

26. Gangestad and Snyder, "Self-Monitoring: Appraisal and Reappraisal."

27. M. Snyder and Gangestad, "On the Nature of Self-Monitoring: Matters of Assessment, Matters of Validity," 126.

28. Ibid., 128. Several studies have criticized the scale, arguing that it does not measure a unified construct. For example, see S. R. Briggs, J. M. Cheek, and A. H. Buss, "An Analysis of the Self-Monitoring Scale," *Journal of Personality and Social Psychology* 38 (1980): 679–86; R. Lennox, "The Problem with Self-Monitoring: A Two-Sided Scale and a One-Sided Theory," *Journal of Personality Assessment* 52 (1988): 58–73; R. Lennox and R. Wolfe, "Revision of the Self-Monitoring Scale," *Journal of Personality and Social Psychology* 46 (1984): 1349–64. However, see Gangestad and Snyder, "Self-Monitoring: Appraisal and Reappraisal."

29. H. Wolf et al., "Self-Monitoring and Personality: A Behavioural-Genetic Study," *Personality and Individual Differences* 47, no. 1 (July 2009): 25–29; S. W. Gangestad, "On the Etiology of Individual Differences in Self-Monitoring and Expressive Self-Control: Testing the Case of Strong Genetic Influence," PhD diss., University of Minnesota, 1984. In a study of the self-monitoring characteristics of monozygotic and dizygotic twins, Robert H. Dworkin, Barbara W. Burke, Brendan A. Maher, and Irving I. Gottesman, "Genetic Influences on the Organization and Development of Personality," *Developmental Psychology* 13, no. 2 (1977): 164–65, found that, if raised in the same environment, pairs of monozygotic twins were far more likely than dizygotic twins to have similar, if not identical, self-monitoring scores. In a similar study, M. Snyder and Gangestad, "On the Nature of Self-Monitoring," found that monozygotic twins were in the same self-monitoring category (high or low) 95 percent of the time, compared to only 74 percent of the time for dizygotic twins. This genetic factor emerges in children at young ages, with girls learning to self-monitor faster than boys on average (Carolyn Saarni, "An Observational Study of Children's Attempts to Monitor Their Expressive Behavior," *Child Development* 55, no. 4 [1984]: 1504–13). Wolf et al., "Self-Monitoring and Personality," find that "behavioral-genetic analyses showed substantial heritability for personality as well as for self-monitoring. Moreover, the relationship between personality and self-monitoring was partly mediated by genetic influences" (25). M. Snyder, *Public Appearances, Private Realities*, notes that, while the nuanced regulation of expressive behavior seen in adults is not immediately present in children, variation in certain traits that emerge before age two (such as differences in temperament and the speed at which children learn languages) may correspond to variation in self-monitoring later in life (136).

30. Fuglestad and Snyder, "Self-Monitoring," 574–91; L. M. Musser and B. Browne, "Self-Monitoring in Middle Childhood: Personality and Social Correlates," *Developmental Psychology*, no. 27 (1991): 994–99.

31. Although self-monitoring exists as a genetically influenced personality trait, researchers have tried to intervene and improve subjects' abilities to monitor certain aspects of their behaviors for desired social ends. Interventions used to curb negative behaviors, such as smoking or interrupting classroom discussions, as well as interventions used to encourage positive behaviors (Rachel L. Loftin, Ashley C. Gibb, Russell Skiba, "Using Self-Monitoring Strategies to Address Behavior and Academic Issues," *Impact* 18, no. 2 [2005]: 12–13). Still, these interventions do not rely on the same self-monitoring that Snyder and colleagues define in their research. Snyder's self-monitoring specifically refers to the ability to control one's expressive behavior in order to convey emotions that may or may not match one's internal feelings, while the "self-monitoring" affected by interventions is merely changing a long-term habit through self-observation. Overall,

interventions cannot turn a "clinically" high self-monitor into a low self-monitor or vice versa but at best try to moderate his or her behavior in the margins.

32. M. Snyder, *Public Appearances, Private Realities*, 130.

33. Martin Kilduff and David Krackhardt, *Interpersonal Networks in Organizations* (Cambridge: Cambridge University Press, 2008), found that women tend to score lower than men on self-monitoring, and they believe that women have had trouble achieving high-level managerial positions because they are not as likely, on average, to self-monitor as men are (174). Adam Berinsky, "Can We Talk? Self-Presentation and the Survey Response," *Political Psychology*, no. 25 (2004): 650, also concluded that women were significantly less likely than men to be high self-monitors (650). However, a literature review conducted by Robert B. Cialdini and Melanie R. Trost, "Social Influence: Social Norms, Conformity and Compliance," in *The Handbook of Social Psychology*, ed. D. T. Gilbert, S. T. Fiske, and G. Lindzey (New York: McGraw-Hill, 1998), found that, across multiple studies, women were more likely to self-monitor and conform to social influence than men, although the differences in most studies were essentially negligible (167).

34. Berinsky, "Can We Talk?," 650. It can sometimes be the case that high self-monitors affiliate with the party that is more popular or that confers greater social status (Don Spurgeon and Randall E. Osborne, "What's in a Chad? Self-Monitoring and Presidential Voting in the 2000 Election," *Psi Chi Journal of Undergraduate Research* 7 (2002): 85–89, 87.

35. See W. B. Gudykunst, G. Gao, T. Nishida, M. H. Bond, K. Leung, G. Wang, et al., "A Cross-Cultural Comparison of Self-Monitoring," *Communication Research Reports*, 6, no. 1 (1989): 7–12.

36. Robert A. Emmons, "Factor Analysis and Construct Validity of the Narcissistic Personality Inventory," *Journal of Personality Assessment* 48, no. 3 (June 1984): 291–300. Finding the correlation between the two traits to be 0.37 and statistically significant is Daniel R. Ames, Paul Rose, and Cameron P. Anderson, "The NPI-16 as a Short Measure of Narcissism," *Journal of Research in Personality* 40, no. 4 (August 2006): 440–50.

37. M. R. Barrick, L. Parks, and M. K. Mount, "Self-Monitoring as a Moderator of the Relationships between Personality Traits and Performance," *Personnel Psychology*, no. 58 (2005): 745–67.

38. Higher self-monitoring is also positively correlated with higher emotional intelligence (Nicola S. Schutte et al., "Emotional Intelligence and Interpersonal Relations," *Journal of Social Psychology* 141, no. 4 [2001]: 523–36), although the causal relationship between the two concepts is unclear.

39. H. Garland and J. F. Beard, "The Relationship between Self-Monitoring and Leader Emergence across Two Task Situations," *Journal of Applied Psychology*, no. 64 (1979): 72–76; R. J. Ellis, "Self-Monitoring and Leadership Emergence in Groups," *Personality and Social Psychology Bulletin*, no. 14 (1988): 681–93; G. H. Dobbins, W. S. Long, E. J. Dedrick, and T. C. Clemons, "The Role of Self-Monitoring and Gender on Leader Emergence: A Laboratory and Field Study," *Journal of Management*, no. 16 (1990): 609–18.

40. A. Mehra, M. Kilduff, and D. J. Brass, "The Social Networks of High and Low Self-Monitors: Implications for Workplace Performance," *Administrative Science Quarterly*, no. 46 (2001): 121–46.

41. M. Kilduff and D. V. Day, "Do Chameleons Get Ahead: The Effects of Self-Monitoring on Managerial Careers," *Academy of Management Journal*, no. 37 (1994): 1047–60.

42. Garland and Beard, "Relationship between Self-Monitoring and Leader Emergence," 72–76.

43. M. D. Whitmore and R. J. Klimoski, "Leader Emergence and Self-Monitoring Behavior under Conditions of High and Low Motivation," paper presented at the annual meetings of the Midwestern Psychological Association (Chicago, May 1984).

44. For example, Preston develops a typology of leader styles that incorporates American presidents' personalities and policy experience. He relies on self-monitoring as a guide to whether the leader is seeking and adapting to feedback about his performance in relation to others, a hallmark of a high self-monitor, compared to a low self-monitor, who does not seek information in order to conform to the political environment. Hermann and Hermann use self-monitoring to examine the predominant leader decision unit, arguing that low self-monitors will be less open to others' opinions, such that their foreign policy views will be more predictive of their behavior than environmental factors. More recently, Keller and Yang extend the theory of poliheuristic decision making to incorporate leader styles. They incorporate self-monitoring as one feature of leader style, arguing that low self-monitors are more likely to challenge political constraints than high self-monitors. See M. G. Hermann and C. F. Hermann, "Who Makes Foreign Policy Decisions and How: An Empirical Inquiry," *International Studies Quarterly* 33, no. 4 (1989): 361–87; J. W. Keller and Y. E. Yang, "Leadership Style, Decision Context, and the Poliheuristic Theory of Decision Making: An Experimental Analysis," *Journal of Conflict Resolution* 52, no. 5 (2008): 687–712; T. Preston, *The President and His Inner Circle: Leadership Style and the Advisory Process in Foreign Policy Making* (New York: Columbia University Press, 2012).

45. Weber et al. have used self-monitoring to study the impact of racial prejudice on individuals. They find that the impact of prejudice is greater among low self-monitors since they should be less subject to social desirability pressures. Christopher R. Weber, Howard Lavine, Leonie Huddy, Christopher M. Federico, "Placing Racial Stereotypes in Context: Social Desirability and the Politics of Racial Hostility," *American Journal of Political Science* 58, no. 1 (2014): 63–78; see also Berinsky, "Can We Talk?"; Adam J. Berinsky and Howard G. Lavine, "Self-Monitoring and Political Attitudes," in *Improving Public Opinion Surveys: Interdisciplinary Innovation and the American National Election Studies*, ed. John Aldrich and Kathleen M. McGraw (Princeton, NJ: Princeton University Press 2011).

46. Keren Yarhi-Milo and Marcus Holmes, "The Psychological Logic of Peace Summits: How Empathy Shapes Outcomes of Diplomatic Negotiations," *International Studies Quarterly* 61, no. 1 (2017): 107–22.

47. Anne E. Sartori, *Deterrence by Diplomacy* (Princeton, NJ: Princeton University Press, 2007).

48. Stephen E. Gent, Mark J. C. Crescenzi, Elizabeth J. Menninga, and Lindsay Reid, "The Reputation Trap of NGO Accountability," *International Theory* 7, no. 3 (2015): 426–43.

49. Kenneth G. DeBono, "Investigating the Social Adjustive and Value Expressive Functions of Attitudes: Implications for Persuasion Processes," *Journal of Personality and Social Psychology*, no. 52 (1987): 279–87.

50. Harold Sigall and David Landy, "Radiating Beauty: Effects of Having a Physically Attractive Partner on Person Perception," *Journal of Personality and Social Psychology*, 28, no. 2 (1973): 281–24; M. Snyder and K. G. DeBono, "Appeals to Image and Claims about Quality: Understanding the Psychology of Advertising," *Journal of Personality and Social Psychology*, no. 49 (1985): 586–97.

51. Kenneth G. DeBono and Mark Snyder, "Understanding Consumer Decision-Making Processes: The Role of Form and Function in Product Evaluation," *Journal of Applied Social Psychology*, no. 19 (1989): 416–24; M. Snyder and DeBono, "Appeals to Image and Claims about Quality."

52. M. Snyder and DeBono, "Appeals to Image and Claims about Quality"; Sigall and Landy, "Radiating Beauty."

53. Dafoe et al., "Reputation and Status as Motives for War."

54. Lebow, *Cultural Theory of International Relations*, 486–88. In contrast, rogue states are positioned at the lowest end of this status hierarchy.

55. Jervis, *Logic of Images in International Relations*; Jervis, "Signaling and Perception: Drawing Inferences and Projecting Images"; Joshua D. Kertzer, *Resolve in International Politics* (Princeton, NJ: Princeton University Press, 2016).

56. Dafoe, Renshon, and Huth, "Reputation and Status as Motives for War," 371–93.

57. Ibid.

58. Ibid.

59. J. D. Morrow, "A Continuous-Outcome Expected Utility Theory of War," *Journal of Conflict Resolution* 29, no. 3 (September 1, 1985): 473–502.

60. See also Renshon, Dafoe, and Huth, "Leader Influence and Reputation Formation in World Politics"; Alexandra Guisinger and Alastair Smith, "Honest Threats," *Journal of Conflict Resolution* 46, no. 2 (2002): 175–200, on the importance of leader-level reputations.

61. Alex Weisiger and Keren Yarhi-Milo, "Revisiting Reputation: How Do Past Actions Matter in International Politics," *International Organization* 69, no. 2 (2015): 473–95; Chin Carter and Yarhi-Milo, "The Political Cost of Territorial Concessions: Dictators, Reputation, and Coups," working paper.

62. For the analytical distinction between status as an intrinsic versus an instrumental good, see Jonathan Renshon, *Fighting for Status: Hierarchy and Conflict in World Politics* (Princeton, NJ: Princeton University Press, 2017), 47–50.

63. W. C. Wohlforth, "Unipolarity, Status Competition, and Great Power War," *World Politics* 61, no. 1 (2009): 28–57; D. S. Markey, "The Prestige Motive in International Relations," PhD diss., Princeton University, 2000; Renshon, *Fighting for Status*.

64. For example, see Shashank Joshi, "Honor in International Relations," Weatherhead Center Working Paper Series No. 2008-0146, citing Steven Lee Myers, "Politicians in Ukraine Near Accord on a Coalition," *New York Times*, June 22, 2006, http://www.nytimes.com/2006/06/22/world/europe/politicians-in-ukraine-near-accord-on-a-coalition.html?mtrref=www.google.com&gwh=E2C441A2509607316C11D04C02CE1C02&gwt=pay.

65. Karin Bäckstrand and Ole Elgström, "The EU's Role in Climate Change Negotiations: From Leader to 'Leadiator,'" *Journal of European Public Policy* 20, no. 10 (2013): 1369–86; Barry G. Rabe, *Statehouse and Greenhouse: The Emerging Politics of American Climate Change Policy* (Washington, DC: Brookings Institution Press, 2004).

66. Jonathan Mercer, *Reputation and International Politics* (Ithaca, NY: Cornell University Press, 1996), 27.

67. That is why leaders believe they can affect their reputations even though the historical record, according to Press, *Calculating Credibility,* Mercer, *Reputation and International Politics,* and Tang, "Reputation, Cult of Reputation, and International Conflict," provide little evidence that reputations form in international politics.

68. Carson and Yarhi-Milo, "Covert Communication." See also Austin Carson, *Secret Wars: Covert Conflict in International Politics* (Princeton, NJ: Princeton University Press, 2018).

69. For a discussion on audience segregation, see Erving Goffman, *The Presentation of Self in Everyday Life* (Garden City, NY: Doubleday Anchor, 1959); as applied to self-monitoring, see M. Snyder, *Public Appearances, Private Realities*.

70. Robert O. Keohane and Joseph S. Nye Jr., "Power and Interdependence," *Survival* 15, no. 4 (1973): 159.

71. Robert Powell, "Absolute and Relative Gains in International Relations Theory," *American Political Science Review* 85, no. 4 (1991): 1303–20.

72. Joseph Grieco, Robert Powell, and Duncan Snidal, "The Relative-Gains Problem for International Cooperation," *American Political Science Review* 87, no. 3 (September 1993): 734.

73. Matthew C. Waxman, "The Use of Force against States That 'Might' Have Weapons of Mass Destruction," *Michigan Journal of International Law*, Research Paper No. 09-216, 31, no. 1

(November 22, 2009): 26. On the revolution in military affairs, see Eliot A. Cohen, "A Revolution in Warfare," *Foreign Affairs*, March/April 1996, https://www.foreignaffairs.com/issues/1996/75/2.

74. Alastair Iain Johnston, "Thinking about Strategic Culture," *International Security* 19, no. 4 (Spring 1995): 46.

75. Martha Finnemore, *The Purpose of Intervention: Changing Beliefs about the Use of Force*, Cornell Studies in Security Affairs (Ithaca, NY: Cornell University Press, 2003).

76. A. Sell et al., "Human Adaptations for the Visual Assessment of Strength and Fighting Ability from the Body and Face," *Proceedings of the Royal Society B: Biological Sciences* 276 (February 7, 2009): 575–84.

77. Peter Liberman, "Punitiveness and US Elite Support for the 1991 Persian Gulf War," *Journal of Conflict Resolution* 51, no. 1 (2007): 3–32.

78. Peter Liberman, "Retributive Support for International Punishment and Torture," *Journal of Conflict Resolution* 57, no. 2 (2013): 285–306.

79. Richard M. Saunders, "Military Force in the Foreign Policy of the Eisenhower Presidency," *Political Science Quarterly* 100, no. 1 (Spring 1985): 98.

80. T. R. Gurr, "War, Revolution, and the Growth of the Coercive State," *Comparative Political Studies* 21, no. 1 (April 1, 1988): 45.

81. Andrew Bennett, "The Guns That Didn't Smoke: Ideas and the Soviet Non-use of Force in 1989," *Journal of Cold War Studies* 7, no. 2 (April 2005): 81–109.

82. Russell J. Leng, "When Will They Ever Learn? Coercive Bargaining in Recurrent Crises," *Journal of Conflict Resolution* 27, no. 3 (1983): 379–419, 382. Jervis originates the concept that policy makers learn general and superficial lessons from history and so apply to current conflicts lessons drawn from the most dramatic parts of previous disputes, such as the outcome. A state will also tend to view its own behavior as the cause of the difference in outcome and so will switch bargaining strategies if the previous interaction was unsuccessful or will maintain the same bargaining strategy if the outcome was as desired. Jervis, *Perception and Misperception in International Politics*, 229–30.

83. Herrmann, Tetlock, and Visser, "Mass Public Decisions to Go to War."

84. Alexander L. George, "The Operational Code": A Neglected Approach to the Study of Political Leaders and Decision-Making," *International Studies Quarterly* 13, no. 2 (1969): 190–222, 199. However, George's discussion of instrumental beliefs, especially about how goals of action should be pursued, also takes into account other factors, such as risk aversion and the ability to control escalation, which I do not incorporate in my consideration of beliefs about the efficacy of force.

85. Bruce Russett, "Doves, Hawks, and U.S. Public Opinion," *Political Science Quarterly* 105, no. 4 (Winter 1990): 516.

86. It is also important to note, in the context of Fearon's argument about the irrationality of war, that a belief in the efficacy of force does not automatically lead to the use of force. If a bargaining solution is possible in the real world, rational leaders would prefer it to fighting. However, the very existence of war—as Fearon himself notes—suggests that the theoretical existence of a bargain often does not translate into a real equivalent. James D. Fearon, "Rationalist Explanations for War," *International Organization* 49, no. 3 (1995), 379–414.

87. G. Snyder and Diesing, *Conflict among Nations*, 188, 381.

88. Although I consider these two cases—high self-monitor doves and low self-monitor hawks—to be illustrative, examination of more cases in the future could provide more robustness for the significance of this difference.

89. Existing research on the use of analogical reasoning—Khong, *Analogies at War*; Jervis *Perceptions and Misperceptions*; Ernest May, *"Lessons" of the Past: The Use and Misuse of History*

in American Foreign Policy (New York: Oxford University Press, 1973)—for example, taps into this vein of belief formation. Pivotal moments in the past can decisively shape a generation of leaders, although leaders may draw different lessons from the same historical episode. Pivotal episodes are also likely to *change* the beliefs leaders hold about the efficacy of force, as was the case with the Soviet invasion of Afghanistan (Bennett, "The Guns That Didn't Smoke") and the American experiences in Korea and Vietnam (Robert J. Art, "To What Ends Military Power?," *International Security* 4, no. 4 [1980], 3–35).

90. The advent of air power, the invention of nuclear weapons, the revolution in military affairs, all mark major shifts in the objective utility of force in international affairs and the beliefs individuals hold about it. Of course, individuals may interpret technological change differently, as evinced by the extensive debates surrounding the potential uses and utility of each new major advance in technology during the twentieth century.

91. There were, of course, substantial domestic changes during the Cold War. Hopf shows how domestic contestation in the Soviet Union over its national identity shaped its foreign policy at critical junctures in the Cold War. Ted Hopf, *Social Construction of International Politics: Identities and Foreign Policies, Moscow, 1955 and 1999* (Ithaca, NY: Cornell University Press, 2002). The same could be argued of the United States and far-reaching domestic changes, such as the civil rights movement. However, the variables most relevant as potentially confounding factors for my theory did not change to any great extent during this period, and the extent that they do, I also treat them as alternative explanations in the statistical and case analysis (see chapters 5 and 6).

It could be argued that the threat environment facing the United States varied across the span of the Cold War, especially during the period of détente, covering the presidencies of Richard Nixon, Gerald Ford, and partially that of Jimmy Carter. While it is plausible that during détente a lower threat from the Soviet Union may have resulted in a lesser willingness to fight for reputation among these presidents, it is clear that the threat did not disappear: the Soviet Union was still a superpower that had achieved nuclear parity with the United States. Moreover, there is sufficient variation in the crisis behaviors of the three détente presidents to suggest that the change in the threat environment alone cannot explain the crisis behavior of any one president.

92. Patrick Morgan, "Saving Face for the Sake of Deterrence," in *Psychology and Deterrence*, ed. Robert Jervis, Richard Ned Lebow, and Janice Stein (Baltimore: Johns Hopkins University Press, 1985); Robert McMahon, "Credibility and World Power: Exploring the Psychological Dimension in Postwar American Diplomacy," *Diplomatic History* 15, no. 3 (1991): 455–72.

93. See Patrick Morgan, "Saving Face for the Sake of Deterrence"; Robert McMahon, "Credibility and World Power"; Stephen Walt, "Why Are U.S. Leaders So Obsessed with Credibility?," *Foreign Policy* (blog), September 11, 2012, http://foreignpolicy.com/2012/09/11/why-are-u-s-leaders-so-obsessed-with-credibility/, and Richard Ned Lebow, *Why Nations Fight: Past and Future Motives for War* (Cambridge: Cambridge University Press, 2010). Some would argue that that consensus continued after the Cold War. As Fettweis puts is, "While all states remain concerned to some degree with their reputation, no country today seems to take the imperative to remain credible as seriously as the United States. Scholars have not been able to detect equivalent levels of concerns for credibility in any other state, even the Soviet Union, who presumably faced many of the same challenges during the Cold War without exhibiting similar influence of the imperative." See Christopher J. Fettweis, *Pathologies of Power: Fear, Honor, Glory, and Hubris in U.S. Foreign Policy* (New York: Cambridge University Press, 2013), 95.

94. There are, of course, countries—such as parliamentary democracies with coalition governments—in which the leader holds lesser sway than the US president over foreign policy. However, when considering regime type more broadly, chief executives are likely to be more constrained in democracies than in nondemocracies. See Bruce Bueno de Mesquita, James D.

Morrow, Randolph M. Siverson, and Alastair Smith, "An Institutional Explanation of the Democratic Peace," *American Political Science Review* 93, no. 4 (1999): 791–807.

95. Jervis, "Do Leaders Matter and How Would We Know?," 153–79.

Chapter 3: Microfoundations

1. Alan Nelson, "Some Issues Surrounding the Reduction of Macroeconomics to Microeconomics," *Philosophy of Science* 51, no. 4 (1984): 575.

2. For a recent discussion on microfoundations in international relations, see Joshua D. Kertzer, *Resolve in International Politics* (Princeton, NJ: Princeton University Press, 2016).

3. Adam J. Berinsky, Gregory A. Huber, Gabriel S. Lenz," Evaluating Online Labor Markets for Experimental Research: Amazon.com's Mechanical Turk," *Political Analysis* 20, no. 3 (2012): 351–68.

4. Michael R. Tomz and Jessica L. P. Weeks, "Public Opinion and the Democratic Peace," *American Political Science Review* 107, no. 4 (2013): 849–65.

5. Andrew Healy and Gabriel S. Lenz, "Substituting the End for the Whole: Why Voters Respond Primarily to the Election-Year Economy," *American Journal of Political Science* 58, no. 1 (2014): 31–47.

6. Douglas Kriner and Francis Shen, "Reassessing American Casualty Sensitivity: The Mediating Influence of Inequality," *Journal of Conflict Resolution* 58, no. 7 (2014): 1174–201.

7. See, for example, Joseph K. Goodman, Cynthia E. Cryder, and Amar Cheema, "Data Collection in a Flat World: The Strengths and Weaknesses of Mechanical Turk Samples," *Journal of Behavioral Decision Making* 26, no. 3 (2013): 213–24; John J. Horton, David G. Rand, and Richard J. Zeckhauser, "The Online Laboratory: Conducting Experiments in a Real Labor Market," *Experimental Economics* 14, no. 3 (2011): 399–425; Winter Mason and Siddharth Suri, "Conducting Behavioral Research on Amazon's Mechanical Turk," *Behavior Research Methods* 44, no. 1 (2010): 1–23; Gabriele Paolacci, Jesse Chandler, and Panagiotis G. Ipeirotis, "Running Experiments on Amazon Mechanical Turk," *Judgment and Decision-Making* 5, no. 5 (2010): 411–19; Michael Buhrmester, Tracy Kwang, and Samuel D. Gosling, "Amazon's Mechanical Turk: A New Source of Inexpensive, Yet High-Quality, Data?," *Perspectives on Psychological Science* 6, no. 1 (2011): 3–5; David G. Rand, "The Promise of Mechanical Turk: How Online Labor Markets Can Help Theorists Run Behavioral Experiments," *Journal of Theoretical Biology* 299 (2012): 172–79. For a different viewpoint, see Yanna Krupnikov and Adam S. Levine, "Cross-Sample Comparisons and External Validity," *Journal of Experimental Political Science* 1, no. 1 (2014): 59–80, though their caution applies particularly to MTurk studies that require subjects to read a significant amount or trust information from an experimenter. These two attributes were not important in the study described here.

8. Herrmann, Tetlock, and Visser, "Mass Public Decisions to Go to War," 569–70. Also used in Kertzer, *Resolve in International Politics*.

9. Milton Rokeach, *The Nature of Human Values* (New York: Free Press, 1973), 7.

10. John Zaller, *The Nature and Origins of Mass Opinion* (Cambridge: Cambridge University Press, 1992); R. Michael Alvarez and John Brehm, *Hard Choices, Easy Answers: Values, Information, and American Public Opinion* (Princeton, NJ: Princeton University Press, 2002).

11. See Dennis Chong and James N. Druckman, "A Theory of Framing and Opinion Formation in Competitive Elite Environments," *Journal of Communication* 7, no. 1 (2007): 99–118; Robert M. Entman: "Framing: Towards Clarification of a Fractured Paradigm," *Journal of Communication* 43, no. 4 (1993): 51–58; Thomas E. Nelson and Donald R. Kinder, "Issue Frames and Group Centrism in American Public Opinion," *Journal of Politics* 58, no. 4 (1996): 1055–78.

12. However, priming is necessary for the public as an educational tool. We can think differently about the implications that "priming" has for leaders' decision making. Advisors play a different role with their presidents than we do in priming our survey participants. Experienced leaders have equal access to information as their advisors and therefore do not need their advisors to "educate" them in the same way. Instead, advisors cue their presidents, or make salient certain considerations about reputation for resolve, to bring those implications to the forefront of their mind. This is illustrated in the case studies. The theory I lay out might suggest that high self-monitor leaders will be more likely to be influenced by reputational cues from their advisors compared to low self-monitor ones. Accordingly, priming is necessary for the public sample, and this form of "cueing" is also relevant to the study of leaders' decision making. The importance of the presidents' self-monitoring dispositions is underscored when they resist advisors' reputational viewpoints that are different from their own, or when faced with the advisors' concerns about reputation, choose to act in a way contrary to recommendation but consistent with their own disposition.

13. See, for example, Max Ernest-Jones, Daniel Nettle, and Melissa Bateson, "Effects of Eye Images on Everyday Cooperative Behavior: A Field Experiment," *Evolution and Human Behavior* 32 (2011): 172–78; and Costas Panagopoulos, "I've Got My Eyes on You: Implicit Social-Pressure Cues and Prosocial Behavior," *Political Psychology* 35, no. 1 (2013): 23–33.

14. A. J. Berinsky and H. Lavine, "Self-Monitoring and Political Attitudes," in *Improving Public Opinion Surveys: Interdisciplinary Innovation and the American National Election Studies*, ed. J. H. Aldrich and K. M. McGraw (Princeton, NJ: Princeton University Press, 2012), 27–45.

15. Herrmann, Tetlock, and Visser, "Mass Public Decisions to Go to War." Also used in Joshua D. Kertzer and Kathleen M. McGraw, "Folk Realism: Testing the Microfoundations of Realism in Ordinary Citizens," *International Studies Quarterly* 56, no. 2 (2012): 245–58.

16. Berinsky, "Can We Talk? Self-Presentation and the Survey Response"; Berinsky and Lavine, "Self-Monitoring and Political Attitudes"; Samara Klar and Yanna Krupnikov, *Independent Politics: How American Disdain for Parties Leads to Political Inaction* (New York: Cambridge University Press, 2016).

17. For example, Pazit Ben-Nun Bloom, Gizem Arikan, and Marie Courtemanche, "Religious Social Identity, Religious Belief, and Anti-immigration Sentiment," *American Political Science Review* 109, no. 2 (2015): 203–21.

18. The Israeli survey was programmed in Hebrew.

19. There are both advantages and disadvantages to this additional quantity of interest: on the one hand, it may more effectively control for participants' perceived reputation costs, since some participants in the pure control may assume reputation costs are high regardless, suppressing the magnitude of the treatment effect. On the other hand, it also primes participants to think about their image, raising the specter of a different kind of noncompliance. Nonetheless, we include it here as a robustness check.

20. Given that the United States and Israel may be unique in their patriotic or nationalist character, it would also be informative to replicate this survey in other countries where the attachment to the state may be less strong.

21. Kosuke Imai, Luke Keele, Dustin Tingley, and Teppei Yamamoto, "Unpacking the Black Box of Causality: Learning about Causal Mechanisms from Experimental and Observational Studies," *American Political Science Review* 105, no. 4 (2011): 765–89; Margaret E. Roberts, Brandon M. Stewart, Dustin Tingley, Christopher Lucas, Jetson Leder-Luis, Shana Kushner Gadarian, Bethany Albertson, and David G. Rand, "Structural Topic Models for Open-Ended Survey Responses," *American Journal of Political Science* 58, no. 4 (2014): 1064–82.

22. This raises the question of the relationship between self-monitoring and other individual difference variables. Indeed, we find that self-monitoring is relatively uncorrelated with

other constructs political scientists routinely study, including militant assertiveness (r=0.105), international trust (r=0.109), political ideology (r=−0.033), partisanship (r=−0.026), education (r=0.089), and personal efficacy (r=0.071). There is a modest correlation between self-monitoring and risk orientation (r=0.27), with high-self monitors more likely to express a willingness to take risks in their daily lives.

23. This pattern is also displayed starkly in panel e, which compares the pooled treatment effect for high self-monitor doves (on the right), with all other subgroups of the sample (on the left). The reputation treatments have a small effect on the other subgroups, but a large effect on high self-monitor doves.

24. See Roberts et al., "Structural Topic Models for Open-Ended Survey Responses," for more details on the application of topic modeling to political science, as well as Ryan Brutger and Joshua D. Kertzer, "Exploring the Microfoundations of Reputation Costs," *International Organization*, forthcoming, for an additional empirical application.

25. The models are estimated using the *stm* package in Roberts et al., "Structural Topic Models for Open-Ended Survey Responses." Because we have no theoretical reason to expect differences across our three different reputation treatments, we pool them together. For model selection, we present the results from a five-topic model, based on semantic coherence and exclusivity.

26. Importantly, high and low self-monitor doves do not systematically differ from one another in topical prevalence in the control.

27. However, the difference in difference between the two groups is not statistically significant: p<0.15.

28. Imai et al., "Unpacking the Black Box of Causality."

29. As before, the results are the same regardless if we use the just low self-monitor doves as the comparison group rather than the pooled comparison.

Chapter 4: Self-Monitoring, US Presidents, and International Crises

1. The online appendix provides additional robustness checks and model specifications, as well as a full "knitr"-ed replication package for all quantitative analysis included in this chapter.

2. On the appropriateness of using MIDs to study reputation for resolve, see Dafoe and Caughey, "Honor and War"; Dafoe, Renshon, and Huth, "Reputation and Status as Motives for War"; James D. Fearon, "Domestic Political Audiences and the Escalation of International Disputes," *American Political Science Review* 88, no. 3 (1994): 577–92.

3. Dafoe and Caughey, "Honor and War."

4. Fearon, "Domestic Political Audiences and the Escalation of International Disputes," 577–92.

5. Kenneth A. Schultz, "Looking for Audience Costs," *Journal of Conflict Resolution* 45, no. 1 (2001): 32–60; Fearon, "Selection Effects and Deterrence," 5–29; Tomz, *Reputation and International Cooperation: Sovereign Debt across Three Centuries* (Princeton, NJ: Princeton University Press, 2007).

6. Jack Snyder and Erica D. Borghard, "The Cost of Empty Threats: A Penny, Not a Pound," *American Political Science Review* 105, no. 3 (2011): 437–56.

7. Alastair Smith, "International Crises and Domestic Politics," *American Political Science Review* 92, no. 3 (1998), 623–38.

8. Fearon, "Signaling Foreign Policy Interests," 68–90.

9. See Cheek, "Aggregation, Moderator Variables, and the Validity of Personality Tests"; and William E. Wymer and Louis A. Penner, "Moderator Variables and Different Types of Pre-

dictability: Do You Have a Match?," *Journal of Personality and Social Psychology* 49, no. 4 (1985): 1002–15. In other words, a person's peers—arguably those who know him or her well, as a president's biographers would—are competent to judge his or her self-monitoring abilities. On the accuracy of peer-ratings, see Gangestad and Snyder, "Self-Monitoring: Appraisal and Reappraisal," 530–55; Babatunde Ogunfowora, Joshua S. Bourdage, and Brenda Nguyen, "An Exploration of the Dishonest Side of Self-Monitoring: Links to Moral Disengagement and Unethical Business Decision Making," *European Journal of Personality* 27, no. 6 (2013): 532–44. It is worth noting that most studies of this nature are conducted with college students as subjects. Compared to these subjects, it is likely that the correlation between self-ratings and peer-ratings will be higher for presidential biographers as a group, given that their careers and intellectual interests revolve around the particular president or presidents they have studied. In this sense, the findings of existing studies with regard to the accuracy of peer-ratings offer a lower bound on what is likely to be a much more accurate measure in the case of biographers.

10. Even for identification of which countries are considered major powers, which is fundamental to international relations scholarship, the most widely used data set—the Correlates of War—relies on a survey of international relations scholars (see J. David Singer and Melvin Small, *The Wages of War, 1816–1965: A Statistical Handbook* [New York: John Wiley and Sons, 1972]).

11. Bear F. Braumoeller, *The Great Powers and the International System: Systemic Politics in Empirical Perspective* (Cambridge: Cambridge University Press, 2013), 86–87.

12. Bear F. Braumoeller, "Systemic Politics and the Origins of Great Power Conflict," *American Political Science Review* 102, no. 1 (2008): 88.

13. The presidents studied were Harry S. Truman, Dwight D. Eisenhower, John F. Kennedy, Lyndon B. Johnson, Richard Nixon, Gerald Ford, Jimmy Carter, Ronald Reagan, George H. W. Bush, Bill Clinton, and George W. Bush.

14. While this procedure overrepresents types of individuals who, for a variety of reasons, are more likely to have their contact information on the Internet, this bias is unlikely to have a systematic effect on item responses in the questionnaire.

15. Sixty-eight individuals took the survey. Of these, four completed three surveys, and five completed two surveys.

16. This method for identifying bias is adapted from Stephen J. Rubenzer and Thomas R. Faschingbauer, *Personality, Character, and Leadership in the White House: Psychologists Assess the Presidents* (Washington, DC: Potomac Books, 2004).

17. Self-monitoring is measured using the eighteen-item revised version of the Self-Monitoring Scale (Mark Snyder and Steven Gangestad, "On the Nature of Self-Monitoring: Matters of Assessment, Matters of Validity," *Journal of Personality and Social Psychology* 51, no. 1 [1986]: 125–39). This scale was developed in response to criticisms of the original version of the Self-Monitoring Scale (Mark Snyder, "Self-Monitoring of Expressive Behavior," *Journal of Personality and Social Psychology* 30, no. 4 [1974]: 526–637) by several other researchers (e.g., Stephen R. Briggs, Jonathan M. Cheek, and Arnold H. Buss, "Analysis of the Self-Monitoring Scale," 679–86; Richard D. Lennox and Raymond N. Wolfe, "Revision of the Self-Monitoring Scale," *Journal of Personality and Social Psychology* 46, no. 6 [1984]: 1349–64). Compared with the original version of the scale, the revised version appears to be more reliable, and to tap more effectively the single latent factor of self-monitoring than did the original twenty-five-item scale (Jon A. Krosnick and Constantine Sedikides, "Self-Monitoring and Self-Protective Biases in the Use of Consensus Information to Predict One's Own Behavior," *Journal of Personality and Social Psychology* 58, no. 4 [1990]: 718–28; Mark Snyder and Gangestad, "On the Nature of Self-Monitoring"; Gangestad and Snyder, "Self-Monitoring: Appraisal and Reappraisal").

18. Briggs et al., "Analysis of the Self-Monitoring Scale."

19. M. Snyder, "Self-Monitoring of Expressive Behavior," 532.

20. For some questions (e.g., "He found it hard to imitate the behavior of other people"), the answer for a high self-monitoring president on a scale of 1–7 would be in the 1–3 range (i.e., "Very Uncharacteristic," "Uncharacteristic," or "Somewhat Uncharacteristic"). For other questions (e.g., "He could put on a show to impress or entertain others"), the answer for a high self-monitoring president would be in the 5–7 range (i.e., "Somewhat Characteristic," "Characteristic," or "Very Characteristic"). For the former category of questions, I have reversed the order of the scale to produce an overall consolidated scale in which higher scores represent higher self-monitoring abilities.

21. Further analysis of the distribution of scores reveals that there are two outliers: one of the Truman surveys (score 88) and one of the Reagan surveys (score 68). Removing the outlier in Reagan's case increases his mean score to 80.83 and does not change the significance of the results. Removing the outlier in Truman's case decreases his mean score to 55.8 and makes his score statistically significant as a low self-monitor. However, given the small sample sizes (n=6 for Truman and n=7 for Reagan), I chose not to omit the results in order to maintain enough data to draw stronger conclusions from the second section of the survey.

22. The scores for those presidents must, of course, be read with caution, since it is somewhat early for historians and biographers to have written fully informed, in-depth histories of these more recent presidents. Hence the judgment of experts regarding these presidents should be taken as provisional.

23. For a review of the Big 5 personality traits, see Oliver P. John and Sanjay Srivastava, "The Big-Five Trait Taxonomy: History, Measurement, and Theoretical Perspectives," in *Handbook of Personality: Theory and Research*, 3rd ed., ed. Lawrence A. Pervin and Oliver P. John (New York: Guilford, 1999), 102–38.

24. Rubenzer and Faschingbauer, *Personality, Character, and Leadership in the White House*, 5.

25. Clara Michelle Cheng and Tanya L. Chartrand, "Self-Monitoring without Awareness: Using Mimicry as a Nonconscious Affiliation Strategy," *Journal of Personality and Social Psychology* 85, no. 6 (2003): 1173.

26. M. Snyder and Gangestad, "On the Nature of Self-Monitoring," 127.

27. I dichotomized the data by coding ones, twos, and threes as zeros; fives, sixes, and sevens as ones; and fours as 0.5. I then compared them to the neutral score of 9 out of 18 points and to the sample median (10.357, Reagan's score) and mean (9.57). Using the sample means and medians on the dichotomized data, Ford is a statistically significant low self-monitor in either continuous or dichotomous scales; Truman is a statistically significant low self-monitor against the median but not the mean on the dichotomous scale only. However, when using the sample mean and sample median of the dichotomized scale, Reagan stops being a significantly high self-monitor.

28. Specifically, I asked experts to rate, on a scale of 1 (Strongly Disagree) to 7 (Strongly Agree), whether "the president was concerned about his international reputation for looking resolved/firm on issues of foreign policy."

29. The average answer to this question was a 6.0, which corresponded to "Agree." The historians scored Truman, Kennedy, Johnson, and Nixon above average on this issue, although Nixon was the only president whose difference from the average was statistically significant. Eisenhower, Carter, and Reagan were all scored below average but not enough to be statistically significant, while George H. W. Bush and Ford scored almost exactly at the mean.

30. Daniel M. Jones, Stuart A. Bremer, and J. David Singer, "Militarized Interstate Disputes, 1816–1992: Rationale, Coding Rules, and Empirical Patterns," *Conflict Management and Peace Science* 15, no. 2 (1996): 163–213.

31. Dara Kay Cohen and Jessica Lea Weeks, "Red Herrings? Fishing Trawler Disputes, Regime Type and Interstate Conflict," Annual Meeting of the International Studies Association, February 16, 2009. Todd Sechser argues that the MIDs data set is inappropriate for evaluating hypotheses about the effectiveness of coercive threats because it includes minor militarized encounters that do not involve an explicit coercive element. However, despite that the theory discusses the use of coercive military instruments to project resolve, this analysis is not wedded to threats alone. Rather, we are interested in how variation in self-monitoring affects any display threat or use of force (except for minor fishing disputes), for which the MIDs data set is relevant. Todd Sechser, "Militarized Compellent Threats, 1918–2001," *Conflict Management and Peace Science* 28, no. 4 (2011): 377–401, 393.

32. For instance, President Nixon did not complete his second term, resigning in August 1974. In that year, President Nixon was engaged in a militarized dispute with Cuba, while President Ford did not enter into any disputes. In the statistical analysis, this is handled by annualizing President Nixon's number of MIDs for that year, while down-weighting the importance attached to this information: Nixon is considered to have a MID rate of about 2 per year in 1974, but this observation is attached about half the importance of 1973, where President Nixon served the full year. For data at the presidency level, I weight observations by the number of years the president was in office, so that data coming from a two-term president like Clinton would receive more importance than data coming from a three-year president like Kennedy. The results are robust to dropping those weights. Dropping the weights implies counting data from all presidents as equally informative, regardless of how much time they spent in office.

33. On permutation tests, see Luke Keele, Corrine McConnaughy, and Ismail White, "Strengthening the Experimenter's Toolbox: Statistical Estimation of Internal Validity," *American Journal of Political Science* 56, no. 2 (2012): 484–99; for application to the study of US presidents, see Dafoe and Caughey, "Honor and War."

34. Specifically, I use the Wilcoxon-Mann-Whitney Exact test, a nonparametric test that does not rely on assumptions about the distribution of the data, and is robust to outliers because it considers only whether one president had more or less MIDs than any other. By reducing the possibility of results being driven by distributional assumptions and extreme values, the Wilcoxon-Mann-Whitney Exact test is thus both a suitable and hard test. Such nonparametric tests also have the benefit of working well in small samples.

35. Across all regression models, I clustered standard errors on the president level. The dyadic analysis was conducted with demeaning at the dyad level (i.e., with dyad fixed effects), which cancels out all potential time invariant effects at the dyadic level (such as distance between the United States and the other country, or whether there previously was a colony-metropole relationship between them).

36. I include the results of the models controlling for each set of predictors separately in the online appendix, with results proving robust in every instance.

37. For example, see Christopher Gelpi and Peter D. Feaver, "Speak Softly and Carry a Big Stick? Veterans in the Political Elite and the American Use of Force," *American Political Science Review* 96, no. 4 (2002): 779–93.

38. As I note in chapter 2, to test the effect of self-monitoring on conflict behavior (i.e., H1 and H2 in this chapter), I use hawkishness as a control. To test H3, however, I either split the sample into high and low hawkishness, and measure the effect of self-monitoring of the president within each sample; or, as a robustness test, use hawkishness as an interaction variable with self-monitoring. Either way, we get similar results supporting this hypothesis, as I report later in this chapter.

39. Michael Laver, Kenneth Benoit, and John Garry, "Extracting Policy Positions from Political Texts Using Words as Data," *American Political Science Review* 97, no. 2 (2003): 311–31.

40. Ibid.; Daniel Coffey, "More Than a Dime's Worth: Using State Party Platforms to Assess the Degree of American Party Polarization," *PS: Political Science and Politics* 44, no. 2 (2011): 331–37; David-Jan Jansen and Jakob de Haan, "An Assessment of the Consistency of ECB Communication Using WordScores," in *Central Bank Communication, Decision-Making and Governance: The Issues, Challenges, and Case Studies*, ed. Jan-Egbert Sturm and Pierre L. Siklos (Cambridge, MA: MIT Press, 2010), 183–201.

41. In a setting with two reference texts, Text A and Text B, if a given word has 10 occurrences per 1,000 words in Text A and 5 occurrences per 1,000 words in Text B, the probability for that word to show up in Text A is $10/(10+5)$ or $2/3$, and the probability for it to show up in Text B is $1/3$. The technique assigns a score—the "WordScore"—to each word included in any of the reference texts: the WordScore is the probability-weighted sum of the texts' assigned numerical policy positions. So if Text A has been assigned a "–10" and Text B a "+10," a word that shows up twice as frequently in Text A as in Text B will get a WordScore of $2/3*(-10) + 1/3*(10) = -10/3$. The technique computes the WordScore for each unique word that is included in at least one reference text. Other texts can then be scored by simply assigning WordScores to all those words for which WordScores have been computed using the reference texts, and those WordScores are subsequently summed to yield the overall score of an unseen text, a "text score." Texts should be evaluated on their *relative* text scores, so in the above example a "–5" score might indicate a more left-leaning policy position than a "+2" score, for instance (depending on the assignment of scores to reference texts).

42. I also collected all addresses marked as "major to the Nation" from the APP. For detail on the collection of speeches, see the American Presidency website, http://www.presidency .ucsb.edu/.

43. Foreign policy in this context was defined in broad geographic terms: for instance, a speech that mentioned Central or South American affairs would be included in the data set. All references to the Soviet Union or to US allies were also included. Some speeches contained no foreign policy element and were therefore discarded.

44. As Laver et al. explain, "Selecting reference texts thus involves crucial substantive and qualitative decisions by the researcher, equivalent to the decisions made in the design or choice of either a substantive coding scheme for hand-coded content analysis or a coding dictionary for traditional computer-coding." Laver et al., "Extracting Policy Positions from Political Texts Using Words as Data," 314.

45. The number of unique words in each reference text is 912 ("American University speech"), 1,044 ("Moscow State University speech"), 703 ("Truman Doctrine speech"), and 965 ("Evil Empire speech") words.

46. Laver et al., "Extracting Policy Positions from Political Texts Using Words as Data," 6.

47. This plot clearly demonstrates that the language used in the public speeches by the Cold War presidents varies significantly. Eisenhower and Truman tended to employ significantly more assertive language in their public speeches compared all other presidents. Moreover, we can see that military assertiveness as measured by public speeches is not correlated with self-monitoring: for example, two consecutive high self-monitoring presidents, Kennedy and Johnson, have very different scores on the military assertiveness scale.

48. Michael Brecher and Jonathan Wilkenfeld, "Codebook for ICB1—International Crisis Behavior Project." System-level data set—July (2010). In particular, I consider all crises in which both the United States and the Soviet Union were involved through propaganda, through covert support, semimilitarily, militarily, or as crisis actors (in accordance with the published ICB coding manual).

49. Michael C. Horowitz, Allan Stam, and Cali M. Ellis, *Why Leaders Fight* (New York: Cambridge University Press, 2015).

50. Adapted from Costel Calin and Brandon Prins, "The Sources of Presidential Foreign Policy Decision Making: Executive Experience and Militarized Interstate Conflicts," *International Journal of Peace Studies* 20, no. 1 (2015): 17–34.

51. Michael Horowitz, Rose McDermott, and Allan C. Stam, "Leader Age, Regime Type, and Violent International Relations," *Journal of Conflict Resolution* 49, no. 5 (2005): 661–85.

52. Gelpi and Feaver, "Speak Softly and Carry a Big Stick?"

53. This indicates whether the congressional majority party is the same as the president's party in both the House and Senate. See William Howell and Jon Pevehouse, "Separation of Powers, Lawmaking, and the Use of Military Force," in *New Directions for International Relations: Confronting the Method-of-Analysis Problem*, ed. Alex Mintz and Bruce Russett (Lanham, MD: Lexington Books, 2005), 135–57.

54. Expanded here up to and including 2009 based on Christopher Gelpi and Peter D. Feaver, "Speak Softly and Carry a Big Stick?"

55. David B. Carter and Curtis S. Signorino, "Back to the Future: Modeling Time Dependence in Binary Data," *Political Analysis* 18, no. 3 (2010): 271–92.

56. This control variable measures the number of days a leader has spent in office from the beginning of his or her term to the beginning of the year in question. At the presidency level, this refers to the number of years the president has been in office.

57. Note that dividing the sample in this way is not viable in the regression analysis that follows, because it reduces the number of observations in each regression by about half. Nevertheless, an interaction term between self-monitoring and hawkishness reveals consistent results in support of H3: the difference in yearly number of MIDs between high and low self-monitoring hawks is smaller than that between high and low self-monitor doves, as reported in the online appendix.

58. Thus, we are able to use the WordScores of presidents Truman through Reagan. Because these were the US presidents during the Cold War, I do not control for Cold War in those models.

59. It is worth noting that adding self-monitoring level as a predictor significantly increases the accuracy of our models. For instance, an analysis of variance tests comparing the models presented in table 4.5 to identical models without self-monitoring level finds that including self-monitoring level gives a better model with confidence at the $p<0.1$ level for MID involvement, and $p<0.001$ level for MID initiation, despite the large number of other predictors.

60. These are MIDs in which the United States is both an original disputant and coded as being on the initiating side.

61. Using an interaction term I find that the difference in MID initiation between a high and a low self-monitor doves is 1.51 MIDs; the difference between high and low self-monitor hawks is only 0.51 MIDs per year.

62. The analysis using the text-based model specification (in the online appendix) thus includes the public foreign policy speeches (not including crisis months) of presidents Truman through Reagan. Adding the WordScore of Bush (41) does not change the results.

63. This is not to argue that foreign policy does not matter in the selection of candidates. In a recent experimental paper with Mike Tomz and Jessica Weeks, we show that candidates' positions on foreign policy matter as much as economic or religious issues. See Mike Tomz, Jessica Weeks, and Keren Yarhi-Milo, "Public Opinion and Decisions about Military Force in Democracies," working paper.

64. Dafoe and Caughey, "Honor and War," 341–81.

65. Since President Clinton is the only president without military experience, he is excluded from the matched analysis reported in table 4.8.

66. The results of this analysis also suggests that Republican presidents were more likely to use military force compared to Democratic presidents, and that such MIDs were less likely to

take place during the Cold War. Still, we see that self-monitoring is a strong predictor of MIDs that involve the use of force even with those controls.

67. In the online appendix I show these results hold using the alternative WordScore measure for hawkishness.

68. Following Dafoe and colleagues, MIDs not resolved by the end of the president's term are coded as a draw. Dafoe and Caughey, "Honor and War," 19.

69. While these results are consistent with the expectation of the theory, they should be interpreted with caution, as MIDs outcomes are often open to interpretation and therefore challenging to code.

Chapter 5: Approaches to Testing the Theory with Case Studies

1. See Elizabeth Saunders, *Leaders at War: How Presidents Shape Military Interventions* (Ithaca, NY: Cornell University Press, 2011), for an excellent use of prepresidential records as an instrument to code presidents' beliefs.

2. Cheek, "Aggregation, Moderator Variables, and the Validity of Personality Tests"; Wymer and Penner, "Moderator Variables and Different Types of Predictability," 1002–15.

3. These measures are adapted from a survey of methods used by C. K. Sigelman and L. Sigelman, "Gender, Physical Attractiveness, and Electability: An Experimental Investigation of Voter Biases," *Journal of Applied Social Psychology* 16, no. 3 (1986): 229–48; Bruce Russett, "Doves, Hawks, and U.S. Public Opinion," *Political Science Quarterly* 105, no. 4 (Winter 1990): 516; Eugene R. Wittkopf, *Faces of Internationalism: Public Opinion and American Foreign Policy* (Durham, NC: Duke University Press, 1990). Measures of hawkish versus dovish foreign policy preferences were adopted from Herrmann, Tetlock, and Visser, "Mass Public Decisions to Go to War"; Ole R. Holsti, *Public Opinion and American Foreign Policy* (Ann Arbor: University of Michigan Press 1996); Ami Pedahzur and Daphna Canetti-Nisim, "Support for Right-Wing Extremist Ideology: Socio-economic Indicators and Socio-psychological Mechanisms of Social Identification," *Comparative Sociology* 3, no. 1 (2004): 1–36.

4. Lack of evidence might be problematic (perhaps we see no evidence because there was a consensus, or because the empirical record is incomplete). It would be better to find evidence of leaders pushing back against reputational concerns raised by their advisors. Still, it is hard to imagine that, if a leader was concerned about reputation, neither the leader nor his or her advisors would raise this, or that it would not appear in secondary literature.

5. Dafoe, Renshon, and Huth, "Reputation and Status as Motives for War," 371–93.

6. Discursive evidence indicating the presence or absence of concerns of reputation for resolve will not allow us to distinguish between a crusader and a believer, or between a skeptic and a critic. This is because both crusaders and believers will similarly and repeatedly voice concerns about reputation for resolve; and both critics and skeptics will either dismiss them or not raise them. We can distinguish among all four types only by examining whether the president chooses military instruments in light of a concern (or lack thereof) for reputation.

7. However, an assertion that the action could result in a disaster, which could cause allies and adversaries to doubt a country's resolve elsewhere, would be consistent with a reputational logic.

8. Kenneth Waltz, *Man, the State, and War* (New York: Columbia University Press, 1959); Kenneth Waltz, *Theory of International Politics* (New York: McGraw-Hill, 1979).

9. Robert Jervis, *System Effects: Complexity in Political and Social Life* (Princeton, NJ: Princeton University Press, 1998), 121–22.

10. Tang, "Reputation, Cult of Reputation, and International Conflict," 34–62.

11. "The emphasis the United States places on reinforcing its reputation for resolve in the face of even the most minimal challenge lingers because of the legacy of bipolarity and the perceived demands of unipolarity." Indeed, according to Fettweis, unipolarity, and with it the desire of American leaders to maintain the status quo, implies that it is perhaps natural for the leaders of the superpowers to be concerned about intangible assets. "If credibility is one concern for those participating in geopolitics on a global scale, today the United States ought to be the state concerned the most." In this sense, he argues, US leaders are not different from other hegemons such as those of the Roman Empire, "who felt that the reputation of their legions was one of the key factors maintaining order in the empire." See Christopher J. Fettweis, *Pathologies of Power*, 135–37.

12. David Lake and Patrick Morgan, *Regional Orders: Building Security in a New World* (University Park: Pennsylvania State University Press, 1997), 62.

13. Christopher Layne, "Why the Gulf War Was Not in the National Interest," *Atlantic* 268, no. 1 (1991): 55, 65–81.

14. Jervis, "What Do We Want to Deter and How Do We Deter It?," in *Turning Point: The Gulf War and U.S. Military Strategy*, ed. L. Benjamin Ederington and Michael J. Mazarr (Boulder, CO: Westview, 1994), 131.

15. See Jervis, *Meaning of the Nuclear Revolution*, 38–42 and 193–96; R. N. Lebow and J. G. Stein, *We All Lost the Cold War* (Princeton, NJ: Princeton University Press, 1995); G. C. Herring, *From Colony to Superpower: US Foreign Relations since 1776* (New York: Oxford University Press, 2008); R. J. McMahon, "US National Security Policy from Eisenhower to Kennedy," in *The Cambridge History of the Cold War*, vol. 1, *Origins*, ed. Melvyn P. Leffler and Odd Arne Westad (New York: Cambridge University Press, 2010), 288–311.

16. On the rationality of domino thinking, see Douglas J. Macdonald, "Falling Dominoes and System Dynamics: A Risk Aversion Perspective," *Security Studies* 3, no. 2 (1993), 225–58.

17. Moreover, even when the costs are extremely high or extremely low, we should still be able to observe variation in leaders' concerns for reputation in their policy discussions. Thus, for instance, crusaders should voice concerns for reputation and push for policies that are consistent with building or restoring reputation for resolve even when the expected costs are high or the likelihood of success is low. They might decide ultimately not to pursue their preferred policies for a variety of other reasons. Still, evidence of their reasoning and advocacy of policies can allow us to distinguish between them and the other ideal-types, such as reputation skeptics or critics.

18. It is possible that over time, these "myths" about reputation become entrenched beliefs (see Jack Snyder, *Myths of Empire* [Ithaca, NY: Cornell University Press, 1991]).

19. Jack Levy, "The Diversionary Theory of War: A Critique," in *Handbook of War Studies*, ed. M. I. Midlarsky (Boston: Unwin Hyman, 1989), 259–88. For a good review of the diversionary literature, see also Brett A. Leeds and David R. Davis, "Domestic Political Vulnerability and International Disputes," *Journal of Conflict Resolution* 41, no. 6 (1997): 814–34; Sara M. Mitchell and Brandon C. Prins, "Rivalry and Diversionary Uses of Force," *Journal of Conflict Resolution* 48, no. 6 (2004): 937–61; T. Clifton Morgan and Christopher J. Anderson, "Domestic Support and Diversionary External Conflict in Great Britain, 1950–1992," *Journal of Politics* 61, no. 3 (1999): 799–814.

20. According to Howell and Pevehouse, Congress is more likely to mount opposition to the use of force when one or more of three conditions apply: (1) the opposing party to the president retains majority in Congress; (2) military operation grows in size; or (3) operations focus on national concerns that are less strategically important to the United States (chapter 2 in *While Dangers Gather*).

21. Bueno de Mesquita, Morrow, Siverson, and Smith, "Institutional Explanation of the Democratic Peace," 791–807.

22. Fearon, "Domestic Political Audiences and the Escalation of International Disputes," 577–92.

23. Audience cost theory is distinct from selectorate theory in that the latter is about the size of the winning coalition, whereas the former is about the strength and salience of domestic constituencies who might, for example, punish a leader for escalating a conflict and then backing down. B. B. De Mesquita, *The Logic of Political Survival* (Cambridge, MA: MIT Press, 2005).

24. Jessica L. Weeks, *Dictators at War and Peace* (Ithaca, NY: Cornell University Press, 2014); Jessica Chen Weiss, *Powerful Patriots: Nationalist Protest In China's Foreign Relations* (Oxford: Oxford University Press, 2014).

25. Dafoe and Caughey, "Honor and War"; Lebow, *Cultural Theory of International Relations*; R. E. Nisbett and D. Cohen, *Culture of Honor: The Psychology of Violence in the South* (Boulder, CO: Westview Press, 1996); S. Joshi, "Honor in International Relations," Weatherhead Center for International Affairs, Harvard University, working paper, 2008, 146; Frank Henderson Stewart, *Honor* (Chicago: University of Chicago Press, 1994); James Bowman, *Honor: A History* (New York: Encounter Books, 2007); Dafoe, "Resolve, Reputation, and War"; Joanne B. Freeman, *Affairs of Honor: National Politics in the New Republic* (New Haven, CT: Yale University Press, 2001); Neill, *Honor, Symbols, and War*.

26. Jervis, *Perception and Misperception in International Politics*; Khong, *Analogies at War*; Levy, "Learning and Foreign Policy."

27. Jervis, *Perception and Misperception in International Politics*; see also Levy, "Psychology and Foreign Policy Decision-Making."

28. If historical precedents are used merely to *explain* their beliefs about the efficacy of force, that would be consistent with the theory presented here, since I am agnostic as to the origins of those beliefs, as I note in chapter 2.

29. Levy, "Learning and Foreign Policy."

30. Clinton's score on the self-monitoring scale is significantly higher than that of Reagan. We would expect both to exhibit a similar behavior during international crisis, although some aspects in the social behavior of Reagan might appear to be less consistent with an extreme case of a high self-monitor. Indeed, as I show in chapter 8, even though Reagan exhibited a high degree of expressive control and social presence, his other-directedness tendencies were lower than Clinton's.

31. Robert Dallek, interview by Bernard Gwertzman for the Council on Foreign Relations, January 3, 2007.

32. Future studies will benefit from testing the theory against leaders of medium or small powers, as well in the pre-Munich crisis period, where the cost of not fighting might have been perceived as lower.

33. Robert Jervis and Jack Snyder, eds. *Dominoes and Bandwagons: Strategic Beliefs and Great Power Competition in the Eurasian Rimland* (New York: Oxford University Press, 1991); Fettweis, *Pathologies of Power*; Earl C. Ravenal, "Counterforce and Alliance: The Ultimate Connection," *International Security* 6, no. 4 (1982): 26–43.

34. The only exception to this is in Afghanistan, but it is also examined during the presidencies of Carter and Reagan, showing variation even where vital interests are at stake.

35. Dafoe, "Resolve, Reputation, and War." See also Scott Wolford, "The Turnover Trap: New Leaders, Reputation, and International Conflict," *American Journal of Political Science* 51, no. 4 (2007): 772–88; Philip B. K. Potter, "Does Experience Matter? American Presidential Experience, Age, and International Conflict," *Journal of Conflict Resolution* 51, no. 3 (2007): 351–78.

36. I am unable to perform the same test for Clinton's advisors because I don't have enough information about what policies they advocated during the crises and the extent to which they were concerned about reputation during those crises.

37. For example, see Bruce W. Jentleson, "Discrepant Responses to Falling Dictators: Presidential Belief Systems and the Mediating Effects of the Senior Advisory Process," *Political Psy-*

chology 11, no. 2 (June 1990), 353–84; Elizabeth N. Saunders, "War and the Inner Circle: Democratic Elites and the Politics of Using Force," *Security Studies* 24, no. 3 (2015): 466–501; Steven B. Redd, "The Influence of Advisers and Decision Strategies on Foreign Policy Choices: President Clinton's Decision to Use Force in Kosovo," *International Studies Perspectives* 6, no. 1 (2005): 129–50; Irving Janis, *Groupthink: Psychological Studies of Policy Decisions and Fiascoes*, 2nd ed. (Boston: Houghton Mifflin, 1982).

Chapter 6: Jimmy Carter and the Crises of the 1970s

1. See, for example, Betty Glad, *An Outsider in the White House: Jimmy Carter, His Advisors, and the Making of American Foreign Policy* (Ithaca, NY: Cornell University Press, 2009). See also Keren Yarhi-Milo, *Knowing the Adversary: Leaders, Intelligence Organizations, and Assessments of Intentions in International Relations* (Princeton, NJ: Princeton University Press, 2014).

2. Mark Snyder, *Public Appearances, Private Realities*, 46.

3. Ibid., 40–41.

4. Randall Balmer, *Redeemer: The Life of Jimmy Carter* (New York: Basic Books, 2014), 18.

5. Ibid., 39.

6. Ibid., 48.

7. Kevin Mattson, *What the Heck Are You Up To, Mr. President? Jimmy Carter, America's "Malaise," and the Speech That Should Have Changed the Country* (New York: Bloomsbury, 2009), 210.

8. Ibid., 5.

9. Balmer, *Redeemer: The Life of Jimmy Carter*, 115.

10. Quoted in ibid., 116.

11. Peter Bourne, *Jimmy Carter: A Comprehensive Biography from Plains to Post-presidency* (New York: Scribner 1997), 464.

12. Walter Isaacson, Christopher Ogden, and Douglas Brew, "A Vow to Zip His Lip," *Time Magazine*, October 20, 1980, 16.

13. Burton I. Kaufman and Scott Kaufman, *The Presidency of James Earl Carter, Jr.* (Lawrence: University Press of Kansas, 2006), 240.

14. Kenneth Morris, *Jimmy Carter: American Moralist* (Athens: University of Georgia Press, 1996), 285–86.

15. Mark H. Davis, "Voting Intentions and the 1980 Carter-Reagan Debate," *Journal of Applied Social Psychology* 12, no. 6 (1982): 486.

16. Howard Melvin Norton and Bob Slosser, *The Miracle of Jimmy Carter* (Plainfield, NJ: Logos International, 1976), 10.

17. Ibid.

18. Ibid., 28.

19. Bourne, *Jimmy Carter: A Comprehensive Biography from Plains to Post-presidency*, 259.

20. Morris, *Jimmy Carter: American Moralist*, 247.

21. Ibid.

22. Balmer, *Redeemer: The Life of Jimmy Carter*, 33.

23. Jimmy Carter, interview by Bill Moyers, *USA: People and Politics*, PBS, May 6, 1976.

24. US House of Representatives, Committee on House Administration, *The Presidential Campaign 1976*, vol. 1, part 1, *Jimmy Carter* (Washington, DC: Government Printing Office, 1978), ProQuest Congressional (CMP-1978-ADH-0001), 444.

25. Memorandum from Zbigniew Brzezinski to Henry Ower and Steve Stark, March 31, 1976, after the March 14 interview.

26. Norton and Slosser, *Miracle of Jimmy Carter*, 44.

27. Committee on House Administration, *The Presidential Campaign 1976*, vol. 1, part 1, *Jimmy Carter*, 406.

28. Julian E. Zelizer, *Jimmy Carter* (New York: Times Books, 2010), 57.

29. Balmer, *Redeemer: The Life of Jimmy Carter*, 42.

30. Frank Moore, interviewed by James Sterling Young, September 18–29, 1981, Miller Center of Public Affairs Presidential Oral History Program, University of Virginia, transcript, 159.

31. Jimmy Carter, interviewed by Charles Jones, H. Clifton McCleskey, Kenneth Thompson, James Sterling Young, Richard Neustadt, David Truman, Richard Fenno, and Erwin Hargrove, November 29, 1982, Miller Center of Public Affairs Presidential Oral History Program, University of Virginia, transcript, 11.

32. Zelizer, *Jimmy Carter*, 262.

33. Jimmy Carter, interview by John Mashek, *U.S. News and World Report*, May 24, 1976, in Committee on House Administration, *The Presidential Campaign 1976*, vol. 1, part 1, *Jimmy Carter*, 201–2.

34. Jimmy Carter, "Address to Alabama American Legion Convention" (speech, Huntsville, July 14, 1973).

35. Donald Williams, *Historical Lessons to Avoid a Hollow Force* (Norfolk, VA: National Defense University School of Advanced Warfighting, 2013), 15.

36. Pat Towell and David M. Maxfield, "Foreign Policy/National Security 1977: Overview," in *Congressional Quarterly Almanac* 33 (1978): 319–22; Executive Office of the President of the United States, Office of Management and Budget, *Fiscal Year 2015 Historical Tables: Budget of the U.S. Government* (Washington, DC: Government Printing Office, 2014), 82.

37. Towell and Maxfield, "Foreign Policy/National Security 1977: Overview."

38. Yael S. Aronoff, "In Like a Lamb, Out Like a Lion: The Political Conversion of Jimmy Carter," *Political Science Quarterly* 121, no. 3 (2006): 440.

39. Jerel A. Rosati, *The Carter Administration's Quest for a Global Community: Belief and Their Impact on Behavior* (Columbia: University of South Carolina Press, 1987), 148.

40. Gaddis Smith, *Morality, Reason, and Power: American Diplomacy in the Carter Years* (New York: Hill and Wang, 1986), 29.

41. Ibid., 30.

42. Jimmy Carter, "State of the Union Address," Washington, DC, January 19, 1978, speech.

43. Loch K. Johnson, *America's Secret Power: The CIA in a Democratic Society* (Oxford: Oxford University Press, 1989) (quoting John McMahon, deputy director of the CIA, remarks, June 12, 1984). However, to some extent it makes sense that Carter and Reagan would utilize covert action less than their predecessors because scrutiny of the intelligence community had become more intense in the early 1970s. In 1974, the Hughes-Ryan Act was enacted, which required the president to report all covert operations of the CIA to one or more congressional committees. This federal law also prohibits the use of appropriated funds unless and until the president issues a "finding" that each such operation is important to national security and submits these findings to the appropriate committees. The Church Committee, which investigated intelligence abuses by federal agencies, released a scathing report in 1975. Following the recommendations of the Church Committee, in 1976 the Senate established the Senate Select Committee on Intelligence to provide "vigilant legislative oversight over the intelligence activities of the United States to assure that such activities are in conformity with the Constitution and laws of the United States." In 1978, Carter signed into law the Foreign Intelligence Surveillance Act (FISA), which established procedures for the executive to request warrants for wiretapping and other surveillance from a specialized FISA court. Therefore, in this environment of scrutiny toward the intelligence community, it is not surprising that Carter's covert actions would be more limited. The comparison with Reagan with respect to covert action is meaningful because both presidents faced the same institutional constraints.

44. Judith Miller, "Reagan Broadens Power of CIA, Allowing Spying Activities in U.S.," *New York Times*, December 5, 1981, http://www.nytimes.com/1981/12/05/us/reagan-broadens-power-of-cia-allowing-spying-activities-in-us.html?pagewanted=all.

45. Committee on House Administration, *The Presidential Campaign 1976*, vol. 1, part 1, *Jimmy Carter*, 202.

46. Stuart Eizenstat, interview by James Sterling Young, Donald Kettl, H. Clifton McCleskey, Frederick Mosher, Robert Strong, Kenneth Thompson, and Erwin Hargrove, Miller Center of Public Affairs Presidential Oral History Program, University of Virginia, January 29, 1982, transcript, 105–6.

47. Zelizer, *Jimmy Carter*.

48. For a good summary of their opposing views, see Glad, *Outsider in the White House*; and Yarhi-Milo, *Knowing the Adversary*.

49. Because I am not employing the clinical self-monitoring assessment, as I did for the presidents' self-monitoring dispositions, I cannot be precisely sure of the advisors' level of self-monitoring, but I am still confident in my relative categorization of Brzezinski as a high self-monitor and Vance as a low self-monitor based on their biographical information.

50. Hamilton Jordan, *Crisis: The Last Year of the Carter Presidency* (New York: G. P. Putnam's Sons, 1982), 49.

51. Cyrus Vance, in Marilyn Berger, "Cyrus R. Vance, a Confidant of Presidents, Is Dead at 84," *New York Times*, January 13, 2002, http://www.nytimes.com/2002/01/13/world/cyrus-r-vance-a-confidant-of-presidents-is-dead-at-84.html.

52. Philip Habib, in "Cyrus Roberts Vance, a Principled Statesman, Died on January 12th, Aged 84," *Economist*, January 17, 2002.

53. Leslie Gelb, "The Vance Legacy," *New Republic*, May 10, 1980, 13–14, in Melchiore Lauchella, "A Cognitive-Psychodynamic Perspective to Understanding Secretary of State Cyrus Vance's Worldview," *Presidential Studies Quarterly* 34, no. 2 (2004): 229.

54. Quoted in Glad, *Outsider in the White House*, 26.

55. Jordan, *Crisis*, 48.

56. Vance, in Berger, "Cyrus R. Vance, a Confidant of Presidents, Is Dead at 84."

57. Quoted in Glad, *Outsider in the White House*, 26.

58. Berger, "Cyrus R. Vance, a Confidant of Presidents, Is Dead at 84."

59. Jordan, *Crisis*, 284. The other was William Jennings Bryan in 1915, who feared that Woodrow Wilson's handling of the German sinking of the HMS *Lusitania* would draw the United States into the First World War.

60. Ibid., 49.

61. Stephen Szabo, "The Professor," in *Zbig: The Strategy and Statecraft of Zbigniew Brzezinski*, ed. Charles Gati (Baltimore: Johns Hopkins University Press, 2013), 210.

62. Jimmy Carter, *Keeping Faith: Memoirs of a President* (New York: Bantam Books, 1982), 54.

63. Justin Vaïsse, "Zbig, Henry, and the New U.S. Foreign Policy Elite," in *Zbig*, ed. Gati, 12.

64. Carter, *Keeping Faith*, 53. Carter could not "remember any dissension at all" in the National Security Council (ibid).

65. Ibid.

66. Yarhi-Milo, *Knowing the Adversary*.

67. Dafoe, "Resolve, Reputation, and War."

68. Peter Mangold, "Shaba I and Shaba II," *Survival* 21, no. 3 (1979): 109.

69. Roger Mann, "Ethiopia Displays Somali Prisoners," *Washington Post*, August 15, 1977, https://www.washingtonpost.com/archive/politics/1977/08/15/ethiopia-displays-somali-prisoners/4a980828-07a3-43b9-97e1-006181a264bb/?utm_term=.6fa6ea9dc1df.

70. Paul B. Henze, "Realities and Lessons of History in the Horn of Africa, January 12, 1978," Declassified Documents Reference System.

71. Nancy Mitchell, *Jimmy Carter in Africa: Race and the Cold War* (Palo Alto, CA: Stanford University Press, 2016), 365.

72. Ibid., 265.

73. *Foreign Relations of the United States, 1977–1980*, vol. 17, *Horn of Africa*, part 1, ed. Louise P. Woodroofe (Washington, DC: Government Printing Office, 2016), document 46. The Special Coordination Committee was a subcommittee of the National Security Council responsible for coordinating covert operations. It included National Security Advisor Zbigniew Brzezinski, Secretaries of State and Defense Cyrus Vance and Harold Brown, the chairman of the Joint Chiefs of Staff, and director of Central Intelligence Admiral Stansfield M. Turner. The chairman of the Joint Chiefs was General George S. Brown until June 20, 1978, and General David C. Jones afterward.

74. Ibid.

75. *Foreign Relations of the United States, 1977–1980*, vol. 1, *Foundations of Foreign Policy*, ed. Kristin Ahlberg (Washington, DC: Government Printing Office, 2014), document 68.

76. Ibid.

77. Ibid.

78. Ibid.

79. Written on ibid.

80. Mitchell, *Jimmy Carter in Africa*, 386.

81. *Foreign Relations of the United States, 1977–1980*, vol. 17, *Horn of Africa*, part 1, document 58.

82. Ibid.

83. Ibid.

84. Ibid.

85. *Foreign Relations of the United States, 1977–1980*, vol. 17, *Horn of Africa*, part 1, document 60.

86. Ibid.

87. *Foreign Relations of the United States, 1977–1980*, vol. 17, *Horn of Africa*, part 1, document 58.

88. Ibid.

89. Ibid.

90. Ibid.

91. Ibid.

92. Ibid.

93. Jimmy Carter, *Keeping Faith*, 235.

94. *Foreign Relations of the United States, 1977–1980*, vol. 17, *Horn of Africa*, part 1, document 62.

95. Ibid.

96. Ibid.

97. Ibid.

98. *Foreign Relations of the United States, 1977–1980*, vol. 17, *Horn of Africa*, part 1, document 63.

99. Ibid., document 62.

100. Mitchell, *Jimmy Carter in Africa*, 392.

101. National Security Council memorandum, "Summary of Conclusions, SCC Meeting on Horn of Africa," January 26, 1978.

102. Weekly Report no. 45 (February 27, 1978); Glad, *Outsider in the White House*, 37.

103. Weekly Report no. 45 (February 27, 1978).

104. Ibid.

105. Louise P. Woodroofe, ed. *Horn of Africa*, part 1, vol. 17 of *Foreign Relations of the United States, 1977–1980* (Washington, DC: Government Printing Office, 2016), 177–82.

106. Ibid.

107. Ibid.

108. Ibid.

109. Ibid.

110. Ibid.

111. Ibid.

112. Ibid. Importantly, Brzezinski and members of the NSC did not advocate sending more troops in support of Somalia. In fact, NSC memos addressing Brzezinski noted that the US military options in the horn were limited because Somali nationalism "was not of the healthy kind."

113. *Foreign Relations of the United States, 1977–1980*, vol. 17, *Horn of Africa*, part 1, document 66.

114. Ibid., document 65.

115. Ibid., document 67.

116. Ibid.

117. Donna R. Jackson, *Jimmy Carter and the Horn of Africa: Cold War Policy in Ethiopia and Somalia* (Jefferson, NC: McFarland, 2007), 89.

118. Ibid., 90.

119. Hamilton Jordan, interview by James Sterling Young, November 6, 1981, Miller Center of Public Affairs Presidential Oral History Program, University of Virginia, transcript, 32, 69.

120. Louis Harris and Associates, Harris Survey, March 1978 (survey question), USHARRIS .041778.R06, Cornell University, Ithaca, NY: Roper Center for Public Opinion Research.

121. Louis Harris and Associates, Harris Survey, March 1978 (survey question), USHARRIS. 041778.R03 and USHARRIS.041778.R02, Louis Harris and Associates (producer), Cornell University, Ithaca, NY: Roper Center for Public Opinion Research.

122. Louis Harris and Associates, Harris Survey, March 1978, USHARRIS.041778.R04, Cornell University, Ithaca, NY: Roper Center for Public Opinion Research.

123. Louis Harris and Associates, Harris Survey, June 1978, USHARRIS.062678.R03, Louis Harris and Associates (producer), Cornell University, Ithaca, NY: Roper Center for Public Opinion Research.

124. Jordan, Miller Center interview, 25.

125. *Foreign Relations of the United States, 1977–1980*, vol. 1, *Foundations of Foreign Policy*, document 76.

126. Ibid. Carter underlined the passages underlined above, and he also highlighted the phrase "demonstration of force."

127. Ibid.

128. *Foreign Relations of the United States, 1977–1980*, vol. 6, *Soviet Union*, ed. Melissa Jane Taylor and Adam M. Howard (Washington, DC: Government Printing Office, 2014), document 98.

129. Ibid.

130. Zbigniew Brzezinski, *Power and Principle: Memoirs of the National Security Advisor, 1977–1981* (New York: Farrar, Straus, and Giroux, 1983), 189.

131. Odd Arne Westad, *The Global Cold War: Third World Interventions and the Making of Our Times* (Cambridge: Cambridge University Press, 2007), 279.

132. I do not argue that Carter never chose to use force as a coercive instrument, but that those few instances included very limited, targeted uses of force.

133. Heading of this section, memo from Brzezinski to Carter, July 27, 1979.

134. NSC Weekly Report no. 95.

135. NSC Weekly Report no. 98.

136. NSC Weekly Report no. 102.

137. *Washington Post*, September 9, 1979, https://www.washingtonpost.com/archive/politics /1979/09/09/the-brigada-an-unwelcome-sighting-in-cuba/f2206663-e39e-4376-8570-751c2b5b 8f7f/?utm_term=.66681e937df4.

138. Letter, Vance to Senator Stone, July 27, 1979.

139. Quoted in ibid.

140. Memo, Brzezinski to Vance, July 12, 1979.

141. Brzezinski, *Power and Principle*, 347.

142. White paper on the Presence of Soviet Troops in Cuba, September 27, 1979 (Document no. NLC 6-16-8-2-8). During the crisis several issues emerged regarding the purpose of this brigade: First, it was concluded that the size and combat capability of the brigade was too small for any conceivable military operation aimed at the United States. Second, the brigade did not violate the 1962 agreement since it did not have "offensive" capability (in the way defined in that agreement). Third, it did not violate the Monroe Doctrine, because that doctrine had never been applied to voluntary military relationships between an independent American state and a non-American state. Fourth, this was the first time since 1962 that the United States had knowledge of a Soviet brigade in Cuba. Fifth, the presence of the Soviet brigade (which clearly had a combat capability) was kept secret by the USSR and Cuba. At the same time "with equipment and advice and support from the Soviet Union, Cuban armed forces continue to take part in civil and border wars in many parts of the world that do not affect the legitimate interests of Cuba. So long as the status quo remained unchanged, there is a reasonable basis for concern that the brigade has a purpose related not to the defense of Cuba, but to the use of Cuban or Soviet force against the territory of another state." Ibid.

143. See Cyrus Vance, *Hard Choices: Critical Years in America's Foreign Policy* (New York: Simon and Schuster, 1983), 360–61; and Brzezinski, *Power and Principle*, 347.

144. Richard C. Thorton, *The Carter Years: Toward a New Global Order* (St. Paul, MN: Paragon House, 1991), 392.

145. Hampson, "Divided Decision-Maker," 135–60.

146. Ibid., 158–60.

147. Glad, *Outsider in the White House*, 190.

148. Vance, *Hard Choices*, 360.

149. Glad, *Outsider in the White House*, 191.

150. Cyrus Vance, "News Conference of September 5," *Department of State Bulletin* 79, no. 2031 (1979): 14.

151. Jimmy Carter, "Soviet Combat Troops in Cuba: President's Remarks, Sept. 7, 1979," *Department of State Bulletin* 79, no. 2031 (1979): 64.

152. Raymond L. Garthoff, *Détente and Confrontation: American-Soviet Relations from Nixon to Reagan* (Washington, DC: Brookings Institution Press, 1994), 915.

153. Gloria Duffy, "Crisis Mangling and the Cuban Brigade," *International Security* 8, no. 1 (1983): 83.

154. *Foreign Relations of the United States, 1977–1980*, vol. 1, *Foundations of Foreign Policy*, document 126.

155. Ibid.

156. Ibid.

157. Ibid., document 127.

158. Ibid.

159. Ibid.

160. NLC-SAFE 4A-16-46-5-7.

161. Ibid.

162. Ibid.

163. Ibid.

164. Glad, *Outsider in the White House*, 191.

165. Memo quoted in ibid., 192.

166. Memorandum for the President from Brzezinski, September 29, 1979.

167. Four percent said "not sure." ABC News/Louis Harris and Associates, ABC News/Harris Survey, July 1979, USABCHS.073179.R2A, Cornell University, Ithaca, NY: Roper Center for Public Opinion Research.

168. One percent were "not sure." NBC News/Associated Press, NBC News/Associated Press Poll, September 1979, USNBCAP.45.R09A, Cornell University, Ithaca, NY: Roper Center for Public Opinion Research.

169. Eleven percent were "not sure." NBC News/Associated Press, NBC News/Associated Press Poll, September 1979, USNBCAP.45.R10, Cornell University, Ithaca, NY: Roper Center for Public Opinion Research.

170. NSC meeting on Soviet Ground Force Presence in Cuba, September 17, 1979 (Document no. NLC-23-53-4-2-2).

171. Brement to Brzezinski, September 12, 1979, Brzezinski Collection, Donated Historical Material, box 37, Jimmy Carter Library, Atlanta, GA.

172. Ibid.

173. Memorandum from Brzezinski to the president, "Options regarding Soviet Brigade in Cuba," September 18, 1979.

174. The letter is quoted in Odd Arne Westad, *The Fall of Détente: Soviet-American Relations during the Carter Years* (Oslo: Scandinavian University Press, 1997), 282.

175. Memorandum for the president from Zbigniew Brzezinski, September 29, 1979.

176. Memorandum from David Aaron to the president, "Dinner Meeting with the Alumni Group," September 28, 1979 (Document no. NLC-126-18-20-1-9).

177. Heading of this section, President Carter, peace and national security address to the nation, October 1, 1979.

178. *Public Papers of the Presidents of the United States: Jimmy Carter, 1979*, book 2, *June 23 to December 31, 1979* (Washington, DC: Government Printing Office, 1980), 1802–4.

179. Ibid., 1803–4.

180. Brzezinski, *Power and Principle*, 346–51.

181. Prime Minister Margaret Thatcher's personal message to President Carter, October, 1979.

182. Sixteen percent had no opinion, Gallup Organization, Gallup Poll (AIPO), October 1979. USGALLUP.1140.Q006C, Cornell University, Ithaca, NY: Roper Center for Public Opinion Research.

183. CBS News/New York Times, CBS News/New York Times Poll, November 1979, USCBSNYT.110779.R34, Cornell University, Ithaca, NY: Roper Center for Public Opinion Research.

184. Three percent not sure. ABC News/Louis Harris and Associates, ABC News/Harris Survey, November 1979, USABCHS.121879.R2C, Cornell University, Ithaca, NY: Roper Center for Public Opinion Research.

185. Thirty-six percent said his reaction was about right; 19 percent don't know. Roper Organization, Roper Report 79-10, December 1979, USROPER.79–10.R07, Cornell University, Ithaca, NY: Roper Center for Public Opinion Research.

186. Heading of this section, President Carter, December 28, 1979.

187. Memorandum from Brzezinski to Carter, "Reflections on Soviet Intervention in Afghanistan," December 26, 1979.

188. Ibid.

189. Ibid.

190. Memo from Brzezinski to Carter, "Our Response to Soviet Intervention in Afghanistan," December 29, 1979.

191. Ibid.

192. *Public Papers of the Presidents of the United States: Jimmy Carter, 1979*, 2287.

193. *Foreign Relations of the United States, 1977–1980*, vol. 1, *Foundations of Foreign Policy*, document 132.

194. Memorandum from Brzezinski to Carter, "Possible Steps in Reactions to Soviet Intervention in Afghanistan," January 2, 1980.

195. Heading of this section, President Carter in National Security Council meeting, March 18, 1980 (Document no. NLC-17-2-19-4-7).

196. Carter, *Keeping Faith*, 471.

197. National Security Council meeting, March 18, 1980 (Document no. NLC-17-2-19-4-7).

198. Garthoff, *Détente and Confrontation*, 1062.

199. "Soviet Invasion of Afghanistan: President's Address, Jan. 4, 1980," *Department of State Bulletin* 80, no. 2034 (1980): A.

200. Jimmy Carter and Don Richardson, *Conversations with Carter* (Boulder, CO: Lynne Rienner, 1998), 181 (emphasis added).

201. Yarhi-Milo, *Knowing the Adversary*, chapters 5–7.

202. NSC Weekly Report no. 134, March 28, 1980.

203. NSC Weekly Report no. 134. I address elsewhere the divisions within the administration about how to assess Soviet intentions. See Yarhi-Milo, *Knowing the Adversary*.

204. NSC Weekly Report, no. 134, March 28, 1980.

205. Yarhi-Milo, *Knowing the Adversary*, chapter 6.

206. In contrast, the purpose of covert action in Afghanistan under Reagan was defeat of the Soviets, reflecting the differing views on the usefulness of force of Reagan, a reputation crusader.

207. Memorandum from Thomas Thornton to Zbigniew Brzezinski, "Regional Cooperation re Afghanistan," September 24, 1979, in *Cold War International History Project Reader*, vol. 1; see also Robert Gates, *From the Shadows: The Ultimate Insider's Story of Five Presidents and How They Won the Cold War* (New York: Simon and Schuster, 1996), 145. Steve Coll notes that debates in mid-1979 about possible covert aid featured concerns that the Soviet retaliation might follow if "they saw an American hand in their Afghan cauldron." See Steve Coll, *Ghost Wars: The Secret History of the CIA, Afghanistan, and Bin Laden, from the Soviet Invasion to September 10, 2001* (New York: Penguin, 2004), 43.

208. An intelligence assessment, "The Invasion of Afghanistan: Implications for Soviet Foreign Policy," January 1980.

209. See Kirsten Lundberg, *Politics of a Covert Action: The US, the "Mujahideen," and the Stinger Missile*, Harvard Kennedy School Case Study Program, 1999, 3–4.

210. Heading of this section, Jimmy Carter, State of the Union Address (Washington, DC, January 23, 1980).

211. National Security Council meeting, January 2, 1980 (Document no. NLC 17-2-18-3/9).

212. Memorandum from Brzezinski to Carter, "A Long-Term Strategy for Coping with the Consequences of the Soviet Action in Afghanistan," January 9 1980.

213. SCC meeting on U.S. Strategy for South West Asia and Persian Gulf, January 14 1980.

214. Yarhi-Milo, *Knowing the Adversary*, chapter 6.

215. Glad, *Outsider in the White House*, 207.

216. Jimmy Carter, "State of the Union Address" (speech, Washington, DC, January 23, 1980).

217. Carter, "State of the Union Address," 1980. To make this policy plausible, increases in US military strength were necessary. To this end, Carter announced an increase in the defense budget for fiscal year 1981 and an intention to improve "the capability to deploy U.S. military forces rapidly to distant areas."

218. CBS News/New York Times, CBS News/New York Times Poll, January 1980.

219. New York Times Poll, January 1980.

220. Harris Survey, https://ropercenter.cornell.edu/CFIDE/cf/action/home/index.cfm.

221. Four percent replied not sure. ABC News/Louis Harris and Associates, ABC News/ Harris Survey, January 1980.

222. Five percent replied not sure. ABC News/Louis Harris and Associates, ABC News/ Harris Survey, March 1980.

223. In fact, a few did speculate that Carter was overreacting to the Soviet invasion. Garthoff, *Détente and Confrontation*, 1082–83.

224. Ibid., 1049.

225. Ibid., 1062.

226. Memorandum from Brzezinski to Carter, "Afghanistan and the Allies," March 17, 1980.

227. Memorandum from Brzezinski to Carter, NSC meeting, March 18, 1980 (Document no. NLC 17-2-19-2-9).

228. Ibid.

229. Ibid.

230. Carter, *Keeping Faith*, 480.

231. Ibid., 482–83.

232. ABC News National Exit Poll, November 1980.

233. Ibid.

234. Jimmy Carter, interviewed by Charles Jones, H. Clifton McClesky, Kenneth Thompson, James Sterling Young, Richard Neustadt, David Truman, Richard Fenno, and Erwin Hargrove, Miller Center of Public Affairs Presidential Oral History Program, University of Virginia, transcript, 57.

235. See Robert Jervis, *System Effects: Complexity and Political and Social Life* (Princeton, NJ: Princeton University Press, 1998); J. Snyder and Jervis, *Dominoes and Bandwagons*.

236. See Yarhi-Milo, *Knowing the Adversary*, 118, and National Security Council, Comprehensive Net Assessment (CNA), 1978.

237. National Security Council, CNA, 1978.

238. The 1975 projections had been favorable to the United States (or near even) with regard to warheads, throw-weight, and launchers into the 1980s; in contrast, the 1978 projections were unfavorable to the United States in warheads and throw-weight. According to Brzezinski's memo to the president from June 1978, these projections assumed a SALT treaty along the lines agreed to as of May 1978, current US programs for the ALCM (air-launched cruise missiles) and Trident II, and Soviet programs projected as the "best estimate" for National Intelligence Estimate (NIE) 1978. In terms of equivalent countermilitary potential, the basic trend, as perceived in 1978, was unfavorable to the United States until 1987, when "it [would] level off at a very substantial Soviet advantage." Yarhi-Milo, *Knowing the Adversary*, 117–19.

239. "The Balance of Nuclear Forces in Central Europe," CIA report, August 1977.

240. Ibid.

241. Ibid.

242. Zbigniew Brzezinski, Madeline Albright, and William Odom, interviewed by James Sterling Young et al., February 18, 1982, Miller Center of Public Affairs Presidential Oral History Program, University of Virginia, transcript, 32. See also NIEs 3–8 during the 1980s.

243. Andrew Z. Katz, "Public Opinion and the Contradictions of Jimmy Carter's Foreign Policy," *Presidential Studies Quarterly* 30, no. 4 (2000): 663.

244. Duffy, "Crisis Mangling and the Cuban Brigade," 83.

245. Jackson, *Jimmy Carter and the Horn of Africa*, 89–90.

246. More broadly, as Hamilton Jordan states, "It was perceived that we had an arrogance toward the Congress." See Jordan, Miller Center interview, 22. Similarly, in 1978, Frank Moore, the president's congressional liaison, appealed to Carter to consider the political ramifications

of his policies with Congress, which he believed were ad hoc, disorganized, contradictory, and without direction. Carter did not take this advice. In the 1978 sale of F-15s in the Middle East, for example, he suffered erosion of support from the Democratic constituency. See Daniel Strieff, "Arms Wrestle: Capitol Hill Fight over Carter's 1978 Middle East 'Package' Airplane Sale," *Diplomatic History* 40, no. 3 (2016): 480, 498.

247. Dafoe and Caughey, "Honor and War" 341–81.

248. Dafoe, "Resolve, Reputation, and War," 72.

Chapter 7: Ronald Reagan and the Fight against Communism

1. Ronald Reagan's score was 56.5 +/− 4.5 on a 100-point scale, with 50 as the midpoint.

2. Lou Cannon, *President Reagan: The Role of a Lifetime* (New York: Touchstone/Simon and Schuster, 1991), 37.

3. Lee Edwards, *Ronald Reagan: A Political Biography* (Houston: Nordland, 1980), 68.

4. Walter Weintraub, "Personality Profiles of American Presidents as Revealed in Their Public Statements: The Presidential News Conferences of Jimmy Carter and Ronald Reagan," *Political Psychology* 7, no. 2 (1986): 285–95, 294.

5. Larry Speakes, *Speaking Out: The Reagan Presidency from Inside the White House* (New York: Scribner, 1988). This was especially true of the Challenger disaster, during which Reagan told the press that the space program would continue in order to honor the memories of the fallen astronauts. This was one of his best-received public engagements (93).

6. Burton Kaufman, *Presidential Profiles: The Carter Years* (New York: Facts on File, 2006), 243.

7. Cannon, *President Reagan*, 50.

8. Ibid., 55.

9. Edwards, *Ronald Reagan*, 71.

10. Cannon, *President Reagan*, 42.

11. Gerard DeGroot, *Selling Ronald Reagan: The Emergence of a President* (London: I. B. Tauris, 2015), 10.

12. Cannon, *President Reagan*, 40.

13. Richard A. Melanson, *Reconstructing Consensus: American Foreign Policy since the Vietnam War* (New York: St. Martin's, 1991), 132.

14. Ibid.

15. Edwards, *Ronald Reagan*, 71.

16. Melanson, *Reconstructing Consensus*, 133.

17. Speakes, *Speaking Out*, 104.

18. Ibid., 104.

19. Ibid., 105.

20. Ibid., 92.

21. John J. Sosik, *Leading with Character: Stories of Valor and Virtue and the Principles They Teach* (Greenwich, CT: Information Age, 2006), 28.

22. H. W. Brands, *Reagan: The Life* (New York: Doubleday, 2015), 270.

23. Both graphs exclude Reagan's hawkish and dovish speeches that were used as two of the four reference texts for the WordScore text analysis.

24. Reagan, "A Time for Choosing," October 27, 1964, Los Angeles, CA, televised campaign speech.

25. Barry Posen and Stephen Van Evera, "Reagan Administration Defense Policy: Departure from Containment," in *Eagle Resurgent? The Reagan Era in American Foreign Policy*, ed. Kenneth A. Oye, Robert J. Lieber, and Donald S. Rothchild (Boston: Little, Brown, 1987), 75–114.

26. Melanson, *Reconstructing Consensus*, 139.

27. Posen and Van Evera, "Reagan Administration Defense Policy," 81.

28. Ibid., 85.

29. Keith L. Shimko, *Images and Arms Control: Perceptions of the Soviet Union in the Reagan Administration* (Ann Arbor: University of Michigan Press, 1991).

30. United States, Office of Management and Budget, "Fiscal Year 2015 Historical Tables, Budget of the U.S. Government" (Washington, DC: Government Printing Office, 2014), 66.

31. Morris H. Morley and James F. Petras, "The Reagan Administration and Nicaragua: How Washington Constructs Its Case for Counterrevolution in Central America," in *Crisis and Confrontation: Ronald Reagan's Foreign Policy*, ed. Morris H. Morley (Totowa, NJ: Rowman and Littlefield, 1988), 168–69.

32. Ibid., 189.

33. Ibid., 169.

34. Ibid., 187.

35. Reagan, "Time for Choosing" speech.

36. Melanson, *Reconstructing Consensus*, 140.

37. Lou Cannon, "Reagan's Peace with the U.N.," *Washington Post*, September 26, 1988, https://www.washingtonpost.com/archive/politics/1988/09/26/reagans-peace-with-the-un /d2561843-6002-41b5-b810-2c3a0958b2a2/?utm_term=.69ac880a9a6f.

38. "Ronald Reagan and the United Nations: Diplomacy without Apology," *Reagan's Country: The Ronald Reagan Presidential Foundation Member Newsletter*, October 2013, 2–3.

39. Ibid., 4.

40. Quoted in Shimko, *Images and Arms Control*, 102. For an excellent discussion of the complexity in Reagan's views regarding nuclear arms control, see Shimko, *Images and Arms Control*.

41. Ronald Reagan, "Foreign Policy Address on Soviet-American Relations," January 16, 1984, White House, Washington, DC.

42. Barbara Farnham, "Reagan and the Gorbachev Revolution," *Political Science Quarterly* 116, no. 2 (2001): 225–52.

43. Keith L. Shimko, "Reagan on the Soviet Union and the Nature of International Conflict," *Political Psychology* 13, no. 3 (1992): 353–77.

44. Ibid.

45. Hedrick Smith, "Shultz-Weinberger Discord Seen in Nearly All Foreign Policy Issues," *New York Times*, December 11, 1984, http://www.nytimes.com/1984/12/11/world/shultz-wein berger-discord-seen-in-nearly-all-foreign-policy-issues.html?pagewanted=all.

46. Weinberger in Dolly Langdon, "Caspar Weinberger," *People* 18, no. 23 (December 6, 1982).

47. Weinberger, *In the Arena: A Memoir of the Twentieth Century* (New York: Gretchen Roberts Regency, 2001), quoted in Robert Novak, "The Life and Times of Cap the Knife," *Weekly Standard*, December 17, 2001, http://www.weeklystandard.com/the-life-and-times-of-cap-the-knife /article/1954.

48. Phillip Taubman, "The Shultz-Weinberger Feud," *New York Times Magazine*, April 14, 1985, http://www.nytimes.com/1985/04/14/magazine/the-shultz-weinberger-feud.html?page wanted=all.

49. Novak, "Life and Times of Cap the Knife."

50. Harold Jackson, "Obituary: Caspar Weinberger," *Guardian*, March 28, 2006, https:// www.theguardian.com/news/2006/mar/29/guardianobituaries.usa.

51. Langdon, "Caspar Weinberger."

52. Edwin Black, "Caspar Weinberger's *In the Arena*," History News Network, March 28, 2006.

53. James Q. Wilson, *Bureaucracy: What Government Agencies Do and Why They Do It* (New York: Basic Books, 1989), 210.

54. Anonymous Reagan official quoted in Taubman, "Shultz-Weinberger Feud."

55. Taubman, "Shultz-Weinberger Feud."

56. Robert Strauss, "Steadfast," *Stanford Magazine*, March/April 2016, https://alumni.stanford.edu/get/page/magazine/article/?article_id=84559.

57. Ibid.

58. Tom Wicker, *New York Times*, 1991, quoted in ibid.; Joe Lonsdale, "Mentorship and Problem Solving with Secretary George Shultz," *8VC News*, 2016, https://medium.com/8vc-news/mentorship-and-problem-solving-with-secretary-george-shultz-aec45b44b8c.

59. Jay Winik, *On the Brink: The Dramatic, Behind-the-Scenes Saga of the Reagan Era and the Men and Women Who Won the Cold War* (New York: Simon and Schuster, 1996), 327.

60. Ibid., 328.

61. Strauss, "Steadfast."

62. Gates, *From the Shadows*, 278.

63. Ibid., 279.

64. Winik, *On the Brink*, 329.

65. Ibid.

66. Gates, *From the Shadows*, 279.

67. Ibid.

68. United States, assistant to the president for national security affairs, *National Security Decision Directive 166: US Policy, Programs, and Strategy in Afghanistan* (Washington, DC, March 27, 1985), 2.

69. "1980 Presidential Forum," transcript, Reagan Library, April, 23, 1980.

70. "October 28, 1980 Debate Transcript: The Carter-Reagan Presidential Debate," Commission on Presidential Debates, October 28, 1980.

71. United States, assistants to the president for national security affairs, *National Security Decision Directive 32: US National Security Strategy* (Washington, DC, May 20, 1982), 2.

72. Ronald Reagan, "The President's News Conference," January 29, 1981, Washington, DC.

73. United States, assistants to the president for national security affairs, *National Security Decision Directive 75: US Relations with the USSR* (Washington, DC, January 17, 1983), 1.

74. Raymond W. Copson and Richard P. Cronin, "The 'Reagan Doctrine' and Its Prospects," *Survival* 29, no. 1 (1987): 41.

75. Brian Glyn Williams, "On the Trail of the 'Lions of Islam': Foreign Fighters in Afghanistan and Pakistan, 1980–2010," *Orbis* 55, no. 2 (2011): 216–39.

76. James M. Scott, *Deciding to Intervene: The Reagan Doctrine and American Foreign Policy* (Durham, NC: Duke University Press, 1996), 87.

77. Ibid., 34.

78. Ibid., 50–51.

79. National security advisor, *National Security Decision Directive 75*, 4.

80. See Scott, *Deciding to Intervene*, 53–54, for a discussion on Wilson's contribution to the Afghan program, and Lundberg, *Politics of a Covert Action*, 15–17, for a variation on Wilson's contributions.

81. Steve Galster, *Afghanistan, Lessons from the Last War*, vol. 2 of *Afghanistan: The Making of US Policy, 1973–1990* (Washington, DC: National Security Archive, 2001).

82. Joseph E. Persico, *Casey: The Lives and Secrets of William J. Casey: From the OSS to the CIA* (New York: Viking, 1990), 313.

83. Bob Woodward, *Veil: The Secret Wars of the CIA, 1981–1987* (New York: Simon and Schuster, 2007), 100.

84. Leslie H. Gelb, "U.S. Said to Increase Arms Aid for Afghan Rebels," *New York Times*, May 4 1983, A1.

85. Scott, *Deciding to Intervene*, 34, 53–54.

86. Lundberg, *Politics of a Covert Action*, 1. Heading for this section, *Los Angeles Times*, February 4, 1985, http://articles.latimes.com/1985-02-04/local/me-4172_1_soviet-union.

87. Scott, *Deciding to Intervene*, 48.

88. Ibid., 5.

89. Ibid.

90. See George E. Curry, "U.S. Supports Afghan Rebels: Policy Shifts to Open Backing of Soviet Foes," *Chicago Tribune*, May 9, 1985, 4.

91. Austin Carson and Keren Yarhi-Milo, "Covert Communication: The Intelligibility and Credibility of Signaling in Secret," *Security Studies* 26, no. 1 (2017): 124–56.

92. See *Washington Post* Foreign Service, "U.S. Flies Weapons to Rebels in Afghanistan, Sadat Says," *Washington Post*, September 23, 1981, ProQuest (147179553); and "Sadat Says US Buys Soviet Arms for Afghan Rebels," *New York Times*, September 23, 1981, ProQuest (121820382). As Edward Juchniewicz said, even if the Soviets did not know exactly how much aid America was giving to the mujahedeen, they were aware from the start that the CIA was involved in the Afghan conflict (Persico, *Casey*, 310).

93. Gelb, "U.S. Said to Increase Arms Aid for Afghan Rebels."

94. Scott, *Deciding to Intervene*, 34.

95. See Leslie H. Gelb, "U.S. Pours Money into Afghan War," *Chicago Tribune*, November 28, 1984, 5.

96. See Associated Press, "CIA aid to Afghan Rebels Skyrockets," *Chicago Tribune*, January 13, 1985, ProQuest (10856706); and Margaret Shapiro, "More Aid Voted for Afghan Rebels: Hill Unit Adds $50 Million for Afghan Rebels," *Washington Post*, July 28, 1984, ProQuest (138212959).

97. Curry, "U.S. Supports Afghan Rebels."

98. Ibid.

99. Lundberg, *Politics of a Covert Action*, 17.

100. Rhea Talley Stewart, "Afghans Deserve Overt Aid," *Chicago Tribune*, June 3, 1984, E3.

101. Paul Kengor, *The Crusader: Ronald Reagan and the Fall of Communism* (New York: Harper Perennial, 2006), 258–59.

102. Yankelovich, Skelly, and White poll for *Time* magazine, September 15–17, 1981. Cornell University, Ithaca, NY: Roper Center for Public Opinion Research.

103. Central Intelligence Agency, "Memorandum for Director, Soviet Analysis, USSR-Afghanistan Exploring Options," by Robert Gates (CIA, Washington, DC, October 17, 1984), in US Congress, Senate, Select Committee on Intelligence, Nomination of Robert H. Gates, vol. 2, 102nd Cong., 1st sess. 1991, 449–50.

104. NSDDs are authorized and signed by the president, often only after detailed discussions with advisors and national security officials. As such, a major policy shift like the choice to evict, instead of harass, Soviet forces could not have occurred without Reagan's deliberate endorsement. Further, Reagan received regular briefings from the CIA on Afghanistan and would have been well informed about the program and its general strategy to modify unsatisfactory language in any NSDD. In this way, Reagan's NSDDs offer excellent insight into the goals Reagan prioritized and the rationale behind his national security strategy.

105. William P. Clark, "U.S. Relations with the USSR," White House, NSDD 75 (Washington, DC, January 17, 1983).

106. Scott, *Deciding to Intervene*, 45.

107. Alan J. Kuperman, "The Stinger Missile and U.S. Intervention in Afghanistan," *Political Science Quarterly* 114, no. 2 (1999): 227.

108. National security advisor, *National Security Decision Directive 75*, 4.

109. Ibid.

110. Ibid.

111. Ibid., 1.

112. Ibid., 4.

113. Scott, *Deciding to Intervene*, 57.

114. Ibid.

115. National security advisor, *National Security Decision Directive 166*, 1.

116. Ibid.

117. Ibid., 2.

118. Ibid.

119. Ibid.

120. Peter Rodman, *More Precious Than Peace: The Cold War and the Struggle for the Third World* (New York: Scribner, 1994). Unfortunately, the existing secondary literature does not offer a satisfactory explanation for why the Reagan administration chose to change policy objectives from harassment to defeat. The government in 2008 declassified NSDD 75, which was signed January 17, 1983. The text of NSDD 75 likewise notes America would seek to force Moscow's "withdraw[al]" from Afghanistan. Even though NSDD 75 does not use the strong language of the later NSDD 166, "withdrawal" implies a cessation of Soviet occupation.

121. Scott, *Deciding to Intervene*, 59.

122. Ibid., 57–59.

123. Lundberg, *Politics of a Covert Action*, 37.

124. Persico, *Casey*, 310. The differences of opinion among Reagan's advisors as to whether Washington should provide Stinger missiles to the mujahedeen caused Reagan to react slowly to the urgings of Iklé and Pillsbury, who drafted the initial memorandum urging the provision of Stinger missiles. Iklé and Pillsbury's proposal confronted a panoply of critics, including officials at the Central Intelligence Agency and the State Department. Both had relatively similar objections, specifically, the destruction of plausible deniability resulting in possible escalation and attack on Pakistan (Lundberg, *Politics of a Covert Action*, 36; Kuperman, "Stinger Missile and U.S. Intervention in Afghanistan," 233); the need to placate President Zia, who vacillated on lending support because Pakistan, did not have Stingers (Diego Cordovez and Selig S. Harrison, *Out of Afghanistan: The Inside Story of the Soviet Withdrawal* (Oxford: Oxford University Press, 1995) 195, quoted in Lundberg, *Politics of a Covert Action*, 32–33; and Lundberg, *Politics of a Covert Action*, 36); and the possibility of unnecessarily upsetting Moscow as Gorbachev came to power and as the two countries began to negotiate arms control agreements (Lundberg, *Politics of a Covert Action*, 37; Kuperman, "Stinger Missile and U.S. Intervention in Afghanistan," 224).

125. Lundberg, *Politics of a Covert Action*, 17.

126. Ibid., 22.

127. Ibid.

128. Kuperman, "Stinger Missile and U.S. Intervention in Afghanistan," 226.

129. Ibid., 227.

130. Lundberg, *Politics of a Covert Action*, 25–26, 62. Although NSDD 166 had few opponents, the decision to supply Stingers was controversial within the administration. The details of the debate over whether to give Stingers to the mujahedeen are provided elsewhere and are beyond the scope of this book. Kuperman, "Stinger Missile and U.S. Intervention in Afghanistan"; Scott, *Deciding to Intervene*.

131. Kuperman, "Stinger Missile and U.S. Intervention in Afghanistan," 234; Scott, *Deciding to Intervene*, 60.

132. George Pratt Shultz, *Turmoil and Triumph: My Years as Secretary of State* (New York: Scribner, 1993), 692.

133. Kengor, *Crusader*, 258–59.

134. Robert Lindsey, "Reagan Urges Bases in Mideast and Missiles for Afghan Rebels," *New York Times*, January 10, 1980, ProQuest (121127228).

135. Ibid.

136. These comments do not appear to have been followed by subsequent endorsements of supplying the mujahedeen with Stingers, because critics used them to paint Reagan as an extreme hawk, which advisors thought would damage his chances of an electoral victory. Furthermore, publicly championing arming the mujahedeen was also disfavored by others in the Reagan administration, as well as Republicans, out of a fear of escalation (Robert Lindsey, "Reagan Is Striving to Protect an Image of Moderation," *New York Times*, January 14, 1980). From the existing evidence it cannot be easily determined why Reagan waited until 1986 to authorize the shipment of Stingers, given that he had endorsed the deployment of heat-seeking anti-aircraft missiles in 1980. Perhaps intelligence reports and advisors convinced him to continue to supply only non-American-made weapons. Or possibly, when referencing heat-seeking anti-aircraft guns, Reagan had never had American-made weapons in mind. Another equally likely explanation is that the CIA and the intelligence committees in both houses of Congress strongly opposed the deployment of Stingers. For whatever reason, Reagan waited to transfer Stingers, although it appears that Reagan had favored this idea from the beginning.

137. United States, Department of State, "Memorandum of Conversation," drafted by M. Palmer (Geneva, Switzerland, November 19, 1985), 7.

138. Ibid.

139. Ibid.

140. United States, the White House, "Memorandum of Conversation: Reagan-Gorbachev Meetings in Geneva, November 1985, Second Plenary Meeting," prepared by Jack Matlock (Geneva, Switzerland, November 19, 1985), 2.

141. Ibid., 2–4.

142. Ibid., 3.

143. Ibid.

144. Reagan, radio address to the nation on the Soviet occupation of Afghanistan, December 28, 1985.

145. Reagan, statement on the seventh anniversary of the Soviet invasion of Afghanistan, December 27, 1986.

146. National security advisor, *National Security Decision Directive 166*, 2.

147. Heading of this section, President Reagan, April 23, 1983.

148. JCS Alert Order of September 23, 1983, to United States European Command (EUCOM).

149. Gallup, July 1982.

150. Gallup, September 1982.

151. Gallup, December 1982.

152. David C. Wills, *The First War on Terrorism: Counter-terrorism Policy during the Reagan Administration* (Oxford: Rowman and Littlefield, 2003), 173.

153. Reagan, *The Reagan Diaries*, ed. Douglas Brinkley (New York: HarperCollins, 2007), 178.

154. United States, assistants to the president for national security affairs, *National Security Decision Directive 64: Next Steps in Lebanon*, Washington, DC, October 28, 1982.

155. The memo itself is undated, but the accompanying memo to Judge Clark has a date of "9/20/83." "Judge, this is the . . . analysis I asked . . . to . . . It clearly points out the pitfalls if we follow the route that the JCS and OSD are headed."

156. NSC memorandum, "Lebanon: Litmus Test for U.S. Credibility and Commitment," undated (emphasis in original).

157. Ibid.

158. Ibid.

159. David C. Martin and John L. Walcott, *Best Laid Plans: The Inside Story of America's War against Terrorism* (New York: Simon and Schuster, 1989), 144.

160. President Reagan, "Address to the Nation on Events in Lebanon and Grenada," October 27, 1983.

161. Detailing how keeping the forces in Lebanon would reinforce US credibility and resolve, Shultz notes: "To ensure a tolerable outcome, it will be more important than even to maintain the balance of forces so that Syria cannot intimidate the other parties and steamroll the conference. The United States must remain actively involved behind the scene. We must keep the *New Jersey* there and not give any hint that we are eager to take our forces out except for some quid pro quo. Reducing our forces unilaterally would send the worst signal and have harmful repercussions in the negotiations." Indeed, crucial for the analysis here is to note Shultz's views of the effects of a US withdrawal from Lebanon. Under the heading "Troop Withdrawal," Shultz explains to the president how a US or an Israeli unilateral withdrawal could affect credibility. "Our credibility in the Arab world and Gemayel's credibility in Lebanon depend on keeping open the prospect of further unilateral Israeli withdrawals, especially from populated areas. . . . At the same time, I am concerned that further unilateral Israeli withdrawal—if it seems the product of Israeli loss of will and yielding to pressure—could also have the effect of removing a psychological counterweight to Syria and thereby weakening Gemayel more than helping him. The key is whether we, Gemayel, and the Israelis seem to be acting from strength and thereby commanding a quid pro quo from those who are now our opponents, or whether it only emboldens the Syrians and strengthens *their* hold on the Shia and the Druze." Memorandum from Shultz to the president, "Our Strategy in Lebanon and the Middle East," October 13, 1983.

162. William E. Pemberton, *Exit with Honor: The Life and Presidency of Ronald Reagan* (Armonk, NY: M. E. Sharpe, 1997), 136.

163. Wills, *First War on Terrorism*, 63.

164. Robert C. McFarlane, with Zofia Smardz, Special Trust (New York: Cadell and Davies, 1994), 268.

165. President Reagan's news conference, October 24, 1983.

166. Gallup, January 1983.

167. Gallup, October 1983.

168. Frank Newport, Jeffrey M. Jones, and Lydia Saad, "Ronald Reagan from the People's Perspective: A Gallup Poll Review," *Gallup News*, 2004, http://news.gallup.com/poll/11887/ronald-reagan-from-peoples-perspective-gallup-poll-review.aspx.

169. Gallup, November 1983.

170. Gallup, January 1984.

171. Pemberton, *Exit with Honor*, 136.

172. Kengor, *Crusader*, 194–95.

173. Reagan, *Reagan Diaries*, 189.

174. Jason Saltoun-Ebin, *The Reagan Files: Inside the National Security Council* (Santa Barbara, CA: Seabec Books, 2014), 261.

175. Shultz, *Turmoil and Triumph*, 331.

176. Caspar Weinberger, *Fighting for Peace: 7 Critical Years in the Pentagon* (New York: Grand Central, 1991), 111.

177. Ibid., 112.

178. Ibid., 114.

179. Weinberger, Miller Center interview, 17.

180. Ronald Reagan: "Address to the Nation on Events in Lebanon and Grenada," October 27, 1983.

181. Heading for this section, Ronald Reagan, "Remarks at the Annual Convention of the Congressional Medal of Honor Society in New York City," December 12, 1983.

182. Saltoun-Ebin, *Reagan Files*, 262.

183. Reagan, *An American Life* (New York: Simon and Schuster, 1990) 451. Shultz similarly viewed the invasion as a signal of US resolve, as he exultantly declared in a cabinet meeting shortly after the invasion had commenced: "This may be a turning point in hostility. We've let the world know that we are going to protect our interests whatever it costs." Jeff McMahan, *Reagan and the World: Imperial Policy in the New Cold War* (New York: Monthly Review Press, 1985), 21.

184. Reagan, "Remarks at the Annual Congressional Medal of Honor Society Convention," December 12, 1983, New York, NY.

185. Reagan, *American Life*, 451.

186. See Steven F. Hayward, *The Age of Reagan: The Conservative Counterrevolution, 1980–1989* (New York: Crown, 2010), 323; and Cannon, *President Reagan*, 390.

187. Reagan, *Reagan Diaries*, 191.

188. Richard Bernstein, "U.S. Vetoes U.N. Resolution 'Deploring' Grenada Invasion," *New York Times*, October 29, 1983, http://www.nytimes.com/1983/10/29/world/us-vetoes-un-reso lution-deploring-grenada-invasion.html.

189. Gallup, October 1983.

190. Gallup, December 1983.

191. CBS News, October 1983.

192. Gail E. S. Yoshitani, "National Power and Military Force: The Origins of the Weinberger Doctrine, 1980–1984," PhD diss., Duke University, 2008, 121, ProQuest (AAT 3297728).

193. Shultz, *Turmoil and Triumph*, 345.

194. Hayward, *Age of Reagan*, 324.

195. Shultz, *Turmoil and Triumph*, 344.

196. Reagan, *Reagan Diaries*, 201.

197. See United States, National Security Council, "National Security Planning Group Meeting, December 1, 1983, Talking Points for Robert McFarlane," by Geoffrey Kemp, special assistant to the president for national security affairs (National Security Council, Washington, DC, December 1, 1983).

198. McFarlane, *Special Trust*, 272.

199. Memorandum from McFarlane to the president, "Putting the Marines Back Aboard Ship," December 21, 1983.

200. Shultz, *Turmoil and Triumph*, 230.

201. Joel Brinkley, "Reagan Asserts Blame Is His in Marine Security Failure; Opposes Punishing Officers," *New York Times*, December 28, 1983, http://www.nytimes.com/1983/12/28 /world/reagan-asserts-blame-his-marine-security-failure-opposes-punishing-officers.html.

202. Caspar Weinberger, interview by PBS *Frontline*, September 2001.

203. United States, assistants to the president for national security affairs, *National Security Decision Directive 117: Lebanon*, Washington, DC, December 5, 1983.

204. United States, White House, assistant to the president for national security affairs, "Talking Points for NSPG on the Next Steps in Lebanon, Tuesday, January 3, 1984, 11:00 am, Situation Room," prepared by Geoffrey Kemp (Washington, DC, January 3, 1984), 1. The documents that Reagan referred to included the DOD Report and General John Kelley's response to it, which were leaked to the media before they were seen by the president.

205. Martin and Walcott, *Best Laid Plans*, 147.

206. Howell and Pevehouse, *When Dangers Gather*, 132.

207. Martin and Walcott, *Best Laid Plans*, 148.

208. Shultz, *Turmoil and Triumph*, 229.

209. Martin and Walcott, *Best Laid Plans*, 150.

210. The Weinberger Doctrine, quoted in the *Washington Post*, November 30, 1984, https://www.washingtonpost.com/archive/politics/1984/11/30/the-weinberger-doctrine/c7f20ffe-b591-4189-ad05-a704aac1935d/?utm_term=.18683c22b105.

211. Shultz, *Turmoil and Triumph*, 345.

212. Ibid.

213. Ibid., 230.

214. Reagan, *Reagan Diaries*, 215.

215. Martin and Walcott, *Best Laid Plans*, 149.

216. Shultz, *Triumph and Turmoil*, 230.

217. Cited in Howell and Pevehouse, *When Dangers Gather*, 132.

218. Wills, *First War on Terrorism*, 81.

219. Reagan, *Reagan Diaries*, 218.

220. Shultz, *Turmoil and Triumph*, 231.

221. Steven R. Weisman, "Reagan Attack on Policy Critics Puts Edge on Campaign," *New York Times*, April 8, 1984, http://www.nytimes.com/1984/04/08/weekinreview/reagan-attack-on-policy-critics-puts-new-edge-on-campaign.html.

222. United States, assistants to the president for national security affairs, *National Security Decision Directive 128: Lebanon*, Washington, DC, February 26, 1984.

223. Importantly, I do not argue that self-monitoring is the only reason explaining the differences between Weinberger and Shultz on the use of force in Lebanon and Grenada; still, the evidence seems consistent with my theoretical predictions.

224. Qaddafi had asserted sovereignty over the entirety of the gulf in 1973, despite the fact that most of it consisted of international waters governed by the 1982 United Nations Convention on the Law of the Sea. Carter had initially authorized naval maneuvers to assert freedom of navigation in these international waters, but the operation had been suspended during the Iranian hostage crisis.

225. Wills, *First War on Terrorism*, 167.

226. Bernard Gwertzman, "U.S. Warns Libya against Attacking AWACs over Sudan," *International New York Times*, March 20, 1984, http://www.nytimes.com/1984/03/20/world/us-warns-libya-against-attacking-awacs-over-sudan.html.

227. United States, White House, assistant to the president for national security affairs, *National Security Decision Directive 138: Combatting Terrorism*, Washington, DC, April 3, 1984.

228. Ibid.

229. Wills, *First War on Terrorism*, 170.

230. Ibid.

231. Ronald Reagan, "Remarks at the Annual Convention of the American Bar Association," Washington, DC, July 8, 1985, https://reaganlibrary.archives.gov/archives/speeches/1985/70885a.htm.

232. Ibid.

233. Wills, *First War on Terrorism*, 173.

234. Joseph T. Stanik, *El Dorado Canyon: Reagan's Undeclared War with Qaddafi* (Annapolis, MD: Naval Institute, 2003), 104.

235. Ronald Bruce St. John, *Libya and the United States: Two Centuries of Strife* (Philadelphia: University of Pennsylvania Press, 2002), 134.

236. Stanik, *El Dorado Canyon*, 112.

237. United States, National Security Council, staff, "NSPG Meeting, January 6, 1986, 11:00–12:00, White House Situation Room, re: Acting against Libyan Support for International Terrorism," by James R. Stark, Oliver L. North, Howard Teicher, Jock Covey, Rod McDaniel, and Elaine Morton (National Security Council, Washington, DC, January 4, 1986), ProQuest DNSA (CO01769), 6.

238. Ibid., 7.

239. Wills, *First War on Terrorism*, 190.

240. This would eventually strain the transatlantic alliance, as Thatcher's opponents would accuse her of being excessively supportive of Reagan. Thatcher told Reagan that this would be the last approved British involvement in such an operation.

241. Nicholas Laham, *The American Bombing of Libya: A Study of the Force of Miscalculation in Reagan Foreign Policy* (Jefferson, NC: McFarland, 2008), 116.

242. United States, White House Office of Public Affairs, "Talking Points on US Action in Libya," by Tom Gibson, White House OPA (Washington, DC, April 16, 1986), ProQuest DNSA (TE00855).

243. Jane Mayer and Doyle McManus, *Landslide: The Unmaking of the President: 1984–1988* (Boston: Houghton Mifflin, 1989).

244. Laham, *American Bombing of Libya*, 158.

245. Caspar Weinberger, *Annual Report to the Congress* (Washington, DC: Government Printing Office, 1983), 51–54.

246. Weinberger, Miller Center interview, 7.

247. United States, director of Central Intelligence and secretary of defense, *Joint Net Assessment: US and Soviet Strategic Forces (Executive Version)*, 1983, 21.

248. Robert Jervis, *The Meaning of the Nuclear Revolution: Statecraft and the Prospect of Armageddon* (Ithaca, NY: Cornell University Press, 1989), 200.

249. See Jervis, *Meaning of the Nuclear Revolution*, 198, for a general discussion of why leaders may take risky actions after suffering some loss or in the event the nuclear balance undergoes an unfavorable shift. Jervis also notes that one reason Reagan gave for supporting the Contras was to improve the US negotiating position in arms control talks with the USSR. Ibid., 195.

250. Ibid., 199.

251. United States, assistants to the president on national security affairs, *National Security Decision Directive 12: Strategic Forces Modernization Program*, October 1, 1981.

252. Weinberger, *Annual Report to the Congress*, 1–39.

253. United States, director of Central Intelligence and secretary of defense, *Joint Net Assessment: US and Soviet Strategic Forces*, 22.

254. Ibid., 19–20.

255. Shultz, Miller Center interview, 10.

256. Shimko, *Images and Arms Control*, 73.

257. The fearful "window of vulnerability" of US strategic missiles depicted in the late 1970s and early 1980s was closed, but not because of enhanced US defense capabilities or diminished Soviet ones. Rather, the conclusion of this episode came about because of the sober report of the Scowcroft Commission in 1983.

258. Weinberger, Miller Center interview, 19.

259. Howell and Pevehouse, *While Dangers Gather*, 134.

260. Beth A. Fischer, *The Reagan Reversal: Foreign Policy and the End of the Cold War* (Columbia: University of Missouri Press, 1997), 59–60.

261. Reagan famously said that he "didn't want to hear [about] the political ramifications of [his] choices" so that he could make the right moral decision. Douglas C. Foyle, *Counting the Public In: Presidents, Public Opinion and Foreign Policy* (New York: Columbia University Press, 1999), 190.

262. Allan Dafoe and Devin Caughey, "Honor, Reputation, and War: Using Southern U.S. Presidents to Identify the Effect of Culture on International Conflict" (presentation, Annual Meeting of the American Political Science Association, Washington, DC, September 3, 2010).

263. Dafoe, "Resolve, Reputation, and War."

Chapter 8: Bill Clinton and America's Credibility after the Cold War

1. David Maraniss, *First in His Class: The Biography of Bill Clinton*, 1st Touchstone ed. (New York: Simon and Schuster, 1995), 43.

2. Ibid., 46.

3. John D. Gartner, *In Search of Bill Clinton: A Psychological Biography*, 1st ed. (New York: St. Martin's, 2008), 94.

4. Joe Klein, *The Natural: The Misunderstood Presidency of Bill Clinton* (New York: Broadway Books, 2002), 43.

5. Ibid., 2.

6. David Gallen, *Bill Clinton: As They Know Him; An Oral Biography* (New York: Gallen, 1994), 13.

7. Meredith L. Oakley, *On the Make: The Rise of Bill Clinton* (Washington, DC: Regnery, 1994), 59.

8. Ibid., 179.

9. Ibid., 176.

10. Ibid., 17.

11. Klein, *Natural*, 41.

12. Ibid., 9.

13. Clinton's own name is an example of his other-directedness. When his mother, Virginia, married Roger Clinton Sr., "Bill [Blythe] adopted his stepfather's surname [Clinton] in an effort to heal the fractured family" and maintain harmonious relations with everyone in his life. Philip Martin in Gallen, *Bill Clinton: As They Know Him*, 6.

14. Ibid., 11.

15. Martin in ibid., 8–9.

16. Martin in ibid., 11.

17. Nigel Hamilton, *Bill Clinton: Mastering the Presidency* (New York: Public Affairs, 2007), 202.

18. Ibid., 46.

19. Ibid., 50.

20. Robert B. Reich, *Locked in the Cabinet* (New York: Knopf, 1997), 133.

21. Thomas Preston, *The President and His Inner Circle: Leadership Style and the Advisory Process in Foreign Policy Making* (New York: Columbia University Press, 2012).

22. Ibid., 234; Reich, *Locked in the Cabinet*; George Stephanopoulos, *All Too Human: A Political Education* (New York: Little, Brown, 2008).

23. Preston, *President and His Inner Circle*, 233.

24. Ibid.; Reich, *Locked in the Cabinet*; Stephanopoulos, *All Too Human*; Elizabeth Drew, *On the Edge: The Clinton Presidency* (New York: Simon and Schuster, 1995); Maraniss, *First in His Class*; Bob Woodward, *The Choice* (New York: Simon and Schuster, 1996).

25. Woodward, *Choice*, 211.

26. Herrmann, Tetlock, and Visser, "Mass Public Decisions to Go to War."

27. Before proceeding, I should note that Bill Clinton came to office with neither a strong ideological view on foreign affairs nor much foreign policy experience. During his presidential

campaign, he had promised to focus on the domestic economy, and not on foreign policy. See James McCormick, "Clinton and Foreign Policy," in *The Postmodern Presidency: Bill Clinton's Legacy in U.S. Politics*, ed. Steven E. Schier (Pittsburgh: University of Pittsburgh Press, 2000).

28. Bill Clinton, "The Economy," Philadelphia, PA, April 16, 1992, speech, https://www.ibiblio.org/nii/econ-posit.html.

29. Office of Management and Budget, table 4.1—Outlays by Agency: 1962–2021, 2015, https://obamawhitehouse.archives.gov/omb/budget/Historicals.

30. Melissa Healy, "Clinton Defense Budget Cuts into Troops, Ships," *Los Angeles Times*, March 27, 1993, http://articles.latimes.com/1993–03–27/news/mn-15800_1_defense-budget.

31. Ibid.

32. Michael O'Hanlon, "Clinton's Strong Defense Legacy," *Foreign Affairs*, November/December 2003, https://www.foreignaffairs.com/articles/2003–11–01/clintons-strong-defense-legacy.

33. James Risen, "The Nation: The Clinton Administration's See-No-Evil C.I.A.," *New York Times*, September 10, 2000, http://www.nytimes.com/2000/09/10/weekinreview/the-nation-the-clinton-administration-s-see-no-evil-cia.html.

34. United States Senate Select Committee on Intelligence, "Special Report: Committee Activities of the Select Committee on Intelligence: January 4, 1993 to December 1, 1994," 22, accessed September 18, 2016, https://www.gpo.gov/fdsys/pkg/CRPT-104srpt4/html/CRPT-104srpt4.htm.

35. Risen, "Nation: The Clinton Administration's See-No-Evil C.I.A."

36. Tim Weiner, *Legacy of Ashes: The History of the CIA* (London: Doubleday, 2007), 440.

37. Ibid.

38. Instead, they relied on an American contracting firm to do overtly what would have been done covertly in the past. Richard A. Best Jr., "Covert Action: An Effective Instrument of U.S. Foreign Policy?," Congressional Research Service (Library of Congress, October 21, 1996), 30, http://congressionalresearch.com/96-844/document.php?study=Covert+Action+An+Effective+Instrument+of+U.S.+Foreign+Policy.

39. Michael Renner, "Peacekeeping and the United Nations," *Foreign Policy in Focus*, December 1, 1996, http://fpif.org/peacekeeping_and_the_united_nations/.

40. Ibid.

41. Bill Clinton, "Statement by US President Bill Clinton, Authorizing the US Signing of the Rome Statute of the International Criminal Court," Camp David, MD, December 31, 2000, http://www.iccnow.org/documents/USClintonSigning31Dec00.pdf.

42. Ibid.

43. Renner, "Peacekeeping and the United Nations."

44. Ibid.

45. I do not provide further analysis of the self-monitoring dispositions of Clinton's advisors, owing to a lack of information on their positions on the issue of reputation for resolve during the international crises I study here.

46. Mark Bowden, *Black Hawk Down: A Story of Modern War* (Grove/Atlantic, 2010).

47. Rebecca Snyder, "Operation Restore Hope, Battle of Mogadishu, 1993," December 27, 2011, accessed September 9, 2016, http://novaonline.nvcc.edu/eli/evans/his135/Events/Somalia93/somalia93.html.

48. Ibid.

49. Ibid.

50. Ibid.

51. United Nations Security Council (SC), Resolution 794, "Somalia," December 3, 1992, 7, 2, http://www.un.org/en/ga/search/view_doc.asp?symbol=S/RES/794(1992).

52. R. Snyder, "Operation Restore Hope."

53. Thomas L. Friedman, "The Somalia Mission: Clinton Reviews Policy in Somalia as Unease Grows," *New York Times*, October 6, 1993, http://www.nytimes.com/1993/10/06/world/the-somalia-mission-clinton-reviews-policy-in-somalia-as-unease-grows.html?pagewanted=all.

54. John R. Bolton, "Wrong Turn in Somalia," *Foreign Affairs* 73, no. 1 (1994): 56–66, 58.

55. Ibid., 61.

56. Ibid.

57. Miller Center, "Interview with Nancy Soderberg," University of Virginia. May 10–11, 2007, accessed September 1, 2016, http://millercenter.org/oralhistory/interview/nancy-soderberg.

58. Bolton, "Wrong Turn in Somalia," 56–66, 59.

59. Miller Center, "Interview with Nancy Soderberg."

60. Miller Center, "Interview with Anthony Lake (2002)," University of Virginia, May 21, 2002, accessed September 8, 2016, http://millercenter.org/oralhistory/interview/anthony-lake-2002.

61. See ibid. for evidence that Clinton agreed to the mission. See also M. K. Albright, "Yes, There Is a Reason to Be in Somalia," *New York Times*, August 10, 1993, A19.

62. Bolton, "Wrong Turn in Somalia," 56–66, 60.

63. Miller Center, "Interview with Nancy Soderberg."

64. William Barna II, "US Military Intervention for Humanitarian Purposes: Exception to Policy or Emerging Norm?," thesis, Hofstra University, 2012, 33.

65. S. Peterson, "Stories and Past Lessons: Understanding U.S. Decisions of Armed Humanitarian Intervention and Nonintervention in the Post–Cold War Era," PhD diss., Ohio State University, 2003.

66. Barna, "US Military Intervention," 33.

67. Albright, "Yes, There Is a Reason to Be in Somalia."

68. Miller Center, "Interview with Anthony Lake (2002)."

69. United Nations Security Council, Resolution 837, "Somalia," June 6, 1993, paragraph 5, http://www.refworld.org/docid/3b00f164c.html.

70. Barna, "US Military Intervention," 34.

71. US Army Center for Military History, "United States Army in Somalia, 1992–1994," 18, http://www.history.army.mil/brochures/somalia/somalia.htm, accessed January 7, 2012.

72. Ibid.

73. Bolton, "Wrong Turn in Somalia," 56–66, 64.

74. National Public Radio, "What a Downed Black Hawk in Somalia Taught America," NPR, October 5, 2013, https://www.npr.org/2013/10/05/229561805/what-a-downed-black-hawk-in-somalia-taught-america, accessed September 9, 2016.

75. Barna, "US Military Intervention," 35; Bowden, *Black Hawk Down*.

76. Barna, "US Military Intervention," 35.

77. Carl Stoffers, "'Blackhawk Down' Vet Reflects on Battle of Mogadishu," *New York Daily News*, October 3, 2015, http://www.nydailynews.com/news/national/blackhawk-vet-reflects-battle-mogadishu-article-1.2383373; Associated Press, "Clinton Supports Somali Policy Despite Latest Deaths," *Tuscaloosa News*, October 4, 1993, 5A.

78. Matthew Baum, "How Public Opinion Constrains the Use of Force: The Case of Operation Restore Hope," *Presidential Studies Quarterly*, June 2004, 218 (CNN/*USA Today* poll, October 5, 1993).

79. William Clinton, "Exchange with Reporters in San Francisco, October 4, 1993," in *Public Papers of the Presidents of the United States: William Clinton, 1993*, book 2, *August 1 to December 31, 1993* (Washington, DC: Government Printing Office, 1994), 1677.

80. Ibid.

81. Ibid., 1682.

82. Associated Press, "Clinton Supports Somali Policy Despite Latest Deaths," 5A.

83. Miller Center, "Interview with Samuel R. Berger," University of Virginia, March 24–25, 2005.

84. Ibid.

85. Friedman, "Somalia Mission."

86. Miller Center, "Interview with Samuel R. Berger."

87. Ibid.

88. Friedman, "Somalia Mission."

89. Michael Ross, "Clinton's Truce with Congress on Somalia Frays," *Los Angeles Times*, October 13, 1993, http://articles.latimes.com/1993-10-13/news/mn-45328_1_somalia-policy.

90. Ibid.

91. Ibid.

92. Ibid.

93. ABC News Poll, "Americans Want Troops Out of Somalia," October 6, 1993, and cross tabs September 27–October 3, 1993.

94. Ibid., 35.

95. Survey by Cable News Network, *USA Today*. Methodology: Conducted by Gallup Organization on October 5, 1993.

96. Work by Larson and Savych reveals no statistically significant difference between Democrats and Republicans in terms of their preference for withdrawal from Somalia. Eric V. Larson and Bogdan Savych, *American Public Support for US Military Operations from Mogadishu to Baghdad* (Santa Monica, CA: Rand, 2005), 38.

97. Friedman, "Somalia Mission."

98. Dana Hughes, "Bill Clinton 'Surprised' at Black Hawk Down Raid," ABC News, April 18, 2014.

99. Donna Cassata, "Leaders Work to Avert Clash: Clinton, Congress Discuss Avoiding Big Showdown on Somalia," *Times Daily*, October 14, 1993, 2A.

100. Shannon Peterson, "Stories and Past Lessons: Understanding US Decisions of Armed Humanitarian Intervention and Nonintervention in the Post–Cold War Era," PhD diss., Ohio State University, 2003, 94.

101. Miller Center, "Interview with Nancy Soderberg."

102. W. S. Poole, *The Effort to Save Somalia: August 1992–March 1994*, Joint History Office, 2005.

103. Anthony Lake, *Six Nightmares* (Boston: Back Bay Books, 2001), 129.

104. William J. Clinton: "Address to the Nation on Somalia," October 7, 1993, online by Gerhard Peters and John T. Woolley, American Presidency Project, http://www.presidency.ucsb.edu/ws/?pid=47180.

105. Poole, *Effort to Save Somalia*, 59.

106. Cassata, "Leaders Work to Avert Clash," 2A.

107. B.M.E. Wennesland, "The U.S. Involvement in Somalia in the Post–Cold War Years: An Illustration of the Tension between Interests and Principles in American Foreign Policy," master's thesis, University of Oslo, 2013, 37.

108. William Clinton, "Address to the Nation on Somalia, October 7, 1993," in *Public Papers of the Presidents of the United States: William Clinton, 1993*, book 2, *August 1 to December 31, 1993*, 1705.

109. Ibid.

110. Michael Ross, "Clinton's Truce with Congress on Somalia Frays."

111. H. Dewar, "Now It's the GOP Asserting Role for Congress on Foreign Policy," *Washington Post*, October 26, 1993, https://www.highbeam.com/publications/the-washington-post-p5554/oct-26-1993.

112. Ryan C. Hendrickson, *The Clinton Wars: The Constitution, Congress, and War Powers* (Nashville, TN: Vanderbilt University Press, 2002), 39. See also Douglas Delaney, "Cutting,

Running, or Otherwise? The US Decision to Withdraw from Somalia," *Small Wars and Insurgencies* 15, no. 3 (2004): 28–46.

113. Delaney, "Cutting, Running, or Otherwise?," 28–46.

114. See Larry Rohter, "Aristide Decides to Quit as Priest," *New York Times*, November 17, 1994, http://www.nytimes.com/1994/11/17/world/aristide-decides-to-quit-as-priest.html; and R. S. Greenberger, "U.S. Faces Dilemma on Restoring Haiti's Leader, as Americans Wonder If Aristide Is Good or Evil," *Wall Street Journal*, September 22, 1994, A12.

115. Strobe Talbott, "Democracy and the National Interest," *Foreign Affairs* 75, no. 6 (1996): 58.

116. Morris Morley and Chris McGillion, "'Disobedient' Generals and the Politics of Re-democratization: The Clinton Administration and Haiti," *Political Science Quarterly* 112, no. 3 (1997): 364–66.

117. Ibid.

118. Henry F. Carey, "US Domestic Politics and the Emerging Humanitarian Intervention Policy: Haiti, Bosnia, and Kosovo," *World Affairs* 164, no. 2 (2001): 79.

119. William Clinton, "Letter to Congressional Leaders on Economic Sanctions against Haiti, July 12, 1993," in *Public Papers of the Presidents of the United States: William Clinton, 1993*, book 1, *January 20 to July 31, 1993* (Washington, DC: Government Printing Office, 1994), 1071.

120. Ibid.

121. Philippe R. Girard, "The Eagle and the Rooster: The 1994 US Invasion of Haiti," PhD diss., Ohio University, 2002, 91.

122. William Clinton, "Address to the Nation on Haiti, September 15, 1994," in *Public Papers of the Presidents of the United States: William Clinton, 1994*, book 2, *August 1 to December 31, 1994* (Washington, DC: Government Printing Office, 1996), 1594.

123. Miller Center, "Interview with Samuel R. Berger."

124. Elaine Sciolino, "Clinton Says U.S. Will Continue Ban on Haitian Exodus," *New York Times*, January 15, 1993, http://www.nytimes.com/1993/01/15/world/clinton-says-us-will-continue-ban-on-haitian-exodus.html.

125. Miller Center, "Interview with Madeleine K. Albright," University of Virginia, August 30, 2006, accessed August 24, 2016, http://millercenter.org/oralhistory/interview/madeleine-k-albright.

126. William Clinton "Exchange with Reporters Prior to Discussions with Secretary General Manfred Woerner of the North Atlantic Treaty Organization, March 2, 1993," in *Public Papers of the Presidents of the United States: William Clinton, 1993*, book 1, *January 20 to July 31, 1993*, 230.

127. B. Gellman and R. Marcus, "U.S. Boosts Pressure on Haitians," *Washington Post* (1974–Current File), May 4, 1994.

128. Members of the administration themselves categorized Haiti a "nonstrategic area." Warren Christopher said, in a later interview, "Haiti is . . . not a vital American interest." Presidential Oral Histories Project, interview with Warren Christopher, Miller Center, University of Virginia.

129. William Clinton, "Statement by the Director of Communications on the Situation in Haiti, March 2, 1993," in *Public Papers of the Presidents of the United States: William Clinton, 1993*, book 1, *January 20 to July 31, 1993*, 231.

130. William Clinton, "Remarks with President Jean-Bertrand Aristide of Haiti and an Exchange with Reporters, March 16, 1993," in *Public Papers of the Presidents of the United States: William Clinton, 1993*, book 1, *January 20 to July 31, 1993*, 309.

131. Ibid.

132. Ibid.

133. William Clinton, "Statement on Sanctions against Haiti, June 4, 1993," in *Public Papers of the Presidents of the United States: William Clinton, 1993*, book 1, *January 20 to July 31, 1993*, 810.

134. William Clinton, "Remarks with President Jean-Bertrand Aristide of Haiti and an Exchange with Reporters, March 16, 1993," in *Public Papers of the Presidents of the United States: William Clinton, 1993*, book 1, *January 20 to July 31, 1993*, 811.

135. United Nations, *United Nations Mission in Haiti (UNMIH)—Background*, http://www .un.org/en/peacekeeping/missions/past/unmihbackgr2.html#two.

136. Ibid.

137. Ibid.

138. Girard, "Eagle and the Rooster," 82.

139. Lake, *Six Nightmares*, 131.

140. Robert S. Greenberger, "Haiti Threatened with New Sanctions after Mobs Attack Americans at Port," *Wall Street Journal*, eastern edition (New York, NY), October 12, 1993, A22.

141. William Clinton, "Exchange with Reporters on Haiti, October 12, 1993," in *Public Papers of the Presidents of the United States: William Clinton, 1993*, book 2, *August 1 to December 21, 1993* (Washington, DC: Government Printing Office, 1994), 1730.

142. Ibid.

143. Ann Devroy and R. J. Smith, "Clinton Reexamines a Foreign Policy under Siege," *Washington Post* (Pre-1997 Fulltext), October 17, 1993, A01, ProQuest.

144. Cited in Philippe Girard, *Clinton in Haiti: The 1994 US Invasion of Haiti* (Springer, 2004), 45.

145. Ibid.

146. Girard, "Eagle and the Rooster," 93.

147. Press Briefing by Secretary of State Warren Christopher, Secretary of Defense William Perry, and Chairman of the Joint Chiefs General John Shalikashvili, September 18, 1994, http:// www.presidency.ucsb.edu/ws/?pid=59788.

148. Cited in Girard, *Clinton in Haiti*, 44.

149. Warren Christopher, *In the Stream of History: Shaping Foreign Policy for a New Era* (Stanford, CA: Stanford University Press, 1998), 176.

150. William Clinton, "Message to the Congress Reporting on the National Emergency with Respect to Haiti, April 25, 1994," in *Public Papers of the Presidents of the United States: William Clinton, 1994*, book 1, *January 1 to July 31, 1994* (Washington, DC: Government Printing Office, 1995), 777.

151. Ibid., 778.

152. Ibid., 776–80.

153. John Goshko, "Clinton's Haiti Course Is Seen as Irreversible," *Washington Post* (1974– Current file), September 12, 1994.

154. Nigel Hamilton, *Bill Clinton: Mastering the Presidency* (New York: Public Affairs, 2007), 197.

155. Ann Devroy and Douglas Farah, "Clinton Weighs Response to Haiti Minister's Slaying," *Washington Post* (1974–Current file), October 15, 1993, ProQuest.

156. Carla Anne Robbins, "U.S. Officials Say Restoring Democracy in Haiti May Require Military Intervention," *Wall Street Journal*, eastern edition (New York, NY), October 18, 1993, A18.

157. Lake, *Six Nightmares*, 135, and Christopher, *In the Stream of History*, 177.

158. Lake, *Six Nightmares*, 134.

159. Ibid.

160. Ibid., 133.

161. Gellman and Marcus, "U.S. Boosts Pressure on Haitians."

162. William Clinton, "Remarks Announcing the Appointment of William H. Gray III as Special Advisor on Haiti and an Exchange with Reporters, May 8, 1994," in *Public Papers of the Presidents of the United States: William Clinton, 1994*, book 1, *January 1 to July 31, 1994*, 862.

163. Lake, Anthony, *Six Nightmares*, 135.

164. J. M. Goshko, "Aristide Denies CIA Report of Treatment for Mental Illness," *Washington Post* (Pre-1997 Fulltext), October 23, 1993.

165. K. Sawyer, "Gore Defends Aristide, Whose Prospects for Return Seem Brighter," *Washington Post* (Pre-1997 Fulltext), October 25, 1993.

166. Ibid.

167. Stephanopoulos, *All Too Human*, 219.

168. "Showdown in Haiti: In the Words of the President; The Reasons Why the U.S. May Invade Haiti," *New York Times*, September 16, 1994, http://www.nytimes.com/1994/09/16/world/showdown-haiti-words-president-reasons-why-us-may-invade-haiti.html?pagewanted=all.

169. "Mission to Haiti: Diplomacy; On the Brink of War, a Tense Battle of Wills," *New York Times*, September 20, 1994, http://www.nytimes.com/1994/09/20/world/mission-to-haiti-diplomacy-on-the-brink-of-war-a-tense-battle-of-wills.html?pagewanted=all.

170. Ibid.

171. Ibid.

172. Miller Center, "Interview with Samuel R. Berger."

173. "Mission to Haiti: Diplomacy."

174. Ibid.

175. Miller Center, "Interview with Strobe Talbott (2010)," University of Virginia, February 25, 2010, accessed August 25, 2016, http://millercenter.org/oralhistory/interview/strobe-talbott-2010.

176. Ibid.

177. Tod Robberson, "Haitian Capital Positively Chaotic; GIs Add to Confusion with Traffic and Trash—Which Locals Turn into Resource," *Washington Post*, October 30, 1994, A31.

178. D. McManus, "News Analysis: Indecisiveness Is Crux of U.S. Policy on Haiti," *Los Angeles Times* (Pre-1997 Fulltext), July 8, 1994.

179. Press Briefing by Secretary of State Warren Christopher, Secretary of Defense William Perry, and Chairman of the Joint Chiefs General John Shalikashvili, September 18, 1994, http://www.presidency.ucsb.edu/ws/?pid=59788.

180. Walter Edward Kretchik, Robert F. Baumann, and John T. Fishel, *Invasion, Intervention, "Intervasion": A Concise History of the US Army in Operation Uphold Democracy* (US Army Command and General Staff College Press, 1999), 45–64.

181. Ibid., 94–95.

182. Ibid., 162.

183. Miller Center, "Interview with William Perry," University of Virginia, February 21, 2006.

184. William Clinton, "Letter to Congressional Leaders on Deployment of United States Armed Forces to Haiti," in *Public Papers of the Presidents of the United States: William Clinton, 1994*, book 1, *January 1 to June 30, 1995* (Washington, DC: Government Printing Office, 1996), 380–81.

185. Ibid.

186. Ibid.

187. William J. Clinton, "Letter to Congressional Leaders on Deployment of United States Armed Forces to Haiti," March 21, 1996.

188. Goshko, "Clinton's Haiti Course Is Seen as Irreversible."

189. Fauirol quoted in McManus, "News Analysis: Indecisiveness Is Crux."

190. Mandelbaum quoted in Goshko, "Clinton's Haiti Course Is Seen as Irreversible."

191. David Broder, "Intervention in Haiti," *Washington Post* (1974–Current file), September 18, 1994.

192. Ibid.

193. D. McManus, "News Analysis: Clinton's Global Gap; Lofty Goals, a Lesser Reality," *Los Angeles Times* (Pre-1997 Fulltext), August 1, 1994.

194. Ibid.

195. Girard, "Eagle and the Rooster," 95.

196. See Ann Devroy and John M. Groshko, "Clinton May Request Reservists for Haiti; Lake Says U.S. 'Reliability' Is at Stake," *Washington Post*, September 13, 1994, A1; Jim Hoagland, "Don't Do It," *Washington Post*, September 15, 1994, A17.

197. Devroy and Groshko, "Clinton May Request Reservists for Haiti," A1.

198. Ibid.

199. William Clinton, "Address to the Nation on Haiti, September 15, 1994," in *Public Papers of the Presidents of the United States: William Clinton, 1994*, book 2, *August 1 to December 31, 1994*, 1594.

200. Paul A. Gigot, "Potomac Watch: Haiti Politics; It's No Cuban Missile Crisis," *Wall Street Journal*, September 16, 1994, A10.

201. Carla Anne Robbins, "President's Resolve to Face More Tests in World Arena," *Wall Street Journal*, September 20, 1994, A10.

202. R. W. Apple Jr., "Showdown in Haiti: In Perspective; Preaching to Skeptics," *New York Times*, September 16, 1994, http://www.nytimes.com/1994/09/16/world/showdown-in-haiti-in-perspective-preaching-to-skeptics.html.

203. David E. Rosenbaum, "Democrats Hope to Avoid Embarrassing Vote on Haiti," *New York Times*, September 14, 1994, A8.

204. Ibid.

205. Ibid.

206. Ibid. The decision not to ask for congressional approval was also controversial because Congress had passed a law forbidding the use of funds for military operations in Haiti unless the legislature gave its express consent.

207. Jeffrey H. Birnbaum and Thomas E. Ricks, "Clinton Must Persuade Haiti's Dictators to Leave or Convince Americans That U.S. Should Invade," *Wall Street Journal*, September 15, 1994, A16.

208. Gigot, "Potomac Watch," A10.

209. "To the Shores of Port-au-Prince," *New York Times*, September 16, 1994, A30.

210. Sarah E. Kreps, "The 1994 Haiti Intervention: A Unilateral Operation in Multilateral Clothes," *Journal of Strategic Studies* 30, no. 3 (2007): 467–68.

211. Ibid.

212. Lake, *Six Nightmares*, 135.

213. Richard Morin, "Poll Shows Clinton with Higher Rating," *Washington Post*, October 25, 1994, A6.

214. Eric V. Larson and Bogdan Savych, *American Public Support for US Military Operations from Mogadishu to Baghdad* (Santa Monica, CA: Rand, 2005), 44.

215. Ibid.

216. Nicolas Bouchet, *Democracy Promotion as US Foreign Policy: Bill Clinton and Democratic Enlargement* (New York: Routledge, 2015).

217. Miller Center, "Interview with Warren Christopher and Strobe Talbott," University of Virginia, April 15–16, 2002.

218. Larson and Savych, *American Public Support for US Military Operations from Mogadishu to Baghdad*, 48.

219. William Clinton, "Letter to Congressional Leaders on Economic Sanctions against Haiti, July 12, 1993," in *Public Papers of the Presidents of the United States: William Clinton, 1993*, book 1, *January 20 to July 31, 1993*, 1071.

220. Leslie A. Benton and Glenn T. Ware, "Haiti: A Case Study in the International Response and the Efficacy of Nongovernmental Organizations in the Crisis," *Emory International Law Review* 12, no. 2 (1998): 873, *Index to Legal Periodicals and Books Full Text (H. W. Wilson)*; and Kreps, "1994 Haiti Intervention," 465.

221. Kreps, "1994 Haiti Intervention," 465.

222. Ibid., 466.

223. Ibid., 461.

224. Ibid., 468, 471.

225. Michael Dobbs and Jeffrey Smith, "Second Carrier Group Sends a Clear Signal," *Washington Post*, March 12, 1996, A10.

226. Jennifer Lin, "U.S. Considers Risking China's Wrath on Taiwan: The Nimitz Could Sail through the Taiwan Strait. China Is Calling That 'Brazen,'" *Philadelphia Inquirer*, March 21, 1996, A1.

227. Martin Lasater, *The Changing of the Guard: President Clinton and the Security of Taiwan* (Boulder, CO: Westview, 1995), 20.

228. Anthony Lake, quoted in Lasater, *Changing*, 20.

229. Lasater, *Changing*, 12–13.

230. Steven Phillips, "Building a Taiwanese Republic: The Independence Movement," in *Dangerous Strait: The U.S.-Taiwan-China Crisis* (New York: Columbia University Press, 2005), 45.

231. Lasater, *Changing*, 6.

232. Robert S. Ross, "The 1995–96 Taiwan Strait Confrontation: Coercion, Credibility, and the Use of Force," *International Security* 25, no. 2 (2000): 88.

233. Dennis Van Vranken Hickey, *United States–Taiwan Security Ties* (Westport, CT: Praeger, 1994), 46.

234. James Mann, *About Face: A History of America's Curious Relationship with China, from Nixon to Clinton* (New York: Knopf, 1999), 225.

235. Ibid., 271.

236. Phillips, "Building a Taiwanese Republic," 45.

237. Wallace Thies and Patrick Bratton, "When Governments Collide in the Taiwan Strait," *Journal of Strategic Studies* 27, no. 4 (2004): 563.

238. Ibid.

239. Mann, *About Face*, 311.

240. Martin L. Lasater, *The Taiwan Conundrum in US China Policy* (Boulder, CO: Westview, 2000), 177.

241. Robert Ross, "1995–96 Taiwan Strait Confrontation," 91.

242. Thies and Bratton, "When Governments Collide," 564.

243. Lee, quoted in Lasater, *Taiwan Conundrum*, 205.

244. Todd Hall, *Emotional Diplomacy: Official Emotion on the International Stage* (Ithaca, NY: Cornell University Press, 2015).

245. Robert Ross, "1995–96 Taiwan Strait Confrontation"; Hall, *Emotional Diplomacy*, 89.

246. Mann, *About Face*, 328.

247. According to Hall, members of the Clinton administration viewed these initial moves as "an opportunity for the PLA to sort of vent its rage." Quoted in Hall, *Emotional Diplomacy*, 65.

248. Michael Dobbs, "Christopher Treads Lightly on China Policy," *Washington Post*, August 1, 1995, A15.

249. Ibid.

250. Robert Ross, "1995–96 Taiwan Strait Confrontation," 96.

251. Associated Press, "U.S.-China Talks Make No Progress," *Dallas Morning News*, August 2, 1995, 12A.

252. Robert Ross, "1995–96 Taiwan Strait Confrontation," 97.

253. Teresa Poole, "US Envoy Fails to Bridge the Gap on Taiwan," *Independent*, August 28, 1995, 3.

254. Robert Ross, "1995–96 Taiwan Strait Confrontation," 101.

255. Thies and Bratton, "When Governments Collide," 567.

256. Ibid., 568.

257. Teresa Poole, "Jiang Bolsters His Claim with Show of Military Might," *Independent*, October 20, 1995, 17.

258. Lasater, *Taiwan Conundrum*, 227.

259. Ibid., 228.

260. Ibid., 23.

261. Allen Whiting, "China's Use of Force, 1996, and Taiwan," *International Security* 26, no. 2 (Fall 2001): 129.

262. Mann, *About Face*, 334.

263. Robert Ross, "1995–96 Taiwan Strait Confrontation," 102.

264. Professor quoted in Whiting, "Use of Force," 129.

265. Lasater, *Taiwan Conundrum*, 248.

266. Robert L. Suettinger, *Beyond Tiananmen: The Politics of U.S.-China Relations 1989–2000* (Washington, D.C.: Brookings Institution Press, 2004), 251.

267. William Perry quoted in Lasater, *Taiwan Conundrum*, 260.

268. Reuters, "US Protests to Chinese over Missile Tests," *Irish Times*, March 9, 1996, 9.

269. Andrew Scobell, "Show of Force: Chinese Soldiers, Statesmen, and the 1995–1996 Taiwan Strait Crisis," *Political Science Quarterly* 115, no. 2 (2000): 227–46. See also Suettinger, *Beyond Tiananmen*, 251–63.

270. Steven Mufson, "China Plans Live-Ammunition Tests; Naval and Air Maneuvers Could Add Pressure before Taiwan's Vote," *Washington Post*, March 10, 1996, A20.

271. Lasater, *Taiwan Conundrum*, 261.

272. Michael Evans, "US Raises the Stakes in Taiwan War Games; Firepower of Seventh Fleet Offers Strong Deterrent to Chinese Forces," *Times*, March 12, 1996, https://search.proquest.com/docview/318568254.

273. Suettinger, *Beyond Tiananmen*, 259–60. On March 19, the PLA started its large exercise on the island of Pingan, off the Fujian coast at the northern end of the Taiwan Strait.

274. Robert Ross, "1995–96 Taiwan Strait Confrontation," 115.

275. Ibid., 112.

276. Steven Erlanger, " 'Ambiguity' on Taiwan," *New York Times,* March 12, 1996, A1.

277. Quoted in Lin, "U.S. Considers Risking China's Wrath on Taiwan," A1.

278. "A Judicious Show of Resolve: Reacting to Chinese Threats, U.S. Moves Carriers Closer to Taiwan," *Los Angeles Times* (Pre-1997 Fulltext), March 12, 1996, 6.

279. Matthew Imbert, "Tough Stance toward China Favored in Poll of U.S. Voters," *Seattle Post-Intelligencer*, February 23, 1996, A2.

280. Louis Harris and Associates, Harris Survey, February 22–29, 1996, Cornell University, Ithaca, NY: Roper Center for Public Opinion Research. For a good review of public opinion polls in the United States about China and Taiwan for 1996–2006 see, http://www.americans-world.org/digest/regional_issues/china/china7-dat.cfm#4.

281. Graham Fraser, "Beijing, Washington Face Off on Taiwan," *Globe and Mail* (1936–Current), March 12, 1996, A12.

282. Thies and Bratton, "When Governments Collide," 561.

283. *Think Twice, Communist China, before You Use Force against Taiwan*, 104th Cong., 2nd sess., February 1, 1996, H 1204.

284. Dobbs and Smith, "Second Carrier Group," A10.

285. Anonymous official, quoted in ibid.

286. William Perry quoted in Lin, "U.S. Considers Risking China's Wrath on Taiwan," A1.

287. Nicholas Burns quoted in Dobbs and Smith, "Second Carrier Group," A10.

288. Kreps, "1994 Haiti Intervention," 467–68.

289. On many domestic issues and those pertaining to his perceived character, Clinton was obsessed with opinion polls. According to Dick Morris, a political consultant close to the president, Clinton was better at reading polls than any pollster Morris knew. See George Stephanopoulos, *All Too Human*, 380–83; John Harris, "A Clouded Mirror: Bill Clinton, Polls, and the Politics of Survival," in *The Postmodern Presidency: Bill Clinton's Legacy in U.S. Politics*, ed. Steven E. Schier (Pittsburgh: University of Pittsburgh Press, 2000).

290. Stephanopoulos, *All Too Human*, 383.

291. Dick Morris, *Behind the Oval Office* (New York: Random House, 1997), 244–65.

292. Bob Woodward, *The Choice* (New York: Simon and Schuster, 1996), 265–66.

293. Foyle, *Counting the Public In*, 246–56; Larson and Savych. *American Public Support for US Military Operations from Mogadishu to Baghdad*.

294. Dafoe and Caughey, "Honor and War."

Chapter 9: Conclusion

1. For example see, M. G. Hermann, "Explaining Foreign Policy Behaviour Using the Personal Characteristics of Political Leaders," 7–46; M. G. Hermann et al., "Who Leads Matters: The Effects of Powerful Individuals," 83–131; Steinberg, *Shame and Humiliation*; Deborah Larson, *Origins of Containment*; Lebow and Stein, *We All Lost the Cold War*; Jervis et al., *Psychology and Deterrence*.

2. Jonathan Mercer, "Emotions and Strategy in the Korean War," *International Organization* 67, no. 2 (April 2013): 221–52.

3. W. Fleeson and E. E. Noftle, "The End of the Person-Situation Debate: An Emerging Synthesis in the Answer to the Consistency Question," *Social and Personality Psychology Compass* 2, no. 4 (2009): 1667–84; W. Fleeson "Toward a Structure- and Process-Integrated View of Personality: Traits As Density Distribution of States," *Journal of Personality and Social Psychology* 80 (2001): 1011–27.

4. Snyder and Diesing, *Conflict among Nations*.

5. For a similar distinction between these two types of reputations see, Kertzer and Brutger, "Decomposing Audience Costs," 234–49.

6. Low self-monitor leaders are likely to care more about maintaining consistency between their words and their deeds compared to high self-monitor leaders, and thus, they might have stronger signaling reputations overall.

7. Indeed, one of the policy implications that follow from the analysis here is that intelligence organizations should collect information about the self-monitoring of the adversary's leadership as a means to gauge their likely behavior in international crises where their reputation or status could be at stake.

8. Acts of self-monitoring in and of themselves are not the evidence observers should use to judge whether a leader is a high or a low self-monitor. Rather, the clinical test of self-monitoring developed by Snyder is what observers should use, and evidence for the behaviors described in that test prior to taking office would be more reliable.

9. Weisiger and Yarhi-Milo, "Revisiting Reputation," 473–95.

10. A rich line of work on self-monitoring has highlighted the link between self-monitoring and social desirability bias in the study of racial policies. For example, Feldman and Huddy found

that high self-monitors disguise their negative racial views owing to social desirability bias, and Weber and colleagues demonstrated that high, but not low, self-monitors are susceptible to local egalitarian social norms. S. Feldman and L. Huddy, "Racial Resentment and White Opposition to Race-Conscious Programs: Principles or Prejudice," *American Journal of Political Science* 49, no. 1 (2005): 168–83. See also Christopher R. Weber, Howard Lavine, Leonie Huddy, and Christopher M. Federico, "Placing Racial Stereotypes in Context: Social Desirability and the Politics of Racial Hostility," *American Journal of Political Science* 58, no. 1 (January 2014): 63–78; Tali Mendelberg, *The Race Card: Campaign Strategy, Implicit Messages, and the Norm of Equality* (Princeton, NJ: Princeton University Press, 2001).

INDEX

Boldface pagination refers to figures and tables

A NOTE ON THE TYPE

This book has been composed in Adobe Text and Gotham.
Adobe Text, designed by Robert Slimbach for Adobe,
bridges the gap between fifteenth- and sixteenth-century
calligraphic and eighteenth-century Modern styles.
Gotham, inspired by New York street signs, was designed
by Tobias Frere-Jones for Hoefler & Co.